Equal Freedom

Equal Freedom

Selected Tanner Lectures on Human Values

Edited by Stephen Darwall

Ann Arbor

THE UNIVERSITY OF MICHIGAN PRESS

2000   1999   1998   1997   5   4   3   2

A CIP catalog record for this book is available from the British Library.

Library of Congress Cataloging-in-Publication Data

Equal freedom / edited by Stephen Darwall.
        p.   cm. — (Selected Tanner lectures on human values)
        ISBN 0-472-10560-4 (alk. paper). — ISBN 0-472-08281-7 (pbk. :
alk. paper)
        1. Liberty. 2. Equality. 3. Libertarianism. I. Darwall,
Stephen L., 1946–   . II. Tanner lectures on human values
(Cambridge, Mass.)
JC585.E675   1995
323.44—dc20   94-35604
                                                                      CIP

The Tanner Lectures included in this volume were reprinted from
The Tanner Lectures on Human Values, volumes 1, 3, 7, 8, 11, and
13, published by the University of Utah Press. Reprinted by
permission.

Contents

Introduction

Egalitarian and libertarian are frequently opposed political labels. A libertarian, in contemporary discussion, is one who endorses the "minimal state"—a government that protects individuals from assault, murder, theft, and other invasions of their "Lockean" rights but otherwise does not interfere with voluntary activity, economic or otherwise. An egalitarian, on the other hand, is someone who is prepared to favor such interference if that is necessary to reduce substantial inequalities of certain kinds and if, perhaps, it is democratically authorized and respects specific "basic" liberties.

Liberty and equality are conflicting ideals when defined in these ways. It seems inevitable that an unrestricted free market will lead to significant inequalities on any index egalitarians have cared about—wealth and resources, opportunities, the meeting of basic needs, well-being, or the worth of liberty itself. Presumably, any attempt to reduce these inequalities will restrict the liberty of individuals to expend resources as they choose, even if only by taxing to support such things as public education.

At the same time, there are senses in which, on anyone's view, liberty and equality are not conflicting but interdependent and mutually reinforcing ideals. Central to libertarianism, for instance, is the doctrine that all persons have equal moral standing by virtue of holding identical natural rights not to be harmed in their "life, health, liberty, or possessions" (in Locke's phrase).[1] Liberty, in the broad sense of freedom from these harms, is a value *among equals;* it is realized when everyone's rights are respected equally. In advancing an ideal of liberty, therefore, the libertarian simultaneously puts forward an ideal of equality. He interprets both as complementary aspects of a comprehensive conception of justice.

Analogously, egalitarians have also thought liberty to have significant importance, if only as one basic interest among others to be

[1] John Locke, *The Second Treatise of Government*, sec. 6. This is frequently claimed by contemporary libertarians as their classical text.

secured equally for all. *Liberal* egalitarians go further. They hold that specific "basic" liberties are the most important interests persons have, and this, according to some writers, because the claim each has to equal treatment as a moral person is itself grounded in the capacity for a kind of freedom—moral freedom or self-governance—that requires substantial political liberty to be exercised properly, or even at all. Unlike libertarians who often treat natural rights as self-evident givens, these writers hold that what rights and duties there are itself depends upon what can be justified to "free and equal" moral persons, in John Rawls's phrase.[2] And, they argue, by this test a just social order requires significantly greater equality in basic liberties, opportunities, and resources than would characterize a libertarian, minimal state.

The essays that follow can all be read as critiques of libertarianism. Several—those of Rawls, T. M. Scanlon, G. A. Cohen, and Ronald Dworkin—advance different versions of liberal egalitarianism. Each maintains that the ideals of freedom and equality enter into moral and political philosophy at a more fundamental level than the substantive, rights-specifying norms on which libertarianism makes its stand. Each proposes a distinctive vision of this fundamental role and argues, on this basis, for egalitarian moral or political principles. Amartya Sen's essay also falls within this tradition, but it is less an argument for substantive equality (and against libertarianism) than a discussion of what form a reasonable egalitarianism might take. Finally, Quentin Skinner directly criticizes libertarianism in ways that arguably tend to support egalitarianism, though this is not his primary aim.

Skinner's starting point is the contemporary distinction between negative and positive liberty as drawn in Sir Isaiah Berlin's pathbreaking essay, "Two Concepts of Liberty."[3] Negative liberty is the

---

[2] John Rawls, *A Theory of Justice* (Cambridge, Mass.: Harvard University Press, 1971). See, e.g., p. 252.

[3] Isaiah Berlin, *Four Essays on Liberty* (Oxford: Oxford University Press, 1971), pp. 118-72.

sort libertarians cherish: namely, the lack of restrictions on individual conduct. Positive liberty, on the other hand, is the "moral freedom" referred to above: autonomy or self-mastery. While negative liberty, or its lack, is part of the context within which an agent acts, positive liberty is something an agent realizes or fails to realize in her own activity.

Any conception of positive liberty requires some distinction between what actually determines conduct and what must determine it for it to be genuinely autonomous. Frequently, however, this has been thought to require a further, metaphysical difference between a self that is rational, real, better, or authentic and one that, while often the source of actual behavior, is nonetheless inauthentic, worse, or somehow less real. For this reason, positive liberty has been a problematic ideal for libertarians, since it appears to warrant tyranny and oppression in the name of freedom itself. As Berlin pointed out, it may encourage states "to ignore the actual wishes of men or societies, to bully, oppress, torture them in the name, and on behalf, of their 'real' selves."[4]

It will be obvious from the essays that follow that liberal egalitarians object no less strenuously to the idea that the state poses no threat to freedom if it only coerces citizens to do what they would have done anyway had they chosen autonomously. For liberal egalitarians, autonomy or positive freedom is not a value that can cancel, or be traded off against, violations of negative liberty. It enters their political philosophy at a more fundamental level, in an ideal of moral or political *justification*—one that aims to explain the importance to justice *both* of egalitarian arrangements and of various forms of negative liberty.

Skinner grants that negative liberty is the only species of freedom a political order ought to protect. But he argues that it does not follow that a society should require no more of its citizens than that they not violate each other's liberty and help maintain the minimal state. Skinner recalls the "classical republican" tradition of political

---

[4] Berlin, "Two Concepts of Liberty," p. 133.

thought—exemplified by theorists of the Roman republic, such as Cicero, and their Renaissance and early modern champions, such as Machiavelli and James Harrington—who held that a political order can adequately protect personal liberty only if it also makes substantial civic demands. This amounts to a "paradox of liberty" not unlike the so-called paradox of egoistic hedonism.[5] Just as the single-minded pursuit of happiness by an individual is likely to be self-defeating, so will a society frustrate itself if it aims solely at the protection of negative liberty. Only independent, self-governing republics can properly safeguard personal freedoms, since other forms of government are ultimately corrupted from within or conquered from without. And self-government is possible only if citizens constitute themselves corporately in a public realm, accepting substantial obligations of public political participation and service. This is not exactly an argument for egalitarianism, but it does imply that a concern for protecting individual liberty might reasonably lead to valuing forms of political order that require significantly greater civic commitment than libertarianism does.

T. M. Scanlon's essay begins, as his title suggests, with some questions regarding the "significance of choice" in morals and politics. Why do we regard choice as essential to moral responsibility? And would our doing so be undermined were we to believe that our behavior invariably results from prior causes? On the political side, why is citizens' choice so important to justice and legitimacy? Why, for example, do we judge the justice of political outcomes, not in terms of how well-being is distributed, but by how resources and opportunities are? To answer these questions Scanlon proposes two different theories, which he calls the Quality of Will and the Value of Choice theories, respectively. Ultimately, however, he connects

[5] See Joseph Butler, *Sermons* (XI.9); and Henry Sidgwick, *The Methods of Ethics*, 7th ed. (London: Macmillan, 1967), pp. 48, 136.

both to a single underlying contractualist account of the nature of morality, and of the moral acceptability of political order.

The problem of moral responsibility, Scanlon stresses, is internal to morality. The worry that someone cannot reasonably be held blameworthy for actions beyond his control arises *within* our practices of moral praise and blame. Thus the thought that our practices would be insupportable if all action resulted from prior causes, because that would put what we do beyond our control, first gets its foothold in those very practices. He argues, consequently, that it should be sufficient to defeat this thought if we can arrive at a compelling understanding and justification of our practice that explains why choice is significant but also why the fact that a chosen act results from prior causes, taken by itself, is not.

Scanlon's thesis is that what underlies morality is the desire "to regulate one's behavior according to standards that others could not reasonably reject insofar as they, too, were looking for a common set of practical principles." Moral praise and blame thus primarily concern "the quality of an agent's will." They involve an assessment of the extent to which an agent actually did regulate her behavior by such principles. So viewed, morality is a "system of co-deliberation" in which all, concerned to justify their actions to others on grounds they could not reasonably reject, are accountable to each other for regulating their conduct in this way. It follows that morality must be "addressed to" persons who have the capacity for "critically reflective, rational self-governance," as Scanlon calls it, since this is required for accountable self-regulation. Morality, by its very nature, presupposes the capacity for moral freedom.

Scanlon argues that this explains why we are accountable for the decisions or intentions we *make* but not for physical features we simply *have*. Once we see morality as a system of co-deliberation we can understand why it is frequently appropriate to ask others for an explanation or justification of the former but not the latter—morality just *is* a practice of holding ourselves and others to reasonable principles for regulating interaction. In addressing others in this way we treat them as part of the (common) moral enterprise.

We can also explain, he thinks, why morally acceptable political institutions must provide scope for individual choice. The "ability to shape their lives and obligations through the exercise of choice under reasonably favorable conditions" has obvious value to self-governing persons. Indeed, some liberty of this sort would seem a necessary condition for the capacity for autonomy to arise or be exercised at all.

Scanlon's contractualism aims to explain why liberties matter for a morally acceptable political order in the first place. Once political liberty is grounded in this way, however, there will also be foundation to argue that liberty may have to be restricted if that is required for arrangements to assure the value of choice for all. Libertarian institutions might seriously undermine the value of choice for some—for instance, for those significantly less able to compete in a free market. If so, libertarian principles might reasonably be rejected by such persons. This creates justificatory pressure toward equality. More fortunate competitors, moreover, would not be able to complain that they are "naturally" entitled to or deserve the fruits of their labors, since any such claim would have to be similarly justified.

The contemporary inspiration for contractualism of this kind is John Rawls's *A Theory of Justice*. Rawls's contribution to the present volume is an attempt to work out in a more comprehensive and convincing way *Theory's* claim that certain basic liberties have priority among the goods that a just social order must distribute equally (or to the greatest benefit of the least advantaged)—that is, that restrictions on basic liberties cannot be justified by increases in wealth and well-being, even if the benefits accrue to all. In the process, Rawls makes clear that he now means to advance his theory of justice ("justice as fairness") as a *political* conception grounded in ideals already implicit in our political institutions and culture, rather than as deriving from some "comprehensive" moral or philosophical view, whether or not we are committed to it by current political practice.[6]

The core idea of justice as fairness is that a just society is a system of fair cooperation between "free and equal" persons. Because it involves the notion of mutual or reciprocal *benefit*, this includes the idea of "the *rational*"—that is, of individuals as rationally advancing their own ends or "conception of the good" through cooperation with others. But the idea of fair cooperation requires as well the notion that individuals are not merely rational, but also *reasonable* in the sense that they can *regulate* their rational pursuits by principles of fair cooperation.

But what are fair terms of social cooperation? What principles would regulate reasonable cooperation between free and equal persons? We have no independent way of answering this question, Rawls argued in *Theory*, other than by asking what principles would be chosen to regulate public political criticism and conduct, were that choice to be made from a (hypothetical) perspective designed to represent the companion ideals of the person as free and equal and of a just social order as a fair cooperation between persons so conceived. This is where Rawls's famous ideas of the *original position* and the *veil of ignorance* enter. A principle is a principle of *justice* if, and only if, it would be rationally chosen by someone who stood to benefit or be harmed by its serving as a standard of public criticism of basic social structure, but who did not know how she would be benefited or harmed *in particular*, because she did not know her own social or personal place—her history, personal preferences, talents, sex, ethnicity, socioeconomic status, and so on. Such a choice of principles represents the idea of fairness to free and equal persons since it is guided only by interests free and equal persons have *as such*, and

---

[6] This theme is developed at length in Rawls's recent *Political Liberalism* (New York: Columbia University Press, 1993), in which this essay appears as a chapter.

is made from the perspective of concern for an arbitrary individual person so conceived.

"Justice as fairness" refers both to the underlying conception and method just described *and* to the principles Rawls argues would be rationally chosen in the hypothetical original position, behind a veil of ignorance. These are, first, that each person has an equal right to a fully adequate scheme of equal basic liberties compatible with a similar scheme for all, and, second, that social and economic inequalities satisfy two conditions: (1) they are attached only to offices and positions that are open to all under conditions of fair equality of opportunity, and (2) they work to the greatest benefit of the least advantaged members of society. The first principle is "lexically prior" to the second in the sense that restrictions of basic liberties cannot be justified by increases in other goods. The second principle is called the "difference principle" because it states the conditions under which differences in these other goods can be justified.

A commitment to equality runs through these principles. Like libertarianism, justice as fairness holds that a just order secures liberty rights equally for all. Unlike libertarianism, however, it proclaims no equal right to liberty *überhaupt*, but only to certain "basic liberties" that are indispensable to free and equal persons: freedom of thought and liberty of conscience, political liberties and freedom of association, liberty and integrity of the person, and liberties covered by the rule of law. These are so important to the interests of rational and reasonable persons, Rawls argues, that securing them takes priority over the social distribution of other goods.[7] Exhibiting grounds for this claim is the primary purpose of Rawls's essay in this volume. Liberty interests beyond the basic liberties, however, have no such priority. They are no different in principle from other

---

[7] This claim can sound very implausible if one does not bear in mind that the two principles are assumed to apply under "reasonably favorable conditions." The claim is not made, for example, for conditions of widespread famine, severe poverty, and underdevelopment.

resources, the distribution of which is governed by the second, "difference" principle.

Justice as fairness is undoubtedly the most comprehensive and systematic liberal egalitarian theory of our time, if not in the history of political thought. In "The Foundations of Liberal Equality," Ronald Dworkin points out one aspect of Rawls's recent elaboration of his theory, that may substantially undermine its capacity actually to support liberal egalitarian institutions, however. Dworkin notes that liberals have traditionally distinguished between a *personal* perspective from which agents properly live their own lives, constituted by the values to which they are most fundamentally committed, and a *political* perspective, detached from personal commitments, from which citizens appropriately consider and discuss issues of political justice. How is the liberal to reconcile these two different standpoints?

Dworkin distinguishes two strategies. The strategy of *discontinuity*, of which Rawls's recent writings are an example, aims to reconcile personal and political standpoints by separating them and keeping each to its own plane or sphere. The thrust of Rawls's recent work is that justice as fairness is a *political* doctrine, and that it is to be defended in the public political realm by steadfastly avoiding comprehensive moral and philosophical issues that divide persons in a pluralistic society. To consider issues of political justice, individuals must therefore bracket their own substantive ethical or philosophical commitments. But, Dworkin objects, this requires individuals to view the political perspective as artificial and external, as an instrument constructed just for political purposes in the way that "a contract might be constructed for some special commercial occasion." Each can agree to occupy the requisite standpoint "without subscribing to its principles as his own, just as he can agree to be bound by a contract without accepting that its terms are perfectly fair or even reasonable." The upshot is that political justice is drained of "categorical force." No explanation can be given why individuals should be bound by it, since it would seem that any such explanation must engage issues of comprehensive moral and philosophical doctrine.

The alternative is to argue that the political perspective is continuous with the personal. Rather than bracketing or setting aside personal convictions, the strategy of *continuity* seeks the seeds of liberal political morality in values individuals can affirm from within their respective personal standpoints. Liberal politics, it maintains, should flow from liberal *ethics*

Dworkin argues that liberal values of freedom and equality are themselves part of what gives value to life. Here he draws from what might seem a surprising source for liberal ideas—Aristotle's thesis that, as Dworkin puts it, a "good life has the inherent value of a skillful performance." Whether a life is valuable has to do with how it is lived, the excellences it manifests in responding to the challenges it faces. What's more, Dworkin argues, the success of a good life must be appreciated by the person who leads it, from the inside. A good life has "ethical integrity"; it is lived in the conviction that it constitutes, by and large, an appropriate response to "the parameters of [the agent's] ethical situation rightly judged." This makes self-mastery part of the good life as a condition of its value.

The "challenge model" thus "fuses value and choice" in insisting on ethical integrity as a condition of life's value. The challenge model is a continuity strategy for justifying political liberty. If a person can have a good life only if she lives out what, in her own conviction, would be an appropriate response to challenges she faces, then a political order will further the conditions for good lives only if it furthers the conditions for ethical integrity. The state will thus lack paternalistic justification for restricting individual liberty, since, if a good life requires ethical integrity, paternalism is likely to be self-defeating. Accepting an *ethical* liberal premise about the value of a life thus leads to political liberal doctrines about liberty.

Dworkin makes a similar argument concerning the relation of egalitarian distributive justice to the good life. Living a good life involves "responding in the right way to the *right* challenges." But among the challenges or "parameters" of a good life are the resources distributed by society. We cannot, Dworkin maintains, specify the good life without describing its "normative parameters," and these include socially distributed resources, and thus, justice. Living within a just order is itself *part* of the good life.

But which distribution is just? Dworkin notes that ethical liberals will reject any answer based on the distribution of well-being, since they believe the idea of benefit itself involves that of just distribution. Rather, ethical liberals must reckon justice by how *resources* are distributed.

But what is a just distribution of resources? The only tenable answer, Dworkin maintains, is "an equal distribution." If there were such a thing as natural individual ethical identity, which defined for an individual the challenges that would give her life value, then it could be argued that differential, unequal distributions are just. But ethical liberals believe there to be no such thing. On the contrary, part of what they judge valuable in a life is the way an individual *defines* her ethical identity for herself. There is, therefore, no case for unequal distribution. At the deepest level, everyone faces the same challenge of self-definition. Since the goodness of an individual's life depends on how she responds to this challenge, Dworkin concludes that a just distribution of resources must be an equal distribution.

Amartya Sen's "Equality of What?" discusses a wide variety of interpretations of the ideal of equality, assessing them by their implications for specific cases. Even utilitarianism (the principle of maximizing total utility) can be considered an interpretation of equality, since it requires that everyone's marginal utility be equal. Additionally, were everyone to have the same preferences or utility function, utilitarianism would require equal utility for all. In fact, however, the "fundamental diversity" of the human condition exposes the profoundly unattractive implications of utilitarian equality, Sen argues, as well as those of some other egalitarian proposals such as Rawls's.

Consider utilitarianism. Sen asks us to imagine a situation in which a cripple, *A*, would derive half the utility a "pleasure-wizard,"

B, would get from the same level of income. Because *B*'s marginal utility would be higher, utilitarianism dictates directing resources to him rather than *A* at the margin. But this makes *A* "doubly worse off" than *B*. Not only does he get less benefit than *B* from a given level of income, but, for this very reason, he also gets less income. Utilitarianism dictates that resources be directed to those most "efficient" in "producing utility." At the least, however, it seems that the claims of the severely disabled should have independent weight.

Next, Sen considers *total utility equality* and related principles. These evaluate distributions by the total utility each individual has under a given distribution. Thus, total utility equality requires that each individual have equal total utility, the *leximin* principle ranks distributions by the total utility of the worst-off group (and then by the next worst-off in cases of ties), and so on. One problem shared by all such proposals is that, owing to their reliance on utilities (which depend on taste or preference) they are insensitive to other, more "objective" indices of benefit such as health and freedom.

Sen returns to the fundamental diversity of human capabilities to criticize Rawls's theory and any other that assesses distributive justice by how resources are distributed without sensitivity to individuals' capabilities to utilize them. Sen's own proposal is that a theory of justice requires some notion of "basic capabilities," of certain basic things that a person should be able (or enabled) to do. *Basic capability equality* would presumably then rank distributions of resources by how close they come to providing everyone a level of basic capability, but Sen does not say here how that might be assessed.

G. A. Cohen's "Incentives, Inequality, and Community" focuses on Rawls's difference principle, and on the kind of situation in which, Rawls and others have argued, the difference principle justifies unequal distributions of wealth. The difference principle, recall, requires that the basic structure of society distribute wealth and other resources so that those who are worse off are better off than they otherwise would be. The condition for justifying departures from equality, therefore, is that inequalities be necessary to increase the total goods distributed, so that even those worst off are better off than they would be under an equal distribution. This might happen, it has been held, if a larger relative share is a necessary incentive to efforts that increase the absolute level of everyone's share.

But are such incentives actually justified? This question has more than academic interest, as Cohen points out. To evaluate it, he argues, we need to think carefully about the claim that incentives of unequal wealth are *necessary* to draw forth the wealth-creating efforts of the talented. The issue is not whether the talented would be *able* to work to the same degree without incentives, but whether they would be *willing* to do so. We need to ask, therefore, whether, if the talented would exert themselves to a given degree only with incentives, this willingness can itself be justified.

Cohen here introduces the thesis that whether something can be justified within a community depends on whether it could be justified by members of that community *to each other*. This amounts to an *interpersonal test* for justification. An argument can justify a policy, Cohen maintains, only if its justificatory force is not undermined when addressed by any *member of society* to any other member. A *justificatory community* exists only if, when "what certain people are disposed to do when a policy is in force is part of the [proffered] justification, it is considered appropriate to ask them to justify the relevant behavior, and it detracts from justificatory community when they cannot do so."

As an example of a simple case where justificatory community fails and the interpersonal test is violated, Cohen asks us to imagine a situation where a child is kidnapped and the parents are told by the kidnapper that he will not return the child without a ransom. We can well imagine the parents believing the kidnapper and deciding on that basis that their best course is to pay the ransom. But we can hardly imagine that they would think the kidnapper's willingness to return the child only if given ransom was justified. The parents and the kidnapper fail to form a justificatory community.

Analogously, Cohen claims, wealth-creators' having larger relative shares can be justified by the fact that their willingness to create greater wealth is contingent on larger shares only if this claim does not ring hollow in their mouths when they address it to those worse-off, as the kidnapper's does when it is addressed to the parents. If it does, then the best-off and the worst-off together fail to form a justificatory community.

What lies behind Cohen's argument is an ideal of democracy and its role in moral and political justification. In order for a social policy or institutional arrangement to be justified, it must be capable of being justified interpersonally, by members speaking to each other. This might be thought of as a Rousseauvian interpretation of the liberal egalitarian line of thought. What policies and institutions are justified depends on what can be justified to free and equal persons, but *that* depends on what they can justify interpersonally, to each other.

The Paradoxes of Political Liberty
Quentin Skinner

These lectures[1] seek to reconsider two connected claims about
political liberty which, from the standpoint of most current debates about the concept, are apt to be dismissed as paradoxical or
merely confused.

First a word about what I mean by speaking, as I have just
done, about the standpoint of most current debates about liberty.
I have in mind the fact that, in recent discussions of the concept
among analytical philosophers, one conclusion has been reached
which commands a remarkably wide measure of assent. It can
best be expressed in the formula originally introduced into the
argument by Jeremy Bentham and recently made famous by Isaiah
Berlin.[2] The suggestion has been that the idea of political liberty
is essentially a negative one. The presence of liberty, that is, is
said to be marked by the absence of something else; specifically,
by the absence of some element of constraint which inhibits an
agent from being able to act in pursuit of his or her chosen ends,
from being able to pursue different options, or at least from being
able to choose between alternatives.[3]

---

[1] For the printed version I have consolidated the two lectures into a single
argument. I am much indebted to those who took part in the staff–student seminar
at Harvard where the lectures were discussed on 26 October 1984. As a result of
that discussion I have recast some of my claims and removed one section of the
opening lecture that met with justified criticism.

[2] See Douglas G. Long, *Bentham on Liberty* (Toronto: Toronto University
Press, 1977), p. 74, for Bentham speaking of liberty as 'an idea purely negative.'
Berlin uses the formula in his classic essay, 'Two Concepts of Liberty', in *Four
Essays on Liberty* (Oxford: Oxford University Press, 1969), at p. 121 and *passim*.

[3] For freedom as the non-restriction of options, see for example S. I. Benn and
W. Weinstein, 'Being Free to Act, and Being a Free Man', *Mind* 80 (1971): 194–
211. Cf. also John N. Gray, 'On Negative and Positive Liberty', *Political Studies* 28
(1980): 507–26, who argues (esp. p. 519) that this is how Berlin's argument in
his 'Two Concepts' essay (cited in note 2 above) is best understood. For the stricter
suggestion that we should speak only of freedom to choose between alternatives, see

Hobbes bequeathed a classic statement of this point of view — one that is still repeatedly invoked—in his chapter 'Of the Liberty of Subjects' in *Leviathan*. It begins by assuring us, with typical briskness, that 'liberty or freedom signifieth (properly) the absence of opposition' — and signifies nothing more.[4] Locke makes the same point in the *Essay*, where he speaks with even greater confidence. 'Liberty, 'tis plain, consists in a power to do or not to do; to do or forbear doing as we will. This cannot be denied'.[5]

Among contemporary analytical philosophers, this basic contention has generally been unpacked into two propositions, the formulation of which appears in many cases to reflect the influence of Gerald MacCallum's classic paper on negative and positive freedom.[6] The first states that there is only one coherent way of thinking about political liberty, that of treating the concept negatively as the absence of impediments to the pursuit of one's chosen ends.[7] The other proposition states that all such talk about negative liberty can in turn be shown, often despite appearances, to reduce to the discussion of one particular triadic relationship be-

---

for example Felix Oppenheim, *Political Concepts: A Reconstruction* (Oxford: Basil Blackwell, 1981), ch. 4, pp. 53–81. For a defence of the even narrower Hobbesian claim that freedom consists in the mere absence of external impediments, see Hillel Steiner, 'Individual Liberty', *Proceedings of the Aristotelian Society* 75 (1975): 33–50. This interpretation of the concept of constraint is partly endorsed by Michael Taylor, *Community, Anarchy and Liberty* (Cambridge: Cambridge University Press, 1982), pp. 142–50, but is criticised both by Oppenheim and by Benn and Weinstein in the works cited above.

   4 Thomas Hobbes, *Leviathan*, ed. C. B. Macpherson (Harmondsworth: Penguin Books, 1968), bk. II, ch. 21, p. 261. (Here and elsewhere in citing from seventeenth-century sources I have modernised spelling and punctuation.)

   5 John Locke, *An Essay Concerning Human Understanding*, ed. Peter H. Nidditch (Oxford: The Clarendon Press, 1975), II.21.56.

   6 Gerald C. MacCallum, Jr., 'Negative and Positive Freedom', in Peter Laslett, W. G. Runciman, and Quentin Skinner, eds., *Philosophy, Politics and Society*, 4th ser. (Oxford: Basil Blackwell, 1972), pp. 174–93.

   7 This is the main implication of the article by MacCallum cited in note 6 above. For a recent and explicit statement to this effect, see for example J. P. Day, 'Individual Liberty', in A. Phillips Griffiths, ed., *Of Liberty* (Cambridge: Cambridge University Press, 1983), who claims (p. 18) 'that "free" is univocal and that the negative concept is the only concept of liberty'.

tween agents, constraints, and ends. All debates about liberty are thus held to consist in effect of disputes either about who are to count as agents, or what are to count as constraints, or what range of things an agent must be free to do, be, or become (or not be or become) in order to count as being at liberty.[8]

I now turn to the two claims about political liberty which, in the light of these assumptions, are apt to be stigmatised as confused. The first connects freedom with self-government, and in consequence links the idea of personal liberty, in a seemingly paradoxical way, with that of public service. The thesis, as Charles Taylor has recently expressed it, is that we can only be free within 'a society of a certain canonical form, incorporating true self-government'.[9] If we wish to assure our own individual liberty, it follows that we must devote ourselves as wholeheartedly as possible to a life of public service, and thus to the cultivation of the civic virtues required for participating most effectively in political life. The attainment of our fullest liberty, in short, presupposes our recognition of the fact that only certain determinate ends are rational for us to pursue.[10]

The other and related thesis states that we may have to be forced to be free, and thus connects the idea of individual liberty,

[8] This formulation derives from the article by MacCallum cited in note 6 above. For recent discussions in which the same approach has been used to analyse the concept of political liberty, see for example Joel Feinberg, *Social Philosophy* (Englewood Cliffs, N.J.: Prentice-Hall, 1973), esp. pp. 12, 16, and J. Roland Pennock, *Democratic Political Theory* (Princeton: Princeton University Press, 1979), esp. pp. 18–24.

[9] Charles Taylor, 'What's Wrong with Negative Liberty', in Alan Ryan, ed., *The Idea of Freedom* (Oxford: Oxford University Press, 1979), pp. 175–93, at p. 181.

[10] For a discussion that moves in this Kantian direction, connecting freedom with rationality and concluding that it cannot therefore 'be identified with absence of impediments,' see for example C. I. Lewis, 'The Meaning of Liberty', in John Lange, ed., *Values and Imperatives* (Stanford: Stanford University Press, 1969), pp. 145–55, at p. 147. (I mention Lewis in particular because, at the request of a Founding Trustee, my lectures at Harvard were dedicated to Lewis's memory.) For a valuable recent exposition of the same Kantian perspective, see the section 'Rationality and Freedom' in Martin Hollis, *Invitation to Philosophy* (Oxford: Basil Blackwell, 1985), pp. 144–51.

in an even more blatantly paradoxical fashion, with the concepts of coercion and constraint. The assumption underlying this further step in the argument is that we may sometimes fail to remember — or may altogether fail to grasp — that the performance of our public duties is indispensable to the maintenance of our own liberty. If it is nevertheless true that freedom depends on service, and hence on our willingness to cultivate the civic virtues, it follows that we may have to be coerced into virtue and thereby constrained into upholding a liberty which, left to ourselves, we would have undermined.

II

Among contemporary theorists of liberty who have criticised these arguments, we need to distinguish two different lines of attack. One of these I shall consider in the present section, the other I shall turn to discuss in section III.

The most unyielding retort has been that, since the negative analysis of liberty is the only coherent one, and since the two contentions I have isolated are incompatible with any such analysis, it follows that they cannot be embodied in any satisfactory account of social freedom at all.

We already find Hobbes taking this view of the alleged relationship between social freedom and public service in his highly influential chapter on liberty in *Leviathan*. There he tells us with scorn about the Lucchese, who have 'written on the turrets of the city of Lucca in great characters, at this day, the word LIBERTAS', in spite of the fact that the constitution of their small-scale city–republic placed heavy demands upon their public-spiritedness.[11] To Hobbes, for whom liberty (as we have seen) simply means absence of interference, it seems obvious that the maximising of our social freedom must depend upon our capacity to maximise the area within which we can claim 'immunity from the service of the commonwealth'.[12] So it seems to him merely absurd of the

---

[11] Hobbes, *Leviathan*, bk. II, ch. 21, p. 266.
[12] Ibid.

Lucchese to proclaim their liberty in circumstances in which such services are so stringently exacted. Hobbes's modern sympathisers regularly make the same point. As Oppenheim puts it, for example, in his recent book *Political Concepts*, the claim that we can speak of 'freedom of participation in the political process' is simply confused.[13] Freedom presupposes the absence of any such obligations or constraints. So this 'so-called freedom of participation does not relate to freedom in any sense'.[14]

We find the same line of argument advanced even more frequently in the case of the other claim I am considering: that our freedom may have to be the fruit of our being coerced. Consider, for example, how Raphael handles this suggestion in his *Problems of Political Philosophy*. He simply reiterates the contention that 'when we speak of having or not having liberty or freedom in a political context, we are referring to freedom of action or social freedom, i.e., the absence of restraint or compulsion by human agency, including compulsion by the State'.[15] To suggest, therefore, that 'compulsion by the State can make a man more free' is not merely to state a paradoxical conclusion; it is to present an 'extraordinary view' that simply consists of confusing together two polar opposites, freedom and constraint.[16] Again, Oppenheim makes the same point. Since freedom consists in the absence of constraint, to suggest that someone might be 'forced to be free' is no longer to speak of freedom at all but 'its opposite'.[17]

What are we to think of this first line of attack, culminating as it does in the suggestion that, as Oppenheim expresses it, neither of the arguments I have isolated 'relate to freedom in any sense'?

[13] Oppenheim, *Political Concepts*, p. 92.

[14] Ibid., p. 162. For a recent endorsement of the claim that, since liberty requires no action, it can hardly require virtuous or valuable action, see Lincoln Allison, *Right Principles* (Oxford: Basil Blackwell, 1984), pp. 134–35.

[15] D. D. Raphael, *Problems of Political Philosophy*, rev. ed. (London: Macmillan, 1976), p. 139.

[16] Ibid., p. 137.

[17] Oppenheim, *Political Concepts*, p. 164.

It seems to me that this conclusion relies on dismissing, far too readily, a different tradition of thought about social freedom which, at this point in my argument, it becomes important briefly to lay out.

The tradition I have in mind stems from Greek moral thought and is founded on two distinctive and highly influential premises. The first, developed in various subsequent systems of naturalistic ethics, claims that we are moral beings with certain characteristically human purposes. The second, later taken up in particular by scholastic political philosophy, adds that the human animal is *naturale sociale et politicum*, and thus that our purposes must essentially be social in character.[18] The view of human freedom to which these assumptions give rise is thus a 'positive' one. We can only be said to be fully or genuinely at liberty, according to this account, if we actually engage in just those activities which are most conducive to *eudaimonia* or 'human flourishing', and may therefore be said to embody our deepest human purposes.

I have no wish to defend the truth of these premises. I merely wish to underline what the above account already makes clear: that if they are granted, a positive theory of liberty flows from them without the least paradox or incoherence.

This has two important implications for my present argument. One is that the basic claim advanced by the theorists of negative liberty I have so far been considering would appear to be false. They have argued that all coherent theories of liberty must have a certain triadic structure. But the theory of social freedom I have just stated, although perfectly coherent if we grant its premises, has a strongly contrasting shape.[19]

---

[18] See for example Thomas Aquinas, *De Regimine Principum*, bk. I, ch. 1, in A. P. D'Entrèves, ed., *Aquinas: Selected Political Writings* (Oxford: Basil Blackwell, 1959), p. 2.

[19] For a fuller exploration of this point see the important article by Tom Baldwin, 'MacCallum and the Two Concepts of Freedom', *Ratio* 26 (1984): 125–42, esp. at 135–36.

The contrast can be readily spelled out. The structure within which MacCallum and his numerous followers insist on analysing all claims about social freedom is such that they make it a sufficient condition of an agent's being at liberty that he or she should be unconstrained from pursuing some particular option, or at least from choosing between alternatives. Freedom, in the terminology Charles Taylor has recently introduced, becomes a pure opportunity concept.[20] I am already free if I have the opportunity to act, whether or not I happen to make use of that opportunity. By contrast, the positive theory I have just laid out makes it a necessary condition of an agent's being fully or truly at liberty that he or she should actually engage in the pursuit of certain determinate ends. Freedom, to invoke Taylor's terminology once more, is viewed not as an opportunity but as an exercise concept.[21] I am only in the fullest sense in possession of my liberty if I actually exercise the capacities and pursue the goals that serve to realise my most distinctively human purposes.

The other implication of this positive analysis is even more important for my present argument. According to the negative theories I have so far considered, the two paradoxes I began by isolating can safely be dismissed as misunderstandings of the concept of liberty.[22] According to some, indeed, they are far worse than misunderstandings; they are 'patent sophisms' that are really designed, in consequence of sinister ideological commitments, to convert social freedom 'into something very different, if not its opposite'.[23] Once we recognise, however, that the positive view of liberty stemming from the thesis of naturalism is a perfectly

[20] Taylor, 'Negative Liberty', p. 177.

[21] Ibid.

[22] See for example the conclusions in W. Parent, 'Some Recent Work on the Concept of Liberty', *American Philosophical Quarterly* 11 (1974): 149–67, esp. 152, 166.

[23] Anthony Flew, ' "Freedom Is Slavery": A Slogan for Our New Philosopher Kings', in Griffiths, ed., *Of Liberty*, pp. 45–59, esp. at pp. 46, 48, 52.

coherent one, we are bound to view the two paradoxes in a quite different light.

There ceases, in the first place, to be any self-evident reason for impugning the motives of those who have defended them.[24] Belief in the idea of 'human flourishing' and its accompanying vision of social freedom arises at a far deeper level than that of mere ideological debate. It arises as an attempt to answer one of the central questions in moral philosophy, the question whether it is rational to be moral. The suggested answer is that it is in fact rational, the reason being that we have an interest in morality, the reason for this in turn being the fact that we are moral agents committed by our very natures to certain normative ends. We may wish to claim that this theory of human nature is false. But we can hardly claim to know *a priori* that it could never in principle be sincerely held.

We can carry this argument a stage further, moreover, if we revert to the particular brand of Thomist and Aristotelian naturalism I have singled out. Suppose for the sake of argument we accept both its distinctive premises: not only that human nature embodies certain moral purposes, but that these purposes are essentially social in character as well. If we do so, the two paradoxes I began by isolating not only cease to look confused; they both begin to look highly plausible.

Consider first the alleged connection between freedom and public service. We are supposing that human nature has an essence, and that this is social and political in character. But this makes it almost truistic to suggest that we may need to establish one particular form of political association — thereafter devoting ourselves to serving and sustaining it — if we wish to realise our own natures and hence our fullest liberty. For the form of association we shall need to maintain will of course be just that form in

[24] At this point I am greatly indebted once more to Baldwin, 'Two Concepts', esp. pp. 139–40.

which our freedom to be our true selves is capable of being realised as completely as possible.

Finally, consider the paradox that connects this idea of freedom with constraint. If we need to serve a certain sort of society
in order to become most fully ourselves, we can certainly imagine
tensions arising between our apparent interests and the duties we
need to discharge if our true natures, and hence our fullest liberty,
are both to be realised. But in those circumstances we can scarcely
call it paradoxical — though we may certainly find it disturbing —
if we are told what Rousseau tells us so forcefully in *The Social
Contract*: that if anyone regards 'what he owes to the common
cause as a gratuitous contribution, the loss of which would be less
painful for others than the payment is onerous for him', then he
must be 'forced to be free', coerced into enjoying a liberty he will
otherwise allow to degenerate into servitude.[25]

III

I now turn to assess the other standpoint from which these
two paradoxes of liberty have commonly been dismissed. The
theorists I now wish to discuss have recognised that there may
well be more than one coherent way of thinking about the idea of
political liberty. Sometimes they have even suggested, in line with
the formula used in Isaiah Berlin's classic essay, that there may be
more than one coherent *concept* of liberty.[26] As a result, they have
sometimes explicitly stated that there may be theories of liberty
within which the paradoxes I have singled out no longer appear
as paradoxical at all. As Berlin himself emphasises, for example,
several 'positive' theories of freedom, religious as well as political, seem readily able to encompass the suggestion that people may

[25] Jean-Jacques Rousseau, *The Social Contract*, trans. Maurice Cranston (Harmondsworth: Penguin Books, 1968), p. 64.

[26] This is how Berlin expresses the point in the title of his essay, although he
shifts in the course of it to speaking instead of the different 'senses' of the term.
See *Four Essays*, esp. p. 121.

have to act 'in certain self-improving ways, which they could be
coerced to do' if there is to be any prospect of realising their
fullest or truest liberty.[27]

When such writers express doubts about the two paradoxes I
am considering, therefore, their thesis is not that such paradoxes
are incapable of being accommodated within any coherent theory
of liberty. It is only that such paradoxes are incapable of being accommodated within any coherent theory of negative liberty — any
theory in which the idea of liberty itself is equated with the mere
absence of impediments to the realisation of one's chosen ends.

This appears, for example, to be Isaiah Berlin's view of the
matter in his 'Two Concepts of Liberty'. Citing Cranmer's epi-
gram 'Whose service is perfect freedom', Berlin allows that such
an ideal, perhaps even coupled with a demand for coercion in its
name, might conceivably form part of a theory of freedom 'without thereby rendering the word "freedom" wholly meaningless'.
His objection is merely that, as he adds, 'all this has little to do
with' the idea of negative liberty as someone like John Stuart Mill
would ordinarily understand it.[28]

Considering the same question from the opposite angle, so to
speak, Charles Taylor appears to reach the same conclusion in his
essay, 'What's Wrong with Negative Liberty'. It is only because
liberty is *not* a mere opportunity concept, he argues, that we need
to confront the two paradoxes I have isolated, asking ourselves
whether our liberty is 'realisable only within a certain form of
society', and whether this commits us 'to justifying the excesses of
totalitarian oppression in the name of liberty'.[29] Taylor's final reason, indeed, for treating the strictly negative view of liberty as an
impoverished one is that, if we restrict ourselves to such an under-

[27] Ibid., esp. p. 152.

[28] Ibid., pp. 160–62.

[29] Taylor, 'Negative Liberty', p. 193.

standing of the concept, these troubling but unavoidable questions do not arise.[30]

What are we to think of this second line of argument, culminating in the suggestion that the two paradoxes I am considering, whatever else may be said about them, have no place in any ordinary theory of negative liberty?

It seems to me that this conclusion depends on ignoring yet another whole tradition of thought about social freedom, one that it again becomes crucial, at this point in my argument, to try to lay out.

The tradition I have in mind is that of classical republicanism.[31] The view of social freedom to which the republican vision of political life gave rise is one that has largely been overlooked in recent philosophical debate. It seems well worth trying to restore it to view, however, for the effect of doing so will be to show us, I believe, that the two paradoxes I have isolated can in fact be accommodated within an ordinary theory of negative liberty. It is to this task of exposition, accordingly, that I now turn, albeit in an unavoidably promissory and over-schematic style.[32]

Within the classical republican tradition, the discussion of political liberty was generally embedded in an analysis of what it means to speak of living in a 'free state'. This approach was

---

[30] See Taylor, ibid., insisting (p. 193) that this is 'altogether too quick a way with them'.

[31] I cannot hope to give anything like a complete account of this ideology here, nor even of the recent historical literature devoted to it. Suffice it to mention that, in the case of English republicanism, the pioneering study is Z. S. Fink, *The Classical Republicans*, 2d ed. (Evanston: Northwestern University Press, 1962). On the development of the entire school of thought, the classic study is J. G. A. Pocock, *The Machiavellian Moment* (Princeton: Princeton University Press, 1975), a work to which I am much indebted.

[32] I have tried to give a fuller account in two earlier articles: 'Machiavelli on the Maintenance of Liberty', *Politics* 18 (1983): 3–15, and 'The Idea of Negative Liberty: Philosophical and Historical Perspectives', in Richard Rorty, J. B. Schneewind, and Quentin Skinner, eds., *Philosophy in History* (Cambridge: Cambridge University Press, 1984), pp. 193–221. The present essay may be regarded as an attempt to bring out the implications of those earlier studies, although at the same time I have considerably modified and I hope strengthened my earlier arguments.

largely derived from Roman moral philosophy, and especially from those writers whose greatest admiration had been reserved for the doomed Roman republic: Livy, Sallust, and above all Cicero. Within modern political theory, their line of argument was first taken up in Renaissance Italy as a means of defending the traditional liberties of the city–republics against the rising tyranny of the *signori* and the secular powers of the Church. Many theorists espoused the republican cause at this formative stage in its development, but perhaps the greatest among those who did so was Machiavelli in his *Discorsi* on the first ten books of Livy's History of Rome. Later we find a similar defence of 'free states' being mounted — with acknowledgements to Machiavelli's influence — by James Harrington, John Milton, and other English republicans as a means of challenging the alleged despotism of the Stuarts in the middle years of the seventeenth century. Still later, we find something of the same outlook — again owing much to Machiavelli's inspiration — among the opponents of absolutism in eighteenth-century France, above all in Montesquieu's account of republican virtue in *De L'esprit des Lois*.

By this time, however, the ideals of classical republicanism had largely been swallowed up by the rising tide of contractarian political thought. If we wish to investigate the heyday of classical republicanism, accordingly, we need to turn back to the period before the concept of individual rights attained that hegemony which it has never subsequently lost. This means turning back to the moral and political philosophy of the Renaissance, as well as to the Roman republican writers on whom the Renaissance theorists placed such overwhelming weight. It is from these sources, therefore, that I shall mainly draw my picture of the republican idea of liberty, and it is from Machiavelli's *Discorsi* — perhaps the most compelling presentation of the case—that I shall mainly cite.[33]

---

[33] All citations from the *Discorsi* refer to the version in Niccolò Machiavelli, *Il Principe e Discorsi*, ed. Sergio Bertelli (Milan: Feltrinelli, 1960). All translations are my own.

IV

I have said that the classical republicans were mainly concerned to celebrate what Nedham, in a resounding title, called the excellency of a free state. It will be best to begin, therefore, by asking what they had in mind when they predicated liberty of entire communities. To grasp the answer, we need only recall that these writers take the metaphor of the body politic as seriously as possible. A political body, no less than a natural one, is said to be at liberty if and only if it is not subject to external constraint. Like a free person, a free state is one that is able to act according to its own will, in pursuit of its own chosen ends. It is a community, that is, in which the will of the citizens, the general will of the body-politic, chooses and determines whatever ends are pursued by the community as a whole. As Machiavelli expresses the point at the beginning of his *Discorsi*, free states are those 'which are far from all external servitude, and are able to govern themselves according to their own will'.[34]

There are two principal benefits, according to these theorists, which we can only hope to enjoy with any degree of assurance if we live as members of free states. One is civic greatness and wealth. Sallust had laid it down in his *Catiline* (7.1) that Rome only became great as a result of throwing off the tyranny of her kings, and the same sentiment was endlessly echoed by later exponents of classical republican thought. Machiavelli also insists, for example, that 'it is easy to understand the affection that people feel for living in liberty, for experience shows that no cities have ever grown in power or wealth except those which have been established as free states'.[35]

But there is another and even greater gift that free states are alone capable of bequeathing with any confidence to their citizens. This is personal liberty, understood in the ordinary sense to mean

[34] Ibid., I.ii, p. 129.
[35] Ibid., II.ii, p. 280.

that each citizen remains free from any elements of constraint (especially those which arise from personal dependence and servitude) and in consequence remains free to pursue his own chosen ends. As Machiavelli insists in a highly emphatic passage at the start of Book II of the *Discorsi*, it is only 'in lands and provinces which live as free states' that individual citizens can hope 'to live without fear that their patrimony will be taken away from them, knowing not merely that they are born as free citizens and not as slaves, but that they can hope to rise by their abilities to become leaders of their communities'.[36]

It is important to add that, by contrast with the Aristotelian assumptions about *eudaimonia* that pervade scholastic political philosophy, the writers I am considering never suggest that there are certain specific goals we need to realise in order to count as being fully or truly in possession of our liberty. Rather they emphasise that different classes of people will always have varying dispositions, and will in consequence value their liberty as the means to attain varying ends. As Machiavelli explains, some people place a high value on the pursuit of honour, glory, and power: 'they will want their liberty in order to be able to dominate others'.[37] But other people merely want to be left to their own devices, free to pursue their own family and professional lives: 'they want liberty in order to be able to live in security'.[38] To be free, in short, is simply to be unconstrained from pursuing whatever goals we may happen to set ourselves.

How then can we hope to set up and maintain a free state, thereby preventing our own individual liberty from degenerating into servitude? This is clearly the pivotal question, and by way of answering it the writers I am considering advance the distinctive claim that entitles them to be treated as a separate school of thought. A free state, they argue, must constitutionally speaking

[36] Ibid., II.ii, p. 284.
[37] Ibid., I.xvi, p. 176.
[38] Ibid., I.xvi, p. 176; cf. also II.ii, pp. 284–85.

be what Livy and Sallust and Cicero had all described and celebrated as a *res publica*.

We need to exercise some care in assessing what this means, however, for it would certainly be an oversimplification to suppose that what they have in mind is necessarily a republic in the modern sense. When the classical republican theorists speak of a *res publica*, what they take themselves to be describing is any set of constitutional arrangements under which it might justifiably be claimed that the *res* (the government) genuinely reflects the will and promotes the good of the *publica* (the community as a whole). Whether a *res publica* has to take the form of a self-governing republic is not therefore an empty definitional question, as modern usage suggests, but rather a matter for earnest enquiry and debate. It is true, however, that most of the writers I have cited remain sceptical about the possibility that an individual or even a governing class could ever hope to remain sufficiently disinterested to equate their own will with the general will, and thereby act to promote the good of the community at all times. So they generally conclude that, if we wish to set up a *res publica*, it will be best to set up a republic as opposed to any kind of principality or monarchical rule.

The central contention of the theory I am examining is thus that a self-governing republic is the only type of regime under which a community can hope to attain greatness at the same time as guaranteeing its citizens their individual liberty. This is Machiavelli's usual view, Harrington's consistent view, and the view that Milton eventually came to accept.[39] But if this is so, we very much need to know how this particular form of government can in practice be established and kept in existence. For it turns out that each one of us has a strong personal interest in understanding how this can best be done.

[39] See Fink, *Classical Republicans*, esp. pp. 103–7, on Milton and Harrington. For Machiavelli's equivocations on the point see Marcia Colish, 'The Idea of Liberty in Machiavelli', *Journal of the History of Ideas* 32 (1971): 323–50.

The writers I am considering all respond, in effect, with a one-word answer. A self-governing republic can only be kept in being, they reply, if its citizens cultivate that crucial quality which Cicero had described as *virtus*, which the Italian theorists later rendered as *virtù*, and which the English republicans translated as civic virtue or public-spiritedness. The term is thus used to denote the range of capacities that each one of us as a citizen most needs to possess: the capacities that enable us willingly to serve the common good, thereby to uphold the freedom of our community, and in consequence to ensure its rise to greatness as well as our own individual liberty.

But what *are* these capacities? First of all, we need to possess the courage and determination to defend our community against the threat of conquest and enslavement by external enemies. A body-politic, no less than a natural body, which entrusts itself to be defended by someone else is exposing itself gratuitously to the loss of its liberty and even its life. For no one else can be expected to care as much for our own life and liberty as we care ourselves. Once we are conquered, moreover, we shall find ourselves serving the ends of our new masters rather than being able to pursue our own purposes. It follows that a willingness to cultivate the martial virtues, and to place them in the service of our community, must be indispensable to the preservation of our own individual liberty as well as the independence of our native land.[40]

We also need to have enough prudence and other civic qualities to play an active and effective role in public life. To allow the political decisions of a body-politic to be determined by the will of anyone other than the entire membership of the body itself is, as in the case of a natural body, to run the gratuitous risk that the behaviour of the body in question will be directed to the attainment not of its own ends, but merely the ends of those who have managed to gain control of it. It follows that, in order to avoid

[40] This constitutes a leading theme of Book II of Machiavelli's *Discorsi*.

such servitude, and hence to ensure our own individual liberty, we must all cultivate the political virtues and devote ourselves whole-heartedly to a life of public service.[41]

This strenuous view of citizenship gives rise to a grave difficulty, however, as the classical republican theorists readily admit. Each of us needs courage to help defend our community and prudence to take part in its government. But no one can be relied on consistently to display these cardinal virtues. On the contrary, as Machiavelli repeatedly emphasises, we are generally reluctant to cultivate the qualities that enable us to serve the common good. Rather we tend to be 'corrupt', a term of art the republican theorists habitually use to denote our natural tendency to ignore the claims of our community as soon as they seem to conflict with the pursuit of our own immediate advantage.[42]

To be corrupt, however, is to forget — or fail to grasp — something which it is profoundly in our interests to remember: that if we wish to enjoy as much freedom as we can hope to attain within political society, there is good reason for us to act in the first instance as virtuous citizens, placing the common good above the pursuit of any individual or factional ends. Corruption, in short, is simply a failure of rationality, an inability to recognise that our own liberty depends on committing ourselves to a life of virtue and public service. And the consequence of our habitual tendency to forget or misunderstand this vital piece of practical reasoning is therefore that we regularly tend to defeat our own purposes. As Machiavelli puts it, we often think we are acting to maximize our own liberty when we are really shouting Long live our own ruin.[43]

---

[41] Book III of Machiavelli's *Discorsi* is much concerned with the role played by great men — defined as those possessing exceptional *virtù* — in Rome's rise to greatness.

[42] For a classic discussion of 'corruption' see Machiavelli, *Discorsi*, I.xvii–xix, pp. 177–85.

[43] Ibid., I.liii, p. 249.

For the republican writers, accordingly, the deepest question of statecraft is one that recent theorists of liberty have supposed it pointless to ask. Contemporary theories of social freedom, analysing the concept of individual liberty in terms of 'background' rights, have come to rely heavily on the doctrine of the invisible hand. If we all pursue our own enlightened self-interest, we are assured, the outcome will in fact be the greatest good of the community as a whole.[44] From the point of view of the republican tradition, however, this is simply another way of describing corruption, the overcoming of which is said to be a necessary condition of maximising our own individual liberty. For the republican writers, accordingly, the deepest and most troubling question still remains: how can naturally self-interested citizens be persuaded to act virtuously, such that they can hope to maximise a freedom which, left to themselves, they will infallibly throw away?

The answer at first sounds familiar: the republican writers place all their faith in the coercive powers of the law. Machiavelli, for example, puts the point graphically in the course of analysing the Roman republican constitution in Book I of his *Discorsi*. 'It is hunger and poverty that make men industrious', he declares, 'and it is the laws that make them good'.[45]

The account the republican writers give, however, of the relationship between law and liberty stands in strong contrast to the more familiar account to be found in contractarian political thought. To Hobbes, for example, or to Locke, the law preserves our liberty essentially by coercing other people. It prevents them from interfering with my acknowledged rights, helps me to draw around myself a circle within which they may not trespass, and prevents me at the same time from interfering with their freedom in just the same way. To a theorist such as Machiavelli, by con-

---

[44] See for example the way in which the concept of 'the common good' is discussed in John Rawls, *A Theory of Justice* (Cambridge: Harvard University Press, 1971), pp. 243, 246.

[45] Machiavelli, *Discorsi*, I.iii, p. 136.

trast, the law preserves our liberty not merely by coercing others, but also by directly coercing each one of us into acting in a particular way. The law is also used, that is, to force us out of our habitual patterns of self-interested behaviour, to force us into discharging the full range of our civic duties, and thereby to ensure that the free state on which our own liberty depends is itself maintained free of servitude.

The justifications offered by the classical republican writers for the coercion that law brings with it also stand in marked contrast to those we find in contractarian or even in classical utilitarian thought. For Hobbes or for Locke, our freedom is a natural possession, a property of ourselves. The law's claim to limit its exercise can only be justified if it can be shown that, were the law to be withdrawn, the effect would not in fact be a greater liberty, but rather a diminution of the security with which our existing liberty is enjoyed. For a writer like Machiavelli, however, the justification of law is nothing to do with the protection of individual rights, a concept that makes no appearance in the *Discorsi* at all. The main justification for its exercise is that, by coercing people into acting in such a way as to uphold the institutions of a free state, the law creates and preserves a degree of individual liberty which, in its absence, would promptly collapse into absolute servitude.

Finally, we might ask what mechanisms the republican writers have in mind when they speak of using the law to coerce naturally self-interested individuals into defending their community with courage and governing it with prudence. This is a question to which Machiavelli devotes much of Book I of his *Discorsi*, and he offers two main suggestions, both derived from Livy's account of republican Rome.

He first considers what induced the Roman people to legislate so prudently for the common good when they might have fallen into factional conflicts.[46] He finds the key in the fact that, under

---

[46] Ibid., I.ii–vi, pp. 129–46.

their republican constitution, they had one assembly controlled by the nobility, another by the common people, with the consent of each being required for any proposal to become law. Each group admittedly tended to produce proposals designed merely to further its own interests. But each was prevented by the other from imposing them as laws. The result was that only such proposals as favoured no faction could ever hope to succeed. The laws relating to the constitution thus served to ensure that the common good was promoted at all times. As a result, the laws duly upheld a liberty that, in the absence of their power to coerce, would soon have been lost to tyranny and servitude.

Machiavelli also considers how the Romans induced their citizen-armies to fight so bravely against enslavement by invading enemies. Here he finds the key in their religious laws.[47] The Romans saw that the only way to make self-interested individuals risk their very lives for the liberty of their community was to make them take an oath binding them to defend the state at all costs. This made them less frightened of fighting than of running away. If they fought they might risk their lives, but if they ran away — thus violating their sacred pledge — they risked the much worse fate of offending the gods. The result was that, even when terrified, they always stood their ground. Hence, once again, their laws forced them to be free, coercing them into defending their liberty when their natural instinct for self-preservation would have led them to defeat and thus servitude.

V

By now, I hope, it will be obvious what conclusions I wish to draw from this examination of the classical republican theory of political liberty. On the one hand, it is evident that the republican writers embrace both the paradoxes I began by singling out. They certainly connect social freedom with self-government, and in con-

---

[47] Ibid., I.xi–xv, pp. 160–73.

sequence link the idea of personal liberty with that of virtuous public service. Moreover, they are no less emphatic that we may have to be forced to cultivate the civic virtues, and in consequence insist that the enjoyment of our personal liberty may often have to be the product of coercion and constraint.

On the other hand, they never appeal to a 'positive' view of social freedom. They never argue, that is, that we are moral beings with certain determinate purposes, and thus that we are only in the fullest sense in possession of our liberty when these purposes are realised. As we have seen, they work with a purely negative view of liberty as the absence of impediments to the realisation of our chosen ends. They are absolutely explicit in adding, moreover, that no determinate specification of these ends can be given without violating the inherent variety of human aspirations and goals.

Nor do they defend the idea of forcing people to be free by claiming that we must be prepared to reason about ends. They never suggest, that is, that there must be a certain range of actions which it will be objectively rational for us to perform, whatever the state of our desires. It is true that, on their analysis, there may well be actions of which it makes sense to say that there are good reasons for us to perform them, even if we have no desire — not even a reflectively considered desire — to do so. But this is not because they believe that it makes sense to reason about ends.[48] It is simply because they consider that the chain of practical reasoning we need to follow out in the case of acting to uphold our own liberty is so complex, and so unwelcome to citizens of corrupt disposition, that we find it all too easy to lose our way in the argument. As a result, we often cannot be brought, even in reflection, to recognise the range of actions we have good reason to perform in order to bring about the ends we actually desire.

---

[48] Although those who attack as well as those who defend the Kantian thesis that there may be reasons for action which are unconnected with our desires appear to assume that this must be what is at stake in such cases.

Given this characterisation of the republican theory of freedom, my principal conclusion is thus that it must be a mistake to
suppose that the two paradoxes I have been considering cannot be
accommodated within an ordinary negative analysis of political
liberty.[49] If the summary characterisation I have just given is correct, however, there is a further implication to be drawn from this
latter part of my argument, and this I should like to end by
pointing out. It is that our inherited traditions of political theory
appear to embody two quite distinct though equally coherent
views about the way in which it is most rational for us to act in
order to maximise our negative liberty.

Recent emphasis on the importance of taking rights seriously
has contrived to leave the impression that there may be only one
way of thinking about this issue. We must first seek to erect
around ourselves a cordon of rights, treating these as 'trumps'
and insisting on their priority over any calls of social duty.[50] We
must then seek to expand this cordon as far as possible, our even-
tual aim being to achieve what Isaiah Berlin has called 'a maximum degree of non-interference compatible with the minimum
demands of social life'.[51] Only in this way — as Hobbes long ago
argued — can we hope to maximise the area within which we are
free to act as we choose.

If we revert to the republican theorists, however, we encounter
a strong challenge to these familiar beliefs. To insist on rights as
trumps, on their account, is simply to proclaim our corruption as

[49] I should stress that this seems to me an implication of MacCallum's analysis
of the concept of freedom cited in note 6 above. If so, it is an implication that none
of those who have made use of his analysis have followed out, and most have explicitly denied. But cf. his discussion at pp. 189–92. I should like to take this
opportunity of acknowledging that, although I believe the central thesis of Mac-
Callum's article to be mistaken, I am nevertheless greatly indebted to it.

[50] See for example Ronald Dworkin, *Taking Rights Seriously* (Cambridge:
Harvard University Press, 1977), p. xi, for the claim that 'individual rights are
political trumps held by individuals', and pp. 170–77 for a defence of the priority
of rights over duties.

[51] Berlin, *Four Essays*, p. 161.

citizens. It is also to embrace a self-destructive form of irrationality. Rather we must take our duties seriously, and instead of trying to evade anything more than 'the minimum demands of social life' we must seek to discharge our public obligations as wholeheartedly as possible. Political rationality consists in recognising that this constitutes the only means of guaranteeing the very liberty we may seem to be giving up.

VI

My story is at an end; it only remains to point the moral of the tale. Contemporary liberalism, especially in its so-called libertarian form, is in danger of sweeping the public arena bare of any concepts save those of self-interest and individual rights. Moralists who have protested against this impoverishment—such as Hannah Arendt, and more recently Charles Taylor, Alasdair MacIntyre and others[52] — have generally assumed in turn that the only alternative is to adopt an 'exercise' concept of liberty, or else to seek by some unexplained means to slip back into the womb of the polis. I have tried to show that the dichotomy here — either a theory of rights or an 'exercise' theory of liberty — is a false one. The Aristotelian and Thomist assumption that a healthy public life must be founded on a conception of *eudaimonia* is by no means the only alternative tradition available to us if we wish to recapture a vision of politics based not merely on fair procedures but on common meanings and purposes. It is also open to us to meditate on the potential relevance of a theory which tells us that, if we wish to maximise our own individual liberty, we must cease to put our trust in princes, and instead take charge of the public arena ourselves.

[52] For Arendt's views see her essay 'What Is Freedom?' in *Between Past and Future*, rev. ed. (New York: The Viking Press, 1968), pp. 143–71. For Taylor's, see 'Negative Liberty', esp. pp. 180–86. For MacIntyre's, see *After Virtue* (London: Duckworth, 1981), esp. p. 241, for the claim 'that the crucial moral opposition is between liberal individualism in some version or other and the Aristotelian tradition in some version or other'.

It will be objected that this is the merest nostalgic anti-modernism. We have no realistic prospect of taking active control of the political processes in any modern democracy committed to the technical complexities and obsessional secrecies of present-day government. But the objection is too crudely formulated. There are many areas of public life, short of directly controlling the actual executive process, where increased public participation might well serve to improve the accountability of our *soi disant* representatives. Even if the objection is valid, however, it misses the point. The reason for wishing to bring the republican vision of politics back into view is not that it tells us how to construct a genuine democracy, one in which government is for the people as a result of being by the people. That is for us to work out. It is simply because it conveys a warning which, while it may be unduly pessimistic, we can hardly afford to ignore: that unless we place our duties before our rights, we must expect to find our rights themselves undermined.

The Significance of Choice

T. M. Scanlon

Lecture 1

1. INTRODUCTION

Choice has obvious and immediate moral significance. The fact that a certain action or outcome resulted from an agent's choice can make a crucial difference both to our moral appraisal of that agent and to our assessment of the rights and obligations of the agent and others after the action has been performed. My aim in these lectures is to investigate the nature and basis of this significance. The explanation which I will offer will be based upon a contractualist account of morality — that is, a theory according to which an act is right if it would be required or allowed by principles which no one, suitably motivated, could reasonably reject as a basis for informed, unforced general agreement.[1]

I believe that it is possible within this general theory of morality to explain the significance of various familiar moral notions such as rights, welfare, and responsibility in a way that preserves their apparent independence rather than reducing all of them to one master concept such as utility. The present lectures are an attempt to carry out this project for the notions of responsibility and choice.

This is a revised version of three lectures presented at Brasenose College, Oxford, on May 16, 23, and 28, 1986. I am grateful to the participants in the seminars following those lectures for their challenging and instructive comments. These lectures are the descendants of a paper, entitled "Freedom of the Will in Political Theory," which I delivered at a meeting of the Washington, D.C., Area Philosophy Club in November 1977. Since that time I have presented many intervening versions to various audiences. I am indebted to members of those audiences and to numerous other friends for comments, criticism, and helpful suggestions.

[1] I have set out my version of contractualism in "Contractualism and Utilitarianism," in Amartya Sen and Bernard Williams, eds., *Utilitarianism and Beyond* (Cambridge: Cambridge University Press, 1982), pp. 103–28. What follows can be seen as an attempt to fulfill, for the case of choice, the promissory remarks made at the end of section III of that paper.

2. The Problems of Free Will

Quite apart from this general theoretical project, however, there is another, more familiar reason for inquiring into the basis of the moral significance of choice. This is the desire to understand and respond to the challenge to that significance which has gone under the heading of the problem of free will. This problem has a number of forms. One form identifies free will with a person's freedom to act otherwise than he or she in fact did or will. The problem, on this view, is the threat to this freedom posed by deterministic conceptions of the universe. A second, related problem is whether determinism, if true, would deprive us of the kind of freedom, whatever it may be, which is presupposed by moral praise and blame. This version of the problem is closer to my present concern in that it has an explicitly moral dimension. In order to address it one needs to find out what the relevant kind of freedom is, and this question can be approached by asking what gives free choice and free action their special moral significance. Given an answer to this question, which is the one I am primarily concerned with, we can then ask how the lack of freedom would threaten this significance and what kinds of unfreedom would do so.

The challenge I have in mind, however, is not posed by determinism but by what I call the Causal Thesis. This is the thesis that the events which are human actions, thoughts, and decisions are linked to antecedent events by causal laws as deterministic as those governing other goings-on in the universe. According to this thesis, given antecedent conditions and the laws of nature, the occurrence of an act of a specific kind follows, either with certainty or with a certain degree of probability, the indeterminacy being due to chance factors of the sort involved in other natural processes. I am concerned with this thesis rather than with determinism because it seems to me that the space opened up by the falsity of determinism would be relevant to morality only if it were filled by something other than the cumulative effects of indeterministic physical processes. If the actions we perform result from the fact that we have a certain physical constitution and have been subjected to certain outside influences, then an apparent threat to morality remains, even if the links between these causes and their effects are not deterministic.

The idea that there is such a threat is sometimes supported by thought experiments such as the following: Suppose you were to learn that someone's present state of mind, intentions, and actions were produced in him or her a few minutes ago by the action of outside forces, for example by electrical stimulation of the nervous system. You would not think it appropriate to blame that person for what he or she does under such conditions. But if the Causal Thesis is true then all of our actions are like this. The only differences are in the form of outside intervention and the span of time over which it occurs, but surely these are not essential to the freedom of the agent.

How might this challenge be answered? One strategy would be to argue that there are mistakes in the loose and naive idea of causality to which the challenge appeals or in the assumptions it makes about the relation between mental and physical events. There is obviously much to be said on both of these topics. I propose, however, to follow a different (but equally familiar) line. Leaving the concepts of cause and action more or less unanalyzed, I will argue that the apparent force of the challenge rests on mistaken ideas about the nature of moral blame and responsibility.[2]

---

[2] In his admirably clear and detailed defense of incompatibilism, Peter van Inwagen observes that if one accepts the premises of his argument for the incompatibility of determinism and free will (in the sense required for moral responsibility) then it is "puzzling" how people could have the kind of freedom required for moral responsibility even under indeterministic universal causation. (See *An Essay on Free Will* [Oxford: Oxford University Press, 1983], pp. 149–50.) On the other hand, he takes it to be not merely puzzling but inconceivable that free will should be impossible or that the premises of his arguments for incompatibilism should be false or that the rules of inference which these arguments employ should be invalid. This leads him, after some further argument, to reject determinism: "If incompatibilism is true, then either determinism or the free-will thesis is false.

It has sometimes been maintained that even if the Causal Thesis holds, this does not represent the kind of unfreedom that excuses agents from moral blame. That kind of unfreedom, it is sometimes said, is specified simply by the excusing conditions which we generally recognize: a person is acting unfreely in the relevant sense only if he or she is acting under posthypnotic suggestion, or under duress, is insane, or falls under some other generally recognized excusing condition. Since the Causal Thesis does not imply that people are always acting under one or another of these conditions, it does not imply that moral praise and blame are generally inapplicable.

I am inclined to think that there is something right about this reaffirmation of common sense. But in this simple form it has been rightly rejected as question begging. It begs the question because it does not take account of the claim that commonsense morality itself holds that people cannot be blamed for what they do when their behavior is the result of outside causes, a claim which is supported by our reactions to imaginary cases like the thought experiment mentioned above and by more general reflection on what a world of universal causality would be like.

In order to show that moral praise and blame are compatible with the Causal Thesis, it is necessary to rebut this claim. The most promising strategy for doing so is to look for a general account of the moral significance of choice, an account which, on

---

To deny the free-will thesis is to deny the existence of moral responsibility, which would be absurd. Moreover, there seems to be no good reason to accept determinism (which, it should be recalled, is *not* the same as the Principle of Universal Causation). Therefore, we should reject determinism" (p. 223).

My response is somewhat different. Determinism is a very general empirical thesis. Our convictions about moral responsibility seem to me an odd basis for drawing a conclusion one way or the other about such a claim. In addition, whatever one may decide about determinism, it remains puzzling how moral responsibility could be compatible with Universal Causation. I am thus led to wonder whether our initial assumptions about the kind of freedom required by moral responsibility might not be mistaken. Rather than starting with a reinterpretation of the principle of alternative possibilities (along the lines of the conditional analysis), my strategy is to ask first, Why does the fact of choice matter morally? and then, What kind of freedom is relevant to mattering in that way?

the one hand, explains why the significance of choice is under-mined both by commonly recognized excusing conditions and by factors such as those imagined to be at work in the thought experi-ment described above and, on the other hand, explains why the moral significance of choice will not be undermined everywhere if the Causal Thesis is true. Such an account, if convincing, would provide a basis for arguing that our initial response to the Causal Thesis was mistaken. At the very least, it would shift the burden of argument to the incompatibilist, who would need to explain why the proffered account of the moral significance of choice was inadequate. Before beginning my search for an account of the significance of choice, however, I will take a moment to examine some other forms of the free-will problem.

The problem of free will is most often discussed as a problem about moral responsibility, but essentially the same problem arises in other forms as well. It arises in political philosophy, for ex-ample, as a problem about the significance of choice as a legitimating condition. We generally think that the fact that the affected parties chose or assented to an outcome is an important factor in making that outcome legitimate. But we also recognize that there are conditions under which acquiescence does not have this legiti-mating force. These include conditions like those listed above: hypnosis, brain stimulation, mental incapacity, brainwashing, and so on. To many, at least, it seems plausible to maintain that these conditions deprive choice of its moral significance because they are conditions under which the agent's action is the result of outside causes. But if the Causal Thesis holds, this is true of all actions, and it would follow that choice never has moral significance as a legitimating factor.

Let me turn to a different example, drawn from John Rawls's book, *A Theory of Justice*.[3] (I believe the example involves a misinterpretation of Rawls, albeit a fairly natural one, but I will

---

[3] *A Theory of Justice* (Cambridge, Mass.: Harvard University Press, 1971), pp. 72–74, 104.

try to correct that later.) Replying to an argument for the justice of a purely laissez-faire economy, Rawls observes that in such a system economic rewards would be unacceptably dependent on factors such as innate talents and fortunate family circumstances, which are, as he puts it, "arbitrary from a moral point of view." In particular, he says that even such factors as willingness to exert oneself will depend to a large extent on family circumstances and upbringing. Therefore we cannot say, of those who might have improved their economic position if they had exerted themselves, that because their predicament is their own doing they have no legitimate complaint. Their lack of exertion has no legitimating force because it is the result of "arbitrary factors."

But this argument, if successful, would seem to prove too much. Consider a society satisfying Rawls's Difference Principle. This principle permits some inequalities, such as those resulting from incentives which improve productivity enough to make everyone better off. When such inequalities exist, they will be due to the fact that some people have responded to these incentives while others have not. If the Causal Thesis is correct, however, there will be some causal explanation of these differences in behavior. They will not be due to gross differences in economic status, since, by hypothesis, these do not exist. But they must be due to something, and it seems clear that the factors responsible, whatever they are, are likely to be as "morally arbitrary" in at least one sense of that phrase as the factors at work in the case of the laissez-faire society to which Rawls was objecting. To sustain Rawls's argument, then, we need a better explanation of how "morally arbitrary" background conditions can undermine the legitimating force of choice, an explanation which will not deprive all choice of moral force if the Causal Thesis is correct.

Let me mention a further, slightly different case. We think it important that a political system should, as we say, "leave people free to make up their own minds," especially about important political questions and questions of personal values. We regard certain conditions as incompatible with this important freedom and therefore to be avoided. Brainwashing is one extreme example, but there are also more moderate, and more common, forms of manipulation, such as strict control of sources of information, bombardment with one-sided information, and the creation of an environment in which people are distracted from certain questions by fear or other competing stimuli. What is it that is bad about these conditions? If they count as conditions of unfreedom simply because they are conditions under which people's opinions are causal products of outside factors, then there is no such thing as "freedom of thought" if the Causal Thesis is correct. It would follow that defenders of "freedom of thought" who accept the Causal Thesis could rightly be accused of ideological blindness: what they advocate as "freedom" is really just determination by a different set of outside factors, factors which are less rational and no more benign than those to which they object. There may be good reasons to favor some determining factors over others, but the issue cannot be one of "freedom." Here again, then, the problem is to show that "determination by outside causes" is not a sufficient condition for unfreedom. To do this we need to come up with some other explanation of what is bad about the conditions which supporters of freedom of thought condemn.[4]

These are versions of what I will call the political problem of free will. As I have said, they have much the same structure as the more frequently discussed problem about moral praise and blame. In addition to these problems there is what might be called the personal problem of free will. If I were to learn that one of my past actions was the result of hypnosis or brain stimulation, I would feel alienated from this act: manipulated, trapped, reduced to the status of a puppet. But why, if the Causal Thesis is correct, should we not feel this way about all of our acts? Why should

[4] I have said more about this version of the problem in section IIB of "Freedom of Expression and Categories of Expression," *University of Pittsburgh Law Review* 40 (1979).

we not feel trapped all the time? This is like the other problems in that what we need in order to answer it is a better explanation of why it is proper to feel trapped and alienated from our own actions in cases like hypnosis, an explanation which goes beyond the mere fact of determination by outside factors. But while this problem is like the others in its form, it differs from them in not being specifically a problem about morality: the significance with which it deals is not *moral* significance. This makes it a particularly difficult problem, much of the difficulty being that of explaining what the desired but threatened form of significance is supposed to be. Since my concern is with moral theory I will not address this problem directly, though the discussion of the value of choice in lecture 2 will have some bearing on it.

I will be concerned in these lectures with the first two of these problems and with the relation between them: to what degree can the "better explanation" that each calls for be provided within the compass of a single, reasonably unified theory? My strategy is to put forward two theories which attempt to explain why the conditions which we commonly recognize as undermining the moral significance of choice in various contexts should have this effect. These theories, which I will refer to as the Quality of Will theory and the Value of Choice theory, are similar to the theories put forward in two famous articles, P. F. Strawson's "Freedom and Resentment," [5] and H. L. A. Hart's "Legal Responsibility and Excuses." [6] My aim is to see whether versions of these two approaches — extended in some respects and modified in others to fit within the contractualist theory I espouse — can be put together into a single coherent account. We can then see how far this combined theory takes us toward providing a satisfactory account of the moral significance of choice across the range of cases I have listed above.

[5] In Strawson, ed., *Studies in the Philosophy of Thought and Action* (Oxford: Oxford University Press, 1968), pp. 71–96.

[6] Chapter 2 of Hart, *Punishment and Responsibility* (Oxford: Oxford University Press, 1968).

3. The Influenceability Theory

Before presenting the Quality of Will theory, it will be helpful to consider briefly an older view which serves as a useful benchmark. This view, which I will call the Influenceability theory, employs a familiar strategy for explaining conditions which excuse a person from moral blame.[7] This strategy is first to identify the purpose or rationale of moral praise and blame and then to show that this rationale fails when the standard excusing conditions are present. According to the Influenceability theory, the purpose of moral praise and blame is to influence people's behavior. There is thus no point in praising or blaming agents who are not (or were not) susceptible to being influenced by moral suasion, and it is this fact which is reflected in the commonly recognized excusing conditions.

The difficulties with this theory are, I think, well known.[8] I will not go into them here except to make two brief points. The first is that the theory appears to conflate the question of whether moral judgment is applicable and the question of whether it should be *expressed* (in particular, expressed to the agent). The second point is that difficulties arise for the theory when it is asked whether what matters is influenceability at or shortly before the time of action or influenceability at the (later) time when moral judgment is being expressed. The utilitarian rationale for praise and blame supports the latter interpretation, but it is the former which retains a tie with commonsense notions of responsibility.

---

[7] See J. J. C. Smart, "Freewill, Praise, and Blame," *Mind* 70 (1961): 291–306; reprinted in G. Dworkin, ed., *Determinism, Free Will, and Moral Responsibility* (Englewood Cliffs, N.J.: Prentice-Hall, 1970; page references will be to this edition). The theory was stated earlier by Moritz Schlick in chapter 7 of *The Problems of Ethics*, trans. D. Rynin (New York: Prentice-Hall, 1939), reprinted as "When Is a Man Responsible?" in B. Berofsky, ed., *Free Will and Determinism* (New York: Harper and Row, 1966; page references will be to this edition).

[8] Some are set forth by Jonathan Bennett in section 6 of "Accountability," in Zak van Staaten, ed., *Philosophical Subjects* (Oxford: Oxford University Press, 1980).

The Influenceability theory might explain why a utilitarian system of behavior control would include something like what we now recognize as excusing conditions. What some proponents of the theory have had in mind is that commonsense notions of responsibility should be given up and replaced by such a utilitarian practice. Whatever the merits of this proposal, however, it is clear that the Influenceability theory does not provide a satisfactory account of the notions of moral praiseworthiness and blameworthiness as we now understand them. The usefulness of administering praise or blame depends on too many factors other than the nature of the act in question for there ever to be a good fit between the idea of influenceability and the idea of responsibility which we now employ.[9]

4. Quality of Will: Strawson's Account

The view which Strawson presents in "Freedom and Resentment" is clearly superior to the Influenceability theory. Like that theory, however, it focuses less on the cognitive content of moral judgments than on what people are doing in making them. The centerpiece of Strawson's analysis is the idea of a reactive attitude. It is the nature of these attitudes that they are reactions not simply to what happens to us or to others but rather to the attitudes toward ourselves or others which are revealed in an agent's actions. For example, when you tread on my blistered toes, I may feel excruciating pain and greatly regret that my toes were stepped on. In addition, however, I am likely to resent the malevolence or callousness or indifference to my pain which your action indicates. This resentment is what Strawson calls a "personal reactive attitude": it is my attitudinal reaction to the attitude toward me which is revealed in your action. Moral indignation, on the other

---

[9] Broadening the theory to take into account the possibility of influencing people other than the agent will produce a better fit in some cases, but at the price of introducing even more considerations which are intuitively irrelevant to the question of responsibility.

hand, is what he calls a "vicarious attitude": a reaction to the attitude toward others in general (e.g., lack of concern about their pain) which your action shows you to have. All of these are what Strawson calls "participant attitudes." They "belong to involvement or participation with others in inter-personal human relationships." [10] This is in contrast to "objective attitudes," which involve seeing a person "as an object of social policy; as an object for what in a wide range of senses might be called treatment; as something certainly to be taken account, perhaps precautionary account, of; to be managed or handled or cured or trained." [11]

It follows from this characterization that the discovery of new facts about an action or an agent can lead to the modification or withdrawal of a reactive attitude in at least three ways: (a) by showing that the action was not, after all, indicative of the agent's attitude toward ourselves or others; (b) by showing that the attitude indicated in the act was not one which makes a certain reactive attitude appropriate; (c) by leading us to see the agent as someone toward whom objective, rather than participant, attitudes are appropriate.

Commonly recognized excusing conditions work in these ways. The most extreme excusing conditions sever any connection between an action (or movement) and the attitudes of the agent. If your stepping on my toes was a mere bodily movement resulting from an epileptic seizure, then it shows nothing at all about your concern or lack of concern about my pain. It would therefore be inappropriate for me to resent your action or for someone else, taking a more impartial view, to feel moral disapproval of you on that account.

Other excusing conditions have the less extreme effect of modifying the quality of will which an action can be taken to indicate, thus modifying the reactive attitudes which are appropri-

[10] Strawson, "Freedom and Resentment," p. 79.
[11] Ibid.

ate. If I learn, for example, that you stepped on my foot by accident, then I can no longer resent your callousness or malevolence,
but I may still, if conditions are right, resent your carelessness. If
I learn that you (reasonably) believed that the toy spider on my
boot was real, and that you were saving my life by killing it before
it could bite me, then I can no longer *resent* your action at all,
although it remains indicative of a particular quality of will on
your part.

Actions produced by posthypnotic suggestion are a less clear
case. Much depends on what we take the hypnosis to do. Hypnosis might lead you to perform the intentional act of stamping your
foot on mine but without any malice or even any thought that you
are causing me harm. In this case a criticizable attitude is indicated by your act: a kind of complacency toward touching other
people's bodies in ways that you have reason to believe are unwanted. But this attitude is not really attributable to *you*. *You*
may not lack any inhibition in this regard: it is just that your
normal inhibition has been inhibited by the hypnotist. The case is
similar if the hypnotist implants in you a passing hatred for me
and a fleeting but intense desire to cause me pain. Here again
there is a criticizable attitude — more serious this time — but it is
not yours. It is "just visiting," so to speak.

Strawson's account of why conditions such as insanity and
extreme immaturity excuse people from moral blame is less satisfactory. The central idea is that these conditions lead us to take an
"objective attitude" toward a person rather than to see him or her
as a participant in those interpersonal human relationships of
which the reactive attitudes are a part. Strawson's claim here can
be understood on two levels. On the one hand there is the empirical claim that when we see someone as "warped or deranged,
neurotic or just a child . . . all our reactive attitudes tend to be profoundly modified." [12] In addition to this, however, there is the

    12 Ibid. My appreciation of this straightforwardly factual reading of Strawson's
argument was aided by Jonathan Bennett's perceptive analysis in "Accountability."

suggestion that these factors render reactive attitudes such as resentment and indignation *inappropriate*. But Strawson's theory does not explain the grounds of this form of inappropriateness as clearly as it explained the grounds of the other excusing conditions. In fact, aside from the references to interpersonal relationships, which are left unspecified, nothing is said on this point.

In other cases, however, Strawson's theory succeeds in giving a better explanation of commonly recognized excusing conditions than that offered by the idea that a person is not to be blamed for an action which is the result of outside causes. The mere fact of causal determination seems to have little to do with the most common forms of excuse, such as accident and mistake of fact. It is a distinct advantage of Strawson's analysis that it accounts for the force of more extreme excuses such as hypnosis and brain stimulation in a way that is continuous with a natural explanation of these less extreme cases as well. Moreover, his theory can explain the relevance of "inability to do otherwise" in several senses of that phrase. Sometimes, as in the case of brain stimulation, the factors which underlie this inability sever any connection between an action and the agent's attitudes. In other cases, "inability to do otherwise" in the different sense of lack of *eligible* alternatives can modify the quality of will indicated by an agent's willingness to choose a particular course of action. For example, if you stamp on my toes because my archenemy, who is holding your child hostage next door, has ordered you to do so, this does not make you less *responsible* for your act. The act is still fully yours, but the quality of will which it indicates on your part is not blameworthy.

As Strawson observes, these appeals to "inability to do otherwise" do not generalize. The truth of the Causal Thesis would not mean that either of these forms of inability obtained generally or that actions never indicated the presence in the agent of those attitudes or qualities of will which make resentment or moral indignation appropriate.

Like the unsuccessful defense of common sense mentioned above, Strawson's analysis is internal to our moral concepts as we now understand them. Its explanation of the conditions which negate or modify moral responsibility rests on a claim that, given the kind of thing that moral indignation is, it is an appropriate response only to actions which manifest certain attitudes on the part of the agent. This internal character may be thought to be a weakness in Strawson's account, and he himself considers an objection of this sort. The objection might be put as follows: You have shown what is and is not appropriate given the moral notions we now have; but the question is whether, if the Causal Thesis is correct, it would not be irrational to go on using those concepts and holding the attitudes they describe. Strawson's direct response to this objection is to say that the change proposed is "practically inconceivable."

> The human commitment to participation in ordinary interpersonal relationships is, I think, too thoroughgoing and deeply rooted for us to take seriously the thought that a general conviction might so change our world that, in it, there were no longer any such things as inter-personal relationships as we normally understand them; and being involved in interpersonal relationships as we normally understand them precisely is being exposed to the range of reactive attitudes and feelings that is in question.[13]

But there is another reply which is suggested by something that Strawson goes on to say and which seems to me much stronger.[14] This reply points out that the principle "If your action was a causal consequence of prior factors outside your control then you cannot properly be praised or blamed for performing it" derives its strength from its claim to be supported by commonsense morality. Consequently, if an analysis such as Strawson's succeeds

---

[13] Strawson, "Freedom and Resentment," p. 82.

[14] Ibid., p. 83.

in giving a convincing account of the requirements of freedom implicit in our ordinary moral views — in particular, giving a systematic explanation of why commonly recognized excusing conditions should excuse — then this is success enough. Succeeding this far undermines the incompatibilist challenge by striking at its supposed basis in everyday moral thought.[15]

Plausible and appealing though it is, there are several respects in which Strawson's analysis is not fully satisfactory. One of these has already been mentioned in connection with insanity. Strawson suggests that the attitudes which moral judgments express are appropriately held only toward people who are participants in certain interpersonal relationships and that these attitudes are therefore inhibited when we become aware of conditions which render a person unfit for these relationships. But one needs to know more about what these relationships are, about why moral reactive attitudes depend on them, and about how these relationships are undermined or ruled out by factors such as insanity.

A second problem is more general. Strawson explains why certain kinds of unfreedom make moral praise and blame inapplicable by appealing to a fact about interpersonal reactive attitudes in general (and moral ones in particular), namely the fact that they are attitudes toward the attitudes of others, as manifested in their actions. But one may wonder whether anything further can be said about why attitudes of moral approval and disapproval are of this general type. Moreover, it is not clear that moral judgments need always involve the *expression* of any par-

---

[15] Compare Thomas Nagel's comments on Strawson's theory in *The View from Nowhere* (Oxford: Oxford University Press, 1986), pp. 124–26. The response I am advocating here does not deny the possibility of what Nagel has called "external" criticism of our practices of moral evaluation. It tries only to deny the incompatibilist critique a foothold in our ordinary ideas of moral responsibility. It claims that a commitment to freedom which is incompatible with the Causal Thesis is not embedded in our ordinary moral practices in the way in which a commitment to objectivity which outruns our experience is embedded in the content of our ordinary empirical beliefs. The incompatibilist response, obviously, is to deny this claim. My point is that the ensuing argument, which I am trying to advance one side of, is internal to the system of our ordinary moral beliefs.

ticular reactive attitude. For example, I may believe that an action of a friend, to whom many horrible things have recently happened, is morally blameworthy. But need this belief, or its expression, involve a feeling or expression of moral indignation or disapproval on my part? Might I not agree that what he did was wrong but be incapable of feeling disapproval toward him?

Here Strawson's analysis faces a version of one of the objections to the Influenceability theory: it links the content of a moral judgment too closely to *one* of the things that may be done in expressing that judgment. Of course, Strawson need not claim that moral judgment always involves the expression of a reactive attitude. It would be enough to say that such a judgment always makes some attitude (e.g., disapproval) appropriate. But then one wonders what the content of this underlying judgment is and whether the requirement of freedom is not to be explained by appeal to this content rather than to the attitudes which it makes appropriate.

In order to answer these questions one needs a more complete account of moral blameworthiness. A number of different moral theories might be called upon for this purpose, but what I will do is to sketch briefly how a Quality of Will theory might be based on a contractualist account of moral judgment.

5. QUALITY OF WILL: A CONTRACTUALIST ANALYSIS

According to contractualism as I understand it, the basic moral motivation is a desire to regulate one's behavior according to standards that others could not reasonably reject insofar as they, too, were looking for a common set of practical principles. Morality, on this view, is what might be called a system of co-deliberation. Moral reasoning is an attempt to work out principles which each of us could be expected to employ as a basis for deliberation and to accept as a basis for criticism. To believe that one is morally at fault is just to believe that one has not regulated one's behavior in the way that such standards would require. This can be so either because one has failed to attend to considerations that such standards would require one to take account of or because one has consciously acted contrary to what such standards would require. If one is concerned, as most people are to at least some extent, to be able to justify one's actions to others on grounds they could not reasonably reject, then the realization that one has failed in these ways will normally produce an attitude of serious self-reproach. But this attitude is distinct from the belief which may give rise to it. Similarly, to believe that another person's behavior is morally faulty is, at base, to believe that there is a divergence of this kind between the way that person regulated his or her behavior and the kind of self-regulation that mutually acceptable standards would require. For reasons like those just mentioned, this belief will normally be the basis for attitudes of disapproval and indignation. This view of morality grounds the fact that moral appraisal is essentially concerned with "the quality of an agent's will" in an account of the nature of moral reasoning and moral motivation. The analysis of moral judgment which it supports is essentially cognitivist. It can explain why moral judgments would normally be accompanied by certain attitudes, but these attitudes are not the basis of its account of moral judgment.

Contractualism also gives specific content to the idea, suggested by Strawson, that moral judgments presuppose a form of interpersonal relationship. On this view, moral judgments apply to people considered as possible participants in a system of co-deliberation. Moral praise and blame can thus be rendered inapplicable by abnormalities which make this kind of participation impossible. (The implications of this idea for excusing conditions such as insanity will be discussed below.)

6. THE SPECIAL FORCE OF MORAL JUDGMENT

Insofar as it goes beyond Strawson's theory in committing itself to a fuller account of the nature of moral blameworthiness, the contractualist view I have described leaves itself open to the objection that this notion of blameworthiness requires a stronger form of freedom, a form which may be incompatible with the Causal Thesis. In order to assess this objection, it will be helpful to compare the contractualist account of blame with what Smart calls "praise and dispraise." According to Smart, we commonly use the word "praise" in two different ways.[16] On the one hand, praise is the opposite of blame. These terms apply only to what a person does or to aspects of a person's character, and they are supposed to carry a special force of moral approval or condemnation. But we also praise things other than persons and their character: the California climate, the flavor of a melon, or the view from a certain hill. In this sense we also praise features of persons which we see as "gifts" beyond their control: their looks, their coordination, or their mathematical ability. Praise in this sense is not the opposite of blame, and Smart coins the term "dispraise" to denote its negative correlate. Praise and dispraise lack the special force of moral approval or condemnation which praise and blame are supposed to have. To praise or dispraise something is simply to grade it.

Smart takes the view that the kind of moral judgment involved in praise and blame as these terms are normally used must be rejected because it presupposes an unacceptable metaphysics of free will. However, we can praise and dispraise actions and character just as we can grade eyes and skill and mountain peaks. The primary function of praise in this "grading" sense, according to Smart, is just "to tell people what people are like." [17] However, since people like being praised and dislike being dispraised, praise and dispraise also have the important secondary function of serving to encourage or discourage classes of actions. Smart suggests that "clear-headed people," insofar as they use the terminology of praise and blame, will use it only in this "grading" sense and will

[16] Smart, "Freewill, Praise, and Blame," p. 210.
[17] Ibid., p. 211.

restrict its use to cases in which this important secondary function can be fulfilled.

Most people would agree that moral praise and blame of the kind involved when we "hold a person responsible" have a force which goes beyond the merely informational function of "telling people what people are like." The problem for a compatibilist is to show that judgments with this "additional force" can be appropriate even if the Causal Thesis is true. The prior problem for moral theory is to say what this "additional force" is. What is it that an account of moral judgment must capture in order to be successfully "compatibilist"?

As I have said, Smart's analysis is not compatibilist. His aim is to replace ordinary moral judgment, not to analyze it. Strawson, on the other hand, is offering a compatibilist analysis of (at least some kinds of) moral judgment, and his analysis clearly satisfies one-half of the compatibilist test. The expression of interpersonal reactive attitudes is compatible with the Causal Thesis for much the same reason that Smart's notions of praise and dispraise are. These attitudes are reactions to "what people are like," as this is shown in their actions. As long as the people in question really are like this — as long, that is, as their actions really do manifest the attitudes in question — these reactive attitudes are appropriate.

Strawson's theory is more appealing than Smart's because it offers a plausible account of moral judgment as we currently understand it, an account of how moral judgment goes beyond merely "saying what people are like" and of how it differs from mere attempts to influence behavior. But his theory is like Smart's in locating the "special force" of moral judgment in what the moral judge is *doing*. The contractualist account I am offering, on the other hand, locates the origin of this distinctive force in what is claimed about the person judged. It is quite compatible with this analysis that moral judgments should often be intended to influence behavior and that they should often be made as expressions of reactive attitudes; but such reforming or expressive intent is not essential. What is essential, on this account, is that a judgment of moral blame asserts that the way in which an agent decided what to do was not in accord with standards which that agent either accepts or should accept insofar as he or she is concerned to justify his or her actions to others on grounds that they could not reasonably reject. This is description, but given that most people care about the justifiability of their actions to others, it is not *mere* description.

This account of the special force of moral judgment may still seem inadequate. Given what I have said it may seem that, on the contractualist view, this special force lies simply in the fact that moral judgments attribute to an agent properties which most people are seriously concerned to have or to avoid. In this respect moral judgments are like judgments of beauty or intelligence. But these forms of appraisal, and the pride and shame that can go with accepting them, involve no attribution of responsibility and hence raise no question of freedom. To the extent that moral appraisal is different in this respect, and does raise a special question of freedom, it would seem that this difference is yet to be accounted for.

One way in which freedom is relevant to moral appraisal on the Quality of Will theory (the main way mentioned so far) is this: insofar as we are talking about praising or blaming a person on the basis of a particular action, the freedom or unfreedom of that action is relevant to the question whether the intentions and attitudes seemingly implicit in it are actually present in the agent. This evidential relevance of freedom is not peculiar to moral appraisal, however. Similar questions can arise in regard to assessments of intelligence or skill on the basis of particular pieces of behavior. (We may ask, for example, whether the occasion was a fair test of her skill, or whether there were interfering conditions.) The objection just raised does not dispute the ability of the Quality of Will theory to explain *this* way in which moral judgments may depend on questions of freedom, but it suggests that this is not enough. It assumes that "blameworthy" intentions and attitudes are correctly attributed to an agent and then asks how, on the analysis I have offered, this attribution goes beyond welcome or unwelcome description. Behind the objection lies the idea that going "beyond description" in the relevant sense would involve holding the agent *responsible* in a way that people are not (normally) responsible for being beautiful or intelligent and that this notion of responsibility brings with it a further condition of freedom which my discussion of the Quality of Will theory has so far ignored.

I do not believe that in order to criticize a person for behaving in a vicious and callous manner we must maintain that he or she is responsible for becoming vicious and callous. Whether a person is so responsible is, in my view, a separate question. Leaving this question aside, however, there is a sense in which we are responsible for — or, I would prefer to say, *accountable for* — our intentions and decisions but not for our looks or intelligence. This is just because, insofar as these intentions and decisions are *ours*, it is appropriate to ask us to justify or explain them—appropriate, that is, for someone to ask, Why do you think you can treat me this way? in a way that it would not be appropriate to ask, in an accusing tone, Why are you so tall? This is not to say that these mental states are the kinds of thing which have reasons *rather than causes* but only that they are states for which requests for reasons are in principle relevant.

Moral criticism and moral argument, on the contractualist view, consist in the exchange of such requests and justifications. Adverse moral judgment therefore differs from mere unwelcome description because it calls for particular kinds of response, such as justification, explanation, or admission of fault. In what way does it "call for" these responses? Here let me make three points. First, the person making an adverse moral judgment is often literally asking for or demanding an explanation, justification, or apology. Second, moral criticism concerns features of the agent for which questions about reasons, raised by the agent him or herself, are appropriate. Insofar as I think of a past intention, decision, or action as *mine*, I think of it as something which was sensitive to my assessment, at the time, of relevant reasons. This makes it appropriate for me to ask myself, Why did I think or do that? and Do I still take those reasons to be sufficient? Third, the contractualist account of moral motivation ties these two points together. A person who is concerned to be able to justify him- or herself to others will be moved to respond to the kind of demand I have mentioned, will want to be able to respond positively (i.e., with a justification) and will want to carry out the kind of first-person reflection just described in a way that makes such a response possible. For such a person, moral blame differs from mere unwelcome description not only because of its seriousness but also because it engages in this way with an agent's own process of critical reflection, thus raising the questions Why did I do that? Do I still endorse those reasons? Can I defend the judgment that they were adequate grounds for acting?

Whether one accepts this as an adequate account of the "special force" of moral judgments will depend, of course, on what one thinks that moral judgment in the "ordinary" sense actually entails. Some have held that from the fact that a person is morally blameworthy it follows that it would be a good thing if he or she were to suffer some harm (or, at least, that this would be less bad than if some innocent person were to suffer the same harm).[18] I do not myself regard moral blame as having this implication. So if a compatibilist account of moral judgment must have this consequence, I am content to be offering a revisionist theory. (The problem of how the fact of choice may make harmful consequences more justifiable will, however, come up again in lecture 2.)

---

[18] This idea was suggested to me by Derek Parfit in the seminar following the presentation of this lecture in Oxford.

7. BLAMEWORTHINESS AND FREEDOM

It remains to say something about how this contractualist version of the Quality of Will theory handles the difficult question of moral appraisal of the insane. Discussion of this matter will also enable me to draw together some of the points that have just been made and to say more about the kind of freedom which is presupposed by moral blameworthiness according to the theory I have been proposing.

As I said earlier, to believe that one's behavior is morally faulty is to believe either that one has failed to attend to considerations which any standards that others could not reasonably reject would require one to attend to or that one has knowingly acted contrary to what such standards would require. Let me focus for a moment on the first disjunct. Something like this is a necessary part of an account of moral blameworthiness, since failure to give any thought at all to what is morally required can certainly be grounds for moral criticism. But the purely negative statement I have given above is too broad. The class of people who simply fail to attend to the relevant considerations includes many who do not seem to be candidates for moral blame: people acting in their sleep, victims of hypnosis, young children, people suffering from mental illness, and so on. We need to find, within the notion of moral blame itself, some basis for a nonarbitrary qualification of the purely negative criterion.

According to contractualism, thought about right and wrong is a search for principles "for the regulation of behavior" which others, similarly motivated, have reason to accept. What kind of "regulation" is intended here? Not regulation "from without" through a system of social sanctions but regulation "from within" through critical reflection on one's own conduct under the pressure provided by the desire to be able to justify one actions to others on grounds they could not reasonably reject. This idea of regulation has two components, one specifically moral, the other not. The specifically moral component is the ability to reason about what could be justified to others. The nonmoral component is the more general capacity through which the results of such reasoning make a difference to what one does. Let me call this the capacity for critically reflective, rational self-governance — "critically reflective" because it involves the ability to reflect and pass judgment upon one's actions and the thought processes leading up to them; "rational" in the broad sense of involving sensitivity to reasons and the ability to weigh them; "self-governance" because it is a process which makes a difference to how one acts.

The critical reflection of a person who has this capacity will have a kind of coherence over time. Conclusions reached at one time will be seen as relevant to critical reflection at later times unless specifically overruled. In addition, the results of this reflection will normally make a difference both in how the person acts given a certain perception of a situation and in the features of situations which he or she is on the alert for and tends to notice.

This general capacity for critically reflective, rational self-governance is not specifically moral, and someone could have it who was entirely unconcerned with morality. Morality does not tell one to have this capacity, and failing to have it in general or on a particular occasion is not a moral fault. Rather, morality is addressed to people who are assumed to have this general capacity, and it tells them how the capacity should be exercised. The most general moral demand is that we exercise our capacity for self-governance in ways that others could reasonably be expected to authorize. More specific moral requirements follow from this.

Since moral blameworthiness concerns the exercise of the general capacity of self-governance, our views about the limits of moral blame are sensitive to changes in our views about the limits of this capacity. We normally believe, for example, that very young children lack this capacity and that it does not govern our actions while we are asleep. Nor, according to some assumptions about hypnosis, does it regulate posthypnotic suggestion, and it is generally believed to be blocked by some forms of mental illness. These assumptions could be wrong, but given that we hold them it is natural that we do not take people in these categories to be morally blameworthy for their actions. (Whether we think it is useful to blame them is of course another question.) It is important to our reactions in such cases, however, that what is impaired or suspended is a *general* capacity for critically reflective, rational self-governance. If what is "lost" is more specifically moral — if, for example, a person lacks any concern for the welfare of others — then the result begins to look more like a species of moral fault.

As a "higher order" capacity, the capacity for critically reflective, rational self-governance has an obvious similarity to the capacities for higher-order desires and judgments which figure in the analyses of personhood and freedom offered by Harry Frankfurt and others.[19] I have been led to this capacity, however, not through an analysis of general notions of freedom and personhood but rather through reflection on the nature of moral argument and moral judgment. Basic to morality as I understand it is an idea of agreement between individuals *qua* critics and regulators of their own actions and deliberative processes. Critically reflective, rational self-governance is a capacity which is required in order for that idea not to be an idle one. It follows that moral criticism is restricted to individuals who have this capacity and to actions which fall within its scope.[20]

---

[19] See Harry Frankfurt, "Freedom of the Will and the Concept of a Person," *Journal of Philosophy* 68 (1971): 5–20; Wright Neely, "Freedom and Desire," *Philosophical Review* 83 (1974): 32–54; and Gary Watson, "Free Agency," *Journal of Philosophy* 72 (1975): 205–20.

[20] The idea that moral criticism is applicable only to actions which are within the scope of a capacity of self-governance which normally makes a difference in what a person does marks a point of tangency between the Influenceability theory and the analysis I am offering. I am not suggesting, however, that particular acts of moral criticism are aimed at influencing people or that moral criticism is always inappropriate when there is no hope of its making any difference to what people do. Morality as I am describing it is in a general sense "action guiding" — moral argument concerns principles for the general regulation of behavior. But moral

In Frankfurt's terms, these restrictions correspond roughly to a restriction to persons (as opposed to "wantons") and a restriction to actions which are performed freely. In my view, however, this last characterization is not entirely apt. Aside from external impediments to bodily motion, what is required for moral appraisal on the view I am presenting is the "freedom," whatever it may be, which is required by critically reflective, rational self-governance. But this is less appropriately thought of as a kind of freedom than as a kind of intrapersonal responsiveness. What is required is that what we do be importantly dependent on our process of critical reflection, that that process itself be sensitive to reasons, and that later stages of the process be importantly dependent on conclusions reached at earlier stages. But there is no reason, as far as I can see, to require that this process itself not be a causal product of antecedent events and conditions.[21] Calling the relevant condition a form of freedom suggests this requirement, but this suggestion is undermined by our investigation into the moral significance of choice.

8. CONCLUSION

The contractualist version of the Quality of Will theory which I have described seems to me to provide a satisfactory explanation of the significance of choice for the moral appraisal of agents.

"ought" judgments need not be intended as action guiding, and insofar as they do guide action they need not do so by being prescriptive in form. Rather, they guide action by calling attention to facts about the justifiability of actions — facts which morally concerned agents care about. In these respects my view differs from R. M. Hare's prescriptivism, though we would say some of the same things about free will. See his "Prediction and Moral Appraisal," in P. French, T. Uehling, and H. Wettstein, eds., *Midwest Studies in Philosophy*, vol. III (Minneapolis: University of Minnesota Press, 1978), pp. 17–27.

21 For more extended discussion of this issue, see Daniel Dennett's *Elbow Room* (Cambridge, Mass.: MIT Press, 1984), especially chs. 3–5. I make no claim to be advancing beyond what other compatibilists have said about the nature of deliberation and action. My concern is with the question of moral responsibility. Here I differ with Dennett, who goes much further than I would toward accepting the Influenceability theory. See ch. 7 of *Elbow Room* and Gary Watson's criticisms of it in his review in *Journal of Philosophy* 83 (1986): 517–22.

This theory offers a convincing and unified account of familiar excusing conditions, such as mistake of fact and duress, and explains our reactions to questions about moral appraisal of very young children, the insane, and victims of hypnosis. It can explain the special critical force which moral judgments seem to have, and it does this without presupposing a form of freedom incompatible with the Causal Thesis. But the theory applies only to what I called earlier the moral version of the free-will problem. A parallel account may, as I will suggest later, have some relevance to the case of criminal punishment, but it does not offer a promising approach to the other problems I have mentioned. The significance of a person's choices and other subjective responses for questions of economic justice and freedom of thought may have something to do with the fact that these responses reflect what might loosely be called "the quality of the person's will," but this is not because what we are doing in these cases is judging this "quality" or expressing attitudes toward it (since this is not what we are doing.) So, in search of an explanation that might cover these other cases, I will look in a different direction.

Lecture 2

1. THE VALUE OF CHOICE

It would have been natural to call these lectures an investigation into the significance of voluntariness. I have spoken of "choice" instead because this term applies not only to something that an agent does — as in "She made a choice" — but also to what an agent is presented with — as in "She was faced with this choice." It thus encompasses both an action and a situation within which such an action determines what will happen: a set of alternatives, their relative desirabilities, the information available to the agent, and so on. My main concern in these lectures is with the significance of choice in the first of these senses: the moral significance of the choices people make. In this lecture, however, I will present a theory which exploits the ambiguity just mentioned by seeking to explain one kind of moral significance of the choices people make in terms of the value of the choices they have. I will call this the Value of Choice theory.[22]

This theory starts from the idea that it is often a good thing for a person to have what will happen depend upon how he or she responds when presented with the alternatives under the right conditions. To take a banal example, when I go to a restaurant, it is generally a good thing from my point of view to have what appears on my plate depend on the way in which I respond when presented with the menu. The most obvious reason why choice has value for me in this situation is simply instrumental: I would like what appears on my plate to conform to my preferences at the time it appears, and I believe that if what appears then is made to depend on my response when faced with the menu then the result is likely to coincide with what I want. This reason for valuing choice is both conditional and relative. It is conditional in that the value of my response as a predictor of future satisfaction depends on the nature of the question and the conditions under which my response is elicited. It is relative in that it depends on the reliability of the available alternative means for selecting the outcomes in question. In the restaurant case this value depends on how much I know about the cuisine in question and on my condition at the time the menu arrives: on whether I am drunk or overeager to impress my companions with my knowledge of French

---

[22] As I have said, the basic idea of this theory was presented by Hart in "Legal Responsibility and Excuses." Since Hart's article others have written in a similar vein, although they have been concerned mainly with the theory of punishment. See, for example, John Mackie, "The Grounds of Responsibility," in P. M. S. Hacker and J. Raz, eds., *Law, Morality, and Society: Essays in Honour of H. L. A. Hart*, (Oxford: Oxford University Press, 1977), and C. S. Nino, "A Consensual Theory of Punishment," *Philosophy and Public Affairs* 12 (1983): 289–306. Like Hart, Nino links the significance of choice (in his terms, consent) as a condition of just punishment with its significance elsewhere in the law, e.g., in contracts and torts. His view of this significance, however, is closer than my own to what I refer to below as the Forfeiture View.

or my ability to swallow highly seasoned food. Thus the same interest which sometimes makes choice valuable — the desire that outcomes should coincide with one's preferences — can at other times provide reasons for wanting outcomes to be determined in some other way. When I go to an exotic restaurant with my sophisticated friends, the chances of getting a meal that accords with my preferences may be increased if someone else does the ordering.

What I have described so far is what might be called the "predictive" or "instrumental" value of choice. In the example I have given, choice is instrumental to my own future enjoyment, but the class of states which one might seek to advance by making outcomes dependent on choices is of course much broader. Aside from such instrumental values, however, there are other ways in which having outcomes depend on my choice can have positive or negative value for me. One of these, which I will call "demonstrative" value, can be illustrated as follows. On our anniversary, I want not only to have a present for my wife but also to have chosen that present myself. This is not because I think this process is the one best calculated to produce a present she will like (for that, it would be better to let her choose the present herself). The reason, rather, is that the gift will have special meaning if I choose it — if it reflects my feelings about her and my thoughts about the occasion. On other occasions, for reasons similar in character but opposite in sign, I might prefer that outcomes *not* be dependent on my choices. For example, I might prefer to have the question of who will get a certain job (my friend or a stranger) not depend on how I respond when presented with the choice: I want it to be clear that the outcome need not reflect my judgment of their respective merits or my balancing of the competing claims of merit and loyalty.

The features of oneself which one may desire to demonstrate or see realized in action are highly varied. They may include the value one attaches to various aims and outcomes, one's knowledge, awareness, or memory, or one's imagination and skill. Many of these are involved in the example cited: I want to make the choice myself because the result will then indicate the importance I attach to the occasion (my willingness to devote time to choosing a gift); my memory of, attention to, and concern for what she likes; as well as my imagination and skill in coming up with an unusual and amusing gift. The desire to see such features of oneself manifested in actions and outcomes is of course not limited to cases in which one's feelings for another person are at issue. I want to choose the furniture for my own apartment, pick out the pictures for the walls, and even write my own lectures despite the fact that these things might be done better by a decorator, art expert, or talented graduate student. For better or worse, I want these things to be produced by and reflect my own taste, imagination, and powers of discrimination and analysis. I feel the same way, even more strongly, about important decisions affecting my life in larger terms: what career to follow, where to work, how to live.

These last examples, however, may involve not only demonstrative but also what I will call "symbolic" value. In a situation in which people are normally expected to determine outcomes of a certain sort through their own choices unless they are not competent to do so, I may value having a choice because my not having it would reflect a judgment on my own or someone else's part that I fell below the expected standard of competence. Thus, while I might like to have the advantage of my sophisticated friends' expertise when the menu arrives tonight, I might prefer, all things considered, to order for myself, in order to avoid public acknowledgment of my relative ignorance of food, wine, and foreign cultures.

I make no claim that these three categories of value are mutually exclusive or that, taken together, they exhaust the forms of value that choice can have. My aim in distinguishing them is simply to illustrate the value that choice can have and to make clear that this value is not always merely instrumental: the reasons people have for wanting outcomes to be (or sometimes not to be) dependent on their choices has to do with the significance that choice itself has for them, not merely with its efficacy in promoting outcomes which are desired on other grounds.

The three forms of value which I have distinguished (predictive, demonstrative, and symbolic) would all figure in a full account of the problem of paternalism. Legal restriction of people's freedom "for their own good" is likely to seem justified where (a) people who make a certain choice are likely to suffer very serious loss; (b) the instrumental value of choice as a way of warding off this loss is, given the circumstances under which that choice would be exercised, seriously undermined; (c) the demonstrative value that would be lost by being deprived of this choice is minimal; and (d) the tendency to "make the wrong choice" under the circumstances in question is widely shared, so that no particular group is being held inferior in the argument for legal regulation. The pejorative ring of "paternalism" and the particular bitterness attaching to it stem from cases in which either the seriousness of the loss in question or the foolishness of the choice leading to it is a matter of controversy. Those who are inclined to make a particular choice may not see it as mistaken and may attach demonstrative value to it. Consequently, they may resent paternalistic legislation, which brands them as less than fully competent when, in their view, they merely differ from the majority in the things they value. But this kind of resentment need not properly extend to other kinds of legislation sometimes called "paternalistic," such as wage and hour laws. Whether there is any reason at all for such resentment will depend on the reasons supporting a piece of legislation and also on the reasons people actually have for valuing freedom of choice which they would lose.

As controversies about paternalism illustrate, people can disagree sharply about the value of particular choices. They disagree, for example, about how important it is to have whether one wears a seat belt depend on how one reacts (in the absence of any coercion) when setting off in a car. Some regard it as a significant loss when some form of coercion or even mild duress (the threat of a fine, or even the monitory presence of a brief buzzer) is introduced. Others, like me, regard this loss as trivial, and see the "constrained" choice as significantly more valuable than the unconstrained one. This disagreement reflects differences in the instrumental, demonstrative, and symbolic value we attach to these choices.

The existence of such differences raises the question of what is to count as "the value" of a choice as I have been using this phrase. One possibility is what I will call "fully individualized value." This is the value of the choice to a particular individual, taking into account the importance that individual attaches to having particular alternatives available, the difference that it makes to that individual which of these alternatives actually occurs, the importance which the individual attaches to having this be determined by his or her reactions, and the skill and discernment with which that individual will choose under the conditions in question. This fully individualized value may not be the same as the value which the individual actually assigns to the choice in question; rather, it is the *ex ante* value which he or she *should* assign given his or her values and propensities.

Fully individualized value is not what normally figures in moral argument, however. Appeals to the value of choice arise in moral argument chiefly when we are appraising moral principles or social institutions rather than when we are discussing particular choices by specific individuals. In these contexts we have to answer such general questions as How important is it to have the selection among these alternatives depend on one's choice? How bad a thing is it to have to choose under these conditions? When we address these questions, fully individualized values are not known. We argue instead in terms of what might be called the "normalized value" of a choice: a rough assignment of values to categories of choice which we take to be a fair starting point for justification. Thus, for example, we take it as given for purposes of moral argument that it is very important that what one wears and whom one lives with be dependent on one's choices and much less important that one be able to choose what other people wear, what they eat, and how they live. And we do this despite the fact that there may be some who would not agree with this assignment of values.

This phenomenon — the use in moral argument of nonunanimously held "normalized" standards of value — is familiar and by no means limited to the case of choice. The status and justification of such standards is a difficult problem in moral theory. I will not address the general question here but will mention briefly two points about the case of choice. First, "giving people the choice" — for example, the opportunity to transfer goods through market trading—is one way to deal with the problem of divergent individual preferences. What has just been indicated, however, is that it is at best a partial solution. "Having a choice" among specified alternatives under specified conditions is itself a good which individuals may value differently — as is "having the choice whether to have the choice" and so on.[23] Second, differences in individualized valuations of choices result not only from differences in preference but also from differences in the personal characteristics which make a choice valuable: differences in foresight, in self-control, in self-understanding, and so on. Moral argument commonly refers to "normal" levels of these capacities as well as to "normal" valuations of outcomes and of demonstrative and symbolic values.

Let me turn now to the question of how the value of choice is related to the Quality of Will theory, discussed above. Like

---

[23] The variability of the value of choice is pointed out clearly by Gerald Dworkin in "Is More Choice Better Than Less?" in P. French, T. Uehling, and H. Wettstein, eds., *Midwest Studies in Philosophy*, vol. VII (Minneapolis: University of Minnesota Press, 1982), pp. 47–62.

what I have here called predictive and demonstrative value, the form of appraisal underlying the Quality of Will theory starts from the obvious fact that subjective responses can indicate or express continuing features of a person and from the equally obvious fact that these responses are better indicators under some conditions than under others. Even in this common starting point, however, there is a difference: the features of the person with which the Quality of Will theory is concerned constitute a narrow subset of those that give choice its value for the agent. For example, I want to choose my own food largely because my choices will be good indicators of what will please me, but my being pleased more by fish than by liver is not part of the quality of my will with which moral judgment is concerned.

Where the two theories differ most importantly, however, is in the way in which they assign moral significance to this indicative aspect of choice. The Quality of Will theory takes the point of view of the moral judge. Variations in the indicative value of subjective responses are significant from this point of view because moral judgment involves an inference from behavior to quality of will. The Value of Choice theory, on the other hand, begins with the value for an agent of having outcomes depend (or not depend) on his or her subjective responses under certain conditions. This (so far purely personal) value takes on moral significance by being the basis for a claim against social institutions (or against other individuals). In my view, to show that a social institution is legitimate one must show that it can be justified to each person affected by it on grounds which that person could not reasonably reject. One thing which people may reasonably demand, however, is the ability to shape their lives and obligations through the exercise of choice under reasonably favorable conditions. Moral principles or social institutions which deny such opportunities when they could easily be provided, or which force one to accept the consequences of choice under extremely unfavorable conditions which could be improved without great cost to others, are likely to be reasonably rejectable for that reason. Let me illustrate by considering some examples.

2. JUSTICE AND CHOICE

Consider first the economic justice example which I mentioned earlier. Suppose a society, not marked by significant economic inequalities, decides that it needs to have a significant proportion of its workforce work overtime at a particular job. To this end, a bonus is offered to anyone willing to undertake the work, at an amount calculated to elicit the required number of volunteers. The choice between extra pay and extra leisure has obvious instrumental value for the people involved, and giving people this choice makes it overwhelmingly likely that those who prefer additional income (with additional labor) will get it, while those who prefer the opposite will get what *they* prefer. If overtime work was not made dependent on choice the scheme would be very difficult to justify; with this feature, justification is much easier. Nonetheless, whether or not a given worker winds up among those with extra pay will no doubt depend on some "morally arbitrary" facts about his or her background. Why then is this situation any better than the one criticized by Rawls?

The difference does not lie in the "fact" that the choices made in one case have causal antecedents while those made in the other case do not. In the egalitarian case, however, we can say that by placing the people in those circumstances, offering them that choice, and letting the outcome be determined by the choice they make under those conditions, we have done as much for them as could reasonably be required. In the other case it may be argued that we cannot say this: once the people are placed in disadvantageous circumstances, circumstances which themselves make it very unlikely that anyone would make the choices necessary to escape, offering these people the opportunity to exert themselves does little to improve their position.

The background conditions under which choices are made in the laissez-faire system are "arbitrary from a moral point of view" in this sense: they could be almost anything. All we know is that they will be conditions which arose from a series of voluntary transactions, and this does nothing to ensure that they will be good conditions under which to choose. Consequently, there is no assurance that these conditions will have the moral property of being conditions under which choices confer legitimacy on their outcomes.

This interpretation of Rawls's objection to the laissez-faire "system of natural liberty" provides the basis for a reply to one line of criticism raised by Nozick and others. Nozick interprets Rawls as arguing that the fact that some people exert themselves, take risks, and excel while others do not do so cannot by itself justify different economic rewards for the two groups because these differences in motivation may be the result of causal factors outside the control of the agents themselves. He goes on to object that

> this line of argument can succeed in blocking the introduction of a person's autonomous choices and actions (and their results) only by attributing *everything* noteworthy about the person completely to certain sorts of "external" factors. So denigrating a person's autonomy and prime responsibility for his actions is a risky line to take for a theory that founds so much (including a theory of the good) upon persons' choices.[24]

The problem which Nozick raises here is a version of the "political problem of free will" as I presented it in my first lecture. My reply (I do not claim that this was also Rawls's intention) is that it is not mere attributability to "external" factors that undermines the legitimating force of the choices in a "system of natural liberty." The problem, rather, is that such a system

[24] Robert Nozick, *Anarchy, State, and Utopia* (New York: Basic Books, 1974), p. 214.

provides no assurance that these factors will not be ones which undermine the value of choice for many people in the society. Suppose that I exert myself to develop my talents and become wealthy. You, on the other hand, suffering the psychological effects of your unfortunate starting position, fail to exert yourself, and as a consequence remain poor. Can I "claim credit" for my initiative and perseverance, given that they resulted from "fortunate family and social circumstances for which [I] can claim no credit"?[25] If to "claim credit" means simply to consider these traits and actions "mine" in the sense required in order to take pride in them, then the answer is clearly yes. My accomplishments reflect personal qualities which I really do have. If, however, what is meant is that these differences in our behavior can be taken to justify my having more income and your having less, then the answer may be no. This is not because my actions, being caused by outside factors, are not "mine," or because your actions, similarly caused by other factors, are therefore not "yours," but rather because presenting a person with a choice of the kind you had is not doing enough for that person.

Of course, Rawls and Nozick disagree over what constitutes "doing enough" for a person. For Nozick, one has "done enough" as long as the person's Lockean rights have not been violated; for Rawls, the standard is set by the principles which would be accepted behind the Veil of Ignorance. As a result, Rawls's remarks about "factors arbitrary from a moral point of view," as I have interpreted them, may seem not to advance his argument against Nozick but merely to restate the disagreement between them. But this restatement seems to me to have several virtues. First, it locates the disagreement in what seems, intuitively, to be the right place — in a question of justice rather than in a separate (and I believe spurious) question of causal determination. Second, framing the argument in terms of the value of choice has

[25] Rawls, *A Theory of Justice*, p. 104; quoted by Nozick, *Anarchy, State, and Utopia*, p. 214.

the effect of disentangling the idea of individual liberty from Nozick's particular system of Lockean rights. This allows opponents of that system to make clear that they, too, value individual choice and liberty and gives them a chance to put forward their alternative interpretations of these values. The argument can then proceed as a debate about the merits of competing interpretations of the moral significance of liberty and choice rather than as a clash between defenders of liberty and proponents of equality or some other pattern of distribution.

The Value of Choice theory represents a general philosophical strategy which is common to Hart's analysis of punishment and Rawls's theory of distributive justice as I have just interpreted it. In approaching the problems of justifying both penal and economic institutions we begin with strong pretheoretical intuitions about the significance of choice: voluntary and intentional commission of a criminal act is a necessary condition of just punishment, and voluntary economic contribution can make an economic reward just and its denial unjust. One way to account for these intuitions is by appeal to a preinstitutional notion of desert: certain acts deserve punishment, certain contributions merit rewards, and institutions are just if they distribute benefits and burdens in accord with these forms of desert.

The strategy I am describing makes a point of avoiding any such appeal. The only notions of desert which it recognizes are internal to institutions and dependent upon a prior notion of justice: if institutions are just then people deserve the rewards and punishments which those institutions assign them. In the justification of institutions, the notion of desert is replaced by an independent notion of justice; in the justification of specific actions and outcomes it is replaced by the idea of legitimate (institutionally defined) expectations.[26]

In order for this strategy to succeed, the conception of justice by which institutions are to be judged must adequately represent

[26] Rawls, *A Theory of Justice*, p. 313.

our intuitions about the significance of choice without falling back on a preinstitutional concept of desert. This is where the idea of the value of choice comes in. Just institutions must make outcomes depend on individuals' choices because of the importance which individuals reasonably attach to this dependence. But there is a serious question whether this strategy can account for the distinctive importance which choice appears to have. Insofar as choice-dependence is merely one form of individual good among others, it may seem that the Value of Choice theory will be unable to explain our intuition that the moral requirement that certain outcomes be made dependent on people's choices is not to be sacrificed for the sake of increases in efficiency, security, or other benefits.

Several defenses can be offered against this charge. The first is to point out the distinctiveness of the value of choice as compared with other elements in a person's welfare. As I have indicated above, the value of choice is not a purely instrumental value. People reasonably attach intrinsic significance to having outcomes depend on their choices. In addition, the moral requirements which this value gives rise to within a contractualist moral theory are not corollaries of a more general duty to look out for people's welfare. In fact, the demand to make outcomes depend on people's choices and the demand to promote their welfare are quite independent, and they can often pull in opposite directions.

A second defense — parallel to Rawls's argument for the priority of liberty — is to argue that in appraising social institutions people would reasonably set a particularly high value on having certain kinds of outcomes be dependent on their choices.[27] A third, more pragmatic defense is to argue that the distinctive significance which choice appears to have is in part an artifact of the position from which we typically view it. This is a position internal to institutions, and one in which choices have special salience because they are the last justifying elements to enter the

[27] See section 82 of *A Theory of Justice.*

picture. When the relevant background is in place — when conditions are right, necessary safeguards have been provided, and so on — the fact that a person chooses a certain outcome may make that outcome one that he or she cannot reasonably complain of. But choice has this effect only when these other factors are present. Because they are relatively fixed features of the environment, these background conditions are less noticeable than the actions of the main actors in the drama, but this does not mean that they are less important.

These defenses are most convincing in those cases in which the first argument is strongest — that is, in cases like the economic justice example just discussed, in which people's desire to shape their own lives gives choice an important, positive value. The Value of Choice theory looks weaker in cases where the only reason for wanting to have a choice is that it makes certain unwanted outcomes (such as punishment) less likely. Here choice has no positive value — rather than have the choice, one would prefer to eliminate these outcomes altogether if that were possible — yet the fact of choice seems to retain its special significance as a justifying condition. Let me turn, then, to an example of this kind.

3. CHOICE AND PROTECTION

Suppose that we, the officials of a town, must remove and dispose of some hazardous waste. We need to dig it up from the illegal dump near a residential area where it has lain for years and move it to a safer spot some distance away. Digging it up and moving it will inevitably release dangerous chemicals into the atmosphere, but this is better than leaving it in its present location, where it will in the long run seep into the water supply. Obviously we must take precautions to minimize the risks involved in this operation. We need to find a safe disposal site, far away from where people normally have to go. We should build a high fence around the new site, and another around the old one where the excavation is to be done, both of them with large signs warning of the danger. We should also arrange for the removal and transportation to be carried out at times when few people are around, in order to minimize the number potentially exposed, and we must be sure to have the material wetted down and transported in covered trucks to minimize the amount of chemicals released into the air. Inevitably, however, enough chemicals will escape to cause lung damage to those who are directly exposed if, because of past exposure or genetic predisposition, they happen to be particularly sensitive, but not enough to pose a threat to anyone who stays indoors and away from the excavation site. Given that this is so, we should be careful to warn people, especially those who know that they are at risk, to stay indoors and away from the relevant area while the chemicals are being moved.

Suppose that we do all of these things but that nonetheless some people are exposed. A few of these, who did not know that they were particularly sensitive to the chemical, suffer lung damage. Let me stipulate that with respect to all of these people we did all that we could reasonably be expected to do to warn and protect them. So in that sense they "can't complain" about what happened. The question which concerns me, however, is what role the signs and warnings play in making this the case. These are the factors which make outcomes depend on people's choices. Are they, like the fences, the careful removal techniques, and the remote location of the new site, just further means through which the likelihood of someone's being injured is reduced? This is what the Value of Choice theory seems to imply. For after all, since no one wants to have the opportunity to be exposed to this chemical, the only value which choice can have in this case is that of making exposure less likely. This may be an adequate explanation of why we would want to be warned and hence "given the choice" whether to be exposed or not. But it may not account for the full moral significance of the fact that those who were injured "knew what they were getting into." Consider the following two cases.

Suppose that one person was exposed because, despite the newspaper stories, mailings, posted signs, radio and television announcements, and sound trucks, he never heard about the danger. He simply failed to get the word. So he went for his usual walk with no idea what was going on. A second person, let us suppose, heard the warnings but did not take them seriously. Curious to see how the task was being done, she sneaked past the guards and climbed the fence to get a better look.

There seems to be a clear difference between these two cases. In the first, we have "done enough" to protect the person simply because, given what we have done, it was extremely unlikely that anyone would be directly exposed to contamination, and we could not have made this even more unlikely without inordinate expense. There is, after all, a limit to the lengths to which we must go to protect others. The second person, on the other hand, bears the responsibility for her own injury, and it is this fact, rather than any consideration of the cost to us of doing more, which makes it the case that she has no claim against us. By choosing, in the face of all our warnings, to go to the excavation site, she laid down her right to complain of the harm she suffered as a result.

4. THE FORFEITURE VIEW

This familiar and intuitively powerful idea about the significance of choice, which I will call "the Forfeiture View," is not captured by either of the theories I have been considering. It is distinct from the Value of Choice theory, since on that theory what matters is the value of the choice a person is presented with: once a person has been placed in a sufficiently good position, the outcome which emerges is legitimate however it may have been produced. On the Forfeiture View, on the other hand, it matters crucially that an outcome actually resulted from an agent's conscious choice, the agent having intentionally passed up specific alternatives. This is why that view accounts so well for our reaction to the person in the second example: not only does she have no one else to blame for her fate; she has *herself* to blame. We could account for this sense of blame by appealing to a prudential version of the Quality of Will theory: the process of deliberation leading to a decision to climb over the fence "just to see what they are doing" is obviously faulty. But the Quality of Will theory is an account of the moral appraisal of agents, while what we are concerned with here is the justification of outcomes. It may be natural to suppose that a difference in the first translates into or supports a difference in the second, but on reflection it is by no means obvious how this is so.

Moreover, the idea of fault is in fact irrelevant here. The intuition to which the Forfeiture View calls attention concerns the significance of the fact of choice, not the faultiness of that choice. We can imagine a person who, unlike the imprudently curious woman in my example, did not run the risk of contamination foolishly or thoughtlessly. Suppose this third person found, just as the excavation was about to begin, that the day was a perfect one for working on an outdoor project to which she attached great value. Aware of the danger, she considered the matter carefully and decided that taking into account her age and condition it was worth less to her to avoid the risk than to advance her project in the time she was likely to have remaining. Surely this person is as fully "responsible for her fate" as the imprudent woman whom I originally described. But her decision is not a foolish or mistaken one.

This illustrates the fact that what lies behind the Forfeiture View is not an idea of desert. That is, it is not an idea according to which certain choices, because they are foolish, immoral, or otherwise mistaken, positively merit certain outcomes or responses. The idea is rather that a person to whom a certain outcome was available, but who knowingly passed it up, cannot complain about not having it: *volenti non fit iniuria*.

It is important to remember here that the challenge of the Forfeiture View lies in the suggestion that the Value of Choice theory gives an inadequate account of the significance of choice *in the justification of institutions, policies, and specific moral principles.* Once we have accepted as justified an institution or policy attaching specific consequences to particular choices, there is no disagreement about whether these choices have the kind of special force which the Forfeiture View claims. This force can be accounted for by appeal to the institutions, principles, or policies in question. The disagreement concerns the way in which such institutions, principles, and policies themselves are to be justified. When the Forfeiture View says that people who make certain choices "cannot complain" about the harms they suffer as a result, what is meant is that these harms lack the force in this process of justification which otherwise comparable harms would have.

It may seem that a view of this kind is in fact forced on us by contractualism. According to contractualism the crucial question about a proposed moral principle is whether anyone could reasonably reject it. In order for rejecting a principle to be reasonable it must at least be reasonable from the point of view of the person doing the rejecting, that is, the person who would bear the burden of that principle. It may seem, therefore, that a harm which an agent has the opportunity to avoid (without great sacrifice) could never serve as a ground for reasonable rejection of a moral principle. Consider the following argument. From the point of view of an agent, an action which he has the choice of performing must be seen as available to him. Suppose that an agent will run the risk of suffering a certain harm if he follows one course of action but that he would avoid this harm if he were to follow an alternative course which is available to him and does not involve significant sacrifice. Given, then, that the harm is from his point of view costlessly avoidable, how could the agent appeal to this harm as grounds for objecting, for example, to a principle freeing others from any duty to prevent such harms from occurring? It would seem that such harms can have no weight in moral argument.

But this conclusion is not forced on us. In moral argument we are choosing principles to apply in general to situations in which we may be involved. Even if we know that actions avoiding a certain unwanted outcome will be available to us in a given situation, we also know that our processes of choice are imperfect. We often choose the worse, sometimes even in the knowledge that it is the worse. Therefore, even from the point of view of an agent looking at his own actions over time, situations of choice have to be evaluated not only for what they make "available" but for what they make it likely that one will choose. It is not unreasonable to want to have some protection against the consequences of one's own mistakes.

5. Rejecting the Forfeiture View

The appeal of the Forfeiture View can and should be resisted. Note, first, that the Value of Choice theory can account for the apparent difference between the two victims of hazardous waste removal described above. We may have "done enough" to protect the first person, who failed to hear of the danger, in the sense that we have gone to as much effort and expense as could be expected. But because we did not succeed in making him aware of the danger we did not make what happened depend on his choice. Given that this kind of "choice-dependence" is something which we all would want for ourselves — we want such risks to be, as far as possible, "under our control" — we did not make this person as well off as we would reasonably want to be. The second person, on the other hand, did have the benefit of "having the choice," even though this turned out to be worth less to her than it would be to most of us. (There was in this case a divergence between "individualized" and "normalized" value.) Given that she had the choice, however, and was provided with the other protections, it was true of her in a way that it was not of the first person that she was placed in as good a position as one could ask for.

From the fact that a person chose, under good conditions, to take a risk, we may conclude that he alone is responsible for what happens to him as a result. But this conclusion need not be seen as a reflection of the special legitimating force of voluntary action. Rather, the fact that an outcome resulted from a person's choice under good conditions *shows* that he was *given* the choice and provided with good conditions for making it, and it is these facts which make it the case that he alone is responsible. A conscious decision to "take the risk" is not necessary. Consider, here, the case of a person who was informed of the risk of contamination but then simply forgot. As a result, he was out in his yard exercising, breathing hard, when the trucks went by. If enough was done to protect and warn him, then this person is responsible for what happens to him and "cannot complain of it" even though he made no conscious decision to take the risk.

The central element of truth in the Forfeiture View is thus a consequence of the Value of Choice theory rather than an alternative to it. Putting this truth in terms of the Forfeiture View, however, has the distorting effect of suggesting that choice has independent deontic force in the justification of institutions and principles. It also exaggerates the importance of the fact of choice relative to that of the conditions under which the choice was made. The Forfeiture View suggests that these conditions are important only insofar as they bear on the voluntariness of the choice. This is a mistake. The fact that a choice was voluntary does not always establish that we "did enough" for an agent by placing him or her in the position from which the choice was made. Nor does the fact that an agent did not voluntarily choose an outcome, or choose to take a certain risk, establish that what resulted was not his fault. Giving him the *opportunity* to choose may have constituted "doing enough" to protect him. It is thus an important virtue of the Value of Choice theory that it gives the conditions of choice their appropriate independent weight and forces us to keep them clearly in view.

6. RESPONSIBILITY AND THE MORAL DIVISION
OF LABOR: BEYOND CHOICE

Within the Value of Choice theory, ideas of responsibility arise as a derived (and often only implicit) moral division of labor. Because most people take themselves to be more actively concerned with the promotion of their own safety and well-being than others are, they want outcomes to be dependent on their choices even when this has only "avoidance value." Given this concern, "giving people the choice" under favorable conditions makes it extremely unlikely that they will suffer easily avoidable harms. We do not want the trouble and expense of supervising others' choices more closely, and do not want them to be supervising us. Therefore, we take the view that giving people the opportunity of avoiding a danger, under favorable conditions, often constitutes "doing enough" for them: the rest is their responsibility. So stated, this is not a principle but only a description of a general tendency in our moral thought. In particular, the idea of "favorable conditions," here left vague, must be filled in before any specific principle of responsibility is obtained, and this filling in will be done differently in the case of different risks and dangers.

This general analysis does, however, shed light on appeals to responsibility in cases in which the notion of choice seems out of place. The idea of freedom of thought, mentioned in my first lecture, is one such case. Another, which I will discuss briefly here, is the idea of responsibility for one's preferences.

This idea arises in the context of debates as to whether, for purposes of assessing claims of justice, people's welfare should be measured in terms of preference satisfaction or in terms of some objective standard of well-being such as what Rawls has called Primary Social Goods. Objective standards of this kind may seem unfair, since the same bundle of objective goods can yield quite different levels of satisfaction for people with different preferences. Rawls has replied that someone who makes this objection "must argue in addition that it is unreasonable, if not unjust, to hold such persons responsible for their preferences and to require them to make out as best they can." To argue this, he says, "seems to presuppose that citizens' preferences are beyond their control as propensities or cravings which simply happen." The use of an objective standard like primary goods, on the other hand, "relies on a capacity to assume responsibility for our ends." The conception of justice which Rawls advocates thus

> includes what we may call a social division of responsibility: society, the citizens as a collective body, accepts responsibility for maintaining the equal basic liberties and fair equality of opportunity, and for providing a fair share of the other primary goods for everyone within this framework, while citizens (as individuals) and associations accept the responsibility for revising and adjusting their ends and aspirations in view of the all-purpose means they can expect, given their present and foreseeable situation. This division of responsibility relies on the capacity of persons to assume responsibility for their ends and to moderate the claims they make on their social institutions in accordance with the use of primary goods. Citizens' claims to liberties, opportunities and all-purpose means are made secure from the unreasonable demands of others.[28]

I am strongly inclined to agree with Rawls here, and I have defended a similar position myself.[29] Nonetheless, I find this argument somewhat worrisome, because it is easily misinterpreted as involving an appeal to the idea of forfeiture which I argued against above. On this interpretation, the argument is that the imagined objection to objective measures of welfare overlooks the fact that people's preferences are under their control. Given this

[28] John Rawls, "Social Unity and Primary Goods," in Amartya Sen and Bernard Williams, eds., *Utilitarianism and Beyond* (Cambridge: Cambridge University Press, 1982), pp. 168, 169, 170.

[29] In "Preference and Urgency," *Journal of Philosophy* 72 (1975): 655–69. The following discussion concerns issues dealt with in my reply to "the voluntariness objection" on pp. 664–66 of that article.

fact, and in view of the basic moral truth that one cannot complain of harms one could have avoided, the objection is no objection at all: people whose preferences are particularly difficult to satisfy have only themselves to blame.

There are two difficulties with this argument. First, for reasons I have already discussed, the "basic moral truth" to which it appeals seems open to serious doubt. Second, even if this "truth" is correct, the argument appears to exaggerate the degree of control which people have over their preferences. To be sure, the argument does not suggest that people can alter their preferences by simply deciding what to prefer; the kind of control which is envisaged is to be exercised through decisions affecting the development of one's preferences over time. Even so, it is questionable how much control of this kind people can realistically be assumed to exercise.

This leads me to look for an alternative interpretation under which the argument avoids these difficulties while still retaining its force. Following the general strategy which I have been advocating in this lecture, this alternative interpretation takes the idea of responsibility for one's preferences to be part of the view being defended rather than an independent moral premise. As Rawls says, the conception of justice which he is defending *includes* "what we may call a social division of responsibility." The question is how this combination — an objective standard of welfare and the idea of responsibility which it entails — can be defended without appeal to anything like the notion of forfeiture.

The issue here is the choice between two types of public standards of justice, objective standards of the sort just described, according to which institutions are judged on the degree to which they provide their citizens with good objective conditions for the development and satisfaction of their preferences, and subjective standards, under which institutions are also judged on the basis of the levels of preference satisfaction which actually result from their policies. In our earlier discussion of individual choice, the argument for a "moral division of labor" rested on three claims: the value which we attach to having outcomes depend on our own choices (even when this is only "avoidance value"), our reluctance to have our choices supervised by others, and our reluctance to bear the costs of protecting others beyond a certain point. The case for the "social division of responsibility" entailed by objective standards of welfare rests on three analogous claims. We reasonably attach a high value to forming our own preferences under favorable conditions, and one reason for this is our expectation that we will to *some* extent be steered away from forming preferences when we can see that they will be difficult to satisfy and will lead mainly to frustration. Second, we do not want others to be taking an active role in determining what we will prefer. And third, we do not want to be burdened with the costs of satisfying other people's preferences when these are much more costly than our own.

The first of these claims accounts for the (limited) force of the idea, to which Rawls appeals, that people can to some extent avoid "costly" preferences. But it does this without invoking a preinstitutional notion of forfeiture, and without assuming the degree of conscious and deliberate control which the Forfeiture View would require.

The second claim is especially important. Particularly in a society marked by sharp disagreements about what is worth preferring, a public standard of justice requiring government policy to be aimed at raising individual levels of satisfaction is an open invitation to unwelcome governmental intervention in the formation of individuals' values and preferences. The "social division of responsibility" which goes with an objective standard of welfare is therefore an attractive alternative.

The case for an objective standard of welfare is thus largely defensive. Giving up the claim to a greater share of resources in the event that one's preferences turn out to be particularly difficult to satisfy is the price one pays for greater security against governmental interference and greater freedom from the possibly burdensome demands of other people's preferences. The role of the possibility of modifying one's preferences (or of avoiding the formation of preferences which are difficult to satisfy) is just to make this price smaller and not, as the Forfeiture View would have it, to license the result.

7. CONCLUSION

In this lecture I have presented the idea of the Value of Choice as part of a general strategy explaining the moral significance of choice in the justification of social institutions and policies. As compared with its main rival, the Forfeiture View, this strategy has the advantage of assigning choice an important positive value without exaggerating its role and significance in justification. It remains to be seen what kind of freedom the Value of Choice theory presupposes and how it fits together with the Quality of Will theory to account for the significance of choice across a range of cases. These questions will be addressed in my next lecture.

Lecture 3

1. PUNISHMENT AND PROTECTION

Let me begin with a schematic comparison of the institution of punishment and the policy of hazardous waste disposal which I discussed in my last lecture. In each case we have the following elements. First, there is an important social goal: protecting the water supply in the one case; protecting ourselves and our possessions in the other. Second, there is a strategy for promoting that goal which involves the creation of another risk: the risk of contamination in the one case, the risk of punishment in the other. Third, the effect of this strategy is to make it the case that there is, literally or metaphorically, a certain affected area which one can no longer enter without danger. In the one case this is the area of excavation, transport, and disposal, in the other the "area" of activities which have been declared illegal. Fourth, although we introduce certain safeguards to reduce exposure to the risk created, it remains the case that many of those who choose to enter the affected area, and perhaps a few others, will suffer harm. Some of these safeguards (such as requirements of due process, and careful methods of excavation and transport) have the effect of protecting those who choose to stay out of the affected area. Other safeguards enhance the value of choice as a protection by making it less likely that people will choose to enter. In the hazardous waste case these include signs, warnings, and publicity to inform people about the nature of the risk, as well as fences, guards, and the choice of an obscure disposal site where no one has reason to go. Analogous features in the case of punishment are education, including moral education, the dissemination of basic information about the law, and the maintenance of social and economic conditions which reduce the incentive to commit crime by offering the possibility of a satisfactory life within the law. Restrictions on "entrapment" by law enforcement officers also belong in this category of safeguards which make it less likely that one will choose badly. Without such safeguards the value of choice as a protection would be reduced to an unacceptable level.

In each case, in order to defend the institution in question we need to claim that the importance of the social goal justifies creating the risk and making the affected area unusable and that, given the prevailing conditions and the safeguards we have put in place, we have done enough to protect people against suffering harm from the threat that has been created.

Now let me turn to some of the differences between the two cases. First, insofar as the activities which make up "the affected area" in the case of punishment are ones which it is morally wrong to engage in, being deprived of the ability to "enter this area" without risk cannot be counted as a morally cognizable loss. This makes the task of justification easier than in the example of hazardous waste.

A second difference makes this task more difficult, however. In neither case is it our aim that people should suffer the new harm, though in both cases the possibility of their doing so is created by our policy. But in the case of punishment this harm, when it occurs, is intentionally inflicted on particular people. It is an essential part of that institution that people who run afoul of the law should be punished; but it is no part of our waste-removal policy that those who enter the affected area should suffer contamination. If, as I believe, intentionally inflicting harm is in most cases more difficult to justify than merely failing to prevent harm, it follows that an institution of punishment carries a heavier burden of justification.

When such an institution *is* justified, however, this justification entails the kind of "forfeiture" which we looked for but did not find in the hazardous waste case. A person who intentionally commits a crime lays down his or her right not to suffer the prescribed punishment. This forfeiture is a consequence of the justification of the institution of punishment, however, not an element in that justification. It is a consequence, specifically, of the "heavier justificatory burden" just mentioned: because the institution assigns punishment to those who fulfill certain conditions, justifying the institution involves justifying the infliction of these penalties. If the conditions for punishment include having made a certain kind of choice, then a justification for the institution justifies making that choice a necessary and, when the other conditions are fulfilled, sufficient condition for punishment. No such assignment and hence no such forfeiture is involved in the justification of the policy of hazardous waste removal. A person who recklessly chooses to enter the affected area does not lay down a right to further protection against contamination: she has already received all the protection she is entitled to. She does not lay down her right to treatment (or rescue) unless this has been prescribed and the policy including this prescription is justified. For-feiture, like economic desert, is the creature of particular social institutions and relatively specific moral principles (such as those governing promising). It is not a moral feature of choice in gen-eral. As I argued in my last lecture, the moral aspect of choice which figures in the justification and criticism of such institutions and principles is not forfeiture but the less-sharp-edged notion of the value of choice.

I have been assuming that "the affected area" is so defined that one can "enter" it only by conscious choice. This will be so if we identify "entering" that area with committing a crime whose definition involves conditions of voluntariness and intent. But a system of criminal law incorporating elements of strict liability could also fit the abstract model I have described. If a legal penalty is attached to selling adulterated milk (not merely to doing so knowingly, recklessly, or negligently), then one "enters the affected area" simply by going into the milk business, and if such a law is justified then doing this involves laying down one's right not to be penalized if the milk one sells turns out to be impure. This enlargement of the affected area is one reason (perhaps not the only one) why such laws are more difficult to justify, especially since the newly affected area includes activities, such as conscien-tious engagement in the milk business, which people are morally entitled to engage in. Having them entail forfeiture of the right not to be punished is a morally cognizable loss.

2. EXCUSES AND THE VALUE OF CHOICE

I said in my first lecture that an acceptable account of the sig-nificance of choice should be able to explain standardly recog-nized excusing conditions in a way that will not generalize to undermine the moral significance of all choice if the Causal Thesis is true. Let me now say something about how the Value of Choice theory fulfills this assignment. My aim here is not to derive par-ticular excusing conditions or to define the notion of voluntariness appropriate to particular social institutions and moral principles. This would be an extremely time-consuming task, since it is reasonable to suppose that these conditions will vary in detail from case to case. My present purpose is merely to point out in a more general way how the Value of Choice theory would account for these conditions and for their variation.

The general point is obvious. If the justification for a principle or institution depends in part on the value of the choices it presents people with, and if the value of these choices in turn can vary greatly depending on the presence or absence of certain conditions, then in order to be justifiable the institution will have to qualify the consequences it attaches to choices by explicitly requiring the presence or absence of the most important of these conditions.

Lack of knowledge of the nature of the alternatives available, lack of time to consider them, and the disruptive effects of fear or emotional distress can all weaken the connection between a person's reaction at a given time and his or her more stable preferences, values, and sensitivities, thus undermining both the predictive and demonstrative value of choice. Coercion and duress can have similar disrupting effects on the process of choice, but also and more often they diminish the value of choice simply by contracting or altering the set of alternatives between which one can choose. Diminishing the set of alternatives or weighting some with penalties can sometimes increase the value of choice — or so those of us must believe who sign up to give lectures we have not yet written and buy automobiles with seat belt buzzers. But this is not usually the case.

Even when duress, false belief, or other conditions clearly diminish the value of choice, however, it does not immediately follow that these conditions must be recognized as negating a particular obligation or liability. Whether it does or not will depend on, among other things, the costs to others of introducing such an exception into the principle or institution in question. This is a further reason why, on the present theory, it is possible for excusing conditions to vary from principle to principle and institution to institution.

Here there is a clear contrast with the genesis of excusing conditions under the Quality of Will theory. Once we learn that an agent acted under duress or under the influence of a mistaken belief, this immediately alters the "will" attributable to that agent. There is no need to ask what the effect would be of recognizing this "excuse." Of course, such considerations are relevant to the further question of which "qualities of will" should be regarded as morally deficient. But the Quality of Will theory plays no role in answering this question; it is an account only of the process of moral appraisal.

A second contrast between the two theories is this. The Value of Choice theory treats changes in the set of alternatives available to a person and changes in the conditions under which he or she chooses among them as factors contributing to the answer to a single question: how good or bad a thing is it to be presented with that choice? Under the Quality of Will theory, on the other hand, there is an important difference here. Some conditions affect the degree to which a "will" can be imputed to the agent; others modify the nature of that will. This difference may explain Hart's remark that while continental jurisprudence has traditionally distinguished between imputability and fault he sees little to be gained by observing this rigid distinction.[30] This difference is to be expected insofar as Hart is speaking as a Value of Choice theorist while the continental tradition may be more concerned with aspects of the law akin to quality of will.

3. The Value of Choice and the Causal Thesis

I turn now to the question of whether choice will retain the moral significance which the Value of Choice theory assigns it if the Causal Thesis is true. Whether it does so or not will depend on

---

[30] *Punishment and Responsibility*, p. 218.

whether choice will retain its value for an individual if the Causal Thesis is true. This is at least part of what I called in my first lecture "the personal problem of free will." So it seems that the most that the Value of Choice theory could accomplish would be to reduce the political problem of free will to the personal problem.

The mere truth of the Causal Thesis would not deprive choice of its predictive value: a person's choices could remain indicative of his or her future preferences and satisfactions even if they had a systematic causal explanation. Nor, it seems to me, need the demonstrative value of choice be undermined. A person's choices could still reflect continuing features of his or her personality such as feelings for others, memory, knowledge, skill, taste, and discernment.

This is how things seem to me, perhaps because I am in the grip of a theory. It is difficult to support these intuitions by argument because it is difficult, for me at least, to identify clearly the basis of the intuitions which move one toward the opposite conclusion. It might be claimed that what I have called the demonstrative value of choice would be undermined because the feelings, attitudes, and so on which a person's choices might be taken to "reflect" will no longer "belong" to that person if the Causal Thesis is true, but it is not clear why this should be the case. It is easy to see that particular kinds of causal history might make a belief or desire "alien." This would happen when, as in the "implantation" examples mentioned above, the special causal genesis of a belief meant also that it lacked connection with the person's other conscious states — that it was not all dependent on other beliefs and desires for support and not subject to modification through the agent's process of critical reflection. But it does not seem that this kind of loss of connection need hold generally if the Causal Thesis is correct.

One can certainly imagine a form of causal determination which would make this kind of alienation hold generally and would make it inappropriate to speak of a person's holding beliefs and attitudes at all. A person's conscious states might be caused to occur in a pattern which made no sense at all "from the inside," following one another in a random and meaningless sequence preserving no continuity of belief or attitude. It might be argued that the "normal case" is more like this than we are inclined to suppose: that our idea of the coherence and regularity of our conscious life is to a large degree an illusion. This might undermine the sense of self on which the value of choice depends. But this, if true, would be the result of a particular substantive claim about the order and coherence of the events that make up our "mental lives." It would not be a consequence of the bare Causal Thesis itself.

4. Freedom and Overdetermination

The kind of freedom required by the Value of Choice theory is in one respect more extensive than that required for moral appraisal of the kind discussed in my first lecture. This difference can be brought out by considering how the ideas of quality of will and value of choice apply to overdetermination cases of the kind introduced by Harry Frankfurt.[31] Frankfurt's central example involves two drug addicts. It is assumed that neither is capable of resisting the pull of his addiction: both will take the drug when it is offered, and neither could do otherwise. But while one, the "unwilling addict," would prefer that the desire to take the drug not be the one which he acts on, the other, "the willing addict," not only has a desire for the drug but also has the "second-order desire" to act on that desire. Frankfurt believes that the latter addict acts freely in the sense required for moral responsibility but that the former does not. What interests me here is the fact that the two theories I have presented appear to give different answers to the question of freedom in cases like that of Frankfurt's willing addict — that is to say, cases in which (for reasons which may or

---

[31] In "Freedom of the Will and the Concept of a Person."

may not be like those in Frankfurt's particular example) a person has no alternative to doing a certain thing but nonetheless gets what he wants or does what he is inclined to do. If the question is whether the action reflects the agent's quality of will, then cases like that of Frankfurt's willing addict seem to be cases of freedom. (This answer agrees with Frankfurt, which is not surprising given that he is concerned specifically with moral responsibility.) If, on the other hand, the question is whether the agent has been given a fair chance to make outcomes conform to or exhibit his or her preferences and abilities, then the answer seems to be no, and the cases count as instances of unfreedom.

It may seem that this difference is illusory. The question under the Value of Choice theory is whether there was the right kind of opportunity for the person's disposition to choose to be discovered and registered. Insofar as it is predictive value we are concerned with, the assumption is that "we" do not generally know in advance what a person's preference is: we are trying to set up a social mechanism to discover this and react to it. In Frankfurt's cases, however, it is assumed that *we* know the addicts' (first- and second-order) preferences. Indeed, we are assumed to know more about this than agents themselves normally do. The question of how these preferences might be discovered is not at issue in Frankfurt's discussion. But this question can arise with respect to moral responsibility. Administering praise and blame is something *we* do, and it is relevant to ask whether we have adequate grounds for doing so: whether it is fair to judge a person on the basis we have. This is like the question which arose in application of the Value of Choice theory: whether there was adequate opportunity for the person's preferences, whatever they may have been, to be revealed.

This same question of fairness can also be raised when we are only forming an opinion about an agent's blameworthiness, without intending to express it. But the question whether the agent is blame*worthy* goes beyond these questions of adequate grounds, and it is the question which is fundamental: if the person's will in doing the action was of the appropriate sort, then a certain moral judgment is in fact applicable, whether or not any particular person is in a position to make it. Insofar as this is the case, the difference between the two theories that was pointed out above still stands.

Of course, parallel to the fact that a person "really was blameworthy" in acting a certain way, there is the fact that a person "really did want X, which was what he got," and this too might be held to be the fundamental fact, on the basis of which we could ask, How can he complain, since he got what he wanted? But this fact of preference is not fundamental in the way that the fact of blameworthiness is: the two facts are differently related to the moral ideas on which the theories in which they figure are based. The Quality of Will theory is based on the idea that the applicability of moral praise and blame depends on what the quality of will expressed in an action actually was. In determining this quality we may need to know what the agent believed the alternatives to be, but the question of which of these were actually available is in at least some cases irrelevant. Under the Value of Choice theory, however, the basic moral idea is not simply that people should get what they want but that things should be set up so that outcomes are made dependent on people's choices. In overdetermination cases this demand may not have been met, even though, as it happens, the person is in certain respects no worse off as a result.

5. The Two Theories Combined

I have described two theories and said something about how they are related to one another. It remains to be seen how these two theories, when combined, cover the territory. I have so far employed the Value of Choice theory mainly to give an account of the significance of choice in "political" cases, and I have relied upon the Quality of Will theory in discussing moral responsibility.

But this division of labor is overly simple. In fact, both analyses are required to account for the significance of choice in morality, and both are required to explain its force in the law.

Let me take the moral case first. Suppose you think that I promised on Monday to pick up your child at school on Tuesday but then failed to do this. There are two ways in which considerations of voluntariness and choice might enter into an assessment of how blameworthy I am on this account. First, such considerations could undermine my blameworthiness by making it the case that I had no obligation to pick up your child in the first place. It could be that I never assented to your request: when I said yes, it was to something else, and I never heard your request at all. Or perhaps I did assent to your request but only because you threatened me or concealed from me the fact that I would have to wait three hours beyond the normal end of the school day. Factors such as these could erase or modify my obligation.

On the other hand, it could be that while I did indeed incur an obligation to you, my not meeting your child was not due to any failure on my part to take my obligation seriously and try to fulfill it. It might be that I was hit over the head and knocked unconscious just before I was to leave, or that my car broke down on the way, leaving me stranded in a deserted spot.

These two kinds of excusing conditions are quite different. Something like the Value of Choice theory seems to provide the best explanation of why moral obligations are qualified by restrictions of the first sort. As Hart suggested, a system for the making of binding agreements, whether moral or legal, is defensible only if it is constrained by restrictions to ensure that the obligations one acquires are obligations one judges to be worth acquiring. The assessment of quality of will has at most a secondary role here.

Things are reversed in a case of involuntary nonfulfillment of a valid obligation. Here the natural value of choice analysis (modeled on that analysis of the choice requirement for criminal punishment) would be that a morality which held agents liable to blame in such cases would be objectionable because it gave people insufficient "protection" against incurring the sanction of moral blame. This is clearly not the right explanation. It is wrong because it treats moral blame simply as a "sanction" which people would like to avoid, which we attach to certain actions although it could just as well be attached to others (e.g., to things that are done involuntarily). This ignores the distinctive content of moral blame, in virtue of which it is not simply another kind of unpleasant treatment, like being shunned. Morality is, at base, a system of mutually authorizable deliberation. To feel oneself subject to moral blame is to be aware of a gap between the way one in fact decided what to do and the form of decision which others could reasonably demand. The absence of such a gap is by itself a sufficient explanation of why blame is inapplicable in cases like that of the person who, despite his or her best efforts, fails to pick up the child. There is no need to refer to the kind of question which the Value of Choice theory addresses.

This internal connection between the nature of "the moral sanction" and the content of morality — between the nature of blame and the things one can be blamed for — differentiates morality from a social institution set up to serve certain extrinsic purposes. Of course there could be a social practice according to which people would be subject to scolding and shunning in cases for actions involving no faulty willing or deliberation, but what was expressed by this behavior would not be moral blame. Even without such a practice there is a question, distinct from that of blameworthiness, of whether one has good reason to engage in "blaming behavior" toward a given person on a given occasion. As I mentioned in my first lecture, even when people are blameworthy it might be callous to scold them, and the reverse may also be true. For example, even though very young children are not blameworthy it may be important for their moral education to treat them as if they were.

The issues raised here are similar to those which arise in connection with what Hart called the "definitional stop" argument against exemplary or vicarious punishment of persons known to be innocent of any offense.[32] A utilitarian justification of punishment, insofar as it is a justification of *punishment*, could not justify such practices, this argument ran, because these practices do not count as punishment, which, by definition, must be of an offender for an offense. The obvious response to this argument is that it is not important what we call it; the question is why it would not be permissible to subject people, known to be innocent, to unpleasant treatment (prison, fines, etc.) as part of a scheme to intimidate others into obeying the law. As I have said above, I agree with Hart that the Value of Choice theory provides a good (though perhaps not fully satisfying) answer to this question. With respect to moral blame, however, I have responded in effect that it matters a great deal what you call it, because blameworthi-*ness*, rather than any form of "blaming behavior," is the central issue. There is also, of course, a question of the desirability and permissibility of expressing or administering blame in a certain way, but this is a separate question and a secondary one.

In the case of criminal punishment this emphasis is reversed: the main question is whether we can justify depriving people of their property, their liberty, or even their lives.[33] Despite the

---

[32] *Punishment and Responsibility*, pp. 5–6.

[33] In a recent article, R. B. Brandt put forward something like the Quality of Will theory as a limitation on legal punishment. See "A Motivational Theory of Excuses in the Criminal Law," in J. R. Pennock and J. W. Chapman, eds., *NOMOS XXVII: Criminal Justice* (New York: New York University Press, 1985), pp. 165–98. Specifically, Brandt defends the principle that a condition should be recognized as excusing a person from legal blame if the presence of that condition "blocks the normal inference" from the fact that the agent performed a certain act to the conclusion that the agent's motivation is defective. His defense of this principle appeals to the value of assuring people that if they lack "defective motivation" they will almost certainly not be punished. This is reminiscent of Hart and the Value of Choice theory, but Brandt's defense is avowedly rule-utilitarian: he sees the value in question merely as a contribution to the general welfare, not as fulfilling a special requirement of fairness to the individual. Moreover, he sees the requirement of "defective motivation" as a replacement for Hart's notion of "capac-

changed emphasis, however, both elements are still present, and consequently it does "matter what you call it" even if this consideration does not settle the crucial question of justification. The law is not just an organized system of threats. It also provides rules and standards which good citizens are supposed to "respect," that is, to employ as a way of deciding what to do — not simply as a way of avoiding sanctions but as a set of norms which they accept as reason-giving. This important feature of law offers a further reason why the Value of Choice theory was not completely satisfying as an explanation of the choice requirement for criminal punishment. Insofar as punishment is in part an expression of "legal blame," as Feinberg and others have pointed out,[34] there is a special inappropriateness in having it fall on persons who have deliberated and acted just as the law says they should. The Value of Choice theory thus fails to be a complete account of the significance of choice in the law for much the same reason that it fails to be a complete account in the case of morality. In each case there is *something* to the "definitional stop."

Something, perhaps, but in the case of the law, how much? Pointing out "the expressive function of punishment" helps us to understand our reactions to punishing particular kinds of people, but what role if any does it have in the justification of punishment? It seems to have no positive role in justifying hard treatment of the legally blameworthy. Insofar as expression is our aim, we could just as well "say it with flowers" or, perhaps more appropriately, with weeds. Nor, it seems, is this idea the central explanation of the apparent wrongfulness of punishing, say, young children or the mentally ill. Assuming that these people lack the

ity and fair opportunity" to avoid punishment (*ibid.*, p. 180). My analysis is similar to Brandt's in a number of respects, but, unlike him, I see quality of will and the value of choice as two independent (though related) *reasons* for the limits of moral and legal blameworthiness. Since they are related, it is not surprising that these two kinds of reasons often support the same limits. But they do not always do so.

[34] Joel Feinberg, "The Expressive Function of Punishment," in *Doing and Deserving* (Princeton: Princeton University Press, 1970).

capacity for critically reflective, rational self-governance, we could argue, as we did in the case of morality, that they cannot be legally blameworthy. But even in the case of morality, the justification of "blaming behavior" is a separate issue from that of blameworthiness, and here it is a much weightier one in view of the losses that the law can inflict.

The Value of Choice theory offers a more plausible explanation. According to that theory the lack of the normal capacity for critically reflective, rational self-governance is relevant because people who lack it are so unlikely to be deterred. This may or may not make punishment pointless for us, but it certainly makes it unfair to them: we must protect them against punishment just as, in my other example, we must post barriers or guards to keep people with Alzheimer's disease away from the hazardous waste. But within the Value of Choice theory the normal capacity for critically reflective, rational self-governance lacks the *distinctive* importance which it has when moral (or legal) blameworthiness is at issue. There are many people who have this capacity yet will not be deterred. It is easy to say why they are blameworthy, but why should we respond differently to their suffering than to that of the mentally ill? We can say that, because they have this normal capacity for self-governance, deterrence is a plausible strategy for us to use in dealing with them and that the possibility of their being deterred is, from their point of view, *some* measure of protection. If it turns out not to be enough, then the best we can say, if it is true, is that we did as much as we could be expected to do to protect them.

At some moments it seems to me that we must be able to say more — that choice has a further significance not captured by either of the theories I have considered, perhaps something more like what the Forfeiture View is straining toward. At other times, however, it seems to me an advantage of the combined theory I have been defending, and a natural consequence of its aspiration to be compatible with the Causal Thesis, that it leaves us in this position: moral and (if there is such a thing) legal indignation toward lawbreakers is entirely in order, and the sufferings we inflict upon them may be justified. But in justifying these sufferings, and inflicting them, we have to say not "You asked for this" but "There but for the grace of God go I."

The Basic Liberties and Their Priority
John Rawls

This is a much revised and longer version of the Tanner Lecture given at the University of Michigan in April 1981. I am grateful to the Tanner Foundation and the Department of Philosophy at the University of Michigan for the opportunity to give this lecture. I should like to take this occasion to express my gratitude to H. L. A. Hart for writing his critical review (see footnote 1) to which I attempt a partial reply. I have tried to sketch replies to what I believe are the two most fundamental difficulties he raises; and this has led to several important changes in my account of liberty. For many valuable comments and suggestions for how to meet the difficulties Hart raises, I am much indebted to Joshua Rabinowitz.

In making this revision I am indebted to Samuel Scheffler and Anthony Kronman for their comments immediately following the lecture and for later conversations. Scheffler's comments have led me to recast entirely and greatly to enlarge the original version of what are now sections V and VI. Kronman's comments have been particularly helpful in revising section VII. I must also thank Burton Dreben, whose instructive advice and discussion have led to what seem like innumerable changes and revisions.

I remark as a preface that my account of the basic liberties and their priority, when applied to the constitutional doctrine of what I call "a well-ordered society," has a certain similarity to the well-known view of Alexander Meiklejohn (see footnote 11). There are, however, these important differences. First, the kind of primacy Meiklejohn gives to the political liberties and to free speech is here given to the family of basic liberties as a whole; second, the value of self-government, which for Meiklejohn often seems overriding, is counted as but one important value among others; and

105

finally, the philosophical background of the basic liberties is very different.

*   *   *

It was pointed out by H. L. A. Hart that the account in my book *A Theory of Justice* of the basic liberties and their priority contains, among other failings, two serious gaps. In this lecture I shall outline, and can do no more than outline, how these gaps can be filled. The first gap is that the grounds upon which the parties in the original position adopt the basic liberties and agree to their priority are not sufficiently explained.[1] This gap is connected with a second, which is that when the principles of justice are applied at the constitutional, legislative, and judicial stages, no satisfactory criterion is given for how the basic liberties are to be further specified and adjusted to one another as social circumstances are made known.[2] I shall try to fill these two gaps by carrying through the revisions already introduced in my Dewey Lectures. I shall outline how the basic liberties and the grounds for their priority can be founded on the conception of citizens as free and equal persons in conjunction with an improved account of primary goods.[3] These revisions bring out that the basic liberties and their priority rest on a conception of the person that would be recognized as liberal and not, as Hart thought, on considerations of rational interests alone.[4] Nevertheless, the structure and content of justice as fairness is still much the same; except for an important change of phrase in the first principle of justice, the statement of the two principles of justice is unchanged and so is the priority of the first principle over the second.

[1] Hart, "Rawls on Liberty and Its Priority," *University of Chicago Law Review*, vol. 40, no. 3 (Spring 1973), pp. 551–55 (henceforth Hart); reprinted in Norman Daniels, ed., *Reading Rawls* (New York: Basic Books, 1975), pp. 249–52 (henceforth Daniels).

[2] Hart, pp. 542–50; see Daniels, pp. 239–44.

[3] See "Kantian Constructivism in Moral Theory," *Journal of Philosophy*, vol. 77, no. 9 (September 1980), especially the first lecture, pp. 519–30.

[4] Hart, p. 555; Daniels, p. 252.

I

Before taking up the two gaps in the account of the basic liberties, a few preliminary matters should be noted. First, the two principles of justice read as follows:

    Two Principles of Justice

1. Each person has an equal right to a fully adequate scheme of equal basic liberties which is compatible with a similar scheme of liberties for all.
2. Social and economic inequalities are to satisfy two conditions. First, they must be attached to offices and positions open to all under conditions of fair equality of opportunity; and second, they must be to the greatest benefit of the least advantaged members of society.

The change in the first principle of justice mentioned above is that the words "a fully adequate scheme" replace the words "the most extensive total system" which were used in *A Theory of Justice*.[5] This change leads to the insertion of the words "which is" before "compatible." The reasons for this change are explained later and the notion of a fully adequate scheme of basic liberties is discussed in section VIII. For the moment I leave this question aside.

A further preliminary matter is that the equal basic liberties in the first principle of justice are specified by a list as follows: freedom of thought and liberty of conscience; the political liberties and freedom of association, as well as the freedoms specified by the liberty and integrity of the person; and finally, the rights and liberties covered by the rule of law. No priority is assigned to liberty as such, as if the exercise of something called "liberty" has a pre-eminent value and is the main if not the sole end of political and social justice. There is, to be sure, a general presumption against imposing legal and other restrictions on conduct without

    Equal basic liberties

[5] The phrase "the most extensive" is used in the main statements of the principles of justice on pp. 60, 250, and 302. The phrase "total system" is used in the second and third of these statements.

sufficient reason. But this presumption creates no special priority for any particular liberty. Hart noted, however, that in *A Theory of Justice* I sometimes used arguments and phrases which suggest that the priority of liberty as such is meant; although, as he saw, this is not the correct interpretation.[6] Throughout the history of democratic thought the focus has been on achieving certain specific liberties and constitutional guarantees, as found, for example, in various bills of rights and declarations of the rights of man. The account of the basic liberties follows this tradition.

Some may think that to specify the basic liberties by a list is a makeshift which a philosophical conception of justice should do without. We are accustomed to moral doctrines presented in the form of general definitions and comprehensive first principles. Note, however, that if we can find a list of liberties which, when made part of the two principles of justice, leads the parties in the original position to agree to these principles rather than to the other principles of justice available to them, then what we may call "the initial aim" of justice as fairness is achieved. This aim is to show that the two principles of justice provide a better understanding of the claims of freedom and equality in a democratic society than the first principles associated with the traditional doctrines of utilitarianism, with perfectionism, or with intuitionism. It is these principles, together with the two principles of justice, which are the alternatives available to the parties in the original position when this initial aim is defined.

Now a list of basic liberties can be drawn up in two ways. One way is historical: we survey the constitutions of democratic states and put together a list of liberties normally protected, and we examine the role of these liberties in those constitutions which have worked well. While this kind of information is not available

> List of basic liberties

---

[6] Hart gives a perceptive discussion of whether the first principle of justice means by "liberty" what I have called "liberty as such." This question arises because in the first statement of the principle on p. 60, and elsewhere, I use the phrase "basic liberty," or simply "liberty" when I should have used "basic liberties." With Hart's discussion I agree, on the whole; see pp. 537–41, Daniels, pp. 234–37.

to the parties in the original position, it is available to us — to you and me who are setting up justice as fairness — and therefore this historical knowledge may influence the content of the principles of justice which we allow the parties as alternatives.[7] A second way is to consider which liberties are essential social conditions for the adequate development and full exercise of the two powers of moral personality over a complete life. Doing this connects the basic liberties with the conception of the person used in justice as fairness, and I shall come back to these important matters in sections III–VI.

Let us suppose that we have found a list of basic liberties which achieves the initial aim of justice as fairness. This list we view as a starting point that can be improved by finding a second list such that the parties in the original position would agree to the two principles with the second list rather than the two principles with the initial list. This process can be continued indefinitely, but the discriminating power of philosophical reflection at the level of the original position may soon run out. When this happens we should settle on the last preferred list and then specify that list further at the constitutional, legislative, and judicial stages, when general knowledge of social institutions and of society's circumstances is made known. It suffices that the considerations adduced from the standpoint of the original position determine the general form and content of the basic liberties and explain the adoption of the two principles of justice, which alone among the alternatives incorporate these liberties and assign them priority. Thus, as a matter of method, nothing need be lost by using a step-by-step procedure for arriving at a list of liberties and their further specification.

Step by step procedure to producing a list.

A final remark concerning the use of a list of liberties. The argument for the priority of liberty, like all arguments from the original position, is always relative to a given enumeration of the

[7] See "Kantian Constructivism in Moral Theory," Lect. I, pp. 533–34, Lect. III, pp. 567–68.

alternatives from which the parties are to select. One of these alternatives, the two principles of justice, contains as part of its specification a list of basic liberties and their priority. The source of the alternatives is the historical tradition of moral and political philosophy. We are to regard the original position and the characterization of the deliberations of the parties as a means of selecting principles of justice from alternatives already presented. And this has the important consequence that to establish the priority of liberty it is not necessary to show that the conception of the person, combined with various other aspects of the original position, suffices of itself to derive a satisfactory list of liberties and the principles of justice which assign them priority. Nor is it necessary to show that the two principles of justice (with the priority of liberty included) would be adopted from any enumeration of alternatives however amply it might be supplemented by other principles.[8] I am concerned here with the initial aim of justice as fairness, which, as defined above, is only to show that the principles of justice would be adopted over the other traditional alternatives. If this can be done, we may then proceed to further refinements.

II

After these preliminaries, I begin by noting several features of the basic liberties and their priority. First, the priority of liberty means that the first principle of justice assigns the basic liberties, as given by a list, a special status. They have an absolute weight with respect to reasons of public good and of perfectionist values.[9] For example, the equal political liberties cannot be denied to certain social groups on the grounds that their having these liberties

---

[8] On this point, see *A Theory of Justice* (henceforth *TJ*), p. 581.

[9] The phrases "public good" and "perfectionist values" are used to refer to the notions of goodness in the teleological moral doctrines of utilitarianism and perfectionism, respectively. Thus, these notions are specified independently of a notion of right, for example, in utilitarianism (and in much of welfare economics also) as the satisfaction of the desires, or interests, or preferences of individuals. See further *TJ*, pp. 24–26.

may enable them to block policies needed for economic efficiency and growth. Nor could a discriminatory selective service act be justified (in time of war) on the grounds that it is the least socially disadvantageous way to raise an army. The claims of the basic liberties cannot be overridden by such considerations.

Since the various basic liberties are bound to conflict with one another, the institutional rules which define these liberties must be adjusted so that they fit into a coherent scheme of liberties. The priority of liberty implies in practice that a basic liberty can be limited or denied solely for the sake of one or more other basic liberties, and never, as I have said, for reasons of public good or of perfectionist values. This restriction holds even when those who benefit from the greater efficiency, or together share the greater sum of advantages, are the same persons whose liberties are limited or denied. Since the basic liberties may be limited when they clash with one another, none of these liberties is absolute; nor is it a requirement that, in the finally adjusted scheme, all the basic liberties are to be equally provided for (whatever that might mean). Rather, however these liberties are adjusted to give one coherent scheme, this scheme is secured equally for all citizens.

In understanding the priority of the basic liberties we must distinguish between their restriction and their regulation.[10] The priority of these liberties is not infringed when they are merely regulated, as they must be, in order to be combined into one scheme as well as adapted to certain social conditions necessary for their enduring exercise. So long as what I shall call "the central range of application" of the basic liberties is provided for, the principles of justice are fulfilled. For example, rules of order

---

[10] This distinction is familiar and important in constitutional law. See, for example, Lawrence Tribe, *American Constitutional Law* (Mineola, N. Y.: The Foundation Press, 1978), ch. 12, section 2, where it is applied to freedom of speech as protected by the First Amendment. In *TJ* I failed to make this distinction at crucial points in my account of the basic liberties. I am indebted to Joshua Rabinowitz for clarification on this matter.

are essential for regulating free discussion.[11] Without the general acceptance of reasonable procedures of inquiry and precepts of debate, freedom of speech cannot serve its purpose. Not everyone can speak at once, or use the same public facility at the same time for different ends. Instituting the basic liberties, just as fulfilling various desires, calls for scheduling and social organization. The requisite regulations are not to be mistaken for restrictions on the content of speech, for example, for prohibitions against arguing for certain religious, philosophical, or political doctrines, or against discussing questions of general and particular fact which are relevant in assessing the justice of the basic structure of society. The public use of our reason[12] must be regulated, but the priority of liberty requires this to be done, so far as possible, to preserve intact the central range of application of each basic liberty.

It is wise, I think, to limit the basic liberties to those that are truly essential in the expectation that the liberties which are not basic are satisfactorily allowed for by the general presumption when the discharge of the burden of proof is decided by the other requirements of the two principles of justice. The reason for this limit on the list of basic liberties is the special status of these liberties. Whenever we enlarge the list of basic liberties we risk weakening the protection of the most essential ones and recreating within the scheme of liberties the indeterminate and unguided balancing problems we had hoped to avoid by a suitably circum-scribed notion of priority. Therefore, I shall assume throughout, and not always mention, that the basic liberties on the list always have priority, as will often be clear from the arguments for them.

---

[11] See Alexander Meiklejohn, *Free Speech and Its Relation to Self-Government* (New York: Harper and Row, 1948), ch. 1, section 6, for a well-known discussion of the distinction between rules of order and rules abridging the content of speech.

[12] The phrase "the public use of our reason" is adapted from Kant's essay "What Is Enlightenment?" (1784), where it is introduced in the fifth paragraph; Academy edi-tion of the *Gesammelte Schriften*, vol. 8 (1912), pp. 36–37. Kant contrasts the public use of reason, which is free, to the private use, which may not be free. I do not mean to endorse this view.

The last point about the priority of liberty is that this priority is not required under all conditions. For our purposes here, however, I assume that it is required under what I shall call "reasonably favorable conditions," that is, under social circumstances which, provided the political will exists, permit the effective establishment and the full exercise of these liberties. These conditions are determined by a society's culture, its traditions and acquired skills in running institutions, and its level of economic advance (which need not be especially high), and no doubt by other things as well. I assume as sufficiently evident for our purposes, that in our country today reasonably favorable conditions do obtain, so that for us the priority of the basic liberties is required. Of course, whether the political will exists is a different question entirely. While this will exists by definition in a well-ordered society, in our society part of the political task is to help fashion it.

Following the preceding remarks about the priority of liberty, I summarize several features of the scheme of basic liberties. First: as I have indicated, I assume that each such liberty has what I shall call a "central range of application." The institutional protection of this range of application is a condition of the adequate development and full exercise of the two moral powers of citizens as free and equal persons. I shall elaborate this remark in the next sections. Second, the basic liberties can be made compatible with one another, at least within their central range of application. Put another way, under reasonably favorable conditions, there is a practicable scheme of liberties that can be instituted in which the central range of each liberty is protected. But that such a scheme exists cannot be derived solely from the conception of the person as having the two moral powers, nor solely from the fact that certain liberties, and other primary goods as all-purpose means, are necessary for the development and exercise of these powers. Both of these elements must fit into a workable constitutional arrangement. The historical experience of democratic institutions and reflection on the principles of constitutional design suggest that a practicable scheme of liberties can indeed be found.

I have already remarked that the scheme of basic liberties is not specified in full detail by considerations available in the original position. It is enough that the general form and content of the basic liberties can be outlined and the grounds of their priority understood. The further specification of the liberties is left to the constitutional, legislative, and judicial stages. But in outlining this general form and content we must indicate the special role and central range of application of the basic liberties sufficiently clearly to guide the process of further specification at later stages. For example, among the basic liberties of the person is the right to hold and to have the exclusive use of personal property. The role of this liberty is to allow a sufficient material basis for a sense of personal independence and self-respect, both of which are essential for the development and exercise of the moral powers. Two wider conceptions of the right of property as a basic liberty are to be avoided. One conception extends this right to include certain rights of acquisition and bequest, as well as the right to own means of production and natural resources. On the other conception, the right of property includes the equal right to participate in the control of means of production and natural resources, which are to be socially owned. These wider conceptions are not used because they cannot, I think, be accounted for as necessary for the development and exercise of the moral powers. The merits of these and other conceptions of the right of property are decided at later stages when much more information about a society's circumstances and historical traditions is available.[13]

Finally, it is not supposed that the basic liberties are equally important or prized for the same reasons. Thus one strand of the liberal tradition regards the political liberties as of less intrinsic

---

[13] As an elaboration of this paragraph, see the discussion in *TJ*, pp. 270–74, 280–82, of the question of private property in democracy versus socialism. The two principles of justice by themselves do not settle this question.

value than freedom of thought and liberty of conscience, and the civil liberties generally. What Constant called "the liberties of the moderns" are prized above "the liberties of the ancients." [14] In a large modern society, whatever may have been true in the city–state of classical times, the political liberties are thought to have a lesser place in most persons' conceptions of the good. The role of the political liberties is perhaps largely instrumental in preserving the other liberties.[15] But even if this view is correct, it is no bar to counting certain political liberties among the basic liberties and protecting them by the priority of liberty. For to assign priority to these liberties they need only be important enough as essential institutional means to secure the other basic liberties under the circumstances of a modern state. And if assigning them this priority helps to account for the judgments of priority that we are disposed to affirm after due reflection, then so far so good.

III

I now consider the first gap in the account of liberty. Recall that this gap concerns the grounds upon which the parties in the original position accept the first principle of justice and agree to the priority of its basic liberties as expressed by the ranking of the first principle of justice over the second. To fill this gap I shall introduce a certain conception of the person together with a companion conception of social cooperation.[16] Consider first the conception of the person: there are many different aspects of our nature that can be singled out as particularly significant depending on our aim and point of view. This fact is witnessed by the use of

[14] See Constant's essay, "De la Liberté des Anciens comparée a celle des modernes" (1819).

[15] For an important recent statement of this view, see Isaiah Berlin's "Two Concepts of Liberty" (1958), reprinted in *Four Essays on Liberty* (Oxford: Oxford University Press, 1969); see, for example, pp. 165–66.

[16] In this and the next section I draw upon my "Kantian Constructivism in Moral Theory," footnote 3, to provide the necessary background for the argument to follow.

such expressions as *Homo politicus, Homo oeconomicus,* and *Homo faber.* In justice as fairness the aim is to work out a conception of political and social justice which is congenial to the most deep-seated convictions and traditions of a modern democratic state. The point of doing this is to see whether we can resolve the impasse in our recent political history; namely, that there is no agreement on the way basic social institutions should be arranged if they are to conform to the freedom and equality of citizens as persons. Thus, from the start the conception of the person is regarded as part of a conception of political and social justice. That is, it characterizes how citizens are to think of themselves and of one another in their political and social relationships as specified by the basic structure. This conception is not to be mistaken for an ideal for personal life (for example, an ideal of friendship) or as an ideal for members of some association, much less as a moral ideal such as the Stoic ideal of a wise man.

The connection between the notion of social cooperation and the conception of the person which I shall introduce can be explained as follows. The notion of social cooperation is not simply that of coordinated social activity efficiently organized and guided by publicly recognized rules to achieve some overall end. Social cooperation is always for mutual benefit and this implies that it involves two elements: the first is a shared notion of fair terms of cooperation, which each participant may reasonably be expected to accept, provided that everyone else likewise accepts them. Fair terms of cooperation articulate an idea of reciprocity and mutuality: all who cooperate must benefit, or share in common burdens, in some appropriate fashion judged by a suitable benchmark of comparison. This element in social cooperation I call the Reasonable. The other element corresponds to the Rational: it refers to each participant's rational advantage; what, as individuals, the participants are trying to advance. Whereas the notion of fair terms of cooperation is shared, participants' conceptions of their own rational advantage in general differ. The unity of social cooperation rests on persons agreeing to its notion of fair terms.

Now the appropriate notion of fair terms of cooperation depends on the nature of the cooperative activity itself: on its background social context, the aims and aspirations of the participants, how they regard themselves and one another as persons, and so on. What are fair terms for joint-partnerships and for associations, or for small groups and teams, are not suitable for social cooperation. For in this case we start by viewing the basic structure of society as a whole as a form of cooperation. This structure comprises the main social institutions — the constitution, the economic regime, the legal order and its specification of property and the like, and how these institutions cohere into one system. What is distinctive about the basic structure is that it provides the framework for a self-sufficient scheme of cooperation for all the essential purposes of human life, which purposes are served by the variety of associations and groups within this framework. Since I suppose the society in question is closed, we are to imagine that there is no entry or exit except by birth and death: thus persons are born into society taken as a self-sufficient scheme of cooperation, and we are to conceive of persons as having the capacity to be normal and fully cooperating members of society over a complete life. It follows from these stipulations that while social cooperation can be willing and harmonious, and in this sense voluntary, it is not voluntary in the sense that our joining or belonging to associations and groups within society is voluntary. There is no alternative to social cooperation except unwilling and resentful compliance, or resistance and civil war.

Our focus, then, is on persons as capable of being normal and fully cooperating members of society over a complete life. The capacity for social cooperation is taken as fundamental, since the basic structure of society is adopted as the first subject of justice. The fair terms of social cooperation for this case specify the content of a political and social conception of justice. But if

[margin note: Fair terms of social co-op: → political & social conception of justice]

persons are viewed in this way, we are attributing to them two powers of moral personality. These two powers are the capacity for a sense of right and justice (the capacity to honor fair terms of cooperation and thus to be reasonable), and the capacity for a conception of the good (and thus to be rational). In greater detail, the capacity for a sense of justice is the capacity to understand, to apply and normally to be moved by an effective desire to act from (and not merely in accordance with) the principles of justice as the fair terms of social cooperation. The capacity for a conception of the good is the capacity to form, to revise, and rationally to pursue such a conception, that is, a conception of what we regard for us as a worthwhile human life. A conception of the good normally consists of a determinate scheme of final ends and aims, and of desires that certain persons and associations, as objects of attachments and loyalties, should flourish. Also included in such a conception is a view of our relation to the world — religious, philosophical or moral — by reference to which these ends and attachments are understood.

The next step is to take the two moral powers as the necessary and sufficient condition for being counted a full and equal member of society in questions of political justice. Those who can take part in social cooperation over a complete life, and who are willing to honor the appropriate fair terms of cooperation, are regarded as equal citizens. Here we assume that the moral powers are realized to the requisite minimum degree and paired at any given time with a determinate conception of the good. Given these assumptions, variations and differences in natural gifts and abilities are subordinate: they do not affect persons' status as equal citizens and become relevant only as we aspire to certain offices and positions, or belong to or wish to join certain associations within society. Thus political justice concerns the basic structure as the encompassing institutional framework within which the natural gifts and abilities of individuals are developed and exercised, and the various associations in society exist.

So far I have said nothing about the content of fair terms of cooperation, or what concerns us here, about the basic liberties and their priority. To approach this question, let's sum up by saying: fair terms of social cooperation are terms upon which as equal persons we are willing to cooperate in good faith with all members of society over a complete life. To this let us add: to cooperate on a basis of mutual respect. Adding this clause makes explicit that fair terms of cooperation can be acknowledged by everyone without resentment or humiliation (or for that matter bad conscience) when citizens regard themselves and one another as having to the requisite degree the two moral powers which constitute the basis of equal citizenship. Against this background the problem of specifying the basic liberties and grounding their priority can be seen as the problem of determining appropriate fair terms of cooperation on the basis of mutual respect. Until the wars of religion in the sixteenth and seventeenth centuries these fair terms were narrowly drawn: social cooperation on the basis of mutual respect was regarded as impossible with those of a different faith; or (in terms I have used) with those who affirm a fundamentally different conception of the good. As a philosophical doctrine, liberalism has its origin in those centuries with the development of the various arguments for religious toleration.[17] In the nineteenth century the liberal doctrine was formulated in its main essentials by Constant, Tocqueville and Mill for the context of the modern democratic state, which they saw to be imminent. A crucial assumption of liberalism is that equal citizens have different and indeed incommensurable and irreconcilable conceptions of the good.[18]

[17] For an instructive survey of these arguments, see J. W. Allen, *A History of Political Thought in the Sixteenth Century* (London: Methuen, 1928), pp. 73–103, 231–46, 302–31, 428–30; and also his *English Political Thought, 1603–1660* (London: Methuen, 1938), pp. 199–249. The views in Locke's *Letter on Toleration* (1689) or in Montesquieu's *The Spirit of Laws* (1748) have a long prehistory.

[18] This assumption is central to liberalism as stated by Berlin in "Two Concepts of Liberty"; see *Four Essays*, pp. 167–71, footnote 15. I believe it is implicit in the writers cited but cannot go into the matter here. For a more recent statement, see Ronald Dworkin, "Liberalism," in Stuart Hampshire, ed., *Public and Private Morality* (Cambridge: Cambridge University Press, 1978).

In a modern democratic society the existence of such diverse ways of life is seen as a normal condition which can only be removed by the autocratic use of state power. Thus liberalism accepts the plurality of conceptions of the good as a fact of modern life, provided, of course, these conceptions respect the limits specified by the appropriate principles of justice. It tries to show both that a plurality of conceptions of the good is desirable and how a regime of liberty can accommodate this plurality so as to achieve the many benefits of human diversity.

My aim in this lecture is to sketch the connection between the basic liberties with their priority and the fair terms of social cooperation among equal persons as described above. The point of introducing the conception of the person I have used, and its companion conception of social cooperation, is to try to carry the liberal view one step further: that is, to root its assumptions in two underlying philosophical conceptions and then to indicate how the basic liberties with their priority can be regarded as belonging among the fair terms of social cooperation where the nature of this cooperation answers to the conditions these conceptions impose. The social union is no longer founded on a conception of the good as given by a common religious faith or philosophical doctrine, but on a shared public conception of justice appropriate to the conception of citizens in a democratic state as free and equal persons.

IV

In order to explain how this might be done I shall now summarize very briefly what I have said elsewhere about the role of what I have called "the original position" and the way in which it models the conception of the person.[19] The leading idea is that the original position connects the conception of the person and its

---

[19] On the original position, see *TJ*, the entries in the index; for how this position models the conception of the person, see further "Kantian Constructivism in Moral Theory," footnote 3.

companion conception of social cooperation with certain specific principles of justice. (These principles specify what I have earlier called "fair terms of social cooperation.") The connection between these two philosophical conceptions and specific principles of justice is established by the original position as follows: The parties in this position are described as rationally autonomous representatives of citizens in society. As such representatives, the parties are to do the best they can for those they represent subject to the restrictions of the original position. For example, the parties are symmetrically situated with respect to one another and they are in that sense equal; and what I have called "the veil of ignorance" means that the parties do not know the social position, or the conception of the good (its particular aims and attachments), or the realized abilities and psychological propensities, and much else, of the persons they represent. And, as I have already remarked, the parties must agree to certain principles of justice on a short list of alternatives given by the tradition of moral and political philosophy. The agreement of the parties on certain definite principles establishes a connection between these principles and the conception of the person represented by the original position. In this way the content of fair terms of cooperation for persons so conceived is ascertained.

Two different parts of the original position must be carefully distinguished. These parts correspond to the two powers of moral personality, or to what I have called the capacity to be reasonable and the capacity to be rational. While the original position as a whole represents both moral powers, and therefore represents the full conception of the person, the parties as rationally autonomous representatives of persons in society represent only the Rational: the parties agree to those principles which they believe are best for those they represent as seen from these persons' conception of the good and their capacity to form, revise, and rationally to pursue such a conception, so far as the parties can know these things. The Reasonable, or persons' capacity for a sense of justice, which here is their capacity to honor fair terms of social cooperation, is represented by the various restrictions to which the parties are subject in the original position and by the conditions imposed on their agreement. When the principles of justice which are adopted by the parties are affirmed and acted upon by equal citizens in society, citizens then act with full autonomy. The difference between full autonomy and rational autonomy is this: rational autonomy is acting solely from our capacity to be rational and from the determinate conception of the good we have at any given time. Full autonomy includes not only this capacity to be rational but also the capacity to advance our conception of the good in ways consistent with honoring the fair terms of social cooperation; that is, the principles of justice. In a well-ordered society in which citizens know they can count on each other's sense of justice, we may suppose that a person normally wants to act justly as well as to be recognized by others as someone who can be relied upon as a fully cooperating member of society over a complete life. Fully autonomous persons therefore publicly acknowledge and act upon the fair terms of social cooperation moved by the reasons specified by the shared principles of justice. The parties, however, are only rationally autonomous, since the constraints of the Reasonable are simply imposed from without. Indeed, the rational autonomy of the parties is merely that of artificial agents who inhabit a construction designed to model the full conception of the person as both reasonable and rational. It is equal citizens in a well-ordered society who are fully autonomous because they freely accept the constraints of the Reasonable, and in so doing their political life reflects that conception of the person which takes as fundamental their capacity for social cooperation. It is the full autonomy of active citizens which expresses the political ideal to be realized in the social world.[20]

---

[20] I use the distinction between the two parts of the original position which correspond to the Reasonable and the Rational as a vivid way to state the idea that this position models the *full* conception of the person. I hope that this will prevent several

[margin notes: full vs rational autonomy.; full autonomy]

Thus we can say that the parties in the original position are, as rational representatives, rationally autonomous in two respects. First, in their deliberations they are not required to apply, or to be guided by, any prior or antecedent principles of right and justice. Second, in arriving at an agreement on which principles of justice to adopt from the alternatives available, the parties are to be guided solely by what they think is for the determinate good of the persons they represent, so far as the limits on information allow them to determine this. The agreement in the original position on the two principles of justice must be an agreement founded on rationally autonomous reasons in this sense. Thus, in effect, we are using the rationally autonomous deliberations of the parties to select from given alternatives the fair terms of cooperation between the persons they represent.

Much more would have to be said adequately to explain the preceding summary. But here I must turn to the considerations that move the parties in the original position. Of course, their overall aim is to fulfill their responsibility and to do the best they can to advance the determinate good of the persons they represent. The problem is that given the restrictions of the veil of ignorance, it may seem impossible for the parties to ascertain these persons' good and therefore to make a rational agreement on their behalf. To solve this problem we introduce the notion of primary goods and enumerate a list of various things which fall under this heading. The main idea is that primary goods are singled out by asking which things are generally necessary as social conditions and all-purpose means to enable persons to pursue their determinate conceptions of the good and to develop and exercise their two moral powers. Here we must look to social requirements and the normal

misinterpretations of this position, for example, that it is intended to be morally neutral, or that it models only the notion of rationality, and therefore that justice as fairness attempts to select principles of justice purely on the basis of a conception of rational choice as understood in economics or decision theory. For a Kantian view, such an attempt is out of the question and is incompatible with its conception of the person.

circumstances of human life in a democratic society. That the primary goods are necessary conditions for realizing the moral powers and are all-purpose means for a sufficiently wide range of final ends presupposes various general facts about human wants and abilities, their characteristic phases and requirements of nurture, relations of social interdependence, and much else. We need at least a rough account of rational plans of life which shows why they normally have a certain structure and depend upon the primary goods for their formation, revision, and execution. What are to count as primary goods is not decided by asking what general means are essential for achieving the final ends which a comprehensive empirical or historical survey might show that people usually or normally have in common. There may be few if any such ends; and those there are may not serve the purposes of a conception of justice. The characterization of primary goods does not rest on such historical or social facts. While the determination of primary goods invokes a knowledge of the general circumstances and requirements of social life, it does so only in the light of a conception of the person given in advance.

The five kinds of primary goods enumerated in *A Theory of Justice* (accompanied by an indication of why each is used) are the following:

5 Kinds of
primary goods:

1. The basic liberties (freedom of thought and liberty of conscience, and so on): these liberties are the background institutional conditions necessary for the development and the full and informed exercise of the two moral powers (particularly in what later, in section VIII, I shall call "the two fundamental cases"); these liberties are also indispensable for the protection of a wide range of determinate conceptions of the good (within the limits of justice).

2. Freedom of movement and free choice of occupation against a background of diverse opportunities: these opportunities allow the pursuit of diverse final ends and give

effect to a decision to revise and change them, if we so desire.

3. Powers and prerogatives of offices and positions of responsibility: these give scope to various self-governing and social capacities of the self.

4. Income and wealth, understood broadly as all-purpose means (having an exchange value): income and wealth are needed to achieve directly or indirectly a wide range of ends, whatever they happen to be.

5. The social bases of self-respect: these bases are those aspects of basic institutions normally essential if citizens are to have a lively sense of their own worth as persons and to be able to develop and exercise their moral powers and to advance their aims and ends with self-confidence.[21]

Observe that the two principles of justice assess the basic structure of society according to how its institutions protect and assign some of these primary goods, for example, the basic liberties, and regulate the production and distribution of other primary goods, for example, income and wealth. Thus, in general, what has to be explained is why the parties use this list of primary goods and why it is rational for them to adopt the two principles of justice.

In this lecture I cannot discuss this general question. Except for the basic liberties, I shall assume that the grounds for relying on primary goods are clear enough for our purposes. My aim in the following sections is to explain why, given the conception of the person which characterizes the citizens the parties represent, the basic liberties are indeed primary goods, and moreover why the principle which guarantees these liberties is to have priority over the second principle of justice. Sometimes the reason for this priority is evident from the explanation of why a liberty is basic,

---

[21] For a fuller account of primary goods, see my "Social Unity and Primary Goods," in Amartya Sen and Bernard Williams, eds., *Beyond Utilitarianism* (Cambridge: Cambridge University Press, 1982).

Explains the rest of the sections.

as in the case of equal liberty of conscience (discussed in sections V–VI). In other cases the priority derives from the procedural role of certain liberties and their fundamental place in regulating the basic structure as a whole, as in the case of the equal political liberties (discussed in section VIII). Finally, certain basic liberties are indispensable institutional conditions once other basic liberties are guaranteed; thus freedom of thought and freedom of association are necessary to give effect to liberty of conscience and the political liberties. (This connection is sketched in the case of free political speech and the political liberties in sections X–XII.) My discussion is very brief and simply illustrates the kinds of grounds the parties have for counting certain liberties as basic. By considering several different basic liberties, each grounded in a somewhat different way, I hope to explain the place of the basic liberties in justice as fairness and the reasons for their priority.

V

equal liberty of the conscious ?

We are now ready to survey the grounds upon which the parties in the original position adopt principles which guarantee the basic liberties and assign them priority. I cannot here present the argument for such principles in a rigorous and convincing manner, but shall merely indicate how it might proceed.

Let us note first that given the conception of the person, there are three kinds of considerations the parties must distinguish when they deliberate concerning the good of the persons they represent. ① There are considerations relating to the development and the full and informed exercise of the two moral powers, each power giving rise to considerations of a distinct kind; and, finally, ② considerations relating to a person's determinate conception of the good. In this section I take up the considerations relating to the capacity for a conception of the good and to a person's determinate conception of the good. I begin with the latter. Recall that while the parties know that the persons they represent have determinate conceptions of the good, they do not know the content of these conceptions; that is, they do not know the particular final ends and aims these persons pursue, nor the objects of their attachments and loyalties, nor their view of their relation to the world — religious, philosophical, or moral — by reference to which these ends and loyalties are understood. However, the parties do know the general structure of rational persons' plans of life (given the general facts about human psychology and the workings of social institutions) and hence the main elements in a conception of the good as just enumerated. Knowledge of these matters goes with their understanding and use of primary goods as previously explained.

[margin note: determinate conception of the good.]

[margin note: we know rational plans ∴ know main elements in the conception of the good.]

To fix ideas, I focus on liberty of conscience and survey the grounds the parties have for adopting principles which guarantee this basic liberty as applied to religious, philosophical, and moral views of our relation to the world.[22] Of course, while the parties cannot be sure that the persons they represent affirm such views, I shall assume that these persons normally do so, and in any event the parties must allow for this possibility. I assume also that these religious, philosophical, and moral views are already formed and firmly held, and in this sense given. Now if but one of the alternative principles of justice available to the parties guarantees equal liberty of conscience, this principle is to be adopted. Or at least this holds if the conception of justice to which this principle belongs is a workable conception. For the veil of ignorance implies that the parties do not know whether the beliefs espoused by the persons they represent is a majority or a minority view. They cannot take chances by permitting a lesser liberty of conscience to minority religions, say, on the possibility that those they represent espouse a majority or dominant religion and will therefore have an even greater liberty. For it may also happen that these persons belong to a minority faith and may suffer accordingly. If the parties were to gamble in this way, they would show

[margin note: goal ↓ liberty of conscience (gained through deliberation behind the veil of ignor.)]

22 In this and the next two paragraphs I state in a somewhat different way the main consideration given for liberty of conscience in *TJ*, section 33.

that they did not take the religious, philosophical, or moral convictions of persons seriously, and, in effect, did not know what a religious, philosophical, or moral conviction was.

Note that, strictly speaking, this first ground for liberty of conscience is not an argument. That is, one simply calls attention to the way in which the veil of ignorance combined with the parties' responsibility to protect some unknown but determinate and affirmed religious, philosophical, or moral view gives the parties the strongest reasons for securing this liberty. Here it is fundamental that affirming such views and the conceptions of the good to which they give rise is recognized as non-negotiable, so to speak. They are understood to be forms of belief and conduct the protection of which we cannot properly abandon or be persuaded to jeopardize for the kinds of considerations covered by the second principle of justice. To be sure, there are religious conversions, and persons change their philosophical and moral views. But presumptively these conversions and changes are not prompted by reasons of power and position, or of wealth and status, but are the result of conviction, reason, and reflection. Even if in practice this presumption is often false, this does not affect the responsibility of the parties to protect the integrity of the conception of the good of those they represent.

It is clear, then, why liberty of conscience is a basic liberty and possesses the priority of such a liberty. Given an understanding of what constitutes a religious, philosophical, or moral view, the kinds of considerations covered by the second principle of justice cannot be adduced to restrict the central range of this liberty. If someone denies that liberty of conscience is a basic liberty and maintains that all human interests are commensurable, and that between any two there always exists some rate of exchange in terms of which it is rational to balance the protection of one against the protection of the other, then we have reached an impasse. One way to continue the discussion is to try to show that the scheme of basic liberties as a family is part of a coherent and workable conception of justice appropriate for the basic structure of a democratic regime and, moreover, a conception that is congruent with its most essential convictions.

Let's now turn to considerations relating to the capacity for a conception of the good. This capacity was earlier defined as a capacity to form, to revise, and rationally to pursue a determinate conception of the good. Here there are two closely related grounds, since this capacity can be viewed in two ways. In the first way, the adequate development and exercise of this capacity, as circumstances require, is regarded as a means to a person's good; and as a means it is not (by definition) part of this person's determinate conception of the good. Persons exercise this power in rationally pursuing their final ends and in articulating their notions of a complete life. At any given moment this power serves the determinate conception of the good then affirmed; but the role of this power in forming other and more rational conceptions of the good and in revising existing ones must not be overlooked. There is no guarantee that all aspects of our present way of life are the most rational for us and not in need of at least minor if not major revision. For these reasons the adequate and full exercise of the capacity for a conception of the good is a means to a person's good. Thus, on the assumption that liberty of conscience, and therefore the liberty to fall into error and to make mistakes, is among the social conditions necessary for the development and exercise of this power, the parties have another ground for adopting principles that guarantee this basic liberty. Here we should observe that freedom of association is required to give effect to liberty of conscience; for unless we are at liberty to associate with other like-minded citizens, the exercise of liberty of conscience is denied. These two basic liberties go in tandem.

The second way of regarding the capacity for a conception of the good leads to a further ground for liberty of conscience. This ground rests on the broad scope and regulative nature of this capacity and the inherent principles that guide its operations (the principles of rational deliberation). These features of this capacity enable us to think of ourselves as affirming our way of life in accordance with the full, deliberate, and reasoned exercise of our intellectual and moral powers. And this rationally affirmed relation between our deliberative reason and our way of life itself becomes part of our determinate conception of the good. This possibility is contained in the conception of the person. Thus, in addition to our beliefs being true, our actions right, and our ends good, we may also strive to appreciate *why* our beliefs are true, our actions right, and our ends good and suitable for us. As Mill would say, we may seek to make our conception of the good "our own"; we are not content to accept it ready-made from our society or social peers.[23] Of course, the conception we affirm need not be peculiar to us, or a conception we have, as it were, fashioned for ourselves; rather, we may affirm a religious, philosophical, or moral tradition in which we have been raised and educated, and which we find, at the age of reason, to be a center of our attachments and loyalties. In this case what we affirm is a tradition that incorporates ideals and virtues which meet the tests of our reason and which answer to our deepest desires and affections. Of course, many persons may not examine their acquired beliefs and ends but take them on faith, or be satisfied that they are matters of custom and tradition. They are not to be criticized for this, for in the liberal view there is no political or social evaluation of conceptions of the good within the limits permitted by justice.

In this way of regarding the capacity for a conception of the good, this capacity is not a means to but is an essential part of a determinate conception of the good. The distinctive place in justice as fairness of this conception is that it enables us to view our final aims and loyalties in a way that realizes to the full extent

---

.[23] See J. S. Mill, *On Liberty*, ch. 3, par. 5, where he says, "To a certain extent it is admitted, that our understanding should be our own; but there is not the same willingness to admit that our desires and impulses should be our own likewise; or that to possess impulses of our own, and of any strength, is anything but a peril and a snare." See the whole of pars. 2–9 on the free development of individuality.

one of the moral powers in terms of which persons are characterized in this political conception of justice. For this conception of the good to be possible we must be allowed, even more plainly than in the case of the preceding ground, to fall into error and to make mistakes within the limits established by the basic liberties. In order to guarantee the possibility of this conception of the good, the parties, as our representatives, adopt principles which protect liberty of conscience.

The preceding three grounds for liberty of conscience are related as follows. In the first, conceptions of the good are regarded as given and firmly rooted; and since there is a plurality of such conceptions, each, as it were, non-negotiable, the parties recognize that behind the veil of ignorance the principles of justice which guarantee equal liberty of conscience are the only principles which they can adopt. In the next two grounds, conceptions of the good are seen as subject to revision in accordance with deliberative reason, which is part of the capacity for a conception of the good. But since the full and informed exercise of this capacity requires the social conditions secured by liberty of conscience, these grounds support the same conclusion as the first.

VI

Finally we come to the considerations relating to the capacity for a sense of justice. Here we must be careful. The parties in the original position are rationally autonomous representatives and as such are moved solely by considerations relating to what furthers the determinate conceptions of the good of the persons they represent, either as a means or as a part of these conceptions. Thus, any grounds that prompt the parties to adopt principles that secure the development and exercise of the capacity for a sense of justice must accord with this restriction. Now we saw in the preceding section that the capacity for a conception of the good can be part of, as well as a means to, someone's determinate conception of the good, and that the parties can invoke reasons based on each of these two cases without violating their rationally autonomous role. The situation is different with the sense of justice: for here the parties cannot invoke reasons founded on regarding the development and exercise of this capacity as part of a person's determinate conception of the good. They are restricted to reasons founded on regarding it solely as a means to a person's good.

To be sure, we assume (as do the parties) that citizens have the capacity for a sense of justice, but this assumption is purely formal. It means only that whatever principles the parties select from the alternatives available, the persons the parties represent will be able to develop, as citizens in society, the corresponding sense of justice to the degree to which the parties' deliberations, informed by common-sense knowledge and the theory of human nature, show to be possible and practicable. This assumption is consistent with the parties' rational autonomy and the stipulation that no antecedent notions or principles of justice are to guide (much less constrain) the parties' reasoning as to which alternative to select. In view of this assumption, the parties know that their agreement is not in vain and that citizens in society will act upon the principles agreed to with an effectiveness and regularity of which human nature is capable when political and social institutions satisfy, and are publicly known to satisfy, these principles. But when the parties count, as a consideration in favor of certain principles of justice, the fact that citizens in society will effectively and regularly act upon them, the parties can do so only because they believe that acting from such principles will serve as effective means to the determinate conceptions of the good of the persons they represent. These persons as citizens are moved by reasons of justice as such, but the parties as rational autonomous representatives are not.

With these precautions stated, I now sketch three grounds, each related to the capacity for a sense of justice, that prompt the parties to adopt principles securing the basic liberties and assigning them priority. The first ground rests on two points: first, on the great advantage to everyone's conception of the good of a just and stable scheme of cooperation; and second, on the thesis that the most stable conception of justice is the one specified by the two principles of justice, and this is the case importantly because of the basic liberties and the priority assigned to them by these principles.

Clearly, the public knowledge that everyone has an effective sense of justice and can be relied upon as a fully cooperating member of society is a great advantage to everyone's conception of the good.[24] This public knowledge, and the shared sense of justice which is its object, is the result of time and cultivation, easier to destroy than to build up. The parties assess the traditional alternatives in accordance with how well they generate a publicly recognized sense of justice when the basic structure is known to satisfy the corresponding principles. In doing this they view the developed capacity for a sense of justice as a means to the good of those they represent. That is, a scheme of just social cooperation advances citizens' determinate conceptions of the good; and a scheme made stable by an effective public sense of justice is a better means to this end than a scheme which requires a severe and costly apparatus of penal sanctions, particularly when this apparatus is dangerous to the basic liberties.

The comparative stability of the traditional principles of justice available to the parties is a complicated matter. I cannot summarize here the many considerations I have examined elsewhere to support the second point, the thesis that the two principles of justice are the most stable. I shall only mention one leading idea: namely, that the most stable conception of justice is one that is clear and perspicuous to our reason, congruent with and unconditionally concerned with our good, and rooted not in abnegation but in affirmation of our person.[25] The conclusion argued for is

---

[24] Here I restate the reasoning for the greater stability of justice as fairness found in *TJ*, section 76.

[25] See *TJ*, pp. 498f.

that the two principles of justice answer better to these conditions than the other alternatives precisely because of the basic liberties taken in conjunction with the fair-value of the political liberties (discussed in the next section) and the difference principle. For example, that the two principles of justice are unconditionally concerned with everyone's good is shown by the equality of the basic liberties and their priority, as well as by the fair-value of the political liberties. Again, these principles are clear and perspicuous to our reason because they are to be public and mutually recognized, and they enjoin the basic liberties directly — on their face, as it were.[26] These liberties do not depend upon conjectural calculations concerning the greatest net balance of social interests (or of social values). In justice as fairness such calculations have no place. Observe that this argument for the first ground conforms to the precautions stated in the opening paragraphs of this section. For the parties in adopting the principles of justice which most effectively secure the development and exercise of the sense of justice are moved not from the desire to realize this moral power for its own sake, but rather view it as the best way to stabilize just social cooperation and thereby to advance the determinate conceptions of the good of the persons they represent.

The second ground, not unrelated to the first, proceeds from the fundamental importance of self-respect.[27] It is argued that self-respect is most effectively encouraged and supported by the two principles of justice, again precisely because of the insistence on the equal basic liberties and the priority assigned them, although self-respect is further strengthened and supported by the fair-value of the political liberties and the difference principle.[28]

[26] In saying that the principles of justice enjoin the basic liberties directly and on their face, I have in mind the various considerations mentioned in *TJ* in connection with what I called "embedding"; see pp. 160f, 261–63, 288–89, and 326–27.

[27] Self-respect is discussed in *TJ*, section 67. For its role in the argument for the two principles of justice, see pp. 178–83. For the equal political liberties as a basis of self-respect, see pp. 234, 544–46.

[28] The fair-value of the political liberties is discussed in *TJ*, pp. 224–28, 233–34, 277–79, and 356. In the discussion of the equal political liberties as a basis of self-

That self-respect is also confirmed by other features of the two principles besides the basic liberties only means that no single feature works alone. But this is to be expected. Provided the basic liberties play an important role in supporting self-respect, the parties have grounds founded on these liberties for adopting the two principles of justice.

Very briefly, the argument is this. Self-respect is rooted in our self-confidence as a fully cooperating member of society capable of pursuing a worthwhile conception of the good over a complete life. Thus self-respect presupposes the development and exercise of both moral powers and therefore an effective sense of justice. The importance of self-respect is that it provides a secure sense of our own value, a firm conviction that our determinate conception of the good is worth carrying out. Without self-respect nothing may seem worth doing, and if some things have value for us, we lack the will to pursue them. Thus, the parties give great weight to how well principles of justice support self-respect, otherwise these principles cannot effectively advance the determinate conceptions of the good of those the parties represent. Given this characterization of self-respect, we argue that self-respect depends upon and is encouraged by certain public features of basic social institutions, how they work together and how people who accept these arrangements are expected to (and normally do) regard and treat one another. These features of basic institutions and publicly expected (and normally honored) ways of conduct are the social bases of self-respect (listed earlier in section IV as the last kind of primary goods).

It is clear from the above characterization of self-respect that these social bases are among the most essential primary goods. Now these bases are importantly determined by the public principles of justice. Since only the two principles of justice guarantee the basic liberties, they are more effective than the other alterna-

---

respect on pp. 544–46, the fair-value of these liberties is not mentioned. It should have been. See also sections VII and XII below.

tives in encouraging and supporting the self-respect of citizens as equal persons. It is the content of these principles as public principles for the basic structure which has this result. This content has two aspects, each paired with one of the two elements of self-respect. Recall that the first element is our self-confidence as a fully cooperating member of society rooted in the development and exercise of the two moral powers (and so as possessing an effective sense of justice); the second element is our secure sense of our own value rooted in the conviction that we can carry out a worthwhile plan of life. The first element is supported by the basic liberties which guarantee the full and informed exercise of both moral powers. The second element is supported by the public nature of this guarantee and the affirmation of it by citizens generally, all in conjunction with the fair-value of the political liberties and the difference principle. For our sense of our own value, as well as our self-confidence, depends on the respect and mutuality shown us by others. By publicly affirming the basic liberties citizens in a well-ordered society express their mutual respect for one another as reasonable and trustworthy, as well as their recognition of the worth all citizens attach to their way of life. Thus the basic liberties enable the two principles of justice to meet more effectively than the other alternatives the requirements for self-respect. Once again, note that at no point in the parties' reasoning are they concerned with the development and exercise of the sense of justice for its own sake; although, of course, this is not true of fully autonomous citizens in a well-ordered society.

The third and last ground relating to the sense of justice I can only indicate here. It is based on that conception of a well-ordered society I have called "a social union of social unions." [29] The idea is that a democratic society well-ordered by the two principles of justice can be for each citizen a far more comprehensive good than the determinate good of individuals when left to their

[29] This notion is discussed in *TJ*, section 79. There I didn't connect it with the basic liberties and their priority as I attempt to do here.

own devices or limited to smaller associations. Participation in this more comprehensive good can greatly enlarge and sustain each person's determinate good. The good of social union is most completely realized when everyone participates in this good, but only some may do so and perhaps only a few.

The idea derives from von Humboldt. He says:

> Every human being . . . can act with only one dominant faculty at a time: or rather, one whole nature disposes us at any given time to some single form of spontaneous activity. It would, therefore, seem to follow that man is inevitably destined to a partial cultivation, since he only enfeebles his energies by directing them to a multiplicity of objects. But man has it in his power to avoid one-sidedness, by attempting to unite distinct and generally separately exercised faculties of his nature, by bringing into spontaneous cooperation, at each period of his life, the dying sparks of one activity, and those which the future will kindle, and endeavoring to increase and diversify the powers with which he works, by harmoniously combining them instead of looking for mere variety of objects for their separate exercise. What is achieved in the case of the individual, by the union of past and future with the present, is produced in society by the mutual cooperation of its different members; for in all stages of his life, each individual can achieve only one of those perfections, which represent the possible features of human character. It is through social union, therefore, based on the internal wants and capabilities of its members, that each is enabled to participate in the rich collective resources of all the others.[30]

To illustrate the idea of social union, consider a group of gifted musicians, all of whom have the same natural talents and who could, therefore, have learned to play equally well every instrument in the orchestra. By long training and practice they have become highly proficient on their adopted instrument, recognizing that human limitations require this; they can never be sufficiently

[30] This passage is quoted in *TJ*, pp. 523–24n. It is from *The Limits of State Action*, J. W. Burrow, ed. (Cambridge: Cambridge University Press, 1969), pp. 16–17.

skilled on many instruments, much less play them all at once. Thus, in this special case in which everyone's natural talents are identical, the group achieves, by a coordination of activities among peers, the same totality of capacities latent in each. But even when these natural musical gifts are not equal and differ from person to person, a similar result can be achieved provided these gifts are suitably complementary and properly coordinated. In each case, persons need one another, since it is only in active cooperation with others that any one's talents can be realized, and then in large part by the efforts of all. Only in the activities of social union can the individual be complete.

In this illustration the orchestra is a social union. But there are as many kinds of social unions as there are kinds of human activities which satisfy the requisite conditions. Moreover, the basic structure of society provides a framework within which each of these activities may be carried out. Thus we arrive at the idea of society as a social union of social unions once these diverse kinds of human activities are made suitably complementary and can be properly coordinated. What makes a social union of social unions possible is three aspects of our social nature. The first aspect is the complementarity between various human talents which makes possible the many kinds of human activities and their various forms of organization. The second aspect is that what we might be and do far surpasses what we can do and be in any one life, and therefore we depend on the cooperative endeavors of others, not only for the material means of well-being, but also to bring to fruition what we might have been and done. The third aspect is our capacity for an effective sense of justice which can take as its content principles of justice which include an appropriate notion of reciprocity. When such principles are realized in social institutions and honored by all citizens, and this is publicly recognized, the activities of the many social unions are coordinated and combined into a social union of social unions.

The question is: which principles available to the parties in the original position are the most effective in coordinating and combining the many social unions into one social union? Here there are two desiderata: first, these principles must be recognizably connected with the conception of citizens as free and equal persons, which conception should be implicit in the content of these principles and conveyed on their face, as it were. Second, these principles, as principles for the basic structure of society, must contain a notion of reciprocity appropriate to citizens as free and equal persons engaged in social cooperation over a complete life. If these desiderata are not satisfied, we cannot regard the richness and diversity of society's public culture as the result of everyone's cooperative efforts for mutual good; nor can we appreciate this culture as something to which we can contribute and in which we can participate. For this public culture is always in large part the work of others; and therefore to support these attitudes of regard and appreciation citizens must affirm a notion of reciprocity appropriate to their conception of themselves and be able to recognize their shared public purpose and common allegiance. These attitudes are best secured by the two principles of justice precisely because of the recognized public purpose of giving justice to each citizen as a free and equal person on a basis of mutual respect. This purpose is manifest in the public affirmation of the equal basic liberties in the setting of the two principles of justice. The ties of reciprocity are extended over the whole of society and individual and group accomplishments are no longer seen as so many separate personal or associational goods.

Finally, observe that in this explanation of the good of social union, the parties in the original position need have no specific knowledge of the determinate conception of the good of the persons they represent For whatever these persons' conceptions of the good are, their conceptions will be enlarged and sustained by the more comprehensive good of social union provided that their determinate conceptions lie within a certain wide range and are compatible with the principles of justice. Thus this third ground is open to the parties in the original position, since it meets the restrictions imposed on their reasoning. To advance the determinate good of those they represent, the parties adopt principles which secure the basic liberties. This is the best way to establish the comprehensive good of social union and the effective sense of justice which makes it possible. I note in passing that the notion of society as a social union of social unions shows how it is possible for a regime of liberty not only to accommodate a plurality of conceptions of the good but also to coordinate the various activities made possible by human diversity into a more comprehensive good to which everyone can contribute and in which each can participate. Observe that this more comprehensive good cannot be specified by a conception of the good alone but also needs a particular conception of justice, namely, justice as fairness. Thus this more comprehensive good presupposes this conception of justice and it can be attained provided the already given determinate conceptions of the good satisfy the general conditions stated above. On the assumption that it is rational for the parties to suppose these conditions fulfilled, they can regard this more comprehensive good as enlarging the good of the persons they represent, whatever the determinate conceptions of the good of these persons may be.

This completes the survey of the grounds upon which the parties in the original position adopt the two principles of justice which guarantee the equal basic liberties and assign them priority as a family. I have not attempted to cover all the grounds that might be cited, nor have I tried to assess the relative weights of those I have discussed. My aim has been to survey the most important grounds. No doubt the grounds connected with the capacity for a conception of the good are more familiar, perhaps because they seem more straightforward and, off-hand, of greater weight; but I believe that the grounds connected with the capacity for a sense of justice are also important. Throughout I have had occasion to emphasize that the parties, in order to advance the determinate conceptions of the good of the persons they represent, are led to adopt principles that encourage the development and allow for the full and informed exercise of the two moral powers. Before discussing how the basic liberties are to be specified and adjusted at later stages (that is, before discussing what I earlier called "the second gap"), I must consider an important feature of the first principle of justice which I have referred to several times, namely, the fair-value of the political liberties. Considering this feature will bring out how the grounds for the basic liberties and their priority depend on the content of the two principles of justice as an interrelated family of requirements.

VII

SUMMARY !
of first gap

We can summarize the preceding sections as follows: given first, that the procedure of the original position situates the parties symmetrically and subjects them to constraints that express the Reasonable, and second, that the parties are rationally autonomous representatives whose deliberations express the Rational, each citizen is fairly represented in the procedure by which the principles of justice to regulate the basic structure of society are selected. The parties are to decide between the alternative principles moved by considerations derived solely from the good of the persons they represent. For the reasons we have just surveyed, the parties favor principles which protect a wide range of determinate (but unknown) conceptions of the good and which best secure the political and social conditions necessary for the adequate development and the full and informed exercise of the two moral powers. On the assumption that the basic liberties and their priority secure these conditions (under reasonably favorable circumstances), the two principles of justice, with the first principle prior to the second, are the principles agreed to. This achieves what I earlier called "the initial aim" of justice as fairness. But to this it will rightly be objected that I have not considered the provisions made for the material means required for persons to advance their good. Whether principles for the basic liberties and their priority are acceptable depends upon the complementing of such principles by others that provide a fair-share of these means.

The question at hand is this: How does justice as fairness meet the long-standing problem that the basic liberties may prove to be merely formal, so to speak.[31] Many have argued, particularly radical democrats and socialists, that while it may appear that citizens are effectively equal, the social and economic inequalities likely to arise if the basic structure includes the basic liberties and fair equality of opportunity are too large. Those with greater responsibility and wealth can control the course of legislation to their advantage. To answer this question, let's distinguish between the basic liberties and the worth of these liberties as follows:[32] the basic liberties are specified by institutional rights and duties that entitle citizens to do various things, if they wish, and that forbid others to interfere. The basic liberties are a framework of legally protected paths and opportunities. Of course, ignorance and poverty, and the lack of material means generally, prevent people from exercising their rights and from taking advantage of these openings. But rather than counting these and similar obstacles as restricting a person's liberty, we count them as affecting the worth of liberty, that is, the usefulness to persons of their liberties. Now in justice as fairness, this usefulness is specified in terms of an index of the primary goods regulated by the second principle of justice. It is not specified by a person's level of well-being (or by a utility function) but by these primary goods, claims to which are treated as claims to special needs defined for the purposes of a

---

[31] I am indebted to Norman Daniels for raising the question I try to resolve in this section. See his "Equal Liberty and Unequal Worth of Liberty," in Daniels, pp. 253–81, footnote 1. I am grateful to Joshua Rabinowitz for extensive comments and discussion.

[32] The rest of this paragraph and the next elaborate the paragraph which begins on p. 204 of *TJ*.

political conception of justice. Some primary goods such as income and wealth are understood as all-purpose material means for citizens to advance their ends within the framework of the equal liberties and fair equality of opportunity.

In justice as fairness, then, the equal basic liberties are the same for each citizen and the question of how to compensate for a lesser liberty does not arise. But the worth, or usefulness, of liberty is not the same for everyone. As the difference principle permits, some citizens have, for example, greater income and wealth and therefore greater means of achieving their ends. When this principle is satisfied, however, this lesser worth of liberty is compensated for in this sense: the all-purpose means available to the least advantaged members of society to achieve their ends would be even less were social and economic inequalities, as measured by the index of primary goods, different from what they are. The basic structure of society is arranged so that it maximizes the primary goods available to the least advantaged to make use of the equal basic liberties enjoyed by everyone. This defines one of the central aims of political and social justice.

This distinction between liberty and the worth of liberty is, of course, merely a definition and settles no substantive question.[33] The idea is to combine the equal basic liberties with a principle for regulating certain primary goods viewed as all-purpose means for advancing our ends. This definition is a first step in combining liberty and equality into one coherent notion. The appropriateness of this combination is decided by whether it yields a workable conception of justice which fits, on due reflection, our considered convictions. But to achieve this fit with our considered convictions, we must take an important further step and treat the equal political liberties in a special way. This is done by including in the first principle of justice the guarantee that the political liberties, and

[33] The paragraph which begins on p. 204 of *TJ* can unfortunately be read so as to give the contrary impression.

only these liberties, are secured by what I have called their "fair-value." [34]

To explain: this guarantee means that the worth of the political liberties to all citizens, whatever their social or economic position, must be approximately equal, or at least sufficiently equal, in the sense that everyone has a fair opportunity to hold public office and to influence the outcome of political decisions. This notion of fair opportunity parallels that of fair equality of opportunity in the second principle of justice.[35] When the parties in the original position adopt the priority of liberty, they understand that the equal political liberties are treated in this special way. When we judge the appropriateness of this combination of liberty and equality into one notion, we must keep in mind the distinctive place of the political liberties in the two principles of justice.

It is beyond the scope of a philosophical doctrine to consider in any detail the kinds of arrangements required to insure the fair-value of the equal political liberties, just as it is beyond its scope to consider the laws and regulations required to ensure competition in a market economy. Nevertheless, we must recognize that the problem of guaranteeing the fair-value of the political liberties is of equal if not greater importance than making sure that markets are workably competitive. For unless the fair-value of these liberties is approximately preserved, just background institutions are unlikely to be either established or maintained. How best to proceed is a complex and difficult matter; and at present the requisite historical experience and theoretical understanding may be lacking, so that we must advance by trial and error. But one guideline for guaranteeing fair-value seems to be to keep political parties independent of large concentrations of private economic and social power in a private-property democracy, and of govern-

[34] While the idea of the fair-value of the equal political liberties is an important aspect of the two principles of justice as presented in *TJ*, this idea was not sufficiently developed or explained. It was, therefore, easy to miss its significance. The relevant references are given in footnote 28 above.

[35] For fair equality of opportunity in *TJ*, see pp. 72–74 and section 14.

ment control and bureaucratic power in a liberal socialist regime. In either case, society must bear at least a large part of the cost of organizing and carrying out the political process and must regulate the conduct of elections. The guarantee of fair-value for the political liberties is one way in which justice as fairness tries to meet the objection that the basic liberties are merely formal.

Now this guarantee of the fair-value of the political liberties has several noteworthy features. First, it secures for each citizen a fair and roughly equal access to the use of a public facility designed to serve a definite political purpose, namely, the public facility specified by the constitutional rules and procedures which govern the political process and control the entry to positions of political authority. As we shall discuss later (in section IX), these rules and procedures are to be a fair process, designed to yield just and effective legislation. The point to note is that the valid claims of equal citizens are held within certain standard limits by the notion of a fair and equal access to the political process as a public facility. Second, this public facility has limited space, so to speak. Hence, those with relatively greater means can combine together and exclude those who have less in the absence of the guarantee of fair-value of the political liberties. We cannot be sure that the inequalities permitted by the difference principle will be sufficiently small to prevent this. Certainly, in the absence of the second principle of justice, the outcome is a foregone conclusion; for the limited space of the political process has the consequence that the usefulness of our political liberties is far more subject to our social position and our place in the distribution of income and wealth than the usefulness of our other basic liberties. When we also consider the distinctive role of the political process in determining the laws and policies to regulate the basic structure, it is not implausible that these liberties alone should receive the special guarantee of fair-value. This guarantee is a natural focal point between merely formal liberty on the one side and some kind of wider guarantee for all basic liberties on the other.

The mention of this natural focal point raises the question of why a wider guarantee is not included in the first principle of justice. While there is a problem as to what a wider guarantee of fair-value would mean, the answer to this question is, I believe, that such a guarantee is either irrational or superfluous or socially divisive. Thus, let's first understand it as enjoining the equal distribution of all primary goods and not only the basic liberties. This principle I assume to be rejected as irrational, since it does not permit society to meet certain essential requirements of social organization, and to take advantage of considerations of efficiency, and much else. Second, this wider guarantee can be understood to require that a certain fixed bundle of primary goods is to be secured to each citizen as a way publicly to represent the ideal of establishing the equal worth of everyone's liberties. Whatever the merits of this suggestion, it is superfluous in view of the difference principle. For any fraction of the index of primary goods enjoyed by the least advantaged can already be regarded in this manner. Third and last, this guarantee can be understood as requiring the distribution of primary goods according to the content of certain interests regarded as especially central, for example, the religious interest. Thus, some persons may count among their religious obligations going on pilgrimages to distant places or building magnificent cathedrals or temples. To guarantee the equal worth of religious liberty is now understood to require that such persons receive special provision to enable them to meet these obligations. On this view, then, their religious needs, as it were, are greater for the purposes of political justice, whereas those whose religious beliefs oblige them to make but modest demands on material means do not receive such provision; their religious needs are much less. Plainly, this kind of guarantee is socially divisive, a receipt for religious controversy if not civil strife. Similar consequences result, I believe, whenever the public conception of justice adjusts citizens' claims to social resources so that some receive more than others depending on the determinate final ends and loyalties belonging to their conceptions of the good. Thus, the principle of proportionate satisfaction is likewise socially divisive. This is the principle to distribute the primary goods regulated by the difference principle so that the fraction K (where $0 < K \leq 1$), which measures the degree to which a citizen's conception of the good is realized, is the same for everyone, and ideally maximized. Since I have discussed this principle elsewhere, I shall not do so here.[36] It suffices to say that one main reason for using an index of primary goods in assessing the strength of citizens' claims in questions of political justice is precisely to eliminate the socially divisive and irreconcilable conflicts which such principles would arouse.[37]

Finally, we should be clear why the equal political liberties are treated in a special way as expressed by the guarantee of their fair-value. It is not because political life and the participation by everyone in democratic self-government is regarded as the pre-eminent good for fully autonomous citizens. To the contrary, assigning a central place to political life is but one conception of the good among others. Given the size of a modern state, the exercise of the political liberties is bound to have a lesser place in the conception of the good of most citizens than the exercise of the other basic liberties. The guarantee of fair-value for the political liberties is included in the first principle of justice because it is essential in order to establish just legislation and also to make sure that the fair political process specified by the constitution is open to everyone on a basis of rough equality. The idea is to incorporate into the basic structure of society an effective political procedure which mirrors in that structure the fair representation of persons achieved by the original position. It is the fairness of this procedure, secured by the guarantee of the fair-value of the political liberties, together with the second principle of justice (with the

---

[36] See "Fairness to Goodness," *Philosophical Review*, vol. 84 (October 1975), pp. 551–53.

[37] See further "Social Unity and Primary Goods," footnote 21, sections IV–V.

difference principle), which provides the answer as to why the basic liberties are not merely formal.

VIII

I now turn to how the second gap may be filled. Recall that this gap arises because once we have a number of liberties which must be further specified and adjusted to one another at later stages, we need a criterion for how this is to be done. We are to establish the best, or at least a fully adequate, scheme of basic liberties, given the circumstances of society. Now, in *A Theory of Justice* one criterion suggested seems to be that the basic liberties are to be specified and adjusted so as to achieve the most extensive scheme of these liberties. This criterion is purely quantitative and does not distinguish some cases as more significant than others; moreover, it does not generally apply and is not consistently followed. As Hart noted, it is only in the simplest and least significant cases that the criterion of greatest extent is both applicable and satisfactory.[38] A second proposed criterion in *A Theory of Justice* is that in the ideal procedure of applying the principles of justice, we are to take up the point of view of the representative equal citizen and to adjust the scheme of liberties in the light of this citizen's rational interests as seen from the point of view of the appropriate later stage. But Hart thought that the content of these interests was not described clearly enough for the knowledge of their content to serve as a criterion.[39] In any case, the two criteria seem to conflict, and the best scheme of liberties is not said to be the most extensive.[40]

[38] See Hart, pp. 542–43; Daniels, pp. 239–40.

[39] Hart, pp. 543–47; Daniels, pp. 240–44.

[40] See *TJ*, p. 250, where I have said in the statement of the priority rule that "a less extensive liberty must strengthen the total system of liberty shared by all." Here the "system of liberty" refers to the "system of equal basic liberties," as found in the statement of the first principle on the same page.

I must clear up this ambiguity concerning the criterion. Now it is tempting to think that the desired criterion should enable us to specify and adjust the basic liberties in the best, or the optimum, way. And this suggests in turn that there is something that the scheme of basic liberties is to maximize. Otherwise, how could the best scheme be identified? But in fact, it is implicit in the preceding account of how the first gap is filled that the scheme of basic liberties is not drawn up so as to maximize anything, and, in particular, not the development and exercise of the moral powers.[41] Rather, these liberties and their priority are to guarantee equally for all citizens the social conditions essential for the adequate development and the full and informed exercise of these powers in what I shall call "the two fundamental cases."

The first of these cases is connected with the capacity for a sense of justice and concerns the application of the principles of justice to the basic structure of society and its social policies. The political liberties and freedom of thought are discussed later under this heading. The second fundamental case is connected with the capacity for a conception of the good and concerns the application of the principles of deliberative reason in guiding our conduct over a complete life. Liberty of conscience and freedom of association come in here. What distinguishes the fundamental cases is the comprehensive scope and basic character of the subject to which the principles of justice and of deliberative reason must be applied. The notion of a fundamental case enables us later to

---

[41] I take it as obvious that acting from the best reasons, or from the balance of reasons as defined by a moral conception, is not, in general, to maximize anything. Whether something is maximized depends on the nature of the moral conception. Thus, neither the pluralistic intuitionism of W. D. Ross as found in *The Right and the Good* (Oxford: The Clarendon Press, 1930), nor the liberalism of Isaiah Berlin as found in *Four Essays on Liberty*, footnote 15, specifies something to be maximized. Neither for that matter does the economists' utility function specify anything to be maximized, in most cases. A utility function is simply a mathematical representation of households' or economic agents' preferences, assuming these preferences to satisfy certain conditions. From a purely formal point of view, there is nothing to prevent an agent who is a pluralistic intuitionist from having a utility function. (Of course, it is well known that an agent with a lexicographical preference-ordering does not have a utility function.)

define a notion of the significance of a liberty, which helps us to outline how the second gap is to be filled.[42]

The upshot will be that the criterion at later stages is to specify and adjust the basic liberties so as to allow the adequate development and the full and informed exercise of both moral powers in the social circumstances under which the two fundamental cases arise in the well-ordered society in question. Such a scheme of liberties I shall call "a fully adequate scheme." This criterion coheres with that of adjusting the scheme of liberties in accordance with the rational interests of the representative equal citizen, the second criterion mentioned earlier. For it is clear from the grounds on which the parties in the original position adopt the two principles of justice that these interests, as seen from the appropriate stage, are best served by a fully adequate scheme. Thus the second gap is filled by carrying through the way the first gap is filled.

Now there are two reasons why the idea of a maximum does not apply to specifying and adjusting the scheme of basic liberties. First, a coherent notion of what is to be maximized is lacking. We cannot maximize the development and exercise of two moral powers at once. And how could we maximize the development and exercise of either power by itself? Do we maximize, other things equal, the number of deliberate affirmations of a conception of the good? That would be absurd. Moreover, we have no notion of a maximum development of these powers. What we do have is a conception of a well-ordered society with certain general features and certain basic institutions. Given this conception, we form the notion of the development and exercise of these powers which is adequate and full relative to the two fundamental cases.

The other reason why the idea of a maximum does not apply is that the two moral powers do not exhaust the person, for persons also have a determinate conception of the good. Recall that such a conception includes an ordering of certain final ends and

---

[42] For clarification of the notion of a fundamental case I am indebted to Susan Wolf.

interests, attachments and loyalties to persons and associations, as well as a view of the world in the light of which these ends and attachments are understood. If citizens had no determinate conceptions of the good which they sought to realize, the just social institutions of a well-ordered society would have no point. Of course, grounds for developing and exercising the moral powers strongly incline the parties in the original position to adopt the basic liberties and their priority. But the great weight of these grounds from the standpoint of the parties does not imply that the exercise of the moral powers on the part of the citizens in society is either the supreme or the sole form of good. Rather, the role and exercise of these powers (in the appropriate instances) is a condition of good. That is, citizens are to act justly and rationally, as circumstances require. In particular, their just and honorable (and fully autonomous) conduct renders them, as Kant would say, worthy of happiness; it makes their accomplishments wholly admirable and their pleasures completely good.[43] But it would be madness to maximize just and rational actions by maximizing the occasions which require them.

IX

Since the notion of a fully adequate scheme of basic liberties has been introduced, I can outline how the scheme of basic liberties is specified and adjusted at later stages. I begin by arranging the basic liberties so as to show their relation to the two moral powers and to the two fundamental cases in which these powers are exercised. The equal political liberties and freedom of thought are to secure the free and informed application of the principles of justice, by means of the full and effective exercise of citizens' sense of justice, to the basic structure of society. (The political liberties, assured their fair-value and other relevant general prin-

---

[43] It is a central theme of Kant's doctrine that moral philosophy is not the study of how to be happy but of how to be worthy of happiness. This theme is found in all his major works beginning with the *First Critique*; see A806, B834.

ciples, properly circumscribed, may of course supplement the principles of justice.) These basic liberties require some form of representative democratic regime and the requisite protections for the
freedom of political speech and press, freedom of assembly, and
the like. Liberty of conscience and freedom of association are to
secure the full and informed and effective application of citizens'
powers of deliberative reason to their forming, revising, and rationally pursuing a conception of the good over a complete life.
The remaining (and supporting) basic liberties — the liberty and
integrity of the person (violated, for example, by slavery and
serfdom, and by the denial of freedom of movement and occupation) and the rights and liberties covered by the rule of law —
can be connected to the two fundamental cases by noting that they
are necessary if the preceding basic liberties are to be properly
guaranteed. Altogether the possession of these basic liberties specifies the common and guaranteed status of equal citizens in a well-
ordered democratic society.[44]

Given this arrangement of the basic liberties, the notion of the
significance of a particular liberty, which we need to fill the second
gap, can be explained in this way: a liberty is more or less significant depending on whether it is more or less essentially involved in, or is a more or less necessary institutional means to
protect, the full and informed and effective exercise of the moral
powers in one (or both) of the two fundamental cases. Thus, the
weight of particular claims to freedom of speech, press, and dis-

---

[44] The arrangement in this paragraph is designed to emphasize the role of the
two fundamental cases and to connect these cases with the two moral powers. Thus
this arrangement belongs to a particular conception of justice. Other arrangements may
be equally useful for other purposes. Vincent Blasi, in his instructive essay "The
Checking Value in First Amendment Theory," *Weaver Constitutional Law Series*,
no. 3 (American Bar Foundation, 1977), classifies First Amendment values under
three headings: individual autonomy, diversity, and self-government, in addition to
what he calls "the checking value." This value focuses on the liberties protected by
the First Amendment as a way of controlling the misconduct of government. I believe
the arrangement in the text covers these distinctions. The discussion in section VII
and below in sections X-XII indicates my agreement with Blasi on the importance of
the checking value.

cussion are to be judged by this criterion. Some kinds of speech are not specially protected and others may even be offenses, for example, libel and defamation of individuals, so-called "fighting words" (in certain circumstances), and even political speech when it becomes incitement to the imminent and lawless use of force. Of course, why these kinds of speech are offenses may require careful reflection, and will generally differ in each case. Libel and defamation of private persons (as opposed to political figures) has no significance at all for the public use of reason to judge and regulate the basic structure, and it is in addition a private wrong; while incitements to the imminent and lawless use of force, whatever the significance of the speakers' overall political views, are too disruptive of the democratic process to be permitted by the rules of order of political debate. A well-designed constitution tries to constrain the political leadership to govern with sufficient justice and good sense so that among a reasonable people such incitements to violence will seldom occur and never be serious. So long as the advocacy of revolutionary and even seditious doctrines is fully protected, as it should be, there is no restriction on the content of political speech, but only regulations as to time and place, and the means used to express it.

It is important to keep in mind that in filling the second gap the first principle of justice is to be applied at the stage of the constitutional convention. This means that the political liberties and freedom of thought enter essentially into the specification of a just political procedure. Delegates to such a convention (still regarded as representatives of citizens as free and equal persons but now assigned a different task) are to adopt, from among the just constitutions that are both just and workable the one that seems most likely to lead to just and effective legislation. (Which constitutions and legislation are just is settled by the principles of justice already agreed to in the original position.) This adoption of a constitution is guided by the general knowledge of how political and social institutions work, together with the general facts about existing social circumstances. In the first instance, then, the constitution is seen as a just political procedure which incorporates the equal political liberties and seeks to assure their fair-value so that the processes of political decision are open to all on a roughly equal basis. The constitution must also guarantee freedom of thought if the exercise of these liberties is to be free and informed. The emphasis is first on the constitution as specifying a just and workable political procedure so far without any explicit constitutional restrictions on what the legislative outcome may be. Although delegates have a notion of just and effective legislation, the second principle of justice, which is part of the content of this notion, is not incorporated into the constitution itself. Indeed, the history of successful constitutions suggests that principles to regulate economic and social inequalities, and other distributive principles, are generally not suitable as constitutional restrictions. Rather, just legislation seems to be best achieved by assuring fairness in representation and by other constitutional devices.

The initial emphasis, then, is on the constitution as specifying a just and workable political procedure without any constitutional restrictions on legislative outcomes. But this initial emphasis is not, of course, final. The basic liberties associated with the capacity for a conception of the good must also be respected and this requires additional constitutional restrictions against infringing equal liberty of conscience and freedom of association (as well as the remaining and supporting basic liberties). Of course, these restrictions are simply the result of applying the first principle of justice at the stage of the constitutional convention. But if we return to the idea of starting from the conception of persons as capable of being normal and fully cooperating members of society and of respecting its fair-terms of cooperation over a complete life, then these restrictions can be viewed in another light. If the equal basic liberties of some are restricted or denied, social cooperation on the basis of mutual respect is impossible. For we saw that fair-terms of social cooperation are terms upon which as equal persons we are willing to cooperate with all members of society over a complete life. When fair-terms are not honored, those mistreated will feel resentment or humiliation, and those who benefit must either recognize their fault and be troubled by it, or else regard those mistreated as deserving their loss. On both sides, the conditions of mutual respect are undermined. Thus, the basic liberties of liberty of conscience and freedom of association are properly protected by explicit constitutional restrictions. These restrictions publicly express on the constitution's face, as it were, the conception of social cooperation held by equal citizens in a well-ordered society.

So much for a bare outline of how the second gap is filled, at least at the constitutional stage. In the next section I shall briefly discuss freedom of speech in order to illustrate how this gap is filled in the case of a particular basic liberty. But before doing this it should be noted that all legal rights and liberties other than the basic liberties as protected by the various constitutional provisions (including the guarantee of the fair-value of the political liberties) are to be specified at the legislative stage in the light of the two principles of justice and other relevant principles. This implies, for example, that the question of private property in the means of production or their social ownership and similar questions are not settled at the level of the first principles of justice, but depend upon the traditions and social institutions of a country and its particular problems and historical circumstances.[45] Moreover, even if by some convincing philosophical argument — at least convincing to us and a few like-minded others — we could trace the right of private or social ownership back to first principles or to basic rights, there is a good reason for working out a conception of justice which does not do this. For as we saw earlier, the aim of justice as fairness as a political conception is to resolve the impasse in the democratic tradition as to the way in

---

[45] For references in *TJ* on this point, see footnote 13 above.

which social institutions are to be arranged if they are to conform to the freedom and equality of citizens as moral persons. Philosophical argument alone is most unlikely to convince either side that the other is correct on a question like that of private or social property in the means of production. It seems more fruitful to look for bases of agreement implicit in the public culture of a democratic society and therefore in its underlying conceptions of the person and of social cooperation. Certainly these conceptions are obscure and may possibly be formulated in various ways. That remains to be seen. But I have tried to indicate how these conceptions may be understood and to describe the way in which the notion of the original position can be used to connect them with definite principles of justice found in the tradition of moral philosophy. These principles enable us to account for many if not most of our fundamental constitutional rights and liberties, and they provide a way to decide the remaining questions of justice at the legislative stage. With the two principles of justice on hand, we have a possible common court of appeal for settling the question of property as it arises in the light of current and foreseeable social circumstances.

In sum, then, the constitution specifies a just political procedure and incorporates restrictions which both protect the basic liberties and secure their priority. The rest is left to the legislative stage. Such a constitution conforms to the traditional idea of democratic government while at the same time it allows a place for the institution of judicial review.[46] This conception of the constitution does not found it, in the first instance, on principles of justice, or on basic (or natural) rights. Rather, its foundation is in the conceptions of the person and of social cooperation most likely to be congenial to the public culture of a modern democratic

---

[46] For a valuable discussion of judicial review in the context of the conception of justice as fairness, see Frank I. Michelman, "In Pursuit of Constitutional Welfare Rights: One View of Rawls' Theory of Justice," *University of Pennsylvania Law Review*, vol. 121, no. 5 (May 1973), pp. 991–1019.

society.[47] I should add that the same idea is used each time in the stages I discuss. That is, at each stage the Reasonable frames and subordinates the Rational; what varies is the task of the rational agents of deliberation and the constraints to which they are subject. Thus the parties in the original position are rationally autonomous representatives constrained by the reasonable conditions incorporated into the original position; and their task is to adopt principles of justice for the basic structure. Whereas delegates to a constitutional convention have far less leeway, since they are to apply the principles of justice adopted in the original position in selecting a constitution. Legislators in a parliamentary body have less leeway still, because any laws they enact must accord both with the constitution and the two principles of justice. As the stages follow one another and as the task changes and becomes less general and more specific, the constraints of the Reasonable become stronger and the veil of ignorance becomes thinner. At each stage, then, the Rational is framed by the Reasonable in a different way. While the constraints of the Reasonable are weakest and the veil of ignorance thickest in the original position, at the judicial stage these constraints are strongest and the veil of ignorance thinnest. The whole sequence is a schema for working out a conception of justice and guiding the application of its principles to the right subject in the right order. This schema is not, of course, a description of any actual political process, and much less of how any constitutional regime may be expected to work. It belongs to a conception of justice, and although it is related to an account of how democracy works, it is not such an account.

X

The preceding outline of how the second gap is filled is extremely abstract. To see in more detail how to proceed, I discuss in this and the next section the freedom of political speech and

---

[47] See "Kantian Constructivism in Moral Theory," pp. 518–19, footnote 3.

press which falls under the basic liberty of freedom of thought and the first fundamental case. Doing this will illustrate how the basic liberties are further specified and adjusted at later stages, and the way the significance of a particular liberty is given by its role in a fully adequate scheme. (For the notion of significance, see the second paragraph of section IX.)

I begin by noting that the basic liberties not only limit one another but they are also self-limiting.[48] The notion of significance shows why this is so. To explain: the requirement that the basic liberties are to be the same for everyone implies that we can obtain a greater liberty for ourselves only if the same greater liberty is granted to others. For example, while we might want to include in our freedom of (political) speech rights to the unimpeded access to public places and to the free use of social resources to express our political views, these extensions of our liberty, when granted to all, are so unworkable and socially divisive that they would actually greatly reduce the effective scope of freedom of speech. These consequences are recognized by delegates to a constitutional convention who are guided by the rational interest of the representative equal citizen in a fully adequate scheme of basic liberties. Thus, the delegates accept reasonable regulations relating to time and place, and the access to public facilities, always on a footing of equality. For the sake of the most significant liberties, they abandon any special claims to the free use of social resources. This enables them to establish the rules required to secure an effective scope for free political speech in the fundamental case. Much the same reasoning shows why the basic liberty of liberty of conscience is also self-limiting. Here too reasonable regulations would be accepted to secure intact the central range of this liberty, which includes the freedom and integrity of the internal life of religious associations and the liberty of persons

---

[48] Hart argues that a strictly quantitative criterion of how to specify and adjust the basic liberties cannot account for this fact, or so I interpret his argument, pp. 550–51; Daniels, pp. 247–48. I agree that some qualitative criterion is necessary and the notion of significance is to serve this role.

to determine their religious affiliations in social conditions that are free.

Let us now turn to freedom of political speech as a basic liberty, and consider how to specify it into more particular liberties so as to protect its central range. Recall that we are concerned with the fundamental case of the application of the principles of justice (and other general principles as appropriate) to the basic structure of society and its social policies. We think of these principles as applied by free and equal citizens of a democratic regime by the exercise of their sense of justice. The question is: What more particular liberties, or rules of law, are essential to secure the free, full and informed exercise of this moral power.

Here as before I proceed not from a general definition that singles out these liberties but from what the history of constitutional doctrine shows to be some of the fixed points within the central range of the freedom of political speech. Among these fixed points are the following: there is no such thing as the crime of seditious libel; there are no prior restraints on freedom of the press, except for special cases; and the advocacy of revolutionary and subversive doctrines is fully protected. The three fixed points mark out and cover by analogy much of the central range of freedom of political speech. Reflection on these constitutional rules brings out why this is so.

Thus, as Kalven has said, a free society is one in which we cannot defame the government; there is no such offense:

> . . . the absence of seditious libel as a crime is the true pragmatic test of freedom of speech. This I would argue is what free speech is about. Any society in which seditious libel is a crime is, no matter what its other features, not a free society. A society can, for example, either treat obscenity as a crime or not a crime without thereby altering its basic nature as a society. It seems to me it cannot do so with seditious libel. Here the response to this crime defines the society.[49]

[49] See *The Negro and the First Amendment* (Chicago: University of Chicago Press, 1966), p. 16.

Kalven is not saying, I think, that the absence of seditious libel is the whole of freedom of political speech; rather, it is a necessary condition and indeed a condition so necessary that, once securely won, the other essential fixed points are much easier to establish. The history of the use by governments of the crime of seditious libel to suppress criticism and dissent and to maintain their power demonstrates the great significance of this particular liberty to any fully adequate scheme of basic liberties.[50] So long as this crime exists the public press and free discussion cannot play their role in informing the electorate. And, plainly, to allow the crime of seditious libel would undermine the wider possibilities of self-government and the several liberties required for its protection. Thus the great importance of *N. Y. Times* v. *Sullivan* in which the Supreme Court not only rejected the crime of seditious libel but declared the Sedition Act of 1798 unconstitutional now, whether or not it was unconstitutional at the time it was enacted. It has been tried, so to speak, by the court of history and found wanting.[51]

The denial of the crime of seditious libel is closely related to the two other fixed points noted above. If this crime does exist, it can serve as a prior restraint and may easily include subversive advocacy. But the Sedition Act of 1798 caused such resentment that once it lapsed in 1801, the crime of seditious libel was never revived. Within our tradition there has been a consensus that the discussion of general political, religious, and philosophical doctrines can never be censored. Thus the leading problem of the freedom of political speech has focused on the question of subversive advocacy, that is, on advocacy of political doctrines an essential part of which is the necessity of revolution, or the use of unlawful force and the incitement thereto as a means of political

[50] See Blasi, "The Checking Value in First Amendment Theory," footnote 44, pp. 529–44, where he discusses the history of the use of seditious libel to show the importance of the checking value of the liberties secured by the First Amendment.

[51] New York Times v. Sullivan, 376 U.S. 254 (1964) at 276. See Kalven's discussion of this case, ibid., pp. 56–64.

change. A series of Supreme Court cases from *Schenck* to *Brandenburg* has dealt with this problem; it was in *Schenck* that Holmes formulated the well-known "clear and present danger rule," which was effectively emasculated by the way it was understood and applied in *Dennis*. Thus I shall briefly discuss the problem of subversive advocacy to illustrate how the more particular liberties are specified under freedom of political speech.

Let us begin by noting why subversive advocacy becomes the central problem once there is agreement that all general discussion of doctrine as well as of the justice of the basic structure and its policies is fully protected. Kalven rightly emphasizes that it is with such advocacy that the grounds for restricting political speech seem most persuasive, yet at the same time these grounds run counter to the fundamental values of a democratic society.[52] Free political speech is not only required if citizens are to exercise their moral powers in the first fundamental case, but free speech together with the just political procedure specified by the constitution provides an alternative to revolution and the use of force which can be so destructive to the basic liberties. There must be some point at which political speech becomes so closely connected with the use of force that it may be properly restricted. But what is this point?

In *Gitlow* the Supreme Court held that subversive advocacy was not protected by the First Amendment when the legislature had determined that advocating the overthrow of organized government by force involves the danger of substantive evils which the state through its police power may prevent. The Court presumed that the legislature's determination of the danger was correct, in the absence of strong grounds to the contrary. *Brandenburg*, which is now controlling and therefore ends the story for

---

[52] Here and throughout this section and the next I am much indebted to Kalven's discussion of subversive advocacy in the forthcoming book *A Worthy Tradition*. I am most grateful to James Kalven for letting me read the relevant part of the manuscript of this very important work.

the moment, overrules *Gitlow* (implied by its explicit overruling of Whitney). Here the Court adopts the principle that "the constitutional guarantees of free speech and press do not permit a State to forbid or to proscribe advocacy of the use of force or of law violation except where such advocacy is directed to inciting or producing imminent lawless action and is likely to incite or produce such action." [53] Observe that the proscribed kind of speech must be both intentional and directed to producing imminent lawless action as well as delivered in circumstances which make this result likely.

While *Brandenburg* leaves several important questions unanswered, it is much better constitutional doctrine than what preceded it, especially when it is read together with *N. Y. Times* v. *Sullivan* and the later *N.Y. Times* v. *United States*.[54] (These three cases between them cover the three fixed points previously mentioned.) The reason is that *Brandenburg* draws the line to protected speech so as to recognize the legitimacy of subversive advocacy in a constitutional democracy. It is tempting to think of political speech which advocates revolution as similar to incitement to an ordinary crime such as arson or assault, or even to causing a dangerous stampede, as in Holmes's utterly trivial example of someone falsely shouting "Fire!" in a crowded theater. (This example is trivial because it has point only against the view, defended by no one, that all speech of whatever kind is protected, perhaps because it is thought that speech is not action and only action is punishable.[55]) But revolution is a very special crime; while

[53] Brandenburg v. Ohio, 395 U.S. 444 (1969) at 447.

[54] New York Times v. United States, 403 U.S. 713. See also Near v. Minnesota, 283 U.S. 697, the major earlier case on prior restraint.

[55] A similar critical view of Holmes's example is found in Kalven's manuscript, footnote 52. Thomas Emerson, in *The System of Freedom of Expression* (New York: Random House, 1970), attempts to give an account of free speech based on a distinction between speech and action, the one protected, the other not. But as T. M. Scanlon points out in his "A Theory of Freedom of Expression," *Philosophy and Public Affairs*, vol. 1, no. 2 (Winter 1972), pp. 207–8, a view of this kind puts the main burden on how this distinction is to be made and is bound to depart widely from the ordinary use

even a constitutional regime must have the legal right to punish violations of its laws, these laws even when enacted by due process may be more or less unjust, or may appear to be so to significant groups in society who find them oppressive. Historically, the question of when resistance and revolution are justified is one of the deepest political questions. Most recently, the problems of civil disobedience and conscientious refusal to military service, occasioned by what was widely regarded as an unjust war, have been profoundly troubling and are still unresolved. Thus, although there is agreement that arson, murder, and lynching are crimes, this is not the case with resistance and revolution whenever they become serious questions even in a moderately well-governed democratic regime (as opposed to a well-ordered society, where by definition the problem does not arise). Or more accurately, they are agreed to be crimes only in the legal sense of being contrary to law, but to a law that in the eyes of many has lost its legitimacy. That subversive advocacy is widespread enough to pose a live political question is a sign of an impending crisis rooted in the perception of significant groups that the basic structure is unjust and oppressive. It is a warning that they are ready to entertain drastic steps because other ways of redressing their grievances have failed.

All this is long familiar. I mention these matters only to recall the obvious: that subversive advocacy is always part of a more comprehensive political view; and in the case of so-called "criminal syndicalism" (the statutory offense in many of the historical cases), the political view was socialism, one of the most comprehensive political doctrines ever formulated. As Kalven observes, revolutionaries don't simply shout: "Revolt! Revolt!" They give reasons.[56] To repress subversive advocacy is to suppress the dis-

---

of the words "speech" and "conduct." For an instructive and sympathetic account of how such a view might be developed, see Alan Fuchs, "Further Steps Toward a General Theory of Freedom of Expression," *William and Mary Law Review*, vol. 18 (Winter 1976).

[56] See Kalven's manuscript, footnote 52.

cussion of these reasons, and to do this is to restrict the free and informed public use of our reason in judging the justice of the basic structure and its social policies. And thus the basic liberty of freedom of thought is violated.

As a further consideration, a conception of justice for a democratic society presupposes a theory of human nature. It does so, first, in regard to whether the ideals expressed by its conceptions of the person and of a well-ordered society are feasible in view of the capacities of human nature and the requirements of social life.[57] And second, and most relevant here, it presupposes a theory of how democratic institutions are likely to work and of how fragile and unstable they are likely to be. The Court said in *Gitlow*:

> That utterances inciting to the overthrow of organized government by unlawful means, present a sufficient danger of substantive evil to bring their punishment within the range of legislative discretion, is clear. Such utterances, by their very nature, involve danger to the public peace and to the security of the State . . . . And the immediate danger is none the less real and substantial, because the effect of a given utterance cannot be accurately foreseen. A single revolutionary spark may kindle a fire that, smouldering for a time, may burst into a sweeping and destructive conflagration.[58]

This passage suggests a view, not unlike that of Hobbes, of the very great fragility and instability of political arrangements. Even in a democratic regime, it supposes that volatile and destructive social forces may be set going by revolutionary speech, to smoulder unrecognized below the surface calm of political life only to break out suddenly with uncontrollable force that sweeps all before it. If free political speech is guaranteed, however, serious grievances do not go unrecognized or suddenly become highly dangerous.

---

[57] See "Kantian Constructivism in Moral Theory," pp. 534–35, footnote 3.

[58] Gitlow v. New York, 268 U.S. 652 (1925) at 669.

They are publicly voiced; and in a moderately well-governed regime they are at least to some degree taken into account. Moreover, the theory of how democratic institutions work must agree with Locke that persons are capable of a certain natural political virtue and do not engage in resistance and revolution unless their social position in the basic structure is seriously unjust and this condition has persisted over some period of time and seems to be removable by no other means.[59] Thus the basic institutions of a moderately well-governed democratic society are not so fragile or unstable as to be brought down by subversive advocacy alone. Indeed, a wise political leadership in such a society takes this advocacy as a warning that fundamental changes may be necessary; and what changes are required is known in part from the more comprehensive political view used to explain and justify the advocacy of resistance and revolution.

It remains to connect the preceding remarks with the deliberations of delegates in a constitutional convention who represent the rational interest of equal citizens in a fully adequate scheme of basic liberties. We simply say that these remarks explain why the delegates would draw the line between protected and unprotected political speech not (as *Gitlow* does) at subversive advocacy as such but (as *Brandenburg* does) at subversive advocacy when it is both directed to inciting imminent and unlawful use of force and likely to achieve this result. The discussion illustrates how the freedom of political speech as a basic liberty is specified and adjusted at later stages so as to protect its central range, namely the free public use of our reason in all matters that concern the justice of the basic structure and its social policies.

XI

In order to fill out the preceding discussion of free political speech I shall make a few observations about the so-called "clear

---

[59] See Locke's Second Treatise of Government, sections 223–30. For the idea of natural political virtue in Locke, see Peter Laslett's introduction to his critical edition:

and present danger rule." This rule is familiar and has an important place in the history of constitutional doctrine. It may prove instructive to ask why it has fallen into disrepute. I shall assume throughout that the rule is intended to apply to political speech, and in particular to subversive advocacy, to decide when such speech and advocacy may be restricted. I assume also that the rule concerns the content of speech and not merely its regulation, since as a rule for regulating speech, it raises altogether different questions and may often prove acceptable.[60]

Let's begin by considering Holmes's original formulation of the rule in *Schenck*. It runs as follows: "The question in every case is whether the words are used in such circumstances and are of such a nature as to create a clear and present danger that they will bring about the substantive evils that Congress has a right to prevent. It is a question of proximity and degree." [61] This rule has a certain similarity with *Brandenburg*; we have only to suppose that the words "clear and present danger" refer to imminent lawless action. But this similarity is deceptive, as we can see by noting the reasons why Holmes's rule, and even Brandeis's statement of it in *Whitney*, proves unsatisfactory. One reason is that the roots of the rule in Holmes's formulation are in his account of the law of attempts in his book *The Common Law*.[62] The law of attempts tries to bridge the gap between what the defendant did and the completed crime as defined by statute. In attempts, and similarly in the case of free speech, actions with no serious consequences can be ignored. The traditional view of attempts required specific intent to do the particular offense. For Holmes

---

John Locke, Two Treatises of Government (Cambridge: Cambridge University Press, 1960), pp. 108–11.

[60] My account of the clear and present danger rule has been much influenced by Kalven's manuscript, footnote 52, and by Meiklejohn's *Free Speech and Its Relation to Self-Government*, ch. 2, footnote 11.

[61] Schenck v. United States, 249 U.S. 47 at 52.

[62] For the significance of this origin of the rule, see Yosal Rogat, "Mr. Justice Holmes: The Judge as Spectator," *University of Chicago Law Review*, vol. 31 (Winter 1964), pp. 215–17.

intent was relevant only because it increased the likelihood that what the agent does will cause actual harm. When applied to free speech this view has the virtue of tolerating innocuous speech and does not justify punishment for thoughts alone. But it is an unsatisfactory basis for the constitutional protection of political speech, since it leads us to focus on how dangerous the speech in question is, as if by being somehow dangerous, speech becomes an ordinary crime.

The essential thing, however, is the kind of speech in question and the role of this kind of speech in a democratic regime. And *of course* political speech which expresses doctrines we reject, or find contrary to our interests, all too easily strikes us as dangerous. A just constitution protects and gives priority to certain kinds of speech in virtue of their significance in what I have called "the two fundamental cases." Because Holmes's rule ignores the role and significance of political speech, it is not surprising that he should have written the unanimous opinions upholding the convictions of *Schenck* and *Debs* and dissented in *Abrams* and *Gitlow*. It might appear that he perceived the political speech of the socialists Schenck and Debs as sufficiently dangerous when the country was at war, while he dissented in *Abrams* and *Gitlow* because he perceived the political activities of the defendants as harmless.

This impression is strengthened by the fact that the words which follow the statement of the rule (cited above) are these: "When a nation is at war many things that might be said in time of peace are such a hindrance to its effort that their utterance will not be endured as long as men fight and that no Court could regard them as protected by any constitutional right. It seems to be admitted that if an actual obstruction of the recruiting service were proved, liability for words that produced that effect might be enforced."

If we look at Holmes's opinion in *Debs*, the socialist candidate for the presidency is not accused of encouraging or inciting imminent and lawless violence, and so of creating a clear and present danger in that sense. As reported in the Court's opinion, Debs in a public speech simply attacked the war as having been declared by the master class for its own ends and maintained that the working class had everything to lose, including their lives, and so on. Holmes finds it sufficient to uphold the sentence of ten years' imprisonment that one purpose of the speech "was to oppose not only war in general but this war, and that the opposition was so expressed that its natural and intended effect would be to obstruct recruiting. If that was intended, and if, in all the circumstances, that would be the probable effect, it would not be protected by reason of its being part of a general program and expressions of a general and conscientious belief." [63] Here the natural and intended effect to which Holmes refers is surely that those who heard or read about Debs's speech would be convinced or encouraged by what he said and resolve to conduct themselves accordingly. It must be the consequences of political conviction and resolve which Holmes sees as the clear and present danger. Holmes is little troubled by the constitutional question raised in *Debs*, even though the case involves a leader of a political party, already four times its candidate for the presidency. Holmes devotes little time to it. He is content to say in one sentence, which immediately follows the passage just quoted, that *Schenck* settles the matter. This sentence reads: "The chief defences upon which the defendant seemed willing to rely were the denial that we have dealt with and that based upon the First Amendment to the Constitution, disposed of in Schenck v. United States . . . ." Holmes is here referring to the fact that Debs had maintained that the statute under which he was indicted is unconstitutional as interfering with free speech contrary to the First Amendment.

Brandeis's concurring opinion in *Whitney* is another matter. Along with Hand's opinion in *Masses*, it was one of the memorable steps in the development of doctrine. Early in the opinion

---

[63] Debs v. United States, 249 U.S. 211 at 215.

Brandeis states that the right of free speech, the right to teach, and the right of assembly are "fundamental rights" protected by the First Amendment. These rights, even though fundamental, are not absolute; their exercise is subject to restriction "if the particular restriction proposed is required in order to protect the State from destruction or serious injury, political, economic, or moral." [64] He then proceeds to refer to the *Schenck* formulation of the clear and present danger rule and seeks to fix more exactly the standard by which it is to be applied; that is, to say when a danger is clear, how remote it may be and yet be held present, and what degree of evil is necessary to justify a restriction of free speech.

The strength of Brandeis's opinion lies in its recognition of the role of free political speech in a democratic regime and the connection he establishes between this role and the requirement that the danger must be imminent and not merely likely sometime in the future. The idea is that the evil should be "so imminent that it may befall before there is opportunity for full discussion. If there is time to expose through discussion the falsehoods and fallacies, to avert the evil by the processes of education, the remedy to be applied is more speech, not enforced silence. Only an emergency can justify repression. Such must be the rule if authority is to be reconciled with freedom." [65] Later on he says, referring to advocacy and not incitement: "The fact that speech is likely to result in some violence or in the destruction of property is not enough to justify its suppression. There must be the probability of serious injury to the State. Among free men the deterrents ordinarily applied to prevent crime are education and punishment for violations of the law, not abridgment of the rights of free speech and assembly." [66] And finally, in rejecting the grounds of the majority opinion, Brandeis concludes: "I am unable to

[64] 274 U.S. 357 at 373. For Hand's opinion in *Masses*, see Masses Publishing v. Patten, 244 Fed. 535 (S.D.N.Y. 1917).

[65] Ibid., at 377.

[66] Ibid., at 378.

assent to the suggestion in the opinion of the Court that assembling with a political party, formed to advocate the desirability of a proletarian revolution by mass action at some date necessarily far in the future, is not a right within the protection of the Fourteenth Amendment." [67] All of this and much else is plainly an advance in fixing the standard by which the clear and present danger rule is to be applied.

Yet in *Dennis* the Court interprets the rule in such a way as to emasculate it as a standard for protecting free political speech. For here the Court adopts Hand's formulation of the rule which runs as follows: "In each case [courts] must ask whether the gravity of the 'evil' discounted by its improbability, justifies such an invasion of free speech as is necessary to avoid the danger." [68] Expressed this way the rule does not require that the evil be imminent. Even though the evil is remote, it may be enough that it is great and sufficiently probable. The rule now reads like a maxim of decision theory appropriate to a constitutional doctrine that justifies all decisions by what is necessary to maximize the net sum of social advantages, or the net balance of social values. Given this background conception, it can seem simply irrational to require that the danger be in any strict sense imminent. This is because the principle to maximize the net sum of social advantages (or the net balance of social values) does not allow us to give any greater weight to what is imminent than what the improbability and the value of future advantages permit. Free political speech is assessed as a means and as an end in itself along with everything else. Thus Brandeis's idea that the danger must be imminent because free speech is the constitutionally approved way to protect against future danger may appear irrational in many situations and sometimes even suicidal. His account of free speech needs to be further elaborated in order to make it convincing. This is because

[67] Ibid., at 379.
[68] 341 U.S. 494 at 510, citing 183 F. 2d. at 212.

the clear and present danger rule originates from a different view than the constitutional doctrine he is attempting to develop.[69] What is required is to specify more sharply the kind of situation which can justify the restriction of free political speech. Brandeis refers to protecting "the state from destruction," and from "serious injury, political, economic and moral." These phrases are too loose and cover too much ground. Let's see how Brandeis's view might be elaborated to accord with the priority of liberty.

The essential thing is to recognize the difference between what I shall call "a constitutional crisis of the requisite kind" and an emergency in which there is a present or foreseeable threat of serious injury, political, economic, and moral, or even of the destruction of the state. For example, the fact that the country is at war and such an emergency exists does not entail that a constitutional crisis of the requisite kind also exists. The reason is that to restrict or suppress free political speech, including subversive advocacy, always implies at least a partial suspension of democracy. A constitutional doctrine which gives priority to free political speech and other basic liberties must hold that to impose such a suspension requires the existence of a constitutional crisis in which free political institutions cannot effectively operate or take the required measures to preserve themselves. A number of historical cases illustrate that free democratic political institutions have operated effectively to take the necessary measures in serious emergencies without restricting free political speech; and in some cases where such restrictions have been imposed they were unneces-

---

[69] The basis of Brandeis's own view is best expressed, I think, in the well-known paragraph which begins: "Those who won our independence believed that the final end of the State was to make men free to develop their faculties; and that in its government the deliberative forces should prevail over the arbitrary." This paragraph ends: "Believing in the power of reason as applied through public discussion, they eschewed the silence coerced by law — the argument of force in its worst form. Recognizing the occasional tyrannies of governing majorities, they amended the Constitution so that free speech and assembly should be guaranteed." It is no criticism of this fine paragraph to recognize that by itself it does not remedy the defect of Brandeis's formulation of the clear and present danger rule.

sary and made no contribution whatever to meeting the emergency. It is not enough for those in authority to say that a grave danger exists and that they are taking effective steps to prevent it. A well-designed constitution includes democratic procedures for dealing with emergencies. Thus as a matter of constitutional doctrine the priority of liberty implies that free political speech cannot be restricted unless it can be reasonably argued from the specific nature of the present situation that there exists a constitutional crisis in which democratic institutions cannot work effectively and their procedures for dealing with emergencies cannot operate.

In the constitutional doctrine proposed, then, it is of no particular moment whether political speech is dangerous, since political speech is by its nature often dangerous, or may often appear to be dangerous. This is because the free public use of our reason applies to the most fundamental questions, and the decisions made may have grave consequences. Suppose a democratic people, engaged in a military rivalry with an autocratic power, should decide that the use of nuclear weapons is so contrary to the principles of humanity that their use must be foresworn and significant steps taken unilaterally toward reducing these weapons, this done in the hope that the other power might be persuaded to follow. This could be a highly dangerous decision; but surely that is irrelevant to whether it should be freely discussed and whether the government is constitutionally obligated to carry out this decision once it is properly made. The dangerousness of political speech is beside the point; it is precisely the danger involved in making this decision which must be freely discussed. Wasn't it dangerous to hold free elections in 1862–64 in the midst of a civil war?

Focusing on the danger of political speech flawed the clear and present danger rule from the start. It failed to recognize that for free political speech to be restricted, a constitutional crisis must exist requiring the more or less temporary suspension of democratic political institutions, solely for the sake of preserving these institutions and other basic liberties. Such a crisis did not exist in 1862–64; and if not then, surely at no other time before or since. There was no constitutional crisis of the requisite kind when *Schenck*, *Debs*, or *Dennis* were decided, no political conditions which prevented free political institutions from operating. Never in our history has there been a time when free political speech, and in particular subversive advocacy, could be restricted or suppressed. And this suggests that in a country with a vigorous tradition of democratic institutions, a constitutional crisis need never arise unless its people and institutions are simply overwhelmed from the outside. For practical purposes, then, in a well-governed democratic society under reasonably favorable conditions, the free public use of our reason in questions of political and social justice would seem to be absolute.

Of course, the preceding remarks do not provide a systematic explanation of the distinction between a constitutional crisis of the requisite kind and an emergency in which there is a threat of serious injury, political, economic, and moral. I have simply appealed to the fact, or to what I take to be a fact, that we can recognize from a number of cases in our history that there is the distinction I have indicated and that often we can tell when it applies. Here I cannot go into a systematic explanation. I believe, however, that the notion of a constitutional crisis of this kind is an important part of an account of free political speech, and that when we explain this notion we must start from an account of free political speech which assigns it priority. In justice as fairness this kind of speech falls under the basic liberties, and while these liberties are not absolute, they can be restricted in their content (as opposed to being regulated in ways consistent with maintaining a fully adequate scheme) only if this is necessary to prevent a greater and more significant loss, either directly or indirectly, to these liberties. I have tried to illustrate how in the case of political speech, we try to identify the more essential elements in the central range of application of this basic liberty. We then proceed to further extensions up to the point where a fully adequate provision for this liberty is achieved, unless this liberty has already become self-limiting or conflicts with more significant extensions of other basic liberties. As always, I assume that these judgments are made by delegates and legislators from the point of view of the appropriate stage in the light of what best advances the rational interest of the representative equal citizen in a fully adequate scheme of basic liberties. If we insist on using the language of the clear and present danger rule, we must say, first, that the substantive evils which the legislature seeks to prevent must be of a highly special kind, namely, the loss of freedom of thought itself, or of other basic liberties, including here the fair-value of the political liberties; and second, that there must be no alternative way to prevent these evils than the restriction of free speech. This formulation of the rule goes with the requirement that a constitutional crisis of the requisite kind is one in which free political institutions cannot operate or take the steps required to preserve themselves.

XII

I now wish to supplement the preceding discussion of political speech in two ways. First, it needs to be emphasized that the basic liberties constitute a family, and that it is this family that has priority and not any single liberty by itself, even if, practically speaking, one or more of the basic liberties may be absolute under certain conditions. In this connection I shall very briefly note the manner in which political speech may be regulated in order to preserve the fair-value of the political liberties. I do this not, of course, to try to resolve this difficult problem, but to illustrate why the basic liberties need to be adjusted to one another and cannot be specified individually. Second, it is helpful in clarifying the notion of the basic liberties and their significance to survey several (non-basic) liberties associated with the second principle of justice. This serves to bring out how the significance of a liberty (whether basic or non-basic) is tied to its political and social role within a just basic structure as specified by the two principles of justice.

I begin in this section with the problem of maintaining the fair-value of the equal political liberties. Although (as I said in section VII) it is beyond the scope of a philosophical doctrine to consider in any detail how this problem is to be solved, such a doctrine must explain the grounds upon which the necessary institutions and rules of law can be justified. Let's assume, for reasons stated earlier, that public financing of political campaigns and election expenditures, various limits on contributions and other regulations are essential to maintain the fair-value of the political liberties.[70] These arrangements are compatible with the central role of free political speech and press as a basic liberty provided that the following three conditions hold. First, there are no restrictions on the content of speech; the arrangements in question are, therefore, regulations which favor no political doctrine over any other. They are, so to speak, rules of order for elections and are required to establish a just political procedure in which the fair-value of the equal political liberties is maintained.

A second condition is that the instituted arrangements must not impose any undue burdens on the various political groups in society and must affect them all in an equitable manner. Plainly, what counts as an undue burden is itself a question, and in any particular case is to be answered by reference to the purpose of achieving the fair-value of the political liberties. For example, the prohibition of large contributions from private persons or corporations to political candidates is not an undue burden (in the requisite sense) on wealthy persons and groups. Such a prohibition may be necessary so that citizens similarly gifted and motivated have roughly an equal chance of influencing the government's policy and of attaining positions of authority irrespective of their economic and social class. It is precisely this equality which defines the fair-value of the political liberties. On the other hand, regulations that restrict the use of certain public places for political speech might impose an undue burden on relatively poor groups

[70] See section VII.

accustomed to this way of conveying their views since they lack the funds for other kinds of political expression.

Finally, the various regulations of political speech must be rationally designed to achieve the fair-value of the political liberties. While it would be too strong to say that they must be the least restrictive regulations required to achieve this end — for who knows what the least restrictive among the equally effective regulations might be — nevertheless, these regulations become unreasonable once considerably less restrictive and equally effective alternatives are both known and available.

The point of the foregoing remarks is to illustrate how the basic liberties constitute a family, the members of which have to be adjusted to one another to guarantee the central range of these liberties in the two fundamental cases. Thus, political speech, even though it falls under the basic liberty of freedom of thought, must be regulated to insure the fair-value of the political liberties. These regulations do not restrict the content of political speech and hence may be consistent with its central role. It should be noted that the mutual adjustment of the basic liberties is justified on grounds allowed by the priority of these liberties as a family, no one of which is in itself absolute. This kind of adjustment is markedly different from a general balancing of interests which permits considerations of all kinds — political, economic, and social — to restrict these liberties, even regarding their content, when the advantages gained or injuries avoided are thought to be great enough. In justice as fairness the adjustment of the basic liberties is grounded solely on their significance as specified by their role in the two fundamental cases, and this adjustment is guided by the aim of specifying a fully adequate scheme of these liberties.

In the preceding two sections I recalled a part of development of doctrine from *Schenck* to *Brandenburg*, a development with a happy ending. By contrast, *Buckley* and its sequel *First National*

Bank are profoundly dismaying.[71] In *Buckley* the Court held unconstitutional various limits on expenditures imposed by the Election Act Amendment of 1974. These limits applied to expenditures in favor of individual candidates, to expenditures by candidates from their own funds, and to total expenditures in the course of a campaign. The Court said that the First Amendment cannot tolerate such provisions since they place direct and substantial restrictions on political speech.[72] For the most part the Court considers what it regards as the primary government interest served by the Act, namely, the interest in preventing corruption of the electoral process, and the appearance of such corruption. The Court also considers two so-called ancillary interests of the Act, namely, the interest in limiting the increasing costs of political campaigns and the interest in equalizing the relative ability of citizens to affect the outcome of elections. Here I am concerned solely with the legitimacy of this second ancillary interest, since it is the only one which falls directly under the notion of the fair-value of the political liberties. Moreover, I leave aside, as irrelevant for our purposes, the question whether the measures enacted by Congress were rationally framed to fulfill this interest in an effective way.

[71] Buckley v. Valeo, 424 U.S. 1 (1976), and First National Bank v. Bellotti, 435 U.S. 765 (1978). For discussions of *Buckley*, see Tribe, *American Constitutional Law*, ch. 13, pp. 800–11; and Skelly Wright, "Political Speech and the Constitution: Is Money Speech?," *Yale Law Journal*, vol. 85, no. 8 (July 1976), pp. 1001–21. For an earlier discussion, see M. A. Nicholson, "Campaign Financing and Equal Protection," *Stanford Law Review*, vol. 26 (April 1974), pp. 815–54. In *First National Bank* the Court, by a 5 to 4 decision, invalidated a Massachusetts criminal law which prohibited expenditures by banks and corporations for the purpose of influencing the outcome of voting on referendum proposals, unless these proposals materially affected the property, business, or assets of the corporation. The statute specified that no referendum question solely concerning the taxation of individuals came under this exception. In a dissent joined by Brennan and Marshall, Justice White said that the fundamental error of the majority opinion was its failure to recognize that the government's interest in prohibiting such expenditures by banks and corporations derives from the First Amendment — in particular, from the value of promoting free political discussion by preventing corporate domination; see 435 U.S. 765 (1978) at 803–4. My discussion in the text is in sympathy with this dissenting opinion, and also with White's dissent in *Buckley* at 257–66, and with Marshall's at 287–90.

[72] Buckley v. Valeo, at 58–59.

What is dismaying is that the present Court seems to reject altogether the idea that Congress may try to establish the fair-value of the political liberties. It says: "the concept that the government may restrict the speech of some elements in our society in order to enhance the relative voice of others is wholly foreign to the First Amendment." [73] The Court then proceeds to cite its own precedents, holding that the First Amendment was designed to secure the widest possible dissemination of information from diverse and opposed sources, and to assure the unrestricted exchange of ideas for bringing about political and social changes favored by the people.[74] But none of the cases cited involves the fundamental question of the fair-value of the political liberties.[75] Moreover, the Court's opinion focuses too much on the so-called primary interest in eliminating corruption and the appearance of corruption. The Court fails to recognize the essential point that the fair-value of the political liberties is required for a just political procedure, and that to insure their fair-value it is necessary to prevent those with greater property and wealth, and the greater skills of organization which accompany them, from controlling the electoral process to their advantage. The way in which this is accomplished need not involve bribery and dishonesty or the granting of special favors, however common these vices may be. Shared political convictions and aims suffice. In *Buckley* the Court runs the risk of endorsing the view that fair representation is representation according to the amount of influence effectively exerted. On this view, democracy is a kind of regulated rivalry between economic classes and interest groups in which the outcome should properly depend on the ability and willingness of each to use its financial resources and skills, admittedly very unequal, to make its desires felt.

[73] Ibid., at 48–49.

[74] Ibid., at 49–51.

[75] See Tribe, *American Constitutional Law*, p. 806.

It is surprising, however, that the Court should think that attempts by Congress to establish the fair-value of the political liberties must run afoul of the First Amendment. In a number of earlier decisions the Court has affirmed the principle of one person, one vote, sometimes relying on Article I, Section 2 of the Constitution, at other times on the Fourteenth Amendment. It has said of the right to vote that it is the "preservative of all rights," and in *Wesberry* it stated: "Other rights, even the most basic, are illusory if the right to vote is undermined." [76] In *Reynolds* the Court recognized that this right involves more than the right simply to cast a vote which is counted equally. The Court said: "Full and effective participation by all citizens in state government requires . . . that each citizen has an equally effective voice in the election of members of the state legislature." [77] Later in the opinion it said: "Since achieving of fair and effective representation for all citizens is concededly the basic aim of legislative apportionment, we conclude that the Equal Protection Clause guarantees the opportunity for equal participation by voters in the election of state legislators." [78] Thus, what is fundamental is a political procedure which secures for all citizens a full and equally effective voice in a fair scheme of representation. Such a scheme is fundamental because the adequate protection of other basic rights depends on it. Formal equality is not enough.

It would seem to follow that the aim of achieving a fair scheme of representation can justify limits on and regulations of political speech in elections, provided that these limits and regulations satisfy the three conditions mentioned earlier. For how else is the full and effective voice of all citizens to be maintained? Since it is a matter of one basic liberty against another, the liberties protected by the First Amendment may have to be adjusted

---

[76] Wesberry v. Sanders, 376 U.S. 1 (1964) at 17.

[77] Reynolds v. Sims, 377 U.S. 533 (1964) at 565.

[78] Ibid., at 565–66.

in the light of other constitutional requirements, in this case the requirement of the fair-value of the political liberties. Not to do so is to fail to see a constitution as a whole and to fail to recognize how its provisions are to be taken together in specifying a just political procedure as an essential part of a fully adequate scheme of basic liberties.

As already noted (in section VII), what kinds of electoral arrangements are required to establish the fair-value of the political liberties is an extremely difficult question. It is not the task of the Court to say what these arrangements are, but to make sure that the arrangements enacted by the legislature accord with the Constitution. The regulations proposed by Congress and struck down in *Buckley* would quite possibly have been ineffective; but in the present state of our knowledge they were admissible attempts to achieve the aim of a fair scheme of representation in which all citizens could have a more full and effective voice. If the Court means what it says in *Wesberry* and *Reynolds*, *Buckley* must sooner or later give way. The First Amendment no more enjoins a system of representation according to influence effectively exerted in free political rivalry between unequals than the Fourteenth Amendment enjoins a system of liberty of contract and free competition between unequals in the economy, as the Court thought in the Lochner era.[79] In both cases the results of the free play of the electoral process and of economic competition are acceptable only if the necessary conditions of background justice are fulfilled. Moreover, in a democratic regime it is important that the fulfillment of these conditions be publicly recognized. This is more fundamental than avoiding corruption and the appearance of corruption; for without the public recognition that background justice is maintained, citizens tend to become resentful, cynical, and apathetic. It is this state of mind that leads to corruption as a serious problem, and indeed makes it uncontrollable. The danger of

[79] Lochner v. New York, 198 U.S. 45 (1905).

Buckley is that it risks repeating the mistake of the Lochner era, this time in the political sphere where, for reasons the Court itself has stated in the cases cited above, the mistake could be much more grievous.

XIII

To clarify further the notion of the significance of the basic liberties I shall briefly discuss several liberties associated with the second principle of justice. The examples I consider are related to advertising; and although some of these liberties are quite important, they are not basic liberties, since they do not have the requisite role and significance in the two fundamental cases.

We may distinguish three kinds of advertising according to whether the information conveyed concerns political questions, openings for jobs and positions, or the nature of products for sale. Political advertising I shall not discuss; I assume that it can be regulated for the reasons just considered in the preceding section, provided that the regulations in question satisfy the conditions already indicated. Let us turn, then, to advertisements of openings for jobs and positions. These contain information important in maintaining fair equality of opportunity. Since the first part of the second principle of justice requires that social and economic inequalities are to be attached to offices and positions open to everyone under conditions of fair equality of opportunity, this kind of advertising is associated with this part of the principle and it is granted protection accordingly. Thus, announcements of jobs and positions can be forbidden to contain statements which exclude applicants of certain designated ethnic and racial groups, or of either sex, when these limitations are contrary to fair equality of opportunity. The notion of fair equality of opportunity, like that of a basic liberty, has a central range of application which consists of various liberties together with certain conditions under which these liberties can be effectively exercised. The advertising of employment opportunities may be restricted and regulated to preserve intact this central range. Just as in the case of basic liberties, I assume that this range of application can be preserved in ways consistent with the other requirements of justice, and in particular with the basic liberties. Observe here that the restrictions in question, in contrast with the basic liberties, may be restrictions on content.

In the case of the advertising of products, let's distinguish two kinds. The first kind is advertising which contains information about prices and the features of products used by knowledgeable purchasers as criteria of evaluation. Assuming that the two principles of justice are best satisfied by a substantial use of a system of free competitive markets, economic policy should encourage this kind of advertising. This is true whether the economy is that of a private-property democracy or a liberal socialist regime. In order for markets to be workably competitive and efficient, it is necessary for consumers to be well informed about both prices and the relevant features of available products. The law may impose penalties for inaccurate or false information, which it cannot do in the case of freedom of thought and liberty of conscience; and for the protection of consumers the law can require that information about harmful and dangerous properties of goods be clearly described on the label, or in some other suitable manner. In addition, it may be forbidden for firms, or for trade and professional associations, to make agreements to limit or not to engage in this kind of advertising. The legislature may require, for example, that prices and accurate information about commodities be readily accessible to the public. Such measures help to maintain a competitive and efficient system of markets and enable consumers to make more intelligent and informed decisions.

A second kind of advertising of products is market-strategic advertising, which is found in imperfect and oligopolistic markets dominated by relatively few firms. Here the aim of a firm's expenditures on advertising may be either aggressive, for example, to expand its volume of sales or its share of the market; or the aim may be defensive: firms may be forced to advertise in order to preserve their position in the industry. In these cases consumers are usually unable to distinguish between the products of firms except by rather superficial and unimportant properties; advertising tries to influence consumers' preferences by presenting the firm as trustworthy through the use of slogans, eye-catching photographs, and so on, all designed to form or to strengthen the habit of buying the firm's products. Much of this kind of advertising is socially wasteful, and a well-ordered society that tries to preserve competition and to remove market imperfections would seek reasonable ways to limit it. The funds now devoted to advertising can be released for investment or for other useful social ends. Thus, the legislature might, for example, encourage agreements among firms to limit expenditures on this kind of advertising through taxes and by enforcing such contracts as legally valid. I am not concerned here with how practicable such a policy would be, but solely with illustrating how in this case the right to advertise, which is a kind of speech, can be restricted by contract, and therefore this right is not inalienable, in contrast to the basic liberties.

I must digress a moment to explain this last point. To say that the basic liberties are inalienable is to say that any agreement by citizens which waives or violates a basic liberty, however rational and voluntary this agreement may be, is void *ab initio*; that is, it has no legal force and does not affect any citizen's basic liberties. Moreover, the priority of the basic liberties implies that they cannot be justly denied to any one, or to any group of persons, or even to all citizens generally, on the grounds that such is the desire, or overwhelming preference, of an effective political majority, however strong and enduring. The priority of liberty excludes such considerations from the grounds that can be entertained.

A common-sense explanation of why the basic liberties are inalienable might say, following an idea of Montesquieu, that the basic liberties of each citizen are a part of public liberty, and therefore in a democratic state a part of sovereignty. The Constitution specifies a just political procedure in accordance with which this sovereignty is exercised subject to limits which guarantee the integrity of the basic liberties of each citizen. Thus agreements which alienate these liberties cannot be enforced by law, which consists of but enactments of sovereignty. Montesquieu believed that to sell one's status as a citizen (and, let's add, any part of it) is an act so extravagant that we cannot attribute it to anyone. He thought that its value to the seller must be beyond all price.[80] In justice as fairness, the sense in which this is so can be explained as follows. We use the original position to model the conception of free and equal persons as both reasonable and rational, and then the parties as rationally autonomous representatives of such persons select the two principles of justice which guarantee the basic liberties and their priority. The grounds upon which the parties are moved to guarantee these liberties, together with the constraints of the Reasonable, explain why the basic liberties are, so to speak, beyond all price to persons so conceived. For these liberties are beyond all price to the representatives of citizens as free and equal persons when these representatives adopt principles of justice for the basic structure in the original position. The aims and conduct of citizens in society are therefore subordinate to the priority of these liberties, and thus in effect subordinate to the conception of citizens as free and equal persons.

This explanation of why the basic liberties are inalienable does not exclude the possibility that even in a well-ordered society some citizens may want to circumscribe or alienate one or more of their basic liberties. They may promise to vote for a certain political party or candidate; or they may enter into a relationship with a party or candidate such that it is a breach of trust not to vote in a certain way. Again, members of a religious association may regard

---

[80] *The Spirit of the Laws*, B 15, ch. 2.

themselves as having submitted in conscience to religious authority, and therefore as not free, from the standpoint of that relationship, to question its pronouncements. Relationships of this kind are obviously neither forbidden nor in general improper.[81]

The essential point here is that the conception of citizens as free and equal persons is not required in a well-ordered society as a personal or associational or moral ideal (see section III, first paragraph). Rather it is a political conception affirmed for the sake of establishing an effective public conception of justice. Thus the institutions of the basic structure do not enforce undertakings which waive or limit the basic liberties. Citizens are always at liberty to vote as they wish and to change their religious affiliations. This, of course, protects their liberty to do things which they regard, or which they may come to regard, as wrong, and which indeed may be wrong. (Thus, they are at liberty to break promises to vote in a certain way, or to apostatize.) This is not a contradiction but simply a consequence of the role of the basic liberties in this political conception of justice.

After this digression, we can sum up by saying that the protection for different kinds of advertising varies depending on whether it is connected with political speech, or with maintaining fair equality of opportunity, or with preserving a workably competitive and efficient system of markets. The conception of the person in justice as fairness ascribes to the self a capacity for a certain hierarchy of interests; and this hierarchy is expressed by the nature of the original position (for example, by the way the Reasonable frames and subordinates the Rational) and by the priorities in the two principles of justice. The second principle of justice is subordinate to the first since the first guarantees the basic liberties

---

[81] There are many other reasons why citizens in certain situations or at certain times might not put much value on the exercise of some of their basic liberties and might want to do an action which limited these liberties in various ways. Unless these possibilities affect the agreement of the parties in the original position (and I hold that they do not), they are irrelevant to the inalienability of the basic liberties. I am indebted to Arthur Kuflik for discussion on this point.

required for the full and informed exercise of the two moral powers in the two fundamental cases. The role of the second principle of justice is to ensure fair equality of opportunity and to regulate the social and economic system so that social resources are properly used and the means to citizens' ends are produced efficiently and fairly shared. Of course, this division of role between the two principles of justice is but part of a guiding framework for deliberation; nevertheless, it brings out why the liberties associated with the second principles are less significant in a well-ordered society than the basic liberties secured by the first.

XIV

I conclude with several comments. First, I should emphasize that the discussion of free speech in the last four sections is not intended to advance any of the problems that actually face constitutional jurists. My aim has been solely to illustrate how the basic liberties are specified and adjusted to one another in the application of the two principles of justice. The conception of justice to which these principles belong is not to be regarded as a method of answering the jurist's questions, but as a guiding framework, which if jurists find it convincing, may orient their reflections, complement their knowledge, and assist their judgment. We must not ask too much of a philosophical view. A conception of justice fulfills its social role provided that persons equally conscientious and sharing roughly the same beliefs find that, by affirming the framework of deliberation set up by it, they are normally led to a sufficient convergence of judgment necessary to achieve effective and fair social cooperation. My discussion of the basic liberties and their priority should be seen in this light.

In this connection recall that the conception of justice as fairness is addressed to that impasse in our recent political history shown in the lack of agreement on the way basic institutions are to be arranged if they are to conform to the freedom and equality of citizens as persons. Thus justice as fairness is addressed not so much to constitutional jurists as to citizens in a constitutional regime. It presents a way for them to conceive of their common and guaranteed status as equal citizens and attempts to connect a particular understanding of freedom and equality with a particular conception of the person thought to be congenial to the shared notions and essential convictions implicit in the public culture of a democratic society. Perhaps in this way the impasse concerning the understanding of freedom and equality can at least be intellectually clarified if not resolved. It is particularly important to keep in mind that the conception of the person is part of a conception of political and social justice. That is, it characterizes how citizens are to think of themselves and of one another in their political and social relationships, and, therefore, as having the basic liberties appropriate to free and equal persons capable of being fully cooperating members of society over a complete life. The role of a conception of the person in a conception of political justice is distinct from its role in a personal or associational ideal, or in a religious or moral way of life. The basis of toleration and of social cooperation on a footing of mutual respect in a democratic regime is put in jeopardy when these distinctions are not recognized; for when this happens and such ideals and ways of life take a political form, the fair-terms of cooperation are narrowly drawn, and free and willing cooperation between persons with different conceptions of the good may become impossible. In this lecture I have tried to strengthen the liberal view (as a philosophical doctrine) by indicating how the basic liberties and their priority belong to the fair-terms of cooperation between citizens who regard themselves and one another according to a conception of free and equal persons.

Finally, an observation about the concluding paragraphs of Hart's essay to which my discussion owes so much. Hart is quite rightly unconvinced by the grounds explicitly offered in *A Theory of Justice* for the priority of the basic liberties. He suggests that the apparently dogmatic course of my argument for this priority may be explained by my tacitly imputing to the parties in the original position a latent ideal of my own. This latent ideal, he thinks, is that of a public-spirited citizen who prizes political activity and service to others so highly that the exchange of the opportunities for such activities for mere material good and contentment would be rejected. Hart goes on to say that this ideal is, of course, one of the main ideals of liberalism; but the difficulty is that my argument for "the priority of liberty purports to rest on interests, not on ideals, and to demonstrate that the general priority of liberty reflects a preference for liberty over other goods which every self-interested person who is rational would have." [82] Now Hart is correct in saying that the priority of liberty cannot be argued for by imputing this ideal of the person to the parties in the original position; and he is right also in supposing that a conception of the person in some sense liberal underlies the argument for the priority of liberty. But this conception is the altogether different conception of citizens as free and equal persons; and it does not enter justice as fairness by imputation to the parties. Rather, it enters through the constraints of the Reasonable imposed on the parties in the original position as well as in the revised account of primary goods. This conception of the person as free and equal also appears in the recognition by the parties that the persons they represent have the two moral powers and a certain psychological nature. How these elements lead to the basic liberties and their priority is sketched in sections V and VI, and there the deliberations of the parties were rational and based on the determinate good of the persons represented. This conception of the person can be said to be liberal (in the sense of the philosophical doctrine) because it takes the capacity for social cooperation as fundamental and attributes to persons the two moral powers which make such cooperation possible. These powers specify the basis of equality. Thus citizens

[82] Hart, p. 555. Daniels, p. 252.

are regarded as having a certain natural political virtue without which the hopes for a regime of liberty may be unrealistic. Moreover, persons are assumed to have different and incommensurable conceptions of the good so that the unity of social cooperation rests on a public conception of justice which secures the basic liberties. Yet despite this plurality of conceptions of the good, the notion of society as a social union of social unions shows how it is possible to coordinate the benefits of human diversity into a more comprehensive good.

While the grounds I have surveyed for the basic liberties and their priority have been drawn from and develop considerations found in *A Theory of Justice*, I failed to bring them together in that work. Furthermore, the grounds I cited for this priority were not sufficient, and in some cases even incompatible with the kind of doctrine I was trying to work out.[83] I hope that the argument in this lecture is an improvement, thanks to Hart's critical discussion.

---

[83] Here I refer to the errors in paragraphs 3–4 of section 82 of *TJ*, the section in which the grounds for the priority of liberty are discussed explicitly. Two main errors are first, that I did not enumerate the most important grounds in a clear way; and second, in paragraph 3, pp. 542–43, that I should not have used the notion of the diminishing marginal significance of economic and social advantages relative to our interest in the basic liberties, which interest is said to become stronger as the social conditions for effectively exercising these liberties are more fully realized. Here the notion of marginal significance is incompatible with the notion of a hierarchy of interests used in par. 4, p. 543. It is this latter notion, founded on a certain conception of the person as a free and equal person, which is required by a Kantian view. The marginal changes I could have spoken of in par. 3 are the marginal, or step-by-step, changes reflected in the gradual realization of the social conditions which are necessary for the full and effective exercise of the basic liberties. But these changes are a different matter altogether from the marginal significance of interests.

Foundations of Liberal Equality
Ronald Dworkin

I. Introduction and Synopsis

In these lectures I try to find ethical foundations for liberalism. Not the kind of foundations mocking critics invent to discredit philosophy. I do not hope to find self-evident, irresistible axioms from which liberal principles flow. I want only to show how liberalism as a political philosophy connects with another part of our intellectual world, our ideas about what a good life is. Since the Enlightenment, in which many of the political ideals of liberalism were formed, its critics have charged that these ideals were fit only for people who did not know how to live well. Nietzsche and the romantic iconoclasts said that liberal morality was a prison made by the jealous to lock up the great. Only small people, they thought, would bother with liberal equality; poets and heroes with new lives to invent and new worlds to rule would treat it with contempt. Later this complaint was reversed. Marxists charged liberals with caring too much rather than too little about individual triumphs, and conservatives said that liberalism ignored the importance of the social stability and rootedness provided by conventional morality.

These three vectors of criticism share a common overall objection, however, which is now often stated in a runic slogan. Liberalism (it is said) pays too much attention to the *right*, by which is meant principles of justice, and too little to the *good*, by which is meant the quality and value of the lives people can lead. The romantics think that liberalism is insensitive to the importance of the creative individual breaking free of petty morality. Marxists think that it overlooks the alienated and impoverished character of life in liberal capitalist democracies. Conservatives claim that it fails to understand that life can be satisfying only when it is rooted in community-defining norms and traditions. In recent decades lib-

190

eral political philosophers have seemed to accept the assumption common to these charges. They say that liberalism subordinates questions about how to live well to questions of justice, that (in a well-known phrase of John Rawls) liberalism makes the right *prior* to the good. They mean that liberalism itself takes no view at all about what a good life is but only stipulates the principles of a just society, leaving it to other theories or disciplines to imagine what living well in such a society would be.

Liberals have an obvious reason for taking that view of their own political theory. It is a fundamental, almost defining, tenet of liberalism that the government of a political community should be tolerant of the different and often antagonistic convictions its citizens have about the right way to live: that it should be neutral, for example, between citizens who insist that a good life is necessarily a religious one and other citizens who fear religion as the only dangerous superstition. This liberal tolerance is easier to understand, and perhaps to defend, if liberalism is understood not itself to be drawn from or dependent on any particular ethical ideal. So liberal philosophers find it both natural and useful to insist that liberalism does not stipulate what a good life is like but merely describes fair political and economic structures within which individual citizens will make their own decisions about which lives are good for them.

They have a further reason for taking that restricted view of their own theory, which is their sense that if liberalism were to be associated with any particular set of ethical convictions about the best way to live, these would be elitist and for many people unappealing convictions. For it is a frequent criticism of liberalism that in spite of its professed neutrality it does presuppose a particular ethics. Some critics who claim to have discovered this inconsistency think that liberalism is drawn from the aristocratic ethics of autonomy, spontaneity, and romantic creativity. According to other critics it presupposes the even less appealing ethics of studied, self-conscious dedication to a program prepared early in life and followed scrupulously thereafter. Liberalism would not much benefit, politically, from association with either of these pictures of how people should live. Once again it seems wiser as well as more accurate to declare liberalism's independence from any theory of the good life at all.

But liberal philosophers who for these and other reasons adopt the restricted view that liberalism is a theory of the right but not the good face the problem of explaining what reason people have to be liberals.[1] They adopt what I shall call the strategy of discontinuity for that purpose: they try to find motives people have, in either self-interest or morality, for setting aside their convictions about the good life when they act politically. I argue that liberals should reject this restricted view of their theory. They should try

[1] The search for the foundations of a political theory, in the sense I have in mind, is somtimes described as the problem of finding *motivation* for the theory. I avoid that description to escape a troublesome ambiguity. There are two senses in which we might hope to discover a motivational basis for liberalism. We might hope to discover arguments that will connect liberal ways of voting and acting with effective motives people already have, showing how liberal policies can be understood as serving or fulfilling what we take to be very widespread personal goals or ambitions. Or, what is plainly different, we might hope to construct an attractive picture of the goals and ambitions we believe people *should* have, and then show that liberal politics in some way flow from or cohere with that picture. Both projects are directed to motives, but in a different sense. The first is concerned wtih motivation descriptively; it lies at the intersection of political philosophy and individual and social psychology. The second takes up questions of motive both normatively and philosophically. It asks whether liberalism, as a political theory, fits easily into a broader system of ideas that also includes a more general theory about how people should live, about what kinds of lives are desirable lives to lead. This issue is at the intersection of politics and, not psychology, but ethics, broadly understood, and it leads, through ethics, into whatever other departments of philosophy or science or art turn out to be pertinent to the question of how to live. We should understand the two different projects as responding to rather different challenges to liberalism. The first replies to the claim that liberalism is unworkable: that it is unlikely to be realized through politics, and could not be sustained if it were realized, because it asks people to behave against what they take to be their own interests even in the broadest sense. The second replies to the different complaint that liberalism is unacceptable because its motivational assumptions are not so much unrealistic as indefensible, that it assumes that people have motives and interests that the most perceptive ethical theory, supported by the soundest opinions in other departments of philosophy, would reject. The second project tries to answer this challenge, and it is for that reason foundational as well as motivational. It aims to discover the true antecedents and relations of liberalism before and beyond political theory, first in ethics and then elsewhere, if and as this turns out to be necessary, in metaphysics, epistemology, biology, psychology, history, and economics, for example.

on the contrary to connect ethics and politics by constructing a view about the nature or character of the good life that makes liberal political morality seem continuous rather than discontinuous with appealing philosophical views about the good life.

The West takes liberalism for granted now, and the recent impatience of some of our philosophers with liberal principles may just be boredom with what seems yesterday's news. But in past centuries liberal ideals were not at all boring; they excited passions and fueled revolutions. Liberalism was not seen, then, as a wise and cautious formula for citizens tired of ideological wars, but as a new and exhilarating way for people to live together in political community. That same excitement is evident in Moscow and Warsaw and Budapest, and it was suppressed in Beijing only through the most hideous savagery. A political tradition that has had such force and magnetism for so long must have roots in very powerful images about what is possible and good for people to do with their lives.

My argument will have the following structure. In the next section I support my claim that liberalism needs foundations in ethics by showing why the charge its critics make, that liberalism is too austere, is an important and grave one. In section III I explain and assess the standard answer contemporary liberals make to that charge, which is that liberalism is a political theory discontinuous with and so not in conflict with personal ethics. In the rest of the lectures I construct and try to defend a competing strategy which argues that liberalism is continuous with the best personal ethics, with the right philosophical view of the good life. In section IV I lay out a version of liberalism, which I call liberal equality, that I believe can most easily be defended in that way, and I identify the features of that conception of liberalism which critics believe incompatible with a decent ethics. In section V, I turn aside from political theory to consider some central issues of philosophical ethics on their own. I describe and contrast two general pictures or models of the kind of goodness a life can have, which I call the model of impact and the model of challenge, and I argue that the choice between these models is of the greatest consequence for a variety of issues and puzzles people face in attempting to make sense of the idea of a good life. In section VI I return to politics. I try to show how people who accept the challenge view of ethics, and its implications for a variety of political issues, will be led naturally toward a theory of justice having the central structural features of liberal equality.

The argument just described is long and at times complex. It might be wise to call attention, in advance, to three themes that run through the argument as a whole. The first is a claim about the right way to understand the heart or essence of liberalism. Liberalism is special and exciting because it insists that liberty, equality, and community are not three distinct and often conflicting political virtues, as other political theories both on the left and right of liberalism regard them, but complementary aspects of a single political vision, so that we cannot secure or even understand any one of these three political ideals independently of the others.[2] That is the emotional nerve of liberalism, the idea that seems so arresting in Eastern Europe and Asia now, and seemed so natural to revolutionaries in Europe and America two centuries ago. It is realized, as I shall try to show, in the conception of liberalism I called liberal equality.

I have already reported my second main claim, which is a preference for what I called the challenge over the impact conception of ethics. These are rival accounts of the character and origin of ethical value, that is, of the kind of goodness or value that a human life has when it is lived well and fails to have when it is lived badly. The challenge account finds ethical value in the per-

---

[2] Contrast this claim about essence of liberalism with my earlier claim that the heart of liberalism is its neutrality among theories of the good. See Ronald Dworkin, *A Matter of Principle* (Cambridge, Mass.: Harvard University Press, 1985), chap. 8. I later abandoned that account as mistaking a theorem for an axiom. See Dworkin, *A Matter of Principle*, chap. 9. In these lectures I substantially elaborate that latter view.

formance of living rather than in the independent value of some product a life leaves behind. Someone lives well, on this view, by having a decent sense of the assignment *he* faces in living — a decent sense of his own ethical identity — and leading that life out of that sense. The value of a life successful on those standards does not consist in the objective value of its impact on the world— on the glory of the nation or the pleasure of God or the reduction of suffering it achieved. It consists in the skillful, in most cases intuitively skillful, managing of a challenge. A good life, on this view, has the kind of value a brilliant dive has and retains when the ripples have died away.

The third main claim provides a link between the first two. It is an old question in political and moral philosophy — part of the more general question about the connection between the right and the good — whether it is always in a person's own interests for him to treat others fairly. I shall argue that if we accept the ethical view I just described, that the goodness of a good life lies in its performance as a response to a set of challenges rather than in its product, then we are drawn to a version of Plato's affirmative answer to that question. We are led to the view that, at least in principle, a just society is a condition of a good life for the individuals who live within it. This Platonic view has great and radical implications for political theory. It casts doubt on the modern tradition of testing theories of justice by asking how far they protect or subordinate the interests of some in the face of competing interests of others. It nevertheless supports a variety of liberal political principles as these are understood and realized in liberal equality.

These are the load-bearing members of the argument that lies ahead. Though only the second is developed in a sustained and detailed way, and the first is hardly developed at all, the interaction among all three fixes the central structure of the argument. I must now add a note about terminology. "Ethics" has a variety of meanings. I shall use it both in its broad sense, to refer to the overall art of living, and in a narrower sense. Ethics in the broad sense has two departments: morality and well-being. The question of morality is how we should treat others; the question of well-being is how we should live to make good lives for ourselves. Ethics in the narrow sense means well-being, and I shall sometimes, when the context warrants, use "ethics" to refer just to that.

I close this introductory section with an apology. Though these lectures are long and complex, they are very much work in progress, and the argument is sketchy and incomplete in many places. I plan to expand and I hope clarify the lectures as part of a book I am preparing on liberal equality which will also include reworked versions of a series of articles about equality I summarize below.

II. Why Does Liberalism Need Foundations?

Two Axes

Liberalism, to most people, means a certain set of rough and unrefined political ideas, which I can state in three propositions.[3] First, liberals are at least modest egalitarians. They deplore the great inequalities of wealth typical of modern industrial nations, and they favor programs of redistribution aimed at reducing those inequalities. A self-described liberal would be reluctant to accept further tax reduction in the United States now at the cost of further cuts in welfare provision for the poor. Second, liberals insist on the sanctity of a certain set of familiar individual rights to liberty; these include rights to freedom of expression, freedom of religious or moral conviction, freedom from racial, ethnic, or gender discrimination, due process of law, and rights of political activity and participation. Liberals treat these rights, in a phrase I have used elsewhere, as *trumps* over other considerations: a liberal

---

[3] It should by now be clear that I am using "liberalism" in the contemporary American sense. I do not mean what British political philosophers sometimes call "classical" or "economic" liberalism.

would disdain the argument promoted by the Thatcher administration in Britain as a justification for newspaper censorship or official secrets acts, that government can be carried out more efficiently if free expression is sometimes stifled. Third, liberals are in general tolerant in matters of personal morality. Liberals oppose legislation making homosexual conduct criminal, for example, or penalizing homosexuals in other ways.

These presumptions and tendencies are instinctive among liberals. They are aspects of character as well as habits of thought. But even taken together they do not constitute a political philosophy. Liberals need a more discriminating, filigreed account of these components of liberalism, that is, of liberal equality, liberty, and tolerance. Any attempt to define either equality or liberty or tolerance as a political goal or ideal raises a variety of difficult questions. Is equality to be measured in welfare, for example? Or in resources, or in opportunity, or in some other way? What are the grounds and limits of the liberal right to free speech? Does free speech extend, for example, to commercial speech, like advertising? It it abridged by legislation limiting political campaign contributions? What are the limits of liberal tolerance? Must a liberal society protect pornography that women find, or should find, deeply insulting and offensive?

These questions lie along the first axis of political philosophy, which I shall call the axis of *political* interpretation. Philosophers construct conceptions of liberalism by proposing general principles of political justice which define and order equality, liberty, and tolerance in a systematic way. The most influential contemporary theory of justice is that proposed by John Rawls, which he calls justice as fairness, and which features two general principles. The first requires, roughly, that certain specified liberties must be protected equally for all, and the second, again roughly, that no inequality in basic goods or resources is acceptable unless that inequality benefits whichever group has least goods or resources. These two principles define a particular conception of liberalism:

they provide an interpretation and refinement of the unrefined liberal predispositions. This is a political interpretation, because the principles, though more general and abstract and systematic than the unrefined ideas, are nevertheless plainly political principles. They state comprehensive standards for the use of coercive political power.

When a philosopher has constructed a conception of liberalism in this way, however, a second set of questions arises, and these require development of that conception along a different axis, the axis of *philosophical* interpretation. On this axis the connection between the conception and other departments of knowledge, belief, and conviction are explored. What ontology (if any) does the conception assume, and is this consistent with our general beliefs about what is in the world? Does the political argument rest on a covert epistemology? If so, does this epistemology match our general opinions about how knowledge is acquired? Does the conception assume motives that defy our psychology, or encourage transactions our economics regards as foolish? We want, in short, consistency not merely within but beyond our distinctly political beliefs. And we want, if we can have it, more than consistency. We want our convictions as a whole to form a system, not just a collection; we hope that our political convictions are nourished, not merely tolerated, by our economics, our psychology, and our metaphysics.

The political interpretation of liberalism must precede, at least in order of exposition, its philosophical interpretation. But of course the axes of interpretation interact in the overall construction of a political philosophy. When we develop a political conception of liberalism, we anticipate the philosophical or foundational axis. We choose, so far as we can, a conception of liberalism that we believe will find roots in our more general intellectual commitments. And the search for foundations itself provides opportunity to review and revise the political conception whose foundations we seek. In these lectures philosophical interpretation will be my main concern. I shall be exploring the philosophical foundations of two developed political conceptions of justice: Rawls's conception of justice as fairness, and a different conception — liberal equality — which I have discussed in a series of earlier articles.[4]

Two Perspectives

The foundations of liberalism lie in a vast number of different intellectual departments: in metaphysics, for example, and economics, social psychology, and even biology. I shall start (and in these lectures remain) in an area of ideas much closer to politics than any of these. I shall begin and remain in the contiguous territory of ethics, by which I mean the study of what it is to live well, because it is there, rather than in any more remote part of our system of ideas, that the foundational problems of liberalism are most apparent and pressing. They arise from an apparent clash of two perspectives.

A perspective is a set of structuring ideas and attitudes adopted or appropriate on some occasions (or by or for some people) but not others. Liberals commonly distinguish what I shall call the personal from the political perspective. People take up the personal perspective in making decisions about their own life and conduct, in deciding, for example, what kind of job to take, or whom to marry, or what help they owe a colleague, or whether to bend some rule on behalf of a friend, or whether their lives are going badly or well. Liberals urge them to take up a different, political perspective for those occasions, like voting or lobbying, when they hope to influence decisions taken and enforced by a political community collectively: decisions about what taxes the state should impose, for example, or who should receive the benefit of public expenditure, or whether homosexual marriages should be recognized.

---

[4] See "What Is Equality?" parts 1 and 2, *Philosophy and Public Affairs* 10 (Summer and Fall 1981): 185–246, 283–345; ibid., part 3, *Iowa Law Journal* 73 (July 1988): 1–54; ibid., part 4, *San Francisco Law Review* 22 (1987): 1–54; and "Liberal Community," *California Law Review* 77 (forthcoming).

This division between the personal and political perspectives is mirrored in the distinction between political philosophy and ethics. Ethics, in the broadest sense in which that term is used, is the art of the personal perspective: it teaches us what our personal ideals and projects and convictions should be, and when and how far we must or should sacrifice our own interests for the sake of others in the name of morality. Political philosophy is the conscience of the political perspective: a political theory of justice describes the ideals and principles we should accept as grounds for collective action. Liberalism, of course, is a political theory: it constructs a political perspective. But ethics must be part of liberalism's foundations: the liberal political perspective must fit with a plausible and attractive account of how people should think and act in their private lives. Liberalism must, at a minimum, not clash with our ethical convictions, and it will be stronger if it can also be seen as drawn from them.

But liberalism seems to require that we detach ourselves from an important part of ethics on important political occasions. It seems to demand that we set aside, though only for these occasions, any convictions we have about what I shall call well-being. I mean convictions about the character of the good life, about which lives are successful or satisfying and which are debased or impoverished or wasted. Liberalism commands tolerance; it commands, for example, that political decisions about what citizens should be forced to do or prevented from doing must be made on grounds that are neutral among the competing convictions about good and bad lives that different members of the community might hold. Liberalism makes a further demand peculiar to political occasions. It insists that we be impartial on those occasions as well: it asks us, when we think or act politically, to support only decisions that treat all members of the political community with equal concern.

Now contrast that austere, gray political perspective, marked by detachment and impartiality, with the attitudes most of us take about our ordinary lives. Our *personal* perspective is everything the liberal political perspective is not: we are not neutral and impartial, day to day, but committed and attached. No one who leads a life can be neutral about success or failure in that enterprise, about what events and experiences and achievements and associates make a life worthwhile and which waste or demean it. No one who holds bright religious convictions can set these aside when he or she considers what his or her own life should be like.[5] Nor are we remotely impartial in the distribution of our resources of emotion, time, and treasure. Our concern tracks allegiance. We have concern even for strangers; we know we should not and most of us cannot wholly ignore the impact on them of what we do. But we care much more for some people than for others, for ourselves and our family and friends, for example, and sometimes for our own ethnic community or compatriots, and we treat their fate as of much greater consequence in deciding how to act. This is not, I must emphasize, only how we are. It is how we want to be, the personal perspective we think right, the ethics we admire. We do not regret our personal commitment and partiality and engagement, or struggle to overcome these as signs of weakness. On the contrary we believe them human and appropriate. Only a zombie, we think, would be neutral about the good life in the decisions he made for others as well as himself, and only a monster would find no more demand in the pain of his child than in the cry of a stranger.

It seems natural for people with those opinions about ethics to carry their views forward into their political activity, because politics is, after all, part of living. If we believe — if we *know* — that the life of someone who lives only for himself is a miserable, unfulfilled life, then why should we not vote or work for legislation that will make such a life impossible, that would force every-

---

[5] I shall henceforth use abstract male pronouns in a gender-neutral sense, unless the context indicates otherwise. I find no other solution to the difficulty raised by our language compatible with clarity and ease of reading.

one to live communally, for example? We work and struggle mainly for our own family and friends and others to whom we feel special allegiance. Why, then, should we not vote for officials whose policies and promises will be specially helpful to those for whom we have most concern?

Liberalism apparently asks us to ignore instincts and attitudes on political occasions that are central to the rest of our lives. It insists that we distribute our concern with fine equality, that we care no more about a brother than a stranger, that we banish the special allegiances we all feel to family or specialized community or neighborhood or institution. It asks us to put our most profound and powerful convictions, about religious faith and moral virtue and how to live, to sleep. Liberalism therefore seems a politics of ethical and moral schizophrenia; it seems to ask us to become, in and for politics, people we cannot recognize as ourselves, special political creatures wholly different from ordinary people who decide for themselves, in their ordinary lives, what to be and what to praise and whom they love.

This sharp contrast between the personal perspective of our ethical ideals, a partial, engaged, and passionate perspective, and the liberal political perspective, austere, neutral, and cold, has attracted the concern of one group of philosophical critics of liberalism, some of whom call themselves communitarians. They do not often identify that problem explicitly; they confront liberalism with more arcane — and in my view confused — claims about epistemology and the mysteries of personal identity. But their challenge is most formidable if we understand it as directed to the ethical foundations of liberalism and provoked by the apparent conflict between the most fundamental political claims of liberalism, about equality and rights and tolerance, and our most compelling personal convictions about the character of a worthwhile life. If we are guided by these critics, as we should be, then our search for the foundations of liberalism must start in this apparent conflict between liberal politics and ordinary ethics. It must start, that is, not in more remote and esoteric areas of science or metaphysics, but closer to politics itself, in our ethical assumptions and ideals, in the character of people we want to be and the lives we want to lead not just in politics but outside it as well.

The apparent conflict between liberalism and ethics has worried political and moral philosophers since liberalism became an influential political theory. Many philosophers have thought the conflict genuine and insurmountable and that one or the other perspective must be reformed. Nietzsche, for example, hated liberalism exactly because it contradicted the passionate commitment he thought essential to the undespised life. He thought that politics should be more like the life of a strong and committed person.[6] Some utilitarians, on the other hand, have thought that the personal perspective should be reformed to look more like the liberal political one. They argued that it is always wrong to be partial to our own interests and projects and those of people we love or who are our friends, except so far as this can be justified, through some two-level strategy, as actually how we would behave if we were basically or fundamentally neutral and impartial.[7] Neither of these reformist campaigns is appealing, however. If we wish to defend liberalism we must reconcile the two perspectives in some other way. We must show how liberal politics can be embedded within foundations that include at least the central or most important part of the ethics most of us embrace. We must show that liberals can lead what most of us would think a good, human life.

Two Strategies

Discontinuity. I must now introduce what I believe to be an important distinction. We can construct two rather different strat-

---

[6] So do the communitarians. Or rather they say they do. It is an arresting fact that actual communitarian policies seem to differ very little from liberal ones. In fact communitarians draw back from any distinctly illiberal policies, and that is in itself significant for the argument to follow.

[7] Bernard Williams directed his most effective arguments against utilitarian theory exactly at this reformist feature of its ethics. See Bernard Williams and J. J. C. Smart, *Utilitarianism For and Against* (Cambridge: Cambridge University Press, 1973).

egies for achieving the reconciliation we need between the two perspectives. The first is a strategy of discontinuity. It argues that the two perspectives are compatible because the second, political perspective is in a special but important sense *artificial*, a social construction whose purpose is exactly to provide a perspective that no one need regard as the application of his full ethical convictions to political decisions, so that people of diverse and conflicting personal perspectives can occupy it together. The discontinuity strategy is both simple and ingenious. If we understand the liberal political perspective as constructed just for politics, in the way a contract is constructed for some special commercial occasion, then no question can arise about the consistency of that political perspective with anyone's personal ethical perspective. Someone can agree to occupy an artificial, purpose-built political perspective without subscribing to its principles as his own, just as he can agree to be bound by a contract without accepting that its terms are perfectly fair or even reasonable. The discontinuity strategy aims to show, not merely that an artificial political perspective is consistent with a committed personal one, but that the former flows from the latter, that people each have reason in their diverse personal convictions and passions for subscribing to the joint project of constructing and occupying the artificial political point of view. The political perspective, on this view, is discontinuous in substance but not in motivation.

The formal structure of this discontinuity strategy is captured as a kind of paradigm by the ordinary, commercial contract, as I just suggested. Prospective business partners each have a personal perspective from which he or she judges, among other things, how responsibilities, costs, and profits should in all fairness be divided between them. But these judgments, made from the personal perspective of each partner, can be expected to differ, and so partners create an artificial perspective — a partnership agreement or contract — which they will henceforth turn to in deciding upon their own responsibilities and making requests or demands on the other.

The terms of that contract do not necessarily represent the personal substantive views of both partners; indeed they may well differ, in each particular, from the views of both. The parties retain their own personal views, but they set these aside, as the proper ground for the arguments and claims they make during their commercial relationship, in favor of the contract as an artificial ground for those claims and arguments. So even when some issue arises that is not settled by the explicit terms of the actual document, the parties try to decide that issue from the perspective of the arrangements set out in the contract, that is, in the spirit of the contract, rather than regarding themselves as free each to retreat to his own private perspective for the occasion.

You will understand why I stress contract as a paradigm of the kind of artificial perspective the strategy of discontinuity supposes the liberal political perspective to be. Liberal philosophers from Locke to Rawls have defined and defended liberalism through the device of a social contract,[8] and Rawls has recently, in a striking series of articles, emphasized that his contractarian theory should be understood as an exercise in discontinuity. He describes the contractarian theory he developed in *A Theory of Justice* as a "political conception" of justice, and explains that a theory of justice is a political conception if it meets three tests. It must, first, be designed specifically for politics. Second, it must not be drawn from — or seen in any way to depend upon the truth or soundness of — any comprehensive ethical or religious or philosophical position. Third, it must instead reflect the intuitive principles of justice and associated ideas latent in the traditions and structures of the society for which it is intended. If a theory of justice is regarded as political in this sense, then though citizens have very different, even antagonistic, ethical and philosophical convictions they can nevertheless accept that theory as providing the basic structure for their political institutions.

[8] I might have begun the social tradition with Thomas Hobbes, who invented the modern form of the device. But though critics of liberalism claim Hobbes as a liberal, I have never understood why.

Some people may, Rawls adds, accept the political conception because their own ethical systems in fact endorse important aspects of it: a religious ethic, for example, might endorse toleration of other religions, as many such ethics do. And Rawls himself argues passionately, in the last part of his great treatise, that a good life must be committed to justice. But it would be, as I understand his argument, a fortunate contingency if most people in any particular community found the political conception of justice to be what their own ethical views fully endorsed. The philosopher who constructs a political conception does not offer it to his community as drawn from any group's comprehensive ethical or religious views, or from what the philosopher himself regards as the right comprehensive view, but on the contrary as a conception setting out fair terms of cooperation among people with widely different comprehensive positions.[9] "Thus the aim of justice as fairness as a political conception is practical," Rawls tells us, "and not metaphysical or epistemological. That is, it presents itself not as a conception of justice that is true, but one that can serve as a basis of informed and willing political agreement between citizens viewed as free and equal persons." [10]

The virtues of the discontinuity strategy, as a means of reconciling the personal and political perspectives liberals embrace, are evident. For if a liberal theory of justice can be seen as providing "a basis of informed and willing political agreement" among people who disagree in the principles and convictions that form their personal perspectives, if people can accept liberalism on that

---

[9] It might be thought that a more careful attention to Rawls's arguments, particularly those about overlapping consensuses, show that he has actually rejected discontinuity, that his idea of a political conception must be understood in some way other than as what I began by calling an artificial conception. But I believe my interpretation makes the best sense of what he has so far been writing in recent years. (My interpretation of *A Theory of Justice* was very different. Indeed, my reading of the recent work is based, among other things, on his rejection of my interpretation of that work as not his own understanding of it. See John Rawls, "Justice as Fairness: Political Not Metaphysical," *Philosophy and Public Affairs* 14 (Spring 1985): 223–51, 236 n. 19). In any case my interpretation provides an example of the discontinuity strategy at what I believe to be its best.

[10] "Justice as Fairness," p. 230.

basis without conceding that its principles are "true," then the liberal political perspective can be regarded as an artificial construction in the sense that a commercial agreement plainly is. There would then be no more problem in reconciling the two perspectives than there is in reconciling the personal views of each partner to a contract with the different and perhaps contradictory terms of the contract he has joined.

Continuity. I shall call the second strategy, in contrast, the strategy of continuity. It appeals to people who want a more integrated moral experience, who want their politics to match their convictions about what it is to live well, rather than requiring them to set these convictions aside, to check them at the voting-booth door. Continuity therefore offers different foundations for liberalism. It tries to construct what we might call a *liberal ethics* — instincts and convictions about the character and ends of human life that seem particularly congenial to liberal political principles — and then to show that these instincts and convictions already form the central part of how many of us imagine living well, living better than we do.

One problem that strategy faces is plain enough. Since liberalism is tolerant, and in some sense neutral among different conceptions people have about how to lead their lives, a liberal ethics must be abstract. It cannot consist in some detailed description of the good life that is controversial within the political community, like the popular view that a life of power flowing from economic success is eminently satisfying and the opposite view that such a life is insensitive and mean. A liberal ethics must have a structural and philosophical rather than substantive character. It must consist in propositions like those I described in the Introduction, supporting a performance rather than a product conception of ethical value, for example, which do not rule out any substantive, detailed conception of a good life likely to be popular in our political community. A liberal ethics must have more than that negative virtue, however. It must be sufficiently muscular to form a distinctive *liberal* ethics, so that anyone embracing the views it deploys would be more likely also to embrace liberal politics. It remains to be seen, later, whether the liberal ethics I shall describe can meet these twin tests: the negative test of abstraction and the positive test of discriminatory power.

Both strategies try to find reasons that people who are engaged and committed in their private lives have for taking up the neutral and austere political perspective of liberalism. Both aim to show how people of diverse substantive ethical convictions can unite in liberal politics. The difference lies in the attitude each encourages people to take toward these ethical convictions. Discontinuity, exemplified in the social contract tradition, asks them to regard the most profound and abstract of these — those Rawls describes as forming a comprehensive ethical view — not as abandoned or renounced but rather as bracketed or set aside on political occasions. Political life is to proceed prescinding from ethical issues of that sort; whatever one might think about the structure or character of the good life is simply not relevant, one way or the other, in one's political activity or decision because the personal perspective in which these issues play a central role is to be seen as supplanted for politics by a different, shared perspective. The strategy of continuity assumes, on the contrary, that all one's ethical convictions are available in politics, that liberal politics follow not from setting some of these aside but on the contrary from giving full effect to the most comprehensive and philosophical convictions among them. On this view, ethics and politics are intertwined so that some of the most far-reaching questions about the character of the good life are political questions too.

You may decide, as the argument progresses, that the two strategies are only different methods toward very much the same substantive conclusions; indeed you may decide that they are only two different ways of describing much the same method. Some suggestive differences have already emerged, however; in particular, the different approaches the strategies take toward liberal tolerance or neutrality. The contractarian discontinuity strategy builds neutrality in at the start of the story it tells. It argues that the political perspective must be created, so far as possible, under a methodological axiom of ethical neutrality, that it is part of the point of the entire constructive exercise to secure as much ethical neutrality as possible. The continuity strategy, on the contrary, hopes to arrive at neutrality in the course of rather than at the beginning of the argument, as a theorem rather than as a methodological axiom. It hopes that the liberal ethics it constructs will not only appeal to people who have very different substantive views about the good life, but also provide reasons why each of them should be tolerant of the others. Though both strategies defend tolerance, they arrive at different interpretations of that virtue, and therefore at different conceptions of liberalism. I shall try to show, in the course of the argument, a variety of other substantive differences as well. If I am right, the contrast between the two strategies illustrates a point I made earlier. The project of searching out foundations for our political convictions is reflexive. When we choose between contract and continuity, as strategies for rooting liberal politics in personal ethics, we are choosing between two forms of liberalism as well.

III. Contract and Controversy

Moral Contractarianism

Social contract theories provide, as I said, a classical example of discontinuity strategy. The parties to an ordinary commercial contract together create, in their contract, a new perspective that is artificial in the sense that it does not aim to represent the convictions or preferences of either party, let alone of both. Each has a reason, or so they think, for agreeing to a new, collective perspective from which disputes between them will be adjudicated. The social contract tradition in political philosophy tries to identify reasons members of a political society might have for a parallel decision, reasons for entering into a global contract defining the basic structure of their political lives. These must be reasons of sufficient power to persuade them, in effect, to agree to exclude all the other convictions that make up their personal perspective from their political deliberations and decisions.

The personal perspective of most people can be seen as a combination of instincts, intuitions, and convictions from two departments of ethics: well-being and morality. Someone's sense of well-being includes preferences that define his self-interest in what is often called the narrow sense: his preferences for money, pleasure and security, for example.[11] It also includes, and more fundamentally, his more general beliefs about what kinds of life it is good or desirable for him to lead: what kinds of experiences he should aim to have, what kind of associations he should try to develop, what character he should hope to have. His moral convictions, in contrast, are his beliefs about how he should or must respond to the needs and ambitions of others.

In commercial contractual situations people are most often, though of course not exclusively, driven by the first of these departments of conviction: they act in their own interests as they understand these. And most often, no doubt, they act in service of the section of their interests I called narrow. The social contractarian tradition has mainly tried to provide a parallel kind of motive for the political contract. In Hobbes's version of the social contract, for example, each party agrees to accept a single sovereign power in order to escape the perils of a nonpolitical state of nature. Other versions of the social contract are more subtle; they recognize greater diversity in the play of interests that give reason for people to enter into a social compact, and also much greater complexity, and protection for the individual, in the terms of the contract they have reasons to construct. Locke's version was

---

[11] I offer what I think a better distinction among beliefs about one's own interests later, in the distinction between volitional and critical interests. See section V below. So the vagueness of the present and more familiar distinction, between narrow and broader self-interest, may safely be ignored.

more subtle than Hobbes's in both those respects, for example, and modern theories based on the prisoners' dilemma are more complex still.

Rawls's contractarian theory is an important departure from this mainstream tradition, because he hopes to locate at least an important part of the reasons people have for taking up a liberal political perspective in the second department of their personal perspective: in morality rather than self-interest. The aim of political philosophy, he says, is to develop a political conception of justice that people will accept not as a mere modus vivendi in the Hobbesian spirit, that is, only so long as it remains in their selfish interest to fall in with its requirements, but as fulfilling their moral interests as well. A political conception, he says, is nevertheless a moral conception of justice. If Rawls is successful in this project, if he is able to show that people have a moral reason and not just a reason of well-being to take up a liberal political conception of justice, then he has dramatically improved the discontinuity strategy as a foundational defense of liberalism, for the more orthodox social contract theories, which appeal narrowly to self-interest rather than morality, are evidently unpersuasive. They cannot show that it is in everyone's narrow self-interest to accept liberal principles of equality, because equality is plainly against the narrow self-interest of some. Rawls argues that many of us share moral convictions that take up where arguments from narrow self-interest or well-being leave off, convictions that recommend discontinuity on moral grounds.

Consensual Promise and Categorical Force

A political conception of justice, constructed to be independent of and neutral among the different ethical positions people in the community hold, is perhaps more likely to prove acceptable to everyone in the community than any conception that is not neutral in that way. If we were statesmen intent on securing the widest possible agreement for some political theory, which could then serve as the basis of a truly and widely consensual government, we might well champion a political conception for that reason. But we need more from a theory of justice than consensual promise; we need categorical force. Liberals insist that political decisions be made on liberal principles now, even before liberal principles come to be embraced by everyone, if they ever will be. A liberal senator thinks he has reason to vote now for expensive improvements in the welfare system, even though he knows that neither these improvements nor the egalitarian principles that support them are popular, let alone uncontroversial. He thinks the community has a collective responsibility to reduce inequality, and he believes that that collective responsibility requires and authorizes him to vote for tax increases many of his constituents resent and think unjust. Any theory that makes categorical demands in that way needs to display the moral basis of its claims, and that basis cannot be found in widespread consent that has not yet been given.

A social contract theory faces a threshold difficulty in claiming categorical force. The crudest form of contract theory (no sane person has ever accepted it) argues that our ancestors in prehistory actually entered into a comprehensive political contract, and that we are now morally bound by the terms to which they agreed. The insane theory at least has the right form to claim categorical force for the contract it fantasizes. If it *were* true that we were morally obligated to respect a political agreement our ancestors had actually made, then that moral obligation would plausibly justify official action in accordance with the terms of that contract, even if the rest of us sincerely denied the obligation. Less crazy social contract theories, which rely on hypothetical, counterfactual rather than actual contracts, seem to lack even the right form to claim categorical force. Even if we did accept their counterfactual claims, we would have no evident reason to accept the justification for contemporary political decision they offer. Suppose it is true that if we all found ourselves in the state of nature Hobbes describes we would undoubtedly sign, as quickly as we could, the contract he would draft, because each of us would see that contract as in his or her self-interest. That counterfactual assumption cannot provide categorical force for a contract we nevertheless never signed. A hypothetical contract, even one in everyone's interests, is not a pale form of contract; it is no contract at all.[12]

Nor is the argument for categorical force improved if we add that we all have reasons of self-interest for entering into a social contract now, or that because of these reasons we are likely to conclude a social contract one day in the future. It is not always, or even typically, true that reasons to enter into an agreement are reasons to act as that agreement would provide were it actually established. I might have very good reasons for agreeing to shovel your snow in winter if you will water my plants in summer. These are not automatically reasons for my shoveling your walk in advance of any such agreement between us, not even if I think it very likely that we will strike that bargain next year.

This is the raw nerve in the social contract tradition. Social contract theories argue that we have good reasons to agree collectively to enforce liberal principles of justice. But it would not follow, even if we did, that we therefore have immediate responsibilities to act individually, one by one, in advance of any collective action. Rawls's moral version of contract theory is better placed to meet this objection, however, just because it is a moral version. If a particular political conception of justice would be agreed upon by artificial people in the right circumstances, he believes, real people each have a moral reason to accept decisions in accordance with that conception of justice now, even though they have not collectively agreed to do so. Can we identify moral reason that have that categorical force, and locate these moral reasons in a plausible personal perspective?[13]

---

[12] I borrow here from my *Taking Rights Seriously* (Cambridge, Mass.: Harvard University Press, 1979), chap. 6.

[13] I assume a certain clarification of Rawls's dictum I quoted earlier, that "a political conception . . . presents itself not as a conception of justice that is true,

These cannot be *familiar* moral reasons, those we recognize in ordinary day-to-day life. Of course ordinary morality forbids us wholly to disregard the interests of other people in pursuing our own. But it does not tell us to be impartial between others and ourselves, nor to ignore our own special allegiances, nor to set aside our convictions about a good life in deciding what the interests of others are or require of us. The personal perspective I described, after all, reflects our convictions *both* about morality and our own well-being. Most of us think that even after giving *full* effect to morality we are rightly guided, in day-to-day life, by passions and partiality. How can the same moral principles have such different force in constructing a political perspective? How can morality permit preference and ethical engagement in ordinary life and yet forbid these in the voting booth?

It would not help to say that ordinary moral principles should be given some greater force in the political perspective. For the difficulty stems not from the weakness of morality in the personal perspective, but from its *content* there. Later in these lectures I shall argue that morality shapes ethics: that our sense of what a good life is draws on our sense of a just distribution of resources. But we should notice at this point how ethics shapes justice, how our sense of what morality requires draws on our sense of what a good life is. Morality should be sharply distinguished from what I called narrow self-interest, of course: my ideas about what is fair should not be colored by what I take to be in my own financial interests. But morality is sensitive to and influenced by convictions about well-being in a broader sense.

Our views about well-being teach us which associations ought to be important to us, for example, and our sense of fairness and

---

but one that can serve as a basis of informed and willing political agreement between citizens viewed as free and equal persons." Liberalism, understood as a political conception, has categorical force only if the moral principles that oblige people to take up that conception in advance of "informed and willing political agreement" *are* conceived as "true" in the sense of binding categorically, in advance of any agreement about *them*.

justice incorporates that sense in distinguishing legitimate special concern from illegitimate discrimination or prejudice. I do not act unfairly when I work mainly for the benefit of myself and my family. So we cannot explain why it would be wrong for me to *vote* for our benefit alone simply by claiming that fairness is of special importance in politics. Our convictions about well-being also teach us which kinds of lives are good and bad lives for people to live, and our sense of fairness also incorporates that advice. It is not unfair, in deciding whether to aid one charity rather than another, for me to discriminate to favor those people and causes who share my ethical views generally. Nor is it unfair, to my children or anyone else, for me to use the influence I have over them in childhood to try to persuade them to my own ethical convictions. So we cannot explain why it would be wrong for me to vote for political policies that promote my own convictions just by appealing to fairness. In ordinary ethical life, the morality of fairness reflects rather than excludes the attachments and ideals of the good life.

We must consider, therefore, whether special moral principles apply in politics because politics is coercive, or because it spends taxes collected from everyone. Thomas Scanlon proposes a principle that might seem specially fit for politics, and he builds his version of the social contract on that principle.[14] He suggests that everyone has an obligation, when he acts in ways that seriously affect other people, to observe principles they could not reasonably reject. That suggestion might seem at first blush no more help to the discontinuity strategy than the more general principle that people should not act unfairly. For my views about what other people would be unreasonable to reject reflect my convictions about what lives are good or bad just as much as my views about fairness do. If I think it obvious that a life without close com-

[14] See Scanlon, "Contractualism and Utilitarianism," in *Utilitarianism and Beyond*, ed. Amartya Sen et al. (London: Cambridge University Press, 1982), pp. 103–28. In fact, Scanlon offers his principle as embracing all morality, not just politics. But I limit discussion to its political role.

munal ties is a waste, or that abortion is wicked, or that welfare is immoral because it saps self-reliance, or that people's wealth should in justice reflect their talent, then I will almost certainly think that it is unreasonable of others to reject the principle I embrace. I may not think them blameworthy for not agreeing with me: they may not have had the benefit of the moral instruction I have had, or they may be too insensitive to see what I have seen. But I can hardly think that they have good reason to disagree, that is, that their failure to agree is not unreasonable.[15]

So on that perhaps natural interpretation, the requirement that people act only on principles they believe others would be unreasonable to reject has too little independent content to support the discontinuity strategy. Someone who thinks that a solitary life is a wasted life can accept the principle of reasonableness, so understood, and still campaign for forced communal living, because he thinks that it is unreasonable for other people to deny his view. Scanlon has in mind, however, a more restricted understanding of reasonableness, according to which the judgment of reasonableness is sufficiently independent of ethical and other moral convictions that it might support the categorical force of a discontinuity strategy. His key idea, as I understand it, is this: there is a special dimension of reasonableness according to which whether it is reasonable for someone to reject a political decision or structure depends only on the disadvantage that decision or structure imposes on him relative to the disadvantage a different solution might impose on someone else. So I can reasonably object to a proposed

---

[15] Thomas Nagel argues that I cannot think it unreasonable of people to reject what I accept if they have no access to the grounds or evidence on which my opinion is based. See his "Moral Conflict and Political Legitimacy," *Philosophy and Public Affairs* 16 (Spring 1987): 215–40. But though this might explain why someone whose religious convictions were based on revelation not available to all should not think a heathen unreasonable, Nagel is unable, in that article at least, to expand his argument to fit other beliefs some people have but others reject without disqualifying too much. In any sense in which I might think that others have no access to any grounds I might have for thinking homosexuality wrong, for example, I must also think they have no access to my evidence for thinking that racial prejudice or untaxed inherited wealth is wrong.

economic arrangement that would work to my special disadvantage if a different arrangement would create no equivalent disadvantage for anyone else. But I could not reasonably object if any other arrangement would be worse for some other person than the proposed arrangement is for me.

This balance-of-burdens version of the reasonableness test would not seem sensible to everyone, because its test compares the relative burden only of different individuals, and so ignores the effects of aggregation. It denies that an economic arrangement can ever be justified on the ground that the *aggregate* burden of any other arrangement on some group would be greater, though not the burden on any single individual.[16] Even if we accept Scanlon's individualized balance-of-burdens version of the reasonableness test, however, it will still not provide the independent moral standard the discontinuity strategy needs. For the defect we noticed in the natural interpretation of the reasonableness test is simply transferred, in this version, from the concept of reasonableness to the concept of a burden or a disadvantage. Our views about what is a burden, and when one burden is greater than another, are not independent of our ethical convictions but sensitive to these. If I believe that homosexuality is a desirable form of life for those who find it natural, then I will think that laws forbidding homosexual acts impose a very great burden on them, and that laws permitting such acts impose comparable burdens on no one else. But if I think homosexuality detestable, and so a grave misfortune for homosexuals and all those who care for them, then I will think that the disadvantages of permitting homosexuality are very great for many people, and that the burdens of forbidding it are relatively slight. If I am committed to a religious faith that commands dangerous rituals, I will think the disadvantages imposed by laws forbidding these rituals to be eternal and enormous. But if I am an atheist I

---

[16] It might seem fair to prevent a business from polluting the atmosphere, for example, even though the burden of the prohibition will be greater for the business than the burden of allowing pollution would be for any other particular person, so long as the aggregate burden of pollution would be greater.

will not.[17] So once again the moral principle supposed to provide categorical force for a contractarian strategy seems to fail. Since our evaluation of burden and benefit is sensitive to our first-person ethical convictions, the principle provides no reason why we should set those ethical convictions aside in politics.[18]

The Interpretive Possibility

Rawls's description of a political conception suggests a different kind of argument for categorical force. He emphasizes that a political interpretation must be drawn from and respect institutions, principles, and ideals "implicit or latent in the public culture of a democratic society." "We collect," he says, "such settled convictions as the belief in religious toleration and the rejection of slavery and try to organize the basic ideas and principles implicit in these convictions into a coherent conception of justice. . . . The hope is that these ideas and principles can be formulated clearly enough to be combined into a conception of political justice congenial to our most firmly held convictions." [19]

---

[17] This problem could not be overcome by using a *subjective* test of the magnitude of a disadvantage or burden, because the balance-of-burdens version of the principle of reasonableness would be very implausible combined with a subjective test. The principle would then require me to accept great disadvantages under an existing economic scheme whenever, under any other arrangement, someone would think himself worse off than I am now, whether I agreed or not. If I have a minimally decent life, I could not argue for a more egalitarian distribution if someone who is rich now thinks his life would be shattered if he were no longer able to collect Renaissance masterpieces.

[18] Scanlon's own use of the comparative-burden principle might be thought less vulnerable to this objection. For he adds that people anxious to find a common basis for political decisions would try to define burdens and benefits in such a way that they could agree on the magnitude of the burdens some arrangement would inflict on them both. But it is not clear how people of widely different ethical convictions could agree on that, except by adopting some special sense of burden that would make the principle of comparative burden seem arbitrary and unappealing. In any case it seems odd to think that I have an obligation to treat others as if they were anxious to enter into an agreement with me about the fundamental terms of government even when it is plain that they are not. And that is what must be shown if the contractarian strategy is to have current categorical force as well as consensual promise.

[19] Rawls, "Justice as Fairness," p. 228.

If a political conception does capture ideas prominent in a nation's political culture, that feature will undoubtedly, as we noticed, contribute to its consensual appeal. People will recognize in the conception ideas and rhetoric to which they are drawn by their cultural inheritance, even when these ideas are arranged, as Rawls suggests, in a different order so that old conflicts are now resolved by being seen in a somewhat new way. Can a political conception of justice gain categorical force as well as consensual promise when its central principles are "latent" in political history? "Latent" is a metaphor, of course, and everything depends on how it is unpacked. On one reading, the principles "latent" in a community's traditions are those that provide the best interpretation of the events that make up its history, and the best interpretation is the interpretation that offers, all things considered, the best political justification for those events.[20] It is an attractive and in my view persuasive idea that the members of a political community do have obligations in virtue of the principles latent, in that sense, in the political traditions of their community. This idea offers one explanation of what the *law* of a community is, and of why law, so understood, has categorical force in normal circumstances just because it is law.[21] Can we adapt this idea, that principles have categorical force when they figure in the best interpretation of political history, to supply categorical force for a political conception of justice constructed so as to embody principles with that pedigree?

I doubt it. No set of political principles constructed by a philosopher can fit all parts of any community's traditions and history perfectly because, as Rawls of course acknowledges, the history of any community includes controversy as well as tradition. Two very different political conceptions, which would justify very different controversial political decisions now, might each fit the record and rhetoric of a community's political history roughly equally well.

[20] See Ronald Dworkin, *Law's Empire* (Cambridge, Mass.: Harvard University Press, 1986).

[21] See ibid.

It may be true, for example, that Rawls's theory of justice as fairness would provide a justification for "such settled convictions [in the American political tradition] as the belief in religious toleration and the rejection of slavery." But it is also true that some form of utilitarianism would also provide a justification for the same settled convictions. Justice as fairness might, it is true, fit better than utilitarianism with some parts of American political tradition. It might better justify, for example, some enduring parts of the New Deal political settlement, like social security. But utilitarianism might fit better than justice as fairness with other parts of that tradition. It might better justify, for example, the large degree of inequality that the American majority is still willing to accept as tolerable.

Rawls suggests that if two compelling political conceptions of justice are both available as interpretations, because each offers a good but not perfect fit with the political history and rhetoric of the community, then a "contest" must decide between them. He means a political contest in which partisans of the two conceptions struggle to gain converts until the balance tips decisively in favor of one conception and the other party recognizes its defeat and joins the victors. This picture of a contest and ultimate victory is drawn with consensual promise in mind; it is offered as an account of how society would decide between two conceptions of roughly equal antecedent consensual promise. It has nothing to do with categorical force, however; it offers no advice to a senator or citizen forced to choose between competitive conceptions that fit rhetoric and tradition roughly equally well.

Suppose we advise the senator or citizen in that position to choose the conception which, in his or her view, provides the *better* justification of the community's history, all things considered. We can mean only one thing by "better" in this context: one conception is better than its rival if the justification it offers is superior as a matter of political morality; it makes the rhetoric and history it interprets a more attractive story politically. But of course the question of which interpretation is superior in that sense will be controversial. Judges can nevertheless decide hard cases at law by answering that question: each judge chooses the interpretation that makes the precedents and statuses more attractive, on the whole, in his judgment. I would give that advice to a senator as well, when I thought that he should be acting to preserve the integrity of his nation's law. I would advise him to choose the interpretation of the nation's history that made it the best, including the most just, it could be, and to carry that interpretation forward through his votes today and tomorrow.

But of course this advice presupposes that the judge or senator already has, or knows how to cultivate, some sense of which of two interpretations *is* more just, or more attractive in some other department of political morality. He cannot decide *that* question in the same way. He cannot ask which of two general theories of justice — justice as fairness, say, or utilitarianism — provides a more just interpretation of his community's history, because he would need a further theory of justice, more abstract still, to decide that question, and so forth into higher and higher levels. At some point we must rely on what (we believe) is *true* about matters of justice in order to decide which interpretation of our own traditions — which way of telling our story — is best. So the attractive idea, that "latency" can be a source of categorical political force, does not supply the argument we need to show how a political conception of justice, composed and defended in accordance with the contractarian strategy of discontinuity, can have that kind of force. We can only decide which principles are latent when we already have in hand some conception of justice whose categorical force we can defend in some *other* way, as not dependent on or derived from its congruence with the community's traditions.[22] We are back where we started.[23]

[22] See *A Matter of Principle*, chap. 10.

[23] Can we use the interpretive strategy to defend the categorical force of a political conception of justice in a different way? We might try to show that some

Summary

The discontinuity strategy hopes to reconcile the liberal political perspective with most people's personal perspective by picturing the liberal perspective as what Rawls calls a political conception of justice. Liberalism, on this story, is constructed not to extend anyone's full or comprehensive personal perspective into politics, but to prescind from at least a part of the personal perspective on political occasions. Perhaps philosophers who join the project Rawls describes—of building a political philosophy around which people of diverse ethical convictions can collect — would do well to construct only political conceptions. But the discontinuity strategy cannot reconcile the two perspectives unless it can also ground the categorical force liberalism claims in some way that respects that strategy. It cannot do that in what seems the most natural way, by showing that ordinary principles of morality require us to adopt a special, austere perspective for politics, because ordinary morality is not independent of but suffused with ethics in the broad sense. Nor can it find categorical force in some special moral principle of reasonableness that supports a discontinuous perspective on political occasions. Nor by arguing that the principles of a political conception are, by design, principles latent in the history and traditions of the community.

---

version of the discontinuity thesis *itself* — the principle that a theory of justice must be a political conception in Rawls's sense, for example — provides a better interpretatation of our political practices than any rival meta-theory about political philosophy. Then, with that conclusion in place, we might try to decide which political conception, of those available, provides a better interpretation than any rival political conception. But the discontinuity thesis does not fit the political history or practices of the United States (for example) particularly well. It cannot justify, for instance, the laws of half the states that make adult, consensual homosexual sex criminal. We could only argue that the discontinuity principle provides a superior interpretation or account of our history by arguing or assuming that, in spite of these difficulties of fit, discontinuity is required by a better abstract theory of justice. So once again the interpretive version of the argument ends back where we began: needing and independent, noninterpretive argument for the categorical force of a political conception of justice.

IV. LIBERAL EQUALITY: THE MAIN OUTLINE

Liberal equality, which differs from justice as fairness in a number of respects, can be described starting from different points. The most efficient exposition, I believe, begins in the account that conception of liberalism gives of the just distribution of property, that is, control over resources. It holds that ideal distribution is achieved only when the resources different people control are equal in the *opportunity costs* of those resources, that is, the value they would have in the hands of other people. The economist's envy test is therefore a test for ideal equality: equality is perfect when no member of the community envies the total set of resources under the control of any other member. Envy, as it figures in this test, is an economic not a psychological phenomenon. Someone envies the resource-set of another person when he would prefer that resource-set to his own, and would therefore trade his own for it. This envy test may be met, of course, and resources therefore judged equal, even when the *welfare* or *happiness* or *well-being* people achieve under the equal resources they control is not equal. If your goals or ambitions or projects are more easily satisfied than mine, or if your personality is otherwise different in some pertinent way, you may be much happier or more satisfied with your life than I am even though I would not trade your resources for mine. Liberal equality is equality of resources not welfare.

Under certain assumptions, which I shall describe in a moment, the envy test would be met and perfect distributional equality secured by a Walrasian auction of all resources among people who begin with an equal number of auction tokens no one wants except for that purpose. If such an auction were repeated until no one wished it to be run again, and it did finally stop, the envy test would be met. No one would prefer the bundle of resources any-one else secured in the auction; if he had preferred another's bundle, he would have acquired that bundle in place of his own. But this ideal situation cannot be achieved, for the following reason.

The resources people control are of two kinds: personal and impersonal. Personal resources are qualities of mind and body that affect people's success in achieving their plans and projects: physical and mental health, strength, and talent. Impersonal resources are parts of the environment that can be owned and transferred: land, raw materials, houses, television sets and computers, and various legal rights and interests in these. The auction we just imagined is an auction of impersonal resources, and, since personal resources will remain unequal after the auction has stopped, the envy test will not be satisfied overall. Even if my material, impersonal resources are the same as yours, I will envy your total set of resources, which also includes your talent and health. Once the auction has stopped, and we begin each to produce and trade from our initial resources, your advantages in talent and health will soon destroy our initial equality even in impersonal resources. So will differences in the luck we have: your investments may prosper and mine decline for reasons we could not have anticipated, for example. So liberal equality insists on compensatory strategies to repair, so far as this can be done, inequalities in personal resources and in luck. We cannot compensate for these inequalities perfectly, and it is in fact difficult to defend compensation schemes with the most obvious initial egalitarian appeal.[24] But compensatory programs modeled on hypothetical insurance markets are available, and though they do not achieve anything like perfect liberal equality, they secure substantial advances toward that goal. Redistributive schemes financed by general taxation can be designed to mimic these insurance-driven programs.[25]

This analysis of distributional justice suggests how liberal equality connects equality and liberty. Since liberal equality depends on economic and political devices that reveal the true opportunity costs of impersonal resources, an egalitarian society must be

[24] Dworkin, "What Is Equality," part 2.
[25] See ibid.

a free society.[26] Invasions of liberty — criminal laws prohibiting activities or ways of life some people might wish to take up, for example — are invasions of equality as well, unless they can be justified as necessary to protect an egalitarian distribution of resources and opportunities by providing security of person and property or in some other way.[27] No laws prohibiting activities on grounds of personal morality could pass that test, and so liberal equality supports one of the strongest of the instinctive principles of liberalism we identified at the outset: its tolerance in matters of personal morality.[28]

Since liberal equality does not treat political power as a private resource, liberal political equality is not a matter of equality of impact on or influence over the community's collective decisions.[29] It is rather a matter of distributing the vote and protecting political liberties so as to serve the other goals of liberal equality. Democracy, for liberal equality, is judged by outcome not input. These other goals, however, include more than the distributive goals already mentioned, important though these are. They include participatory goals as well: liberal equality supposes, for example, that a worthwhile life includes political activity as an extension of moral experience and insists that the opportunity for genuine political engagement be available to all who are willing to take it up. That means more than a formal opportunity to vote; it means that politics must be organized so that it can be a theater of moral argument and commitment based in the responsibilities of community rather than only another market for discovering passive revealed preferences.[30] The familiar liberal political rights, embedded in a political culture of expression and reason, are at least as important as full suffrage.[31]

26 See ibid., part 3.
27 See ibid.
28 See ibid.
29 See ibid., part 4.
30 See Dworkin, "Liberal Community."
31 See Dworkin, "What Is Equality," part 4.

That brief sketch must be amplified in certain respects later in the argument, but it gives a sufficient account for now of the way in which liberal equality represents equality, liberty, and community as fused together in an overall political ideal. (The same story could have been told beginning not in distributive equality, as I did, but in liberty or community.) It is also sufficiently complex to allow us to identify liberal equality's leading and most controversial ideas, of which I believe there are four. First, liberal equality depends on a sharp and striking distinction between personality and circumstance. People are to be equal, so far as possible, in the resources they control, which include personal as well as impersonal resources. But they are not to be equal in their welfare. They are to take responsibility, themselves, for their tastes and projects and ambitions and the other features of personality in virtue of which one person may count his life better or worse than another who has identical resources. So no one is considered entitled to more resources just because his tastes are more expensive or his ambitions more perilous or the demands he makes on himself more arduous. The distinction liberal equality makes between personality and circumstance is therefore of capital importance to the theory as a whole.

There is an obvious objection to this distinction. We no more control our tastes and convictions than we do our talents or our luck. Since liberal equality treats the latter as part of our circumstances, and so in principle a matter in which people should be equal, it is inconsistent, according to this objection, not to treat the former that way as well. We cannot reply to this strong objection by arguing that people do choose their tastes. We can, it is true, cultivate tastes at some level. We can try to be the kind of person who likes classical music or skiing. But if we decide to try to acquire these tastes, we do so only in virtue of a conviction we have that it is desirable to be a person with the tastes in question, and we do not choose to acquire that conviction, or any of the other convictions that make up our personality, any more than we decide to acquire other beliefs we have. So liberal equality must reply to this objection in some other way.

The second leading idea of liberal equality is closely connected to the first, but since it attracts a different objection I list it independently. Liberal equality, as we noticed, rejects welfare or well-being as the metric of justice, in favor of resources. It contemplates as ideal a situation in which people are equal in resources even though they might then be very unequal in welfare. Critics therefore object that liberal equality mistakes means for ends. Sane people care about resources only as instruments to their welfare or well-being; anyone who cares about resources for their own sake, just for the sake of acquiring them, is a pathological fetishist. It therefore seems irrational to try to make people equal in resources, which they want only derivatively, and to ignore the distribution of well-being, which they care about intrinsically. We can reframe this objection to show how it connects with the clash between personal and political perspectives. From the personal perspective we clearly care about our own or others' well-being primarily and the resources that produce well-being only derivatively. We care whether we are content or miserable, whether our plans are prospering or in ruin, whether those we love are happy or sad. We worry about our wealth only when and because it affects these really important matters. Why should we care only about material resources and not about happiness or success or pain when we take up the political perspective?

The third leading idea of liberal equality is the complement of the second. It insists not only that justice is a matter of resources but that it is a matter of *equal* resources. Equality seems a dubious political ideal, judged from the personal perspective, for a variety of reasons. First, equality ignores the impact of the virtues. We would think it wrong, in our personal lives, to treat everyone the same way with no discrimination between those who are generous and those who are mean, between those who have helped us, and thus earned our gratitude and loyalty, and those who have been indifferent or hostile. Why should we embrace a politics that is insensitive to these virtues? Second, equality ignores commitment and attachment. In private life we favor those we love or with whom we feel a bond of kinship or other special association: we favor our family or neighbors or friends or colleagues. This kind of favoritism expresses natural impulses; if there is nothing wrong with favoritism in day-to-day life — if there is something wrong with *excluding* favoritism there — why is an austere equality required in politics? Why is austerity not also inhuman — there?[32]

The fourth leading idea of liberal equality is tolerance: it insists that government must be neutral in ethics in the following sense. It must not forbid or reward any private activity on the ground that one set of substantive ethical values, one set of opinions about the best way to lead a life, is superior or inferior to others. This version of neutrality seems particularly problematic from the ethical perspective; I have already set out the obvious objection. Why should people not use whatever political power they have in a democratic society to improve the lives they and others lead, according to their best judgment about what a good life is? We cannot, after all, give up the idea that some lives are better than others. We could not give that idea up and continue to live in anything like the way we do. And each of us is confident at least that some *particular* lives are inferior. Some of us think we *know* that homosexuality is degrading, for example. Others

---

[32] These objections do not, of course, exhaust even the most familiar objections politicians now make to egalitarian programs. Politicians are more likely to complain that equality is inefficient, or that it saps the initiative and character of the poor because the poor have fewer incentives to improve their situation in an egalitarian regime. These latter objections are less pertinent as objections to liberal equality than they might be to other egalitarian theories, because (though I will not pursue these points now) equality of resources, grounded in an opportunity-cost test and based on a sharp distinction between personality and circumstance, may not be inefficient and is not open to the charge that it allows the lazy to profit. In any case, I chose the two objections to the egalitarian character of liberal equality that I listed because they are objections distinctly rooted in ethics, and in the supposed incompatibility between liberalism and an attractive personal perspective. So like the other objections in our growing catalog, they are objections I must meet in order to provide ethical foundations for that conception of liberalism.

think they *know* that a life of material consumerism is impoverished and contemptible. Why should a majority not be able to enforce its ethics through the criminal law, as it enforces its other convictions of policy? And if there are reasons why it should not use the criminal law in that way, why should it not enact legislation that would improve ethical consciousness in other, less coercive ways?

This last objection to liberal equality poses a particularly difficult problem for the continuity strategy. The contractarian strategy is well suited to explaining neutrality: there is no conflict, it points out, between commitment in one's personal perspective and neutrality as part of a distinct and discontinuous political one. But the strategy of continuity rejects this distinction, and so must explain how political neutrality grows out of ethical commitment directly, without an intervening contract or joint social construction. I have already suggested the main lines of the explanation I shall offer: it rests on a distinction between the philosophical level of ethics, where liberalism takes sides, and more substantive levels, where the side it takes at the philosophical level dictates neutrality. But I must prepare the way for this answer, and for the replies I shall make to the other objections to liberal equality I described, by turning aside from political issues for several pages and studying certain issues in philosophical ethics directly.

V. Philosophical Ethics

Volitional and Critical Interests

I shall be considering not the details but the idea of a good life. What *kind* of goodness does a good life have? Philosophers in the utilitarian tradition have by and large assumed that any correct answer to that question would reduce all the elements of well-being to a single common denominator. They debate the merits of two competing claims: first, that well-being consists in desirable experiences, like pleasure, and, second, that it consists in the phenomenon of having one's desires satisfied. It now seems plain enough that though each of these — pleasurable experience and the satisfaction of aims and desires — must find some place in any acceptable overall philosophical account of well-being, neither tells the whole story, nor even the most interesting part of it.

We must suppress the reductionist impulse of these philosophers, and accept not only complexity but structure within the idea of well-being. We must recognize, first, a distinction between what I shall call volitional well-being, on the one hand, and critical well-being on the other. Someone's volitional well-being is improved, and just for that reason, when he has or achieves what in fact he wants. His critical well-being is improved by his having or achieving what he *should* want, that is, the achievements or experiences that it would make his life a worse one *not* to want.[33] Avoiding dental work and sailing well are part of my own volitional well-being: I want them both, and my life therefore goes better, in the volitional sense, when I have them. I take a different view of other things I want: having a close relationship with my children, for example, securing some success in my work, and — what I despair of achieving — some minimal grasp of the state of advanced science of my era. These I believe to be important to my critical well-being in a way in which the first group are not. My life is not a worse life to have lived — I have nothing to regret, still less to take shame in — because I have suffered in the dentist's chair.[34]

---

[33] In a fuller exposition I would distinguish a third category of well-being that is more elemental or biological, such as health and freedom from pain and sexual or other frustration. Someone's life can go worse when he is sick even though he doesn't particularly want to be healthy and even when his illness doesn't prevent him from achieving a worthwhile life for him. But it will be enough for the arguments I shall make here to see how these biological interests can figure within the two categories I name. Avoiding pain is something I want, and so it counts, for me, as part of my volitional interests. I also believe that avoiding pain counts as part of my critical interest as well, though in a different and generally smaller way than it counts in my volitional interest.

[34] That is established, among other ways, by the fact that my attitude toward dental suffering is dramatically time sensitive: I am indifferent about pain I suffer in the chair once it is past.

And though I do want to sail well, and am disappointed when I do not, I cannot think that my life would be a worse one if I had never conceived that desire. It is important for me to sail well because I want to sail well, not vice versa. But all this is reversed when I consider the importance of being close to my children. I do think my life would have been worse had I never understood the importance of this, if I had not suffered pain at estrangement. I do not think that having a close relationship with my children is important just because I happen to want it; on the contrary, I want it because I believe a life without such relationships is a worse one.

This distinction between volitional and critical well-being is not the distinction between what is sometimes called subjective and objective well-being. It is true that critical interest has an objective dimension that volitional interest does not: it makes sense to suppose that I have made a mistake about my critical interest, though not, at least in the same direct sense, that I could be wrong in my volitional interests. But that is not to say that my volitional interests are only my present judgments, which I may later decide are mistakes, about where my critical interests lie. The two kinds of interests, the two modes of well-being, are distinct: I can intelligibly just want something without thinking that it makes my life a better life to have it; indeed a life in which someone only wanted what he thought it was in his critical interests to have would be a sad, preposterous mess of a life.

Critical and volitional interests are interconnected in various ways. Critical interest normally tracks volitional interest. Once I have embraced some desire — to sail well — it is normally in my critical interest to succeed, not because sailing well is critically important but because a fair measure of success in what I happen to want is. And volitional interest normally tracks critical interest: people generally want what they think it is in their critical interests to have. If they think it in their critical interest to have close relationships with their children, they will want to do so. But that is not inevitably the case.[35] At least part of the complex problem philosophers call *akrasia* arises because people do not actually want what they believe it in their critical interest to have. So I may think that my life would be a better life, in the critical sense, if I worked less and spent more time with my family, and yet I find that I actually don't want to, or don't want to enough.

Are the categories of volitional and critical well-being only components of a larger, more inclusive category that we might call well-being all things considered? We might think that well-being, all things considered, consisted in the right mix or trade-off between success in volitional and critical interests. That is a tempting idea, because it supposes a standard for resolving possible conflicts between the two modes of well-being. But the idea makes no sense, however tempting it is. There can be no standards for judging whether the right mix or trade-off has been achieved between volitional and critical well-being except the standards of one of the two modes of well-being themselves. We can ask what we should do in order to have the right sort of life. Then the answer is given by reflecting on our critical interests alone. Or we can ask what we want to do, and then the answer is given by consulting (if that is the right word) our volitional interests. But if the two conflict, as when I want to do something I know is against my critical interest, there is no third or higher-order concept of my interest to which I can appeal. What I should do in these circumstances, in order to lead a good life, is to follow my critical interests, and there is no *other*, higher-order sense of my best interests that might require or permit me to set my critical interests aside. We must therefore accept the dualism of perspectives, recognizing that practical conflicts between the two perspectives can be frequent and vivid. So far as morality provides different standards for conduct from the standards of critical well-being, then

---

[35] The common assumption among philosophers that I cannot think something best, all things considered, without wanting it seems to ignore the distinction between the two kinds of well-being.

morality offers a different perspective yet. But of course morality is not a more comprehensive category of well-being that includes both volitional and critical interests as components to be traded off against one another.

So we have volitional and critical interests and no more inclusive category of well-being that can adjudicate conflicts between them. I shall from this point on assume that our project of finding a liberal ethics as a foundation for liberal politics must concentrate on critical as distinct from volitional well-being. We need an account of what people's critical interests are that will show why people who accept that account and care about their own and other people's critical well-being will be led naturally toward some form of liberal polity and practice. I do not mean, of course, that political liberals should care about improving people's lives only in the critical as distinguished from the volitional (or biological) sense. Fighting pain and disease is important no matter in which of these categories it figures. Nor am I making the mistake I warned against a moment ago, of assuming that people worry only about their critical interests, or even that most people think about their critical interests very often. I mean only to distinguish our project from others that ask rather different questions about the connection between liberalism and the motives people bring to politics.

Of course it is a sensible question — and a politically crucial one — whether liberal political principles would serve the volitional interests of most people in a democracy and, if so, how liberal politicians can convince a majority that this is so. Our question is about motivation in a different sense, not so immediately political though perhaps of more far-reaching political importance. Political principles are normative in the way critical interests are: one defines the political community we should have, the other how we should live in it. Our search for foundations is therefore a search for normative integrity. We ask whether people who do take their critical interests seriously would have that motive for adopting the liberal political perspective. In the long run that question is, as I just suggested, a practical one, because in the long run political programs fail unless they find space in people's self-image and not just in what they happen to want.

Worries and Puzzles about Critical Interests

Most people believe they have critical interests. They think it important to make something of their lives, whether or not that conviction much affects how they actually live. But most of us are also aware how problematic and obscure the idea of critical interests is, and many people fear that it is a cosmic illusion. People who believe in an afterlife are not troubled by that worry, of course, because heaven and hell convert ethics into prudence. But most us lack that comfort, and though we manage to shake off our skeptical moments, and regain whatever ethical conviction we had before, we have not come to terms with our anxieties but only postponed them. In the next several pages, I offer a kind of catalog of these anxieties in the form of philosophical issues about the character of ethics. I begin with the familiar dead-of-night worry, that life is meaningless, and then add a series of further issues or puzzles about ethics that, while not so intimidating or familiar, are nevertheless of philosophical dimension because they also call into question our grasp of the very idea of critical ethical value.

Significance. People who are self-conscious about living well treat this as a matter of capital importance; they think it very important not merely or even whether their lives are enjoyable, but whether they are good or bad lives to lead. In what sense or from what perspective *could* that be important? How can it matter what happens in the absurdly tiny space and time of a single human life? Or even in the tiny episode of all sentient life taken together? The universe is so big and has lasted so long that our best scientists struggle even to give sense to the question of how big it is or how long it has lasted. One day — any moment now in the history of time — the sun will explode and then there may be nothing left that can even wonder about how we lived. How can we reconcile these two ideas: that life is nothing and that how we live is everything?

Transcendent or Indexed? It is part of the idea of someone's having critical interests that these are not just a matter of what he happens to want, but of what he should want, and that he can be deeply mistaken about what his critical interests are. That seems to suggest that ethical values are *transcendent*, that is, that the components of a good life are always and everywhere the same. But that conflicts with the opposite assumption many of us find irresistibly reasonable: that there is no such thing as the single good life for everyone, that ethical standards are in some way *indexed* to culture and ability and resource and other aspects of one's circumstance, so that the best life for a person in one situation may be very different from the best life for someone else in another. Which of these two views, each supported by strong intuitions and convictions, is correct, and which must be abandoned? Can we reject the transcendent view of ethical value and still retain our conviction that ethics is not merely subjective, that it is not merely a matter of discovering what we really want?

Ethics and Morality. Now consider Plato's question. What is the connection between self-interest and morality? When we have volitional interests in mind, it is plain that my own interests and morality are very different matters. They often conflict; I can often have more of what I want by cheating or stealing or lying. But the matter is more complex when we take self-interest in the critical rather than the volitional sense. Then three views seem possible. First, we might think that living well, even in the critical sense, is wholly independent of living justly. Someone who believes that the truly good life is the life of great power, for example, may well think his critical interests conflict with justice because he could increase his power by lying or stealing. Second, we might think that justice is a component of critical well-being, but not the whole story. No one lives really well unless he is at least reasonably just (we might say) so that a person who is forced to choose between extending his power and acting justly has a choice to make *within* ethics, and not just between ethics and morality. He must decide whether, all things considered, his life goes better with more power at the cost of some injustice, or vice versa. Third, we might take Plato's view: that there is never a conflict between justice and self-interest because one can never lead a critically better life through unjust acts. If it is necessary to act unjustly to gain more power, then gaining more power cannot count, even *pro tanto*, as an improvement in the critical value of one's life.[36]

Most people's intuitions seem to favor one of the first two views over the third. Paul Cézanne was a draft dodger not out of conscientious objection but from a desire to paint, and many people think that even if he acted wrongly he had a greater life as a result.[37] Suppose someone builds a fortune in a ruthless and immoral business career, and then uses it to finance a dazzling Renaissance life of refined and exotic experience, of artistic creation and patronage, of exploration and discovery. We will say he was wrong to do it, that a *morally* better person would have resisted the opportunities he took. But almost everyone would say that his dazzling life was a better *life* than the more honest person would have had. Plato denied that, however, and some of our intuitions support his view. For critical interests are normative — they are the interests one *ought* to have — and it therefore seems odd that they should conflict with any other normative demand. Why ought I want power or artistic achievement or a dazzling life if I (or others) ought not to do what will produce these? Would it not be more accurate to say that we ought to want the *kind* of

[36] There are two versions of this third view. The first holds that justice is only one component of the good life, as the second view does, but insists that it is dominantly more important than any other component, so that no gain in any other component could outweigh even the smallest compromise of justice. The second holds that the connection between justice and the good life is more intimate still. But I cannot explain in what way until I have developed what I call the model of challenge. See the subsection "The Model of Challenge."

[37] I owe this example to A. J. Ayer, who emphatically rejected the third view.

power or achievement or life that can be achieved consistently with justice? How can we ought in *any* sense to want more power than that? Our intuitions are in disorder, yet again.

Additive or Constitutive? We can reflect on someone *else's* life with two questions in mind. We can ask, first, how far his life includes whatever experiences or relationships or events or achievements we count as components of a good or decent life. We can ask, second, how far he recognizes whatever components of the good life his own life contains, whether he sought them, regarded them as valuable, in short endorsed them as serving his critical interests. But how should we combine these two types of questions? Two views are possible. The *additive* view holds that we can judge his life a good or bad one without consulting his opinions of its value. If his life has the components of a good life, then it is good for that reason. If he endorses those components, then this increases the goodness of his life; it is frosting on the cake. But if he does not, the ethical value of the components remains. He may have a very good life in virtue of experiences and achievements he does not endorse, though not so good a life, perhaps, as if he had endorsed them.

The *constitutive* view, on the other hand, argues that no component may even so much as contribute to the value of a person's life without his endorsement. So if a misanthrope is much loved but disdains the love of others as worthless, his life is not more valuable for their affection. The constitutive view is *not* the skeptical view that someone's life is good or bad in the critical sense only when and because he thinks it good or bad. Someone might be wrong in thinking his life a good one, and wrong because he counts something as a component of a good life that in fact is not. And he might be wrong in not recognizing and endorsing some feature of his life that, had he recognized it, would have made his life better. The constitutive view denies only that some event or achievement can make a person's life better against his opinion that it does not.

Which of these views should we adopt? Once again, each seems to be supported and assumed by some familiar intuitions and convictions. Our sense that critical value is not merely subjective, which seemed to support the transcendent view of ethical standards, also seems to support the additive view of ethical value. If it is not just up to me to decide what kind of a life is good, then why should it matter, for the value of my life, what I think about it? In some, extreme cases, common sense confirms that argument. Would Hitler not have led a better life if he had been locked up from adolescence, even if he spent the rest of his life dreaming of the horror he could have caused? But other, less dramatic examples provoke contrary intuitions. Even if we think that religion must be part of a good life, can it improve someone's life to force him into religious observance he counts worthless? Can it really make sense to say that the misanthrope's life was improved by having the love he did not want? In these cases, we do not feel that just the value of something good — religion or the love of friends — is diminished when it is not appreciated. We feel that its value is obliterated, that there is no value at all unless that value is in some way sponsored by recognition. Once again some of our intuitions seem in conflict with others, and ethics seems more mysterious as a result.

Ethics and Community. The final set of puzzles I shall describe raise the question of the *unit* of ethical value, that is, of the entity whose life ethics aims to make good. On the one hand, we feel that ethics is entirely personal. Each of us has ultimate responsibility for deciding what kind of life is right for him; even a person who unreflectively settles into social grooves is responsible for that nonchoice if less conforming lives were available. And each of us has a personal *stake* in the life he lives, whether or not he chose it. It is *my* life that is at stake when I decide where to live or what career to take up or whether to lie for advantage, and though I may have great concern for the lives of others — my family and friends, for example — there is nevertheless a crucial distinction between what I do for the sake of my own life, to make *it* more successful, and what I do for their lives. But yet on some occasions and in some circumstances that confident division of the ethical world into our own life and the lives of others fails. We sense that the most fundamental ethical unit is collective not individual, that the question of whether my life is going well is subordinate to the question whether, for some group of which I am a member, *our* life is going well.

We must take care not to dissipate this apparent conflict by confusing it with other connections between personal and social concerns that, however important, do not challenge the distinctly individual character of ethics. Of course the lives of other people are important to me; I know that a good life cannot be a selfish or self-centered one. And of course I know that my ethical convictions are socially conditioned and constrained, that I cannot even contemplate lives that seem natural in other cultures. If I believe that ethics is indexed rather than transcendent, moreover, I will think that the connection between conviction and culture is not merely psychological or conceptual but ethics as well, because the right life for me depends in part on which time and nation and culture I live it in. There is no conflict between believing that my ethical life is fully and only my responsibility and that it is connected to community in these various ways.

I have in mind, as raising a puzzle for ethics, a different and more radical way of connecting my ethical life to my community. This supposes that a community has an ethical life of its own and that the critical success of any individual's life depends to some degree on the critical success of the life of his community. That assumption is, for many people, a common part of their political sensibility. They feel a personal failure when their own nation acts unjustly or wickedly, even when they have played no part in the injustice and have even tried to prevent it, which they do not feel when some other nation acts in the same way. The most notorious and powerful example of this attitude in our time is the responsibility Germans who played no part in the Holocaust feel for the sins of their political community; some Germans who were not born until the Nazi era was only sad history feel this responsibility. Most people fuse their lives in a parallel way to nonpolitical communities. Partners in joint projects — people thrown together in a rescue operation, for example — do not distinguish personal success from the success of the venture. If the venture fails they have failed, even when their own part was a success.

Mysteries teem. Does this kind of ethical group priority, in which an individual's critical interests are dependent on and merged into the critical interests of some group, presuppose ontological priority as well? Does it suppose that the fundamental human units of the universe are actually groups rather than the individual people who make them up, as some philosophers have thought? If not, how else can ethical priority be explained? Is it consistent to believe, as many of us seem to do, that ethics is both individual and communal? If this is consistent, then which unit of ethical priority — personal or communal — is the appropriate one to adopt when?

Models of Critical Value

These various puzzles and worries about the character of ethics and critical interests arise, I believe, because our ethical instincts and impulses reflect two different and in some respects antagonistic ways of conceiving the source and nature of the value a life can have for the person whose life it is. We draw on two different *models* of value that we use in other spheres or form more limited judgments, and we co-opt these models of value for ethics on different occasions. Both models have some grip on us, and our ethical intuitions will remain divided and inconclusive until we settle on one or the other, or for some more comprehensive model that includes and orders both, if that is possible. The first of these models, which I call the model of impact, holds that the value of a good life consists in its product, that is, in its consequences for the rest of the world. The second, which I call the model of challenge, argues that the value of a good life lies in the inherent value of a skillful performance of living. I shall try to show how these two abstract ideas about the fundamental character of ethics guide our reactions to the worries and puzzles I listed, and how far the perplexing character of ethics arises from unnoticed conflicts between the two, and our failure, or perhaps our inability, to resolve them.

I warned that our excursion into philosophical ethics would take us away from liberalism and political philosophy, but I can offer some reassurance at what will seem the furthest distance from where we began. In the next several pages we shall actually begin the return trip, because I shall try to show, in the sections that follow, that we find the key to liberal ethics in the distinctions we now begin to explore. Liberal ethics, I shall argue, are ethics that take the challenge model seriously and give it a prominent if not exclusive role in ethical imagination.

But that argument is some way off yet, and I shall ask you still to consider the ethical issues I shall be discussing next on their own terms, as matters important for us in themselves. I should offer a warning about the limited power of the two philosophical models of ethics we shall be discussing. Neither of the two models purports to offer any general argument for ethical value from the ground up, that is, against someone who claims no temptation to think that it matters what he does with his life so long as he enjoys it. The two models are rather *interpretations* of ethical experience, attempts to organize the convictions or intimations of ethical value which most of us do have into a coherent picture. The puzzles I described do not begin, after all, in any general Cartesian challenge to the basic assumption that we have critical as well as volitional interests, that it matters how we live. They arise because we have too many rather than too few ethical convictions; some of these seem to conflict with others. On the one hand we believe that significance depends on proportion, so that nothing of infinitesimal size relative to the universe can be really important, for example. On the other hand we believe — most of us cannot help believing — that it is crucially important how we live in spite of our insignificance. Any skeptical force this and the other puzzles have arises from despair at reconciliation. That kind of skepticism is internal rather than external to ethics — it uses one set of convictions to attack another, rather than attacking ethics from outside as a whole. The philosophical models try to defend ethics from that dangerous internal attack by showing how most of our convictions, at least, can be saved from one another if we look at them all in a certain light.

The Model of Impact

The impact of a person's life is the difference his life makes to the objective value of the world. Impact plainly figures in our judgments about whose life was a good one. We admire the lives of Alexander Fleming and Mozart and Martin Luther King, and we explain why we do by pointing to penicillin and *The Marriage of Figaro* and what King did for his race and his country. The model of impact generalizes from these examples; it holds that the ethical value of a life — its success in the critical sense — is entirely dependent on and measured by the value of its consequences for the rest of the world. The model hopes to dissipate the mysteries of ethical value by tying it to another, apparently less mysterious, kind of value: the value that objective states of affairs of the world can have. A life can have more or less value, the model claims, not because it is intrinsically more valuable to live one's life in one way rather than another, but because living in one way can have better consequences.

We all have opinions about when the world is going better or worse, though of course our opinions differ. Most of us think that things are better when disease is cured or great works of art are created, or social justice is improved. Some people — mainly philosophers — think the world goes better when the sum of human happiness or pleasure has been increased. The model of impact does not in itself declare for or against these various opinions about which states of affairs are objectively valuable. It merely fuses anyone's opinions about the critical value of his or other lives to whatever opinions he has about objective value in states of the world. If I think the world is better for a great work of art then, according to the model of impact, I must think the life of its author a better life to have lived for his having painted it. If, more controversially, I think the world better when commerce thrives, I will think that successful entrepreneurs live distinguished lives for that reason. The model connects not just the type but the metric of ethical value to consequence value. If I think that one artist's work is, as a whole, much greater than the art of another, then I must think the former's life a much greater life, at least so far as value is given to the lives of each by their art.

The model of impact finds support, as I said, in much conventional ethical opinion and rhetoric. It has great difficulty fitting and explaining other common ethical views and practices, however. Many of the ethical goals people regard as very important are not matters of consequence at all. I said earlier that I think my own critical interests include having close relations with my children and securing at least some feeble grasp of contemporary science. Other people have parallel convictions: they think it important to do at least something well, important that they master some field of learning or craft or learn to play a musical instrument, for example, not because they will make the world better by so doing — what can it matter that one more person can do something with average skill that other people can do much better — but just in order that *they* have done it. Many people set wholly adverbial goals for themselves: they want to live, they say, with integrity, doing things their way, with the courage of their convictions. These various ambitions make no sense in the vocabulary of impact. I hope it makes my children's lives better if I am close to them, but I am not sure that it does, and I should still want it as something important for *my* life even if I thought it did not. I know it will make no positive difference to anyone else how much or little grasp I have of cosmology: I will contribute nothing to knowledge of the universe in any case. The model of impact makes many popular views about critical interests seem silly and self-indulgent.

The Model of Challenge

The impact model does not deny the phenomenon of ethical value: it does not deny that people have critical interests and that their lives are better or worse depending on how far these interests are satisfied. But it describes those critical interests in a way that, as we have seen, is constricting of ethical value. It claims that lives go better only in virtue of their impact on the objective value of states of affairs. The alternate model I shall now develop — the model of challenge — rejects that limitation. It adopts Aristotle's view that a good life has the inherent value of a skillful performance. So it holds that events and achievements and experiences can have ethical value even when they have no impact beyond the life in which they occur. The idea that a skillful performance has an inherent value is perfectly familiar as a kind of value within lives. We admire a complex and elegant dive, for example, and we admire people who climbed Mount Everest because, as they said, it was there. The model of challenge holds that living a life is itself a performance that demands skill, that it is the most comprehensive and important challenge we face, and that our critical interests consist in the achievements, events, and experiences that mean that we have met the challenge well.

The model of challenge therefore offers room to the convictions about critical interest that the model of impact rejects as self-indulgent. It makes sense to support, even though it is by no means obvious or uncontroversial, that part of living well is acquiring some sense of the state of the art of knowledge of one's time. Nor does the model of challenge reject the intuitions that the model of impact accepts. For it also makes sense to think — indeed this might be obvious — that one way brilliantly to meet the challenge of living well is to reduce the world's suffering by conquering disease. The ecumenical character of the model of challenge might strike you as a weakness, as showing that the model is empty or at least uninformative. The model of impact ties ethical value to objective world value, and so seems at least to offer some guidance as to the actual substance of a good life. The model of challenge, by comparison, allows the idea of ethical value to float free of any other kind of value. If we are free to count doing or having anything at all as meeting the challenge of living well, then the model (it might seem) is not so much a model as a truism: living well is doing whatever counts as living well.

That complaint would be misjudged. Both models rely on convictions they assume we already have. The model of impact assumes we have convictions about what states of the world are independently valuable; it does not offer to judge these, but simply to explain our ethical values by showing the connection between our opinions about the two kinds of value. The model of challenge also assumes we have convictions about how to live; it does not judge these but tells us that we will understand our ethical life better if we see them in the way it recommends, as opinions about the skillful performance of an important self-assignment, rather than just as opinions about how we can change the world for the better. It is true, as we saw, that the model of impact makes certain ethical convictions some people have seem silly: they would probably not survive if the model were taken to heart as exclusive. But the model of challenge also makes certain convictions seem odd, as we shall see. The difference between the two models, in this respect, is that the convictions the model of challenge makes odd are anyway convictions few if any people would actually hold.

Ethics and Significance

We must now consider the different responses the two models suggest to the various puzzles of ethics, and I shall begin with the first puzzle I listed: the problem of significance. Since the model of impact locates the value of living a particular way in the independent value of its consequences, it is particularly vulnerable to the challenge that the difference even the most powerful human being can make to the state of the universe is indescribably puny. Impact can rescue ethics from this objection only by deploying some theory about objective value that stands up to infinity, some theory, that is, that makes the difference people can make to the universe seem much greater than the objection claims it can be. Perhaps that fact explains the appeal, for some people, of the romantic claim that the greatest value in the universe is aesthetic value, so that the transcendent value of a great work of art is in no way undercut by the fact that it is surrounded by light years and eons of aesthetic nullity. That theory of value, connected to the model of impact, could explain why artistic geniuses have great lives. But if art were the only significant value in the universe, it would not matter how most people lived. Ethics would be only for great souls.

There are other, less relentlessly elitist, theories of value, however, that might also stand up to the universe. One is theological anthropocentrism. Suppose there is a God who, in spite of the amplitude of his creation, takes special interest in human beings made in his own image, whose lives can please or displease him mightily. If that were true, then people could make an important difference, judged objectively, to the universe. Or consider a currently much more popular view: hedonistic anthropomorphism. On this view, human pleasure or happiness is the only objective value, even though human beings exist only on a tiny mote and only for a tiny moment. This view of consequent value, tied to the model of impact, produces a recognizably utilitarian ethics: our lives are good, in the critical sense, to the degree to which we create pleasure or happiness for ourselves and others. Theological and utilitarian ethics are, in most versions, elitist to some degree but not in the obviously unacceptable way in which the aesthetic theory is elitist. Some people, because they are chosen or blessed or gifted or lucky, will be able to lead critically better lives, measured in the theological or utilitarian way, than others can. But no one is frozen out of ethics, since we can all have some impact on God's satisfaction or on the general level of happiness in the world. Someone can lead a perfectly good life, on the utilitarian version, simply by living in a way that produces great pleasure for himself. So the model of impact can provide an answer to the first puzzle of ethics if we can accept some theory of objective value that makes what people can do seem genuinely important to the universe, like aestheticism or theological anthropomorphism or human utilitarianism.

The model of challenge responds to the problem of significance in a very different way: by denying that ethical value has or is meant to have impersonal value. For the value of a performance, as an exercise of skill in the face of a challenge, is complete in itself in a way that does not depend on anything we might call objective value or value to everyone. We do not have to think that the world is in any way an objectively better place when someone has mastered a complex dive or climbed Everest, that it is then the repository of greater objective value, in order to see the point of diving or climbing. This response does not *overcome* the objection that nothing human beings can do is important in the face of infinity, as the model of impact tries to do by imagining theories of transcendent human achievement. It simply sets the objection aside as based on a misconception of the kind of value ethical value is.

Nor does this model rely on the objective importance of achievement even when it recognizes the importance of making a difference in the world. It is obviously compelling that making great music or conquering pneumonia or restoring the pride of a race are among the good ways to live, and we could not accept the model of challenge if it could not find as comfortable a place for these ambitions as the model of impact can. There is no difficulty in finding a place for these ambitions, however: it does not distort the idea of performance or challenge to say that someone who has eliminated a great deal of misery in the world has done a skillful job of leading his life. That is not, however, simply a way of incorporating the model of impact within the model of challenge, as a compartment, because the former will not, as the latter must, make the objective value of the achievement the measure of its ethical value. For the contribution someone's invention or discovery or creation makes to the goodness of his life, on the challenge model, will undoubtedly be sensitive to much besides the objective value of what he has created. The *ethical* contribution of an invention might be thought to depend, for example, on the degree of difficulty involved in its making, or in its originality, or in the degree to which its author made full use of or stretched his abilities, or in the intensity of his dedication, or in the way in which his work flowed from his sense of his role in or his dedication to a particular community or tradition. The model of challenge does not, of course, in itself stipulate which of these or hundreds of other possible considerations should enter into deciding how great a contribution a particular achievement makes to the overall skill with which someone has lived his life. My point is the same one again: that treating achievements as having ethical value in that way, rather than just in virtue of their impact alone, allows more subtlety to our judgments of the success of our own and other people's lives.[38]

---

[38] In these lectures I am concentrating on the difference between the two models of ethical value and generally ignoring the possibility of a higher-level model that incorporates aspects of each, or recognizes the value of both. As I hope the argument of this paragraph suggests, however, each of the two models is comprehensive, in the sense that each offers a distinctive reading of the claims of the other, in a way that would make any simple union of the two impossible. In any case, my arguments about the ethical foundations of liberalism would hold, as I have already claimed, for any higher-order model that gave the model of challenge a prominent place.

The challenge model also allows us to celebrate some kinds of achievement — the creation of great art, for example — without the elitist consequence that only lives capable of that kind of success are really worth leading. Or that, if the lives of two artists are good lives in virtue of the art they have created, the one who has created better art has for that reason had a greater life. I recognize that, in this respect, the name "model of challenge" might be misleading. I do not mean that only lives full of internal challenge, given over to heroic deeds like climbing impossible mountains, can be successful lives on this model. I mean rather that life itself is to be seen as a challenge; skill at that challenge might be thought to require avoiding rather than embracing arduous exploits in favor of a life more suited to one's talents or situation or satisfactions or cultural expectations. The point, once again, is formal. Seeing ethical value as the value of a performance rather than as tied to the independent value of a product allows a further range of considerations and beliefs to enter ethical judgment, though it does not itself select among any particular set of these as more appropriate than others.

Transcendent or Indexed?

Since the model of impact ties ethical value to the independent value of states of affairs, ethical value must be transcendent under that model because it is very implausible that the objective value of states of affairs depends on their time or location. We might, perhaps, imagine bizarre theories of value that would index the value of states of affairs temporally or geographically. But any plausible or familiar theory would be immune to indexing. If we think that the only objective good is God's pleasure or the happiness of human beings, then we cannot think that the same amount of God's pleasure or overall human happiness could be less valuable at some moment of the world's history than another. That must also be true of more complex theories about objective value that assign, for example, different value to different components of an overall state of affairs. Any particular complex structure of independent value must have the same total value whenever or wherever it occurs. So the model of impact, on any plausible interpretation of the value it assumes, implies that ethical value is transcendent. Of course what creates ethical value, according to any particular interpretation, will depend on circumstances. What makes people happy in developed economies may be different from what makes them happy in economically simpler societies. But the metric of value, of how far someone's life has succeeded in being good, must remain everywhere the same. How much objective and timeless value, on the right theory of independent value, has he added to the world's stock?

The model of challenge, on the other hand, tempts those who accept it to the view that ethical value is indexed rather than transcendent. Someone who accepted the model could conceivably, it is true, adopt a transcendent view of what a good performance of living is. He might think, for example, that living well only means living with style and might hold some timeless view about what style consists in. But any such timeless account of living well would be fatally superficial. It seems irresistible that living well, judged as a performance, means among other things living in a way responsive and appropriate to one's culture and other circumstances. A life of chivalrous and courtly virtue might have been a very good one in twelfth-century Bohemia but not in Brooklyn now.

An analogy to art will be useful, though dangerous, here. I mentioned earlier the opinion some people have that great art has independent and timeless product value, so that the world is objectively better for having a brilliant painting in it no matter how that painting arrived. But that opinion, we should now notice, overlooks an important feature of art. A painting does have an independent value which we might call its product value: this is the power it has to excite aesthetic and other forms of valuable experiences. But this product value is different from a painting's *artistic* value, which is the value it has not independently but in virtue of how it was produced; we need the distinction between product and artistic value to explain the different value of an original and a perfectly, mechanically produced and undetected fake. The value we attach to great art reflects not just its value as a product, but our respect for the performance that produced it considered as a skillful response to a well-judged artistic challenge.

Art offers a better analogy to living, according to the challenge model, than the analogies I used earlier. For the challenge of art, unlike the challenge of diving well or climbing a difficult mountain, includes the challenge of defining as well as securing success, and if living well is regarded as a challenge, defining what it is to live well must be part of that challenge too. Artists are not furnished with blueprints, even in the most academic or conventionalized moments. When Duccio drew the Siennese tradition out of the Byzantine, or Duchamp hung his urinal on a gallery wall, each was making as well as answering a claim about the character of artistic achievement. There is no settled view about what artistic achievement is, as there is (I imagine) about achievements in diving. We expect artists to make claims that, if successful, might expand or at least change what the tradition counts as artistic achievement. These claims (we might say) offer to make something of nothing, to make value out of a kind of performance in which none was recognized before. If we treat ethical value as the value of a performance rather than the independent value of a product, then we shall have to take the same view of what a skillful performance of living is. There is no settled canon of skill in living, and some people's lives, at least, make claims about a skillful performance that if widely accepted would change prevailing views on the subject and might even launch what would seem a new mode of living well, making, once again, ethical value from nothing.[39]

---

[39] I do not mean that living a life well must also require breaking with an ethical custom or tradition or even developing it in some particularly original way.

It is therefore important to notice how implausible it would be
to think that artistic value is transcendent, that painting in the
same way always has the same artistic value, that there is, in principle, one absolutely greatest way to make art against which all
others must be judged. For artists enter the history of art at a particular time, and the artistic value of their work must be judged
in that light, not because their circumstances limit how close they
can come to the perfect ideal of artistry but for the opposite reason, that their circumstances affect what for them *is* a skillful performance of defining and extending and executing art. An artist's
situation in the history of art, and the political, technological, and
social conditions of his age, enter we might say into the *parameters*
of the challenge he faces. Duccio's challenge was very different
from, say, Caro's or Duchamp's. Even if we think that contemporary sculpture must explore and comment on the materials of mod-

---

The model of challenge makes room for that suggestion: it makes room for the
romantic ideal that one should make of one's life a work of art, understood in that
specially romantic way. But it does not require it. It might help to guard against
other misinterpretations of the analogy between ethics and art by noticing a variety
of senses we can give to the familiar injunction that we should try to make our life
a work of art. The simplest reading construes the injunction as a recommendation
that everyone create as much and as great art as possible in his life, which would be
a silly recommendation for almost everyone because not even all those with the
necessary talent would find a good life in exploiting it. We can understand the injunction in a different and almost equally silly way: that we should give over our
lives to aesthetic sensibility, making a response to artistic excellence, whether created
by ourselves or others, our dominant concern and experience. Some of us know
people who have taken that view of how to live; in any case we can find examples
in the novels, for instance, of Henry James, but it does not seem a particularly
attractive ethical ideal. On a third reading the ideal asks us to live in such a way
that our life is a fit object of artistic contemplation and aesthetic satisfaction. That
cannot be made plausible except by so diluting the idea of an aesthetic judgment or
response or experience as to make the suggestion practically empty. We do not contemplate or savor or experience our own lives, let alone those of other people, in the
way the idea that our ethical convictions are aesthetic seems to suggest. In fact the
injunction makes sense only if understood in the structural sense I mean the analogy
between art and ethics to reveal: we make our lives works of art by treating ethical
value in the challenge way, and therefore as having the same structure as artistic
value. If there is any genetic connection between ethics and art, its direction is probably the opposite from the direction the more romantic readings of the injunction
assume. Perhaps we can recognize artistic value only because it has the same structure as the developmentally prior idea that there is value in the way someone lives,
that elegance in art is parasitic on elegance in living, for example.

ern technology, we do not count it a limitation on an artist of the trecento that he did not have steel or resin or epoxy. Even if we think Christian mythology would be an impoverished religious subject now, we do not count Duccio's work banal.

So the artistic analogy reminds us that the value of a performance can be indexed without being subjective, because the indexing can be provided by parameters of challenge that change with time and situation but that nevertheless can pose categorical demands. Living well, like painting well, can be seen as responding in an appropriate way to one's situation, though of course the ethical challenge of a particular time and place is very different from the artistic challenge. Art and ethics, on this view, are indexed in the same way. Both call for a decision, as part of the challenge they present, about the right response to the complex circumstances in which the decision must be made. It is, in both cases, a further question what the right response for any particular artist or person in any particular circumstances actually is, or whether there is a single right response even for a particular person or circumstance or only a set of these. The model of challenge, at the level of abstraction we are exploring, does not answer that further question. It only emphasizes what kind of a question it is: that it requires a personal response to the full particularity of situation, not the application, to that situation, of a timelessly ideal life.

Limitations and Parameters

We must now explore the distinction we have just noticed. Under any plausible version of the model of impact, all the circumstances of any person's actual life act as limitations on the quality of the life he can have. The ideal life is always the same: it is a life creating as much independent value — as powerful a pleasing of God or as much human happiness — as it is conceivable for a human being to create. Circumstances act as limits on the degree to which the ideal can be achieved. Mortality, for example, is a very important limit: most people could create more pleasure if they lived longer. Talent, wealth, personality, language, technology, and culture provide other limits, and their force as limits will be much greater for some people, and in some times and places, than others. If we take an indexed challenge view of ethics, however, and treat living well as responding in the right way to one's situation, then we must treat some of the circumstances in which a particular person lives differently, as parameters that help define what a good performance of living would be for him.

Living well includes defining what the challenge of living, properly understood, is, just as painting well includes sensing which aspects of the artist's overall circumstances define the right tradition for him to continue or to defy. We have no settled template for that decision, in art or in ethics, and no philosophical model can provide one, for the circumstances in which each of us lives are enormously complex. They include our health, our physical powers, our tenure of life, our material resources, our friendships and associations, our commitments and traditions of family and race and nation, the constitutional and legal system under which we live, the intellectual and literary and philosophical opportunities and standards offered by our language and culture, and thousands of other aspects of our world as well. Anyone who reflects seriously on the question which of the various lives he might lead is right for him will consciously or unconsciously discriminate among these, treating some as limits and others as parameters. I might treat the fact that I am an American, for example, as just a fact that in some cases might help and in others hinder my leading the life I think best. Or I must treat my nationality as a parameter and assume, whether or not self-consciously, that being an American is part of what makes a particular life the right one for me.

No philosophical model can decide these issues; certainly not in any detail. Most people will sort their circumstances into the two camps, discriminating between limits and parameters, almost

automatically, and those who do reflect on the distinction are unlikely to draw the convictions they reach from any overall theory.
But if I do not think ethics transcendent — if I do not think one
life would be the greatest for all human beings who will ever have
lived — then I must treat *some* of the facts that distinguish my
situation from that of other human beings as parameters rather
than limitations. My biological, social, and national associations,
those I was born or fell into, not those I chose, seem obvious candidates to me, though they may not to others. The fact that I am
a member of the American political community is not a limitation
on my ability to lead a good life I could describe in isolation from
that connection. It rather states a condition of a good life for me:
it is a life appropriate to someone whose situation includes that
connection.

But of course I cannot treat *everything* about my situation as a
parameter without destroying ethics for myself altogether. Suppose I took my own character, desires, resources, opportunities,
and predilections to mark parameters for me; I say that the life
good for me is a life good for someone with exactly my present
material wealth and education and ambitions. I would have indexed my account of the good life so thoroughly to my own immediate situation that it could no longer offer a challenge at all. So
living well requires more discrimination about limits and parameters than either of the extreme views that counts everything as
limitation or everything as parameter.

It is fortunate for us that most of the discriminations we need
are more or less automatic, carried in our culture like so much else
about ethics. But we can nevertheless identify some of the decisions we have in effect made, and we can force ourselves to consider whether they have been made in the right way.[40] I might
come to think, for example, that my professional or religious or

---

[40] Of course we cannot review them all together, though much of Michael
Sandel's criticism of liberalism seems to assume that liberals think we can. See
Michael J. Sandel, *Liberalism and the Limits of Justice* (Cambridge: Cambridge
University Press, 1982).

some other connections are even more fundamental in defining the challenge I face in living than my political ones are, and I may seek citizenship in some other nation in consequence. When we reflect on the structure of our ethical convictions in this way we notice important complexities. We notice, for example, that many of our parameters are normative: they define our ethical situation not in terms of our actual situation but of our situation as it should be. Our lives may go badly, in other words, not just because we are unwilling or unable properly to respond to the circumstances we have, but because we have the wrong circumstances. We do not even face the challenge we identify as the right one; even if we do the best we can in the circumstances we do face, we do badly measuring our success against the chance we believe we ought to have been given, and it is the latter that defines a good life for us.

Consider, for example, the way most of us treat our mortality. We do not count the fact that we will die someday, much as we might fear or resent it, as a limitation on the value of the life we can have. We do not think that our lives can be at best only a tiny fraction as good as the lives people could lead if they lived to biblical ages, or forever. We count a life good on that score if it lasts long by human standards, so that it can have the kinds of interrelatedness of age and generation and the other kinds of internal complexity that our cultural standards of a good life presuppose.[41] But we do not judge the goodness of someone's life only by asking how well it occupied whatever span of years it in fact had. If someone dies young by our standards, we count that a tragedy; his life was only partly as good as it might have been. Many of our ethical parameters are normative in that way: they define the challenge that people should face in the *ethically* normative sense that a life not permitted that challenge is for that very reason a worse one.

[41] See A Concise Encyclopedia of the Italian Renaissance (New York: Oxford University Press, 1981), p. 17, under "Age."

That points the way to a further complexity. We must distinguish between what I shall call hard and soft parameters. Parameters, as I said, enter into the description of any challenge or assignment: they describe the conditions of successful performance. Hard parameters state essential conditions: if they are violated the performance is a total failure, no matter how successful in other respects. The formal structure of a sonnet imposes hard parameters: we cannot make a sonnet better by adding an extra line, no matter how beautiful it is. Soft parameters are those aspects of assignment that, when violated, reduce the value of the performance but do not annihilate it: they act as standards of good performance that permit defects to be compensated by high success against other standards. Compulsory figures in competitive ice skating are treated as soft parameters. It is part of the assignment that the performance execute a particular figure, and any deviations, no matter how beautifully executed, count as faults. But deviations are not absolutely fatal to winning any points at all, and a performance that includes a brilliant deviation may win more overall than a lackluster but perfectly faithful one.

For most of us, at least, the parameters that define success in living a life are all soft. It counts against the goodness of someone's life that it was cut short by an early death because a good life for a human being is a life that occupies and makes good use of at least a normal life span. But a short life can nevertheless be a brilliant success, as Mozart's was. Some soft parameters require choices, and these may pose conflicts or dilemmas. Suppose I think that my life must be a life appropriate for an American and also for a Jew, and then I come to think that recognizing both these allegiances would tear my life apart. I might think that the best life for me required some compromise, or that it required accepting one parameter and rejecting the other. Or I might think that no choice, in these circumstances, could really be thought better than the other, that I must just choose knowing that my life will be marred either way. The challenge model gives more sense and point to all these circumstances and dilemmas than the impact model can.

Justice as Parameter

The fourth set of puzzles I described involves the connection between well-being and morality: can someone lead a better life in virtue of injustice? I want now to distinguish two versions of that question. How is the critical value of someone's life affected by his own unjust behavior? How is it affected by the injustice of others or by an unjust situation, by living in a community in which resources are unjustly distributed, for example? The impact model, in its abstract form, takes up no position on the first of these questions, for we can find interpretations of it that are compatible with each of the three views I listed earlier. On one interpretation, for example, we do good for the world only when we make it less unjust, and on that interpretation no one could have a better life through behavior that produced more injustice in the world. On another interpretation the greatest life is a life of producing great art; on that interpretation Cézanne's draft dodging made his life a greater one even if it was indefensibly unjust.

But the model of impact, even in its abstract form, does take up a position about the second question: how the value of one's life can be affected by the injustice of others, or by an unjust situation. It holds that third-party injustice, as such, can make no difference to ethics. It is undeniable that in the United States now some people — I shall call them the rich — have more wealth than justice allows and others — the poor — have less. A rich man may use his wealth to make a positive impact on the world on any interpretation of what a positive impact would be. He may use it to create or sponsor great art, or to finance his own or others' research into antibiotics, or even to reduce the overall level of injustice in the world by giving his money away. However we interpret objective value, the impact of his life has more value than it would have had if he had only average wealth, and, since the unjust situation (we are assuming) is not of his making, there is no negative impact value, in *his* life, to set against the gain. Of course it does not follow that he should approve of the injustice, or that he should not vote and work to correct it so far as he can. But these are moral not ethical requirements. Now consider the poor man. He almost undoubtedly will have a worse life, measured by its impact, than he could have had if he had more wealth. But that is in no way the consequence of the fact that his having less wealth is unjust: it is not the injustice of his share of resources, but the absolute amount of that share, that sets limits to the impact he can have. We would not judge his life a better one if we changed our mind about justice and decided that his share was just after all.

The model of challenge suggests a dramatically different answer to the question of whether a person can have a better life in virtue of an unjust situation. Someone who accepts that model, and so accepts that some aspects of our circumstances must count as normative parameters of living well, will find it difficult not to regard justice as figuring among those normative parameters. Certainly resources must figure as parameters in some way, because we cannot describe the challenge of living well without making some assumptions about the resources a good life should have available to it. Resources cannot count only as limitations, because we can make no sense of the best possible life abstracting from its economic circumstances altogether. We must therefore find some suitable account of the way in which resources enter ethics as parameters of the good life, and we have, I think, no alternative but to bring justice into that story by stipulating that a good life is a life suitable to circumstances in which resources are justly distributed.

I said, earlier, that it seems odd to say that we ought to want resources we can have only by acting as we think we or others ought not to act. The model of challenge absorbs and explains that intuition. If living well includes assigning ourselves the right challenge in living, and that in turn includes stipulating the right resource parameters, then any normative convictions we have about the right distribution of resources must be brought to bear on that assignment. It makes no sense to say that it is appropriate for people to have only a fair share of resources, and then add that the circumstances we should regard as appropriate, in deciding how to live well, can be unfair ones. It does not help to say that we mean morally appropriate in the first clause and ethically appropriate in the second, because the concept of normative parameters is insensitive to that distinction. We must set the resource parameters of a life well lived, so far as we can, so that these respect our sense of justice.

If living well means responding in the right way to the right challenge, then a life goes worse when the right challenge cannot be faced. That explains why injustice, just on its own, is bad for people. Someone who is denied what justice entitles him to have leads a worse life just for that reason; he leads a worse life than he would with the same absolute resources in, say, a poorer age when no one has more than he does. I do not mean, of course, that the absolute value or quality of the resources a person commands makes no difference to the life he can lead, so long as he has a just share of whatever there is. Someone who lives in a richer community or age, with a just share of its wealth, faces a more interesting and valuable challenge, and can lead a more exciting, diverse, complex, and creative life just for that reason, much as someone playing chess has a more valuable opportunity than someone playing tic-tac-toe. Lives can be better in different ways, and facing a more valuable challenge is one of them. Recognizing justice as a parameter of ethics does, however, limit the goodness of the life someone can lead in any given economic circumstances. I could have a better life, I assume, if circumstances changed so that justice allowed me more resources. Recognizing justice as a parameter denies, or at least calls into question, that I could have a better life with an unjust share of resources now.

But is it really true that no one can ever, in any circumstances, lead a better life by having more than justice permits? That was

Plato's view, and it would seem absurd, as I said earlier, if he meant a life better in terms of volitional interests. But the Platonic view has great appeal and some plausibility if we understand him to mean that justice is a hard parameter of living well, that no one can improve his life in the critical sense by using more resources than he is entitled to have, any more than someone can improve a sonnet by adding more lines. Once we accept that the best life means a life responding well to the right circumstances, and that the right circumstances are circumstances of justice, we become aware of how difficult it is to lead anything like the right life when circumstances are far from just. We become aware, indeed, of how difficult it is even to imagine a really good life then.

Our own society is unjust. So our culture offers no examples we can study of lives that flourished or were deemed successful in circumstances as they should be. Those of us who are rich cannot establish the relations with other people, particularly those who are poor because we are rich, that would be important to a good life in a just society. We may try to live with only the resources we think we would have in a fair society, doing the best we can, with what is left, to repair injustice through private charity. But since a just distribution cannot be established counterfactually, but only through just institutions, we are unable to judge what share of our wealth is fair. In any case our lives would be distorted by a genuinely thoroughgoing attempt to lead it in such an artificial way. On the other hand, simply ignoring the fact of injustice, and spending what we have in satisfying the volitional interests our culture recommends to people of our means, hardly seems an appropriate response. We may work in politics. But we will likely fail to do much good, and that, too, makes our life worse because the community's failure is ours as well. So once we identify the conditions of a really good life for us, in a clearheaded way, we will have some sympathy with Plato's view that justice is a hard parameter of ethics, that nothing can redeem a life spoilt by the misfortune of living in an unjust state.

Nevertheless that seems too strong. The alternative view, that justice is a soft parameter, is less destructive of recalcitrant ethical intuitions. On this view, though someone supported by unjust wealth cannot succeed fully in meeting the appropriate challenge, which is to live a life suited to someone in a just community, his life is nevertheless not automatically worthless. It might be a very good life. Indeed, like a skating performance that deviates from compulsory figures, it might even, in rare cases, be a better life than he could have led in a society perfectly just. That will not be true of most people who have more wealth than they should, however. They will do nothing so brilliant or amazing with the surplus over justice that it will compensate for their inability to lead a life good for a just community. Some of them may enjoy their life more than they would in a just community, of course. But that does not mean that their lives are any better in the critical sense. Nevertheless some genius financed by unjust wealth — Michelangelo by the Medici — may achieve a life greater than anyone could in a more just state.[42] And a child whose life is saved by medicine available to him only because of his parents' unjust wealth will very likely lead a better life in consequence. These concessions seem required by our sense of ethical possibility. But they are statistically insignificant. On the model of challenge, Plato was nearly right.

Additive or Constitutive?

Our next set of puzzles worries about the connection between convictions and the good life. How far and in what way does my having a good life depend on my thinking it good? We make no sense of ethical experience except on the supposition that these are objective: a particular life cannot be good for me just because I think it is, and I can make a mistake in thinking a particular life

[42] As Harry Lime told us in *The Third Man*, the Italian quattrocento produced tyranny and the Renaissance. Switzerland in the same period produced democracy and the cuckoo clock.

good. But convictions seem to play a more important part in ethics than that flat statement allows. It seems preposterous that it could be in someone's interests, even in the critical sense, to lead a life he despises and thinks unworthy. How can that life be good *for* him? We are tempted, then, to say that ethical value must be subjective after all: having a good life must be a matter of ethical *satisfaction*, which means, in the end, that it must be a matter of thinking one's life good. But then the wheel turns again: I cannot think my life good unless I think that its goodness does *not* depend on my thinking it so.

The model of impact, on any plausible interpretation, cuts that knot by insisting that ethical value is fully objective, so that someone can indeed lead a better life than some alternative even when he thinks it much worse. Ethical value is additive rather than constitutive on the impact model, because ethical value is a matter of the objective value a life adds to the universe, and except on bizarre views, like the possible view that God is pleased by a person's life only if that person thinks his life pleasing to God, that cannot depend on how much value a person thinks he is adding. Creating art might require a belief that one is creating art. But it certainly does not require the belief that creating great art makes a great life. Nor does improving the happiness of others require the belief that it is in one's own ethical interests to do so. In some cases the ethical convictions of the actor might add to the impact of what he does. Perhaps I can create more pleasure by what I do if others know that I believe it does me good, too. But that extra impact is incremental. The impact model would therefore have no trouble explaining the common feeling I reported earlier: that Hitler would have had a better life for himself, as well as for the rest of the world, if he had been locked up or even killed soon after birth. The impact of Hitler's life would then have been much more favorable, even if he would then have had no impact at all, and so his life would have been a much better one, in the critical sense, for him as well.

The challenge view, however, resolves these puzzles in a very different way. On any plausible interpretation of that model, the connection between conviction and value is constitutive: my life cannot be better for me in virtue of some feature or component I think has no value. Even in its abstract form the model presses toward that constitutive view. For intention is part of performance: we do not give credit to a performer for some feature of his performance he was struggling to avoid, or would not recognize, even in retrospect, as good or desirable. A painter's artistic performance is not improved when a master pushes his hand across the canvas, or drags it back from a stroke that would ruin what he has already done. The misanthrope's life is not made better by the friendship he thinks pointless. Of course it would have been better for everyone else if Hitler had died in his cradle. But on the challenge view it makes no sense to say that his own life would have been better, as distinct from no worse, if that had happened. There is nothing comparable under that model to a negative impact on the world.

It will be useful to consider, at this point, how this difference between the two models affects an issue in political philosophy: the legitimacy of coercive critical paternalism. The question is often raised, at least in philosophy texts, whether it is proper for the state to try to make people's lives better by forcing them to act in ways they think make their lives worse. A good deal of actual coercive paternalism is not critical but volitional in character: the state makes people wear seat belts in order to keep them from harm it assumes they already want to avoid. But some people claim that the state has a right or even an obligation to make people's lives better in the *critical* sense, not only against their will, that is, but against their conviction. I doubt that that motive for coercion has ever been of much practical importance; certainly it is not in our time. Theocratic colonizers aim at their own salvation, not the well-being of those they force to convert, and sexual bigots act out of hatred, not concern for those whose behavior they find immoral. Nevertheless some political movements do claim pater-nalistic motives: they want to compel people to act in civic ways, for example, on the ground that civic-minded people lead better lives.

The model of impact accepts the theoretical basis of critical paternalism. I do not mean that anyone who accepts that model must approve paternalism. He might think that officials would misuse their power, or make worse judgments about ethical value than ordinary people would on their own. But he would see the *point* of ethical paternalism: it could make sense to him, for ex-ample, that people's lives would go better if they were forced to pray, because in that case they might please God more and so have a better impact, even though they were atheists. The challenge view, on the other hand, is suspicious of critical paternalism be-cause it rejects its root assumption: that a person's life can be im-proved just by forcing him into some act or abstinence he thinks valueless. Someone who accepts the challenge model might well think that religious devotion is an essential part of how human beings should respond to their place in the universe, and therefore that devotion is part of living well. But he cannot think that in-voluntary religious observance, prayer in the shadow of the rack, has any ethical value. He may think that an active homosexual blights his life by a failure to understand the point of sexual love. But he cannot think that a homosexual who abstains, against his own convictions and only out of fear, has therefore overcome that defect in his life. On the challenge model, that is, it is performance that counts, not mere external result, and the right motive or sense is necessary to the right performance. It overstates the point to say that the challenge model rules out *any* form of paternalism, how-ever, because the defect it finds in paternalism can be cured by endorsement if the paternalism is sufficiently short-term and lim-ited that it does significantly constrict choices if the endorsement never comes. We know that a child who is forced to practice music is very likely later to endorse the coercion by agreeing that it did, in fact, make his life better; if he does not, he has lost little ground in a life that makes no use of his training. In any case, endorsement must be genuine, and it is not genuine when someone is hypnotized or brainwashed or frightened into conversion. Endorsement is genuine only when it is itself the agent's performance, not the result of another person's thoughts being piped into his brain.[43]

The examples I have used so far are cases of surgical paternalism: coercion is justified on the ground that the behavior implanted is good or the behavior excised is bad for people. Now consider a more sophisticated form of paternalism. Substitute paternalism justifies a prohibition not by pointing to the badness of what it prohibits but to the positive value of the substitute lives it makes available. Suppose people in power think that a life of religious devotion is wasted and therefore prohibit religious orders. Citizens who might have spent their lives in orders will then lead other lives with other experiences and achievements they find valuable, even though (unless they change their convictions and endorse the paternalism) they will think these lives worse than the life they were denied. Someone who would have spent his life in monastic orders might, for example, take up a life in politics that is eminently successful and valuable to others in ways that he agrees make his life a better one. Now the dilemma we noticed earlier reappears. Suppose we agree that a life of religious devotion is wasted. The politician's life has plainly not been wasted. He cannot take credit, it is true, for the decision to prefer politics to devotion, because that is not something he did or endorsed. But he can take credit for the various acts and decisions that made his life in politics a success; he chose that life and made those decisions with a sense of their value. How can we not think that the decent life he in fact led was better than the life we believe would have been worthless, whatever he thinks? But yet the oddness remains: how can the life he led be better *for* him when he goes

[43] I say a bit more in "Liberal Community."

to his grave thinking it has been worse? In what sense was it more in *his* interests to lead a life that left him bitter, believing that he was leading a false, distorted life, at war with his own ethical sense?

The model of challenge (though not the model of impact) has the resources to resolve this dilemma. If we accept the challenge model we can insist on the priority of ethical *integrity* in any judgments we make about how good someone's life is. Ethical integrity is the condition someone achieves who is able to live out of the conviction that his life, in its central features, is an appropriate one for him, that no other life he might live would be a plainly better response to the parameters of his ethical situation rightly judged. The priority of integrity makes a stronger claim than merely that disappointment and regret mar a life, that these are features of a life that *pro tanto* make it worse. If that were all, then these negative components might easily be outweighed by the positive features of the substitute life. We would be comfortable saying that even though the politician would much have preferred a life in religious orders, his political career was nevertheless, on balance, taking his own feelings into account, a better life than the wasted life he would have had. Giving priority to ethical integrity makes a merger of conviction and life a parameter of ethical success, and it stipulates that a life that never achieves that kind of integrity cannot be critically better for someone to lead than a life that does.

Of course ethical integrity may fail for many reasons. It fails when people live mechanically, with no sense of having and responding to ethical convictions at all. It fails when people set their convictions aside and serve their volitional interests with a vague but persistent sense that they are not living as they should. It fails when people believe, rightly or wrongly, that the correct normative parameters have not been met for them, when they have less resources than justice permits, for example. And it fails conspicuously when people are made to live in a way they regret, and never endorse, by the fiat of other people.

Recognizing the priority of ethical integrity does not make ethics subjective in the first person, that is, for someone considering how he himself should live. The principle of priority does not make the mistake we noticed earlier: it does not make any person's convictions parameters for him in the sense that his assignment is only to live comfortably with whatever ethical assumptions he happens to have. On the contrary, living *out* of conviction — treating my beliefs *as* convictions — requires reflection, coherence, and openness to the examples of others. It requires me to reflect, from time to time, on whether I do find the life I am living satisfactory, and to take doubts and twinges to heart. It also requires me to open my mind to the advice and example of others, and to the kinds of issues we have been exploring here: whether an unjust society is in my interest, for instance, and whether my society is a just one. In other words: ethical integrity is not a different demand, in the first person, from the demand of ethics itself. I must want to live a good life, and not merely one I think good, to satisfy either. Nevertheless, even in the first person, ethical integrity sometimes acquires an independent force. I cannot agonize over ethics all my life; I must come to terms, at least temporarily, with convictions that survive a decent and honest scrutiny. Then I treat these convictions no longer just as hypotheses about ethical value but, right or wrong, as stipulating what ethical integrity requires of *me*. I claim a distinct virtue in holding to them for that reason — I say that I can act only as I do — even though I know others disagree and that they might, in some sense, be right.

The role of ethical integrity is very different in the third person, however. When I consider what life is best for someone else, I must take his settled convictions into account, just as facts, in my judgment about what kind of life he should lead. If my friend, after much self-examination, and after having opened his mind to arguments the other way, decides to enter religious orders, I can imagine three lives he might lead. He might change his mind (perhaps after reflecting on further argument) and enter politics, successfully, for the good of the country, and with full satisfaction and confidence in the value of what he does and the wisdom of his choice. Or he might hold to his course and live a life of religious devotion, again with full satisfaction and confidence in his choice. Or he might for some reason bow to the advice of his friends, against his own instincts and convictions, and enter politics; he will be successful there but will find no genuine satisfaction or self-approval, and will therefore never cease regretting his choice.

I have no doubt that the first life is better, for him, than either of the other two. But I equally have no doubt that the second is better than the third, and that reflects my commitment to the priority of integrity in the third person. There is no skepticism in my ranking. I do not mean that the life of religious devotion is the best for him because he thinks it best. I have not changed my view that his life will be wasted, and I will continue to argue with him if I think I can change his mind on that score. I mean that, given his unshaken convictions, it is the only life he can lead at peace with himself, and it is therefore the best he can do in meeting the challenge of his situation now understood to include that fact. Of course some ethical convictions are so terrible or base that we would not encourage someone who was unable to shake them off to live at peace with them. But that is because a wicked life is bad for other people, not because we think a life against the grain would be better for him.

If we accept the priority of ethical integrity, why are we concerned at all about how good a life other people lead, so long as they find it satisfying? Why should we try to persuade someone who finds value only in wealth and power to think again, if he has no doubt that his materialistic convictions are sound? The answer may lie simply in what seems a very abstract benevolence: that we believe people should lead better lives, find integrity at a higher level, even if the satisfaction they take in their new lives is no greater than that which they took in their lives before. The principle of priority of course offers no reason why we should not try to improve people's lives, by persuasion and example, in that way. But in most circumstances the principle provides a more positive reason why benevolence should take that form. For we suspect that the materialist and the misanthrope will not in the end find their lives fulfilling or satisfactory; we suspect that their ethical sense will one day reveal their lives as barren and unrewarding, though perhaps tragically too late. We also know that integrity, over some range, is a matter of degree: even if they think their lives successful now, and would continue to do so, we think they could unite life and conviction even more successfully with different convictions in place.

But does the priority of integrity therefore recommend a deeper form of paternalism than those we have so far been considering? I have in mind cultural paternalism: the suggestion that people should be protected from choosing wasteful or bad lives not by flat prohibitions of the criminal law but by educational decisions and devices that remove bad options from people's view and imagination. People do not make decisions about how to live in a cultural vacuum. They respond in various ways to what their culture makes available by way of possibility and example and recommendation. Why, then, should we not try to make that cultural environment as sound as we can, in the interests of people who will decide how to live influenced by it?

Of course our circumstances, including the ethical vocabulary and example of our culture, affect our ethical responses. But to some degree these circumstances are up to us, collectively, and when they are we must ask what these should ideally be. We must ask, that is, what circumstances are appropriate for people who give value to their lives by showing skill in living. In the last section we saw how justice becomes an ethical as well as political question in that way. We need normative parameters to define the challenge of living, and justice enters ethics when we ask how resources should figure in people's understanding of what that challenge is. Questions about critical paternalism enter ethics, on the challenge model, in a similar way. Those who defend paternalism claim, in effect, that the circumstances appropriate for ethical reflection are those in which bad or wasted lives have been screened out collectively so that the decisions each individual is to make are from a deliberately restricted menu. If that were a sensible view of what ethical reflection sholud be like, then my argument that paternalism undermines ethical value, because it destroys ethical integrity, would be entirely misplaced. Living well would mean taking the best choices from a culled list, and paternalism would be indispensable rather than threatening to ethical success. But that view is not sensible: a challenge cannot be more interesting, or in any other way a more valuable challenge to face, when it has been narrowed, simplified, and bowdlerized by others in advance, and that is as much true when we are ignorant of what they have done as when we are all too aware of it.

Suppose someone replies that the challenge is more valuable when the chances of selecting a truly good life are improved, as they would be if the list of possibilities was filtered by wise collective rulers. That reply misunderstands the challenge model profoundly, because it confuses parameters and limitations. It assumes that we have some standard of what a good life is that *transcends* the question of what circumstances are appropriate for people deciding how to live, and so can be used in answering that question, by stipulating that the best circumstances are those most likely to produce the really correct answer. On the challenge view, living well is responding appropriately to circumstances rightly judged, and that means that the direction of argument must go in the other way. We must have some *independent* ground for thinking it is better for people to choose in ignorance of lives other people disapprove; we cannot, without begging the question, argue that people will lead better lives if their choices are narrowed.

Once that point is grasped, any temptation toward conceptual paternalism must disappear.[44]

The issue of paternalism therefore adds a new dimension to the differences we have noticed among the various kinds and models of ethical value. Superficial paternalism — forcing people to take precautions that are reasonable within their own structure of preferences — is easily defended even from the perspective of volitional interests. A deeper form of paternalism might be defended from that point of view as well; someone might think that people should be forced to high culture, for example, because the pleasures of art are more satisfying, to those trained to appreciate them, than any other form of pleasure, as John Stuart Mill thought. The impact model allows its adherents to defend coercive critical paternalism with no such assumption, because that model divorces ethical value from ethical choice in the necessary way. The challenge model fuses value and choice, however. It insists that nothing can improve the critical value of a life unless it is seen as an improvement by the person whose life it is, and that makes surgical paternalism self-defeating. A compelling interpretation of the model — the principle of ethical priority — shows substitute paternalism to be self-defeating as well when the substitute life will be one without ethical integrity. The challenge model undermines conceptual paternalism, finally, because that form of

[44] That does not mean that government has no responsibility for the cultural background against which people decide how to live. A sensible answer to the question of normative parameters might well insist that citizens should choose against a background that includes opportunities and examples that have been thought to be part of living well by reflective people in the past and that are part of a cultural heritage. See Dworkin, *A Matter of Principle*, chap. 11. It might also insist that, consistently with the requirements of justice, the right background requires collective decisions about which lives to promote or recommend as better, particularly when popular culture presses the other way and so provides too few examples of those lives. My arguments in chap. 11 of *A Matter of Principle* did not include that reason for government support of the arts, because I was attempting to reply there to the argument that such support was unjust when the funds could be used to help relieve disease and unjustified poverty. But nothing in my argument here denies that a state that has fulfilled the requirements of justice can properly use public funds to support art that the market will allow to perish, on the substantive ground that art improves the value of lives available in the community.

paternalism assumes an independent, transcendent picture of ethical value the model begins by rejecting. The challenge model does not rule out the possibility that the community should collectively endorse and recommend ethical ideals not adequately supported by the culture. Nor does it rule out compulsory education and other forms of regulation which experience shows are likely to be endorsed in a genuine rather than manipulated way, when these are sufficiently short-term and noninvasive and not subject to other, independent objection. All this follows from the central, constitutive role the model of challenge assigns to reflective or intuitive *judgment*.

We should return to our original puzzle. Is ethical value subjective or objective? The connection the challenge model reveals between convictions and value in ethics now seems too complex to be captured neatly in the distinction, which is geared to discriminations within lives, not to judging lives as a whole. We do better to set the distinction aside in favor of the kind of description we began in this section. We capture the quality of ethical value only by exposing its phenomenology, taking adequate care to notice the complexity of that phenomenology, and the differences that arise on different occasions, particularly the differences between judging for ourselves and others.

Ethics and Community

The last set of problems I described raised the question whether and how far ethics can be social rather than individual. Does it make sense for an individual to accept the idea of ethical priority, that is, that his critical interests depend not only on his own experiences and achievements but also on the success of groups to which he belongs? Though the contrast between the two models with respect to this issue will not figure in the later argument of these lectures, it is of interest in itself for the further light it throws on the two models, and because it affects political theory dramatically in spite of its neglect here.[45]

[45] See Dworkin, "Liberal Community."

The model of impact supposes that each person's critical good consists in the impact that *he* makes on the world. It can defend ethical priority only by arguing that an individual actually has a more valuable impact, on his own, when he thinks *not* of his own impact but of the impact of a group to which he belongs. Games theory, and moral and political philosophy in its wake, have defined one situation, the so-called prisoners' dilemma, in which this is true. In these situations individuals each acting rationally to advance his own interests will together do what is worse for each, and this may be true not only when people aim at what is in their own interests in the narrow, volitional sense but when they aim to have an objectively valuable impact on the world.[46] In these circumstances, each would do better to ask, not how he could have the maximum impact, but how some group might, and then to do his part in that group's project. In that way each secures a greater impact by what he himself does, and so he leads, according to the model of impact, a critically better life for himself.

But the impact model cannot explain our actual intuitions in this way. For though we do have intuitions of ethical priority, we have these only along what we might call preestablished lines. I mean that we feel ethically integrated only into groups to which we already belong in some other way, and then only for acts of that group that are already established in the group's practices as collective. So we feel ethically integrated only into political communities of which we are citizens, and only for the acts of those communities, like their political decisions, that are institutionally collective.[47] It follows that we recognize ethical priority on many occasions when there appear, at least, to be no advantages to projects we favor in doing so. I have no games-theoretical reasons for thinking my life goes worse if my community does what I want it not to do: collective rationality cannot explain my personal shame at Vietnam. It also follows that we often have no sense of ethical

[46] See Derek Parfit, *Reasons and Persons* (Oxford: Clarendon Press, 1984).
[47] See Dworkin, "Liberal Community."

integration when cooperation is plainly appropriate. My fellow prisoner and I each have a strong reason to sign an agreement not to confess that neither of us will profit by breaking, and each of us may have a moral reason not to confess even in the absence of such an agreement. But unless we are friends or relatives, neither of us is likely to feel the reason of ethical priority: that his own life goes badly unless the group of the two of us prospers. So the order of explanation the model of impact offers for ethical priority goes the wrong way. Ethical integration sometimes provides the motivation needed for collective rationality. But not vice versa.

The model of challenge puts ethical priority in an entirely different light. It need not show, as the impact model must, that an individual has more impact through a community's collective action than on his own. It need only show how it might sensibly be thought that accepting ethical priority is an appropriate response to an important part of an individual's circumstances — the fact that he lives bound up with other people in a variety of communities — and is for that reason an important part of living well in community with other people. In fact that is a very widely shared view about living well, and so the challenge model is able to make sense of ethical priority in a natural rather than strained way. I should probably repeat, once again, that the model of challenge is not a mechanism for supporting convictions like that one. I do not cite the abstract claim of that model, that the goodness of living well is a matter of performance not impact, as part of the case for ethical priority. I mean only to point out, for the final time in this long section, that interpreting the convictions we do have as convictions about a skillful response to a complex challenge gives them more sense and coherence than the alternate general interpretation, that they are convictions about having the best impact, can.

VI. FROM ETHICS TO POLITICS

Ethical Liberals

We have completed our excursion into philosophical ethics. We have convictions about our ethical interests, about what kinds of lives are good in the critical sense, and these give rise to puzzles and problems. We can structure these convictions around two different models. The first ties the goodness of a life to the objective value of its independent product. The second ties a life's goodness to the skill with which it is lived, valued as a performance. These are both formal models: neither purports to define which products are valuable or which performances are skillful. Nevertheless they organize our convictions in different ways with different likely consequences. Some intuitions about what is valuable in life that have a grip from the perspective of one model seem silly from the point of view of the other. The model we favor at the moment is likely to affect our response to internal ethical skepticism, and to the questions of whether ethical values are universal or personal, how our circumstances figure in fixing the best life for us, what role our predilections and convictions play, and when and how far it is right to subordinate our ethical interests to the good of some larger community. I hope that as you made your way through these various arguments you felt yourself attracted more to the model of challenge than to its rival. I believe it offers a better interpretation, all things considered, of our ethical practices and instincts. In any case I hope you felt persuaded that the challenge model must have at least an important place in any overall ethics. Nevertheless the next phase of my argument is independent of those hopes, for my thesis, that the ethical roots of liberalism are to be found in the model of challenge, can be fairly judged by someone who rejects both liberalism and that model.

The continuity strategy hopes to show how liberalism develops naturally from ethics so that ethics merges into politics, the personal into the political perspective. In the next several pages I shall conduct a thought experiment of a kind familiar in philosophy. I want to test the plausibility of my claim that an actual deliberative conversation embracing the different ethical traditions of our political community would settle on liberal principles if it began in the ethics of challenge. So I imagine a group of people discussing (or reflecting each for himself) about which principles should govern their community's political life. Their comprehensive convictions about the good life are very different one from another, and taken together these convictions represent the range of opinions people in our world actually have. But this is a group of people each of whom is assumed to hold a certain ethical position. They all understand their different ethical convictions in the fashion of the challenge conception. They endorse the very abstract implications of that conception that I described in the last section. Each is concerned to advance his own interests, but each understands these to be his critical interests, that is, his interests in leading a life good for him because it responds in the right way to his circumstances as they ought to be.

Since I believe these to be the central features of liberal ethics, I shall call these people ethical liberals. I shall try to suggest that ethical liberals have good reason to become political liberals, and in particular to adopt the conception of liberalism I called liberal equality. When I described that conception, I picked out four features that seemed most controversial and most in need of ethical support. First, liberal equality builds justice on the space of resources rather than well-being or welfare. It defines the ideal society not in terms of the goodness of the lives people live but in terms of the share of resources each has available. Second, liberal equality is, of course, egalitarian: it insists that the share of resources each person has in an ideal society is an equal share. Third, it draws a sharp distinction in its account of when people's resources are equal between handicaps of various sorts, which it insists are part of a person's circumstances, and tastes, ambitions, and preferences, which it assigns to personality instead. So liberal equality tries to compensate people who have physical and mental handicaps but not people whose tastes or ambitions are particularly expensive. Fourth, liberal equality is tolerant: it condemns using the criminal or other law to limit liberty when the only justification is the assumed ethical inferiority of the life some people in the community wish to lead.

Taken together, these features seem to ratify the tension I described at the beginning of these lectures: they seem to describe a politics at war with the ethical convictions that are natural from what I called the personal perspective. Most of us (as I said) reject equality in our personal lives: we reject the idea that we must treat even fellow citizens with equal concern day by day. And we reject neutrality about what lives are good: we care deeply about the kinds of lives we lead and those we hope our children will find. So liberal equality provides an appropriate test for my overall claim that liberalism is supported by ethics on the challenge model, and can therefore be defended as continuous rather than discontinuous with ethics so understood. I shall try to show that ethical liberals, who do not treat everyone else with equal concern in their daily lives and who have no doubts about the superiority of their own ethical convictions, will nevertheless settle on the principles of liberal equality as most in their own critical interests, as most continuous with their own ethical lives.

I should emphasize the contrast between the argument through which I hope to show this and the imaginary social-contract device associated with the strategy of discontinuity. Contractarianism identifies, as sound principles of justice, the principles that emerge from a congress of people each seeking to advance his own interests in a special kind of negotiation conducted under certain assumptions or limitations. In Rawls's version of the social contract, for example, each party negotiates to advance the interests of people he represents, but of whose actual concrete interests he is nearly wholly ignorant. Justice lies in the agreement negotiators in that position would ultimately reach.

My present argument begins, on the contrary, with a developed normative position — the challenge conception of ethics — which ethical liberals are assumed to accept. We want to learn two things: first, whether that normative ethical position yields a particular theory of justice, and, second, whether that theory of justice is liberal. So ethical liberals, in my argument, are subject to no constraints of information at all. They know everything actual people know about their own interests and convictions and situation. (Indeed, if the challenge model of ethics is the best interpretation of most people's ethical convictions, ethical liberals know more than they do, because ethical liberals know that it is.) Ethical liberals are actual people: they are you and me and enough further hundreds so that they represent all the main variations in concrete ethical convictions in familiar political communities.

The problem ethical liberals face is also radically different from the problem confronting contractors in the contractarian tradition, including Rawls's version. In that tradition the imaginary negotiators must be moved by their own interests (or the interests of those they represent) prescinding from any questions of justice; each negotiates with the sole aim of making his share unconditionally as large as possible. Otherwise justice could not *emerge* from the contractual situation. Ethical liberals each have an interest in the decisions their community reaches about justice, but only, as we have noticed, in a certain special sense. A person's life can go better if he is at a higher level of challenge, which means, generally, if a larger share of resources is a just share for him. So ethical liberals deliberating about what justice is requires each to hope that the correct answer to that question awards him more rather than less resources: he hopes that a just share for him is a large share. But that gives him no reason to negotiate for, or in any other way to try to persuade others to accept, a theory of justice that gives him a greater share, for it is only *conditionally* in his interests that such a theory be adopted by the community; it is only good for him if it is the *right* theory of justice. On that view, justice cannot emerge from the negotiations and calculations of people who have no concern for it themselves, as it does in the social-contract tradition. Self-interest and a concern for justice merge, because the latter is part of the former. That fact has very great implications for a theory of justice constructed to be continuous with the challenge model of ethics, as we shall straightaway begin to see.

Justice and Resource

Liberal equality insists on a resource-based conception of justice. It holds that justice is measured in the resources people have, not the welfare or well-being they achieve with those resources. That feature attracts (as I said) the objection that people care about resources only if and because these will improve their well-being. Why try to give people a fair share of resources, which are only means to an end, rather than a fair share of well-being, which is what we all think really important?

Imagine, then, that ethical liberals, who do take their well-being to be what really matters, are invited to consider whether justice should be regarded as a matter of the division of well-being or of resources. They ask how a system of justice based on the division of welfare would proceed, and they are told it would require a two-stage procedure. At the first stage each citizen decides what level of well-being he would reach under different proposed institutional and economic arrangements. At the second stage officials select those arrangements under which well-being, as so reported, is divided in whatever way is deemed fair under the version of justice finally adopted. If justice commands an equal division of welfare, for example, officials will choose the institutions under which people's judgments of their welfare will be most nearly equal. If justice commands that welfare be maximized overall, they will choose the distribution that according to the first-stage reports secures that result. I have argued elsewhere that no conception of welfare or well-being could be found that would make that procedure workable and attractive for anyone.[48] But

[48] See Dworkin, "What Is Equality," part 1.

ethical liberals will have special and important reasons for rejecting it out of hand.[49]

Welfare-based theories of justice seem particularly well suited
to a view about the good life that they have rejected: that the only
interests people have are volitional interests, or that these are the
only interests that matter in politics. If we took that view, then
the two-stage procedure would be feasible and its appeal apparent
even if not compelling. If we were officials managing an economic

---

[49] In the text I consider substantive reasons that are drawn from a challenge
view of ethics. In fact ethically aware people could not make the two-stage procedure work at all, at least not in the way welfare egalitarians and utilitarians
imagine its working. Notice first how people who are ethically aware must understand the question put to them at the first stage of the procedure. Other people, who
think of their well-being only in volitional terms, may be able to answer that question in a relatively straightforward way: they state how well they believe themselves
able to satisfy, under each of the proposed economic arrangements, the desires they
happen to have. But since ethically aware people are concerned about their critical
interests, and count justice as a parameter of critical well-being, they must make
assumptions about the justice of the alternative arrangements just in order to decide
how well-off they are in each. So the two-stage procedure would be unworkable for
them, because circular, if they were asked that simple question. They would have to
know what arrangements were just, which is supposed to be decided at the second
stage, in order to report their well-being under each proposed arrangement at the
first stage. So the two-stage procedure can work, for them, only if the question put
to them at the first stage is different and more awkward. It must be a hypothetical
question of the following form: how good would your life be under each alternative
arrangement on the assumption in each case that the arrangement in question is just?
Ethically aware people can, I suppose, give that question some sense. In general,
the challenge a person faces is more interesting and valuable as his and his community's prosperity increases; so we prefer to have a greater to a lesser stock of
resources, provided that in each case our stock is just. Nevertheless the fact that
justice must figure at the first as well as the second stage of the procedure, even in
this hypothetical way, has a crucial consequence. Presumably citizens who accept
a welfare-based account of justice politically will use the same account ethically. So
each in effect reports, at the first stage, that he will have a certain welfare level
under each proposed distribution provided that others have the same well-being (or
provided that well-being is maximized) under that particular distribution. But since
citizens disagree about what their and others' critical interests are, they will disagree about when these conditions are fulfilled. So even if (for example) everyone
conditionally reported his welfare at .5 for a particular distribution, only a few
people would think the justice condition actually satisfied at that distribution, and
so welfare would not in fact be equal (or maximized) as judged by most people if
that distribution were chosen. Officials would have to substitute their own critical
judgments about how good different peoples lives were, under different economic
arrangements, in making that decision, and they might well end by proclaiming welfare equal when everyone else thought it vastly unequal, or welfare maximized when
everyone else thought their lives miserable.

structure, we could take people's reports of their well-being under alternative arrangements at face value, in the fashion of welfare economics. Even if their ambitions for themselves happened to reflect intuitions they had about justice, we would be free to ignore that fact. It would be important for us only that they preferred, for whatever reason, whatever they did prefer. We would be free to declare, at the second stage, that justice for us consisted in the situation in which people's volitional interests were satisfied best on average, according to some theory we might have or invent about what that means. It would make sense, under those assumptions, to regard well-being as competitive. The degree to which some people would be able to have what they in fact want would plainly depend on the degree to which others have what they want. And there would be some appeal, at least, in the idea that treating people as equals means either arranging matters so that welfare is equal, as in welfare-egalitarianism, or so that the community as a whole prospers, taking the success or failure of each into account on the same terms, as utilitarianism requires.

Ethical liberals of course reject volitionalism. They also reject a more sophisticated view: that politics should attend to critical rather than volitional interests but that critical interests should be understood on the impact rather than the challenge model. Assume we took that view of ethics and that we believed, as our substantive interpretation of it, that human pleasure is the only objective good, and that the ethically best life is the one that produces most total pleasure. (I choose that version of ethical hedonism as simplest; the point will hold for more complex versions.) Once again we would think the two-stage procedure workable, and we are even more likely to think it desirable in its utilitarian version than the volitionalist would. If we know what pleasure is, and how to measure it, we can in principle calculate how much net pleasure each person will have under competing economic arrangements. (Once again, some person's pleasure under some arrangement may be increased by his view that the arrangement is a just one; but all that would matter, for us, is the sum of pleasure he would find in it, not why.) Then we could sensibly aim, at the second stage, to choose economic institutions and arrangements that will maximize the amount of human pleasure, which we believe inherently valuable, in the world.

But on the challenge model none of this makes sense, because ethics and justice are dynamically interrelated. People who see their well-being in those terms rely on instincts or assumptions about their fair share of resources, as well as other assumptions about how their life connects with and relates to their neighbors' and fellow citizens' lives, in every decision they make about which of possible ways of living would be living well for them. So they cannot accept any theory of justice that presupposes that well-being and justice are two separate things, as any theory that takes welfare to be the metric of justice must. They need an account of justice that responds to the requirement we identified, that resources enter ethics as normative parameters, and only a resource-based view of justice can do that. Nor does it make sense on a challenge model to suppose that well-being is in any way competitive, that it is something to be divided, and so something whose division must be fair. Your living a good life, appropriate to just circumstances, in no way reduces my chances of doing so; on the contrary it enhances it. So there is no moral bite or appeal to the idea that the success of one person in finding the right life for him, should bear some constraining relationship to the success of others. Why should you have less resources because, as you think, most other people in your community hold an impoverished view of what makes life worth living? Why should you have any less than you would have if they held your views of the good life instead?

So ethical liberals cannot use a well-being–based conception of justice ethically — it simply does not fit their view of what well-being is — and so they must reject any such conception politically. They have a second, equally revealing, reason for rejecting a well-being–based conception: the two-stage procedure would undermine the challenge of living on which, for them, the goodness of a life depends. Part of that challenge, in some ways the most important and exciting part, lies in a person's identifying which of the lives he might lead is in fact a life good for him. It is true that in conformist societies that challenge is dulled by lack of imagination; but the challenge is still there, and someone aware of other possibilities will be aware of their importance for him. But the two-stage procedure sets out to undermine the challenge in a fatal way, because officials try to ensure that people lead lives that are equally as good, or on average collectively as good, no matter which choice of lives they make for themselves.

Of course that goal will probably fail, because officials will make mistakes of different kinds. They may do a bad job of deciding which lives are good ones for different people; indeed they are very likely to do so. In that case the enterprise will be ruinous for the ethical quality of people's lives, because officials will be shifting resources to encourage mistakes. But suppose officials are right: suppose they do a superbly sensitive job of identifying good lives, and of designing arrangements so that each person's life is equally good no matter what views that person has taken of where his good lies. If some group has made a serious mistake, then officials make sure, perhaps by giving that group very great resources, that its members do not suffer from that mistake in the overall value of the lives they end by living. So an individual has no genuine responsibility for the design of his life. It will be equally good, judged by the right standards, no matter how ethically perceptive or insensitive he has been. That story is crazy of course: the ethical equivalent of bad science fiction. But we would have to think that officials could administer equality or utilitarianism of well-being with reasonable success in order seriously to contemplate these ideals, and it is therefore important to see why, even if officials could succeed in measuring and comparing the ethical success of different lives, and shifting resources to make these more equal, they would end by making a good life impossible to lead on the challenge conception.

So the challenge view of ethics proposes a definite view about the proper role of government in helping people to lead good lives. If living well means responding well to circumstances as these ought to be, then it must be one function of government to try to bring it about that circumstances are as they should be. Government should set the right stage; it should provide the background against which people can decide which role is for them the right one. That formula leaves open the question, of course, of what circumstances are right. It leaves open the question, for example, of how far it is appropriate for government to educate citizens in the variety and competing virtues of lives open to them, or to keep alive, by subsidy or other support, forms of life in which other people have found great value. Taking up the challenge model of ethics does not commit us to noncaring or noncommittal government but only to a particular conception of what a caring and committed government must and must not do. Ethical liberals will be drawn to that conception of government whatever their concrete view of what living well is like. For I made no assumption, in arguing that they would reject welfare-based conceptions of justice, that they held any particular detailed views about the form a good life takes, beyond the very abstract and compelling view that justice is at least a soft parameter of living well.

Equality

Ethical liberals insist that justice is a matter of resources, not well-being. But what share of resources is a just share? Liberal equality replies: an equal share. Do ethical liberals have some reason, just in the view they take about the character of their critical interests, to accept that answer? Is the challenge model of ethics inherently egalitarian?

We begin by taking the full measure of a point we have now several times noticed: that under the challenge model of ethics justice and ethics merge because whether my life is good depends, among other things, on whether the share of resources available to me is a just share. If so, then a striking conclusion follows: most contemporary arguments for or against theories of justice are of no help to ethical liberals. We anticipated this point when we noticed that ethical liberals could not negotiate in their own interests prescinding from questions of justice as artificial people do in Rawls's original position. Each might hope that the just share for him is a large share, but he knows that a large share is unlikely to be good for him unless it is a just one. That fact limits not only the possibilities any member has to advance his own interests at the cost of others', but also the arguments he can deploy, to himself and them, about which conception of justice is the best one.

If justice is a parameter of a life's value, then any argument that defines justice in terms of some function of different people's interests will be either circular, if these interests are taken to be critical interests, or arbitrary, if these interests are defined in some way that disconnects them from critical interests. Consider, for example, Rawls's argument for the principle that (provided other conditions are met) a just society will arrange its fundamental economic structure so as to make the position of the worst-off group, in primary goods, as good as it can be. That argument assumes what Rawls calls a "thin" theory of the good: that though people disagree about what kinds of lives are good, all agree that the more primary goods someone has the more likely he is to achieve his conception of a good life. This assumption allows Rawls to define justice in terms of a narrow or "thin" theory of what people's interests are, and then to embrace the view, as he does, that a broader notion of interest includes living in a just society. If justice is a parameter and not merely a component of a good life, however, it is not true that having more primary goods makes, even pro tanto, for a critically better life. There is no "thin" sense of interests such that justice can be defined in a noncircular way as the distribution that is most in the interests of the worst-off group.

If justice is a parameter, then popular arguments for other theories of justice are also undermined. It is widely thought a powerful argument for economic inequality, for example, that a scheme of justice that allows rich people to keep the full profits of their investments is in the interests of nearly everyone, in the end, because people will have an incentive to invest more under such a scheme. But this general kind of argument is ruled out once we accept, as the challenge model insists, that justice is at least a soft parameter of people's critical interests. It cannot then be an argument for a theory of justice that a community run on that theory will have more aggregate resources; that would beg the question whether having more is actually in the interests of those who will in fact have more. We will not think that more wealth *is* in the interests of the majority unless the scheme that provides this is just.[50] No doubt a just economic scheme would produce more resources for *some* section of the community than would any alternative scheme. Perhaps a just scheme would produce more resources for everyone. But ethical liberals cannot argue that a scheme is just *because* it has those consequences, since they are not consequences they can approve, as in people's interests, unless they have some other reason for thinking the arrangement that produces them a just one.

But then how can ethical liberals think about justice? We are used to the competitive model the contractarian tradition exploits. We imagine people with different interests coming to see that they must reach some compromise in order to serve some higher-order interest each has: to live together without war, as in Hobbes, or with the right kind of respect for one another, as in Rawls, or fulfilling the motive each has to be able to explain himself to the

---

[50] The same point holds, though it may seem even more counterintuitive, for the worst off. It is in their interest to have more only if the scheme that provides it is a just scheme. It would be against their critical interest, for example, if their initially smaller share of social resources was a just share — perhaps because they had worked less than others had — and the extra wealth given them was stolen from others, who were entitled to keep it.

others, as in Scanlon. That picture guides our thinking about justice in a particular way: we judge the reasonableness of different
people's suggestions, as in Scanlon's version, by comparing the size
and importance of the different interests people would be asked
to sacrifice or abandon under different suggestions. This general
approach is finally unsatisfactory, as I suggested earlier, because
our intuitions about justice are already built into our sense of what
it is reasonable of someone to ask. But the approach nevertheless
seems an appropriate way to organize and deploy these intuitions.
Equality does well, though not necessarily *very* well, in political
philosophies that proceed in this way. In principle it is unreasonable to ask people who already have less than others to give up
more, so the approach has an egalitarian drift. But under some
circumstances insisting on equality will seem unreasonable and
doctrinaire: if small gains for the poor can be achieved only
through large sacrifices by everyone else, for example.[51]

In any case, however, the picture on which this whole approach is based, of justice as a compromise among interests, is not
available for ethical liberals. Then how should such people think
about justice? The difficulty arises because the challenge model
makes ethics depend on justice. Now we should turn that coin
over and consider how, if that is true, justice can be seen to depend
on ethics. Justice, we said, plays a dynamic role within the life of
an ethical liberal; it stipulates the resources it is appropriate for
him to use, and so helps to fix the challenge he faces, in living his
life. So if we cannot test a theory of justice consequentially, by
asking whether it has the right consequences for people's interests,
we can test it ethically, by asking whether it fits well with our
other beliefs about how it is appropriate for people to live.

Ethical liberals must treat the question of justice as part of
ethics. They decide what share of resources each should have by
deciding what parameters it is appropriate for each to accept as

---

[51] Rawls's difference principle, which requires any inequality to be in the interests of the worst-off group, is often criticized as doctrinaire on that ground.

defining the character of a life good for him. Suppose they adopt, as a starting point, the presumption that all members of a political community should face the same abstract ethical challenge and that it is therefore appropriate that each have an equal share of resources. What counterarguments are then available? The arguments that are now most often urged to justify a nonegalitarian distribution are not available, for reasons we have just noticed. It is not a counterargument, for example, that a nonegalitarian community will be a more prosperous community, because that argument begs the question whether prosperity is in the interests of those who would benefit from it. So the *only* counterarguments that may be pressed in a discussion among ethical liberals are arguments, now happily out of fashion, that appeal to the inherent difference in the worth or value of different people or groups.

People have always made claims of special importance justifying special privilege by pointing to a vast variety of distinctions: that they are descendants of Richard Plantagenet, or white, or part of a nation favored by God, or people of special lineage or talent or beauty or even wealth. But ethical liberals will have a special reason for not pressing any such claim, and for insisting that equality is the right theory of justice for them. They cannot accept that the social and economic institutions of a community should predefine different challenges in living for different kinds of people—different challenges for aristocrats or for talented people, for example. They think that it is part of each person's ethical responsibility to decide an ethical identity for himself — to decide for *himself* whether it *is* a parameter of his life that he is an aristocrat or talented or whether these properties are only opportunities or limitations he faces in leading a life properly defined in some quite different way.

For ethical liberals, living well includes — begins in — trying to answer that kind of question, and the question assumes that the challenge of living is more abstract than the challenge of living in any particular role. It obscures and demeans the stark challenge of ethics, the categorical force of the imperative to live well, to locate its source in anything more contingent than our being persons with lives to live. Nonegalitarian theories of justice, seen from the perspective of the challenge view, demean ethics in just that way. They suppose that it belongs to politics, rather than to people, to construct the parameters of ethical identity. Ethical liberals will therefore reject all such theories and endorse equality of resources as the only theory of justice that matches their sense of the character of the ethical challenge each faces.

The argument that has led us to this point has a certain symmetry. It begins in the idea that justice limits ethics, that someone leads a less good life with the same resources when and because these are unjustly low. Now we have turned the coin over and we have seen how ethics limits justice. A scheme of justice must fit our sense of the character and depth of the ethical challenge, and that supports equality as the best theory of justice. I do not mean that a different view of ethics—the volitional or the impact view— could not support equality, though as I suggested, strict equality is likely to seem an extreme and doctrinaire position on these models of ethics. I mean only that the challenge view supports equality of resources directly, as flowing from people's sense of their own best interests critically understood. When we have reached that point, the argument becomes reciprocal, for the fact that equality is a natural theory of justice on the challenge model in turn supports the idea with which we began, that justice is a parameter of ethics. Living well has a social dimension, and I live less well if I live in community with others who treat my efforts to lead a good life as unimportant. Indeed, everyone is insulted by a political and economic system dedicated to inequality, even those who profit in resources from the injustice, because a structure of community that assumes that the challenge of living is hypothetical and superficial denies the self-definition that is part of dignity. On the challenge model, critical self-interest and political equality are allies. Hegel said that masters and slaves are prisoners together; equality unlocks the prison for both.

Ethics and Partiality

But now we have a further issue to face. Assume our group of ethical liberals has decided on equality for politics, but they reject equality from the personal perspective. They think that someone who tried to show no more interest in his own fate, and in the fate of family and friends, than he shows for strangers would be an ethical idiot. So we have reached a problem anticipating right at the beginning when we distinguished the political from the personal perspective in people's lives. Is it inconsistent for people to insist on equality in politics and condemn it in ordinary life? Must ethical liberals be embarrassed by their apparent ambivalence about equality?

Political equality and personal partiality would indeed be inconsistent if equality meant equality of welfare or well-being. If we struggle together in politics, for a decade, to make the welfare of each person in the community equal as of a particular date, but then lapse back into a private life in which each of us spends whatever resources he has improving his own well-being, and that of his family and friends, then only by the most freakish coincidence could welfare remain equal among us. We would have undermined individually what we achieved collectively, and we should have to start again.[52] But that is not true, at least not in principle, if for us equality means equality of resources. On that theory of justice, I show equal respect for others when I do not use resources that are properly theirs, when I do not exceed my fair share at their expense. Suppose the auction I described as illustrating that theory begins in equal bidding resources and ends in mutual satisfaction. Then my decision to look after my own well-being in my

---

[52] Compare Robert Nozick's argument that patterned theories of justice require constant intervention in *Anarchy, State and Utopia* (New York: Basic Books, 1974).

plans and investments, and to work for the welfare of family and friends, could not on its own impair the equality the auction achieved.[53] The goods distributed to me under a fair and equal auction are, that is, *morally*, mine, in a way nothing can be morally mine under welfare egalitarianism or another welfare-based conception of justice. Equality of resources in that way *licenses* partiality.

We might put this point another way: under equality of resources there is a division of labor between the political and the private perspectives. People are free to take up partisan aims and attachments in their private lives with complete conviction, if and because politics has secured a distribution that is egalitarian publicly. Of course this division of labor must not be taken to mean that private individuals have no concern with distributive justice, that they are entitled simply to consume whatever resources the reigning system distributes to them indifferent to the demands of others who have less, as if distributive justice were always someone else's business. It would be incredible that a theory of justice should make no private demands on citizens living in unjust affluence. But, as we noticed when we first considered the connection between justice and ethics, it is a complex and perhaps unanswerable question what equality of resources asks of us here and now. That is part of the reason why according to the challenge model our lives go worse if we live amid injustice. So we should say, of our own indelible partiality in the private perspective, not that it

---

[53] I mean to set aside a more complex problem, whose solution I believe would require elaborating the hypothetical insurance feature of equality of resources beyond what I or others have yet done. Suppose I consume all my resources but you economize and leave most of yours to your children. Or that you have invested skillfully and have more to leave for that reason. Or that I have more children than you and so must divide their inheritance in smaller shares. Then, although neither of us has invaded resources properly belonging to another, our children will not have equal resources: some will envy what others have. Equality of resources must find some way to recognize and at least reduce inequality generated in that way, perhaps, as I just suggested, by regarding one's situation as a beneficiary as an in principle insurable hazard. In the text I consider only the central problem: whether it is inconsistent to work for equality in politics and yet try to improve partially in ordinary life.

is in conflict with a genuinely egalitarian political perspective but rather that it is in conflict with any *other* kind of politics.

Personality and Circumstance

Liberal equality demands equality of circumstances, but it takes a particular view about when circumstances are equal. It distinguishes between two kinds or aspects of the circumstances a person faces. Someone's impersonal resources consist in the independent control he exercises over transferable goods which he can use, as he chooses, in leading his life as he wishes. Liberal equality assumes that impersonal resources are equal, in principle, when the opportunity cost of the set of each person's resources is equal as measured in an auction from the right egalitarian base line. Someone's personal resources are the qualities of physical and mental health and skill, and other talents and capabilities, which he may also put at the disposal of his life. People envy the impersonal resources others have: they would often prefer the health and skills of another person to their own. But personal resources cannot be made the subject of any auction. Instead liberal equality requires that impersonal resources be adjusted to compensate for differences in personal resources, in amounts determined by some exercise like the hypothetical insurance scheme I described earlier.

Several features of this account need justification or at least explanation. Why should impersonal resources be deemed equal when and only when the opportunity cost of these is equal, for example? But I single out, here, the feature that has troubled most critics and that seems most closely connected to the question of ethical foundations we are exploring. Liberal equality does not count, as among the personal resources which affect the equality of someone's circumstances, the preferences, tastes, convictions, predilections, ambitions, attachments and other features of personality that will in fact play an important role when he decides how content he is with the life he leads. So even though one person aims high — he has costly tastes or great and expensive ambitions —

and another needs only modest resources to lead the life he wants, liberal equality does not adjust impersonal resources to take account of that difference in their situations. Is this arbitrary? Would the ethical liberals have any reason for drawing the line liberal equality draws between physical and mental handicaps, for which it does seek to compensate, and expensive ambitions, for which it does not?

Consider this objection: that line is drawn in the wrong place. It should be drawn between differences in people's situations which are *voluntary* and those that are not. If someone deliberately cultivates costly tastes — forcing himself to eat caviar until finally he likes it — then there is no reason in social justice why others should give up part of their resources so that he can satisfy his new craving. But not all costly tastes are deliberately cultivated in that way: some people just do want expensive things. They no more choose to enjoy caviar, they no more decide to feel driven to build cathedrals, than other people choose to be lame or blind. So the line liberal equality draws, where it does, is arbitrary and unjustified.

Will ethical liberals accept this objection? Part of the objection, as I said earlier, is just mistaken.[54] People do cultivate tastes, but they do so in response to higher-order ambitions that are not in turn deliberately cultivated. The odd person who forces himself to eat caviar does so out of some misshapen ethical conviction: he thinks people with rarefied tastes, or tastes expensive to gratify, lead better lives, and he did not choose to have that higher-order conviction. So if the objection has any merit, its force must be that all tastes, preferences, convictions, and the rest must be counted part of circumstances. The result is, of course, to collapse equality of circumstances back into equality of welfare: the only way to compensate for someone's taste for caviar is to give him additional resources until the total welfare he achieves is no less than any-

[54] And why would it matter if some tastes were voluntary? See the discussion of Jude's case in Dworkin, "What Is Equality," part 1.

one else's. I said that ethical liberals cannot accept equality of welfare or any other welfare-based theory of justice. So we must construe the present objection as an objection, from a different quarter, to that claim. It argues that liberal equality rests on an arbitrary distinction, and that ethical liberals should reject it for that reason.

But it was no part of any argument I have used so far that some or any or all convictions and other preferences are voluntarily chosen. Liberal equality does not assume that people choose their beliefs about ethics any more than their beliefs about geography. It does suppose that they *reflect* on their ethical beliefs and that they choose how to behave on the basis on those reflections. And it supposes a certain structure to that reflection: the structure we have been exploring for many pages now. The distinction between talents and handicaps, on the one hand, and tastes and convictions on the other is a distinction *within* that structure, and it is crucial for liberal equality exactly for that reason.

Liberal equality is designed for ethical liberals: it aims to make them equal in their circumstances, and it understands someone's circumstances as the set of opportunities and limitations he encounters in identifying and pursuing what he deems, after reflections, to be an appropriate life for him. Talents and handicaps are plainly circumstances in that sense.[55] But convictions and preferences are plainly not. It would be incoherent for me to regard some ethical conviction I have — that the only important thing to do with my life is to create religious monuments, for example — as a limitation on the goodness of the life I can lead. If that is my view about what a good life would be for me, then I must think my having that view *essential* to leading a good life; it cannot be a *limitation* because I would be worse, not better, off without it.

---

[55] This needs qualification in one way not relevant to the present argument. As I suggested earlier, talents may sometimes play a role in people's ethical reflection as components of the challenge they face. Someone who believes he has a great talent for art may feel ethically compelled to spend his life developing and exploiting that talent: he may feel that art is the only challenge appropriate for him.

So the distinction between handicaps and personality is as little arbitrary as ethics itself. People insist on the distinction not because they make the silly mistake of thinking they choose their ethical convictions like their neckties but because the distinction is at the center of their ethical lives. So once again a controversial aspect of liberal equality can be traced back to a particular conception of ethical reflection. Liberal equality aims to be continuous with the reflections of ethical liberals; it aims to provide a theory of justice such people can use ethically, in their own lives from their personal perspective, as well as publicly from their political perspective. If people cannot regard their own convictions and preferences as limitations, they cannot accept and use a theory of justice that treats blindness and conviction in the same terms.

But the claim that the distinction between handicaps and convictions is arbitrary, because people do not necessarily choose their convictions, has proved a popular one, and we should try to discover the perspective from which that distinction *would* seem arbitrary. It would seem arbitrary, of course, within a voluntarist ethics which supposed that people all want, at bottom, the same thing: utility or pleasure or the satisfaction of the desires they happen to have. If that is what I really want, then I will certainly regard my conviction, that the only thing worth doing is building cathedrals, as a handicap as great as some physical infirmity. Both are obstacles to my having utility or pleasure or the satisfaction of desires. That simply ratifies, however, our sense that a voluntarist ethics is untrue to most people's actual ethical experiences. For we do not think of our deep ambitions as obstacles to our achieving the life we most want to lead. On the contrary, we most want to lead the life the ambitions lay out before us.

But now consider a different and more complex suggestion. When we considered whether convictions could act as ethical parameters, as part of our brief general tour of philosophical ethics, I emphasized the importance of distinguishing third-person from first-person ethical judgments. Suppose you think the best life for you would begin in professional sports. Of course you cannot regard that belief — so long as you hold it — as a limitation on your ability to lead a good life. But *I* can regard it that way, and in fact I probably would. So from my third-person perspective, there is no difference between a physical handicap you might have and this conviction. They will both prove obstacles to your leading the life I think good for you.

Does that suggest an argument why people should be compensated for having the wrong ethical convictions? No, at least not from the point of view of ethical liberals. It is hard to imagine how a scheme of that kind could actually be constructed. There is the obvious problem that some official would have to make the decision about which ethical convictions were right and which wrong. And the further problem that no one could apply for compensation with a straight face. And the even graver problem that compensation would be self-defeating: if you had more money, in virtue of your supposedly mistaken ambition for sports, you would only train harder and lead, in my view, a worse life. But ethical liberals would have to reject any scheme of that sort, even if some farfetched scheme for administering it could be constructed, because it would not be a scheme that could play the dynamic role within ethics that they want a theory of justice to play. No one could identify the resources he ought to have to compensate for mistaken beliefs he could not think mistaken. If politics is to be continuous with ethics, it must be continuous with ethics in the first person.

Neutrality of Appeal

We come finally to the last problematic feature of liberal equality, which is tolerance. We should distinguish two ways in which a political theory might be neutral or tolerant about the different ethical convictions members of a political community might hold. First, it might be neutral in its appeal, that is to say ecumenical. It might set out principles of political morality that can be accepted by people from a very great variety of ethical traditions. Second, it might be neutral in its operation, that is to say, tolerant. It might specify, as one of its principles of political morality, that government must in no way punish or discriminate against people of any particular ethical party or conviction. Obviously these two aspects of neutrality are very closely connected. In many (though not all) circumstances the best hope of attracting wide support from different groups lies in some general guaranty against the persecution of any. But the two aspects are nevertheless different: a majority — or even a minority — might succeed in establishing a political scheme that requires tolerance of those who do not and could not accept it, as liberalism requires general tolerance of illiberal bigots.

The contractarian tradition I discussed earlier begins in the ambition to make liberalism ecumenical or neutral in appeal. Its strategy of discontinuity is tailored to that purpose, and it urges tolerance, neutrality in operation, to that end. Our continuity strategy must come upon neutrality of both kinds, as I said earlier, in the course of its argument, as theorems. The strategy begins in ethics, and so it can achieve neutrality of appeal only if it can show that the ethical foundations to which it appeals are already very generally accepted, or at least that these could be widely accepted without people having to abandon convictions they are unlikely to give up. It draws political principles from these ethical foundations, and so it can achieve neutrality in operation only if these ethical foundations have that consequence. I shall consider how far our argument has shown that liberal equality succeeds in these aims, and I begin, in this section, with neutrality of appeal.

The challenge model of ethics does not discriminate, as a formal matter, among substantive ethical convictions. People who think the good life lies in religious devotion and others who think it requires unconventional sexual variety may all treat their convictions as opinions about the most skillful performance of living. But I conceded, right at the start, that the challenge model captures and organizes only some of the intuitions people have about ethics, and I argued that the model, once studied, has implications that many people have certainly not accepted. The argument that followed relied, for example, on a proposition most people would find dubious: that justice is a parameter of good lives, so that a person's life goes worse, at least in one important respect, if he has more resources because his society is unjust. So I certainly cannot claim that the ethical foundations from which I have so far drawn features of liberal equality are already accepted in full.

I must settle for the weaker claim that liberal ethics could be generally accepted without people having to abandon what I believe is important to them. I have in mind, first, their convictions of ethical identity: their intuitions about which aspects of their circumstances — their religion or nation or vocation or some other feature — supply the most basic parameters of a life good for them. And, second, their substantive views and assumptions about what living a life well, given that ethical identity, is like. Neither of these sets of convictions would be threatened by accepting that living well also means living within the constraints of justice. But notice an important qualification built into this suggestion. No one would have to abandon or qualify the convictions I describe so far as these touch his first-person ethical beliefs: his beliefs about the life right or best for him. But people also have third-person ethical convictions, about the life best for others, and some people's third-person beliefs would indeed be altered by accepting the challenge model with the implications I have drawn from it. We have already noticed how someone's third-person ethics might be changed by accepting the challenge model's views about the efficacy of coercive critical paternalism, for example.

So our answer to the question — how ecumenical or neutral in appeal can liberal equality be — is somewhat complex. Liberal equality cannot be drawn from abstract ethical convictions almost everyone already holds, at least self-consciously. I had to imagine a group of self-conscious ethical liberals, who organize their con-

victions around the challenge model of ethics understood to carry
certain forceful implications, in order to make it plausible that
people of different convictions would agree to liberal equality out
of reflective self-interest. But the challenge model captures intuitions which almost everyone has about ethics. It captures them in
a more satisfactory way than rival views about the nature of ethical
value do, and it resolves puzzles and dilemma in these intuitions
that they cannot; the model should appeal to people for that reason. Indeed the enduring power of liberalism suggests that the
challenge model, or at least central aspects of it, already has a grip
on the ethical imagination of a great many people, and reflection
should increase its appeal to others. It is important, to that opti-
mistic view, that almost anyone could occupy the position of an
ethical liberal without abandoning the heart of his ethical convictions understood in the first person, that is, as convictions about
how he should live to live well. Taken together, this is hardly a
discouraging or unpromising assessment. A political theory should
carry what I called consensual promise: we should be able to present it to enlightened democratic politics with some prospects of
success. Liberal equality is ethically ecumenical enough, and in the
right way, to offer that hope. For it is far less utopian to hope that
people will change their third-person than their first-person views,
particularly if arguments are available to show how these can be
de-coupled. That sanguine opinion does not apply, of course, to
the fanatic who thinks God will punish him, for eternity, unless he
kills us. We must not turn our backs to him, or to his luggage,
but he cannot be part of our liberal community.

Liberal Tolerance

Liberal equality is neutral in its operation in the following
sense. It distinguishes two kinds of reasons a political community
might offer as justification for denying liberty The first is a reason
of justice: a community might outlaw conduct because, in its view,
the best theory of justice so requires. It might think, for example,

that it must outlaw theft to protect people's rights to security of property. The second is a reason of ethics: a community might think that the conduct it outlaws, though not against justice, is demeaning or corrupting or otherwise bad for the life of its author. It might think, for example, that the life of a homosexual is a degrading life and outlaw homosexual relations on that ground. Liberal equality denies the legitimacy of the second, ethical reason for outlawing conduct.[56]

That does not mean, of course, that liberal equality is ethically neutral in result, or that it aims to be. Under any political and economic scheme some kinds of lives are more difficult or expensive to lead than they would be under other schemes. For example, it is much less likely that anyone will be in a position to gather a great collection of Renaissance masterpieces under liberal equality than under unrestrained capitalism. But liberal equality makes some lives more expensive than others in virtue of its conception of justice, not because it condemns art collecting as unworthy or degrading or selfish, or because it holds that people are less likely to lead good lives in a community in which collections flourish. So liberal equality disagrees sharply with the view the Supreme Court recently said was part of American constitutional law: that a majority may properly make homosexuality a crime just because most people think homosexuals lead bad lives.[57]

Our imagined group of ethical liberals includes some who do think that homosexuals lead bad lives. And others who think that commerce is contemptible, that atheists destroy their lives, that America has become a nation of pitiful couch potatoes, that wel-

---

[56] In this discussion I ignore paternalism that can be justified on the ground that those who are coerced are very likely later to endorse, in a genuine way, the coercion. It may be that coercive education of the young is an example of that form of paternalism. And it may be that a culture that provides that kind of collective educational power provides a better background for ethical reflection than one that does not. In any case, I do not now claim that liberal equality will have no room for paternalism of that sort. I have in mind, in this discussion, coercion that is indifferent or cynical about the views of its subject, or which hopes to secure endorsement through fear or the stifling of imagination.

[57] *Bowers v. Hardwick*, 106 S. Ct. 2841 (1986).

fare benefits rust people's souls, that people need to return to nature, that people need to preserve their ethnic or religious identi-
ties, that people need a sense of patriotism, and so forth. Many
members of our group hold these views passionately; they live
and preach them, and they despair when their children reject them.
How can a group of people like that endorse the tolerance of liberal equality? Why should they not agree with the view the Supreme Court said the Constitution accepts? If politics is an extension of ethics, as the continuity strategy insists it is, why should
ethical liberals not campaign in politics for what they think is
good?

The question, however, is not whether they should campaign
for the good, but how. Liberal equality denies them one weapon:
even if they are in the majority, they must not forbid anyone to
lead the life he wants, or punish him for doing so, just on the
ground that they think his ethical convictions are wrong. Ethical
liberals have what seems a conclusive reason for accepting that
constraint: they accept an account of justice that demands equality
of circumstances and resources. The law is plainly part of people's
circumstances, and circumstances are plainly unequal when the
law forbids some to lead the lives they think best for them only
because others disagree.[58] So ethical liberals, who accept equality
of circumstance as what justice requires, must accept liberal tolerance too. Liberty and equality, for them, merge as different
aspects of the same political ideal. Of course someone who thinks
that the best life is one lived in a religiously homogeneous community will think it best for him if his community is both just and
homogeneous. But on the challenge conception of ethics it is best
only if it is just, because injustice would spoil the advantage, and
homogeneity is not just if it is coerced.

---

[58] That is a brief statement of an argument that should be explored in much
more detail, as I have tried to do in "What Is Equality," part 3. There is all the
difference, from the point of view of justice, between someone finding a life he
wants too expensive, because others want old masters too, for example, and finding
the life he wants forbidden because others think it contemptible.

It is crucial to the continuity strategy, moreover, that ethical liberals will not *resent* this tolerance, or feel that they have in any way compromised or set aside or bracketed their own ethical convictions in deciding not collectively to impose them on a dissenting minority when they have the opportunity to do so. On the contrary, tolerance gives full force to their abstract ethical convictions about how they and others can live best, because the theory of justice that requires tolerance is not a competing department of morality that checks their ethical convictions, but, on the contrary, is drawn from and *serves* these ethical convictions in the ways we have been exploring. Their substantive convictions, in other words, offer no advice or incentive or motive that *could* override tolerance if these were somehow given freer reign, because there is nothing these convictions ask or require of them that tolerance forbids. They cannot make their own lives better by ignoring the limits justice sets to their power to have a cultural or social environment more congenial to them, because justice is a parameter of the life good for them. They cannot make other people's lives better by the coercive means liberal tolerance forbids, because on the challenge model, as we discovered, someone's life cannot be improved against his steady conviction that it has not been. Ethical liberals will treat each other's convictions as parameters in the way I described. Even if they think someone's life would be better if he changed his convictions, they know they cannot make it better unless he does change them, and in the right way. They accept that he leads a better life at peace with his own settled convictions than he can live, under external pressure, at war with them. This point is a companion to the one we noticed when we considered the distinction liberal equality makes between personality and circumstances. Just as no one deserves compensation because his ethical beliefs are (as we judge) mistaken, so no one should be denied liberty on the same ground. In both cases, paternalism is misguided because it wrongly treats convictions as limitations or handicaps.

So ethical liberals will accept liberal tolerance in the sense I described, as continuous rather than discontinuous with their own comprehensive ethical convictions. But notice that the tolerance liberal equality offers falls short of the kind of neutrality some critics believe liberalism aims to have. I have already said that liberal equality cannot be neutral in consequences: it will have the result that some lives, which it neither approves nor disapproves, will be more difficult to lead than they would be in other political systems. And liberal equality leaves room, in appropriate circumstances, for short-term educational paternalism that looks forward, with confidence, to genuine, unmanipulated endorsement. Nor is liberal equality's tolerance global. Any political theory must disapprove other theories that dispute its principles; liberal equality cannot be neutral toward ethical ideals that directly challenge its theory of justice. So its version of ethical tolerance is not compromised when a thief is punished who claims to believe that theft is central to a good life. Or when a racist is thwarted who claims that his life's mission is to promote white superiority. It would be disingenuous to suggest that liberalism neither approves nor disapproves of those ethical convictions, but only makes both impossibly expensive. It does disapprove them, because they oppose its fundamental principles of justice, and it cannot treat them as if that were not true.[59]

It follows that liberal equality is not neutral in operation in one quite general respect, and we noticed this in considering how far it is neutral in appeal. Liberal equality is not neutral about third-person ethics. It insists, for example, on the proposition I just cited: that no one can improve another's life by forcing him to behave differently, against his will and his convictions. Ethical liberals agree with that proposition; but not everyone does, and liberal equality cannot give equal respect or attention to the latter view. We can imagine cases in which someone's first-person convictions, about the best way to lead his own life, are parasitic on

[59] See Dworkin, *A Matter of Principle*, chap. 17.

third-person convictions liberal equality rejects: someone might find his own life's meaning and mission, for example, in coercing others to improve their lives as he thinks. Liberal equality cannot be neutral about those first-person convictions either, of course, because they require what it deems unjust.

Long ago in these lectures I said that our deliberations about ethics and justice would arrive at a version of ethical neutrality most people could accept in politics, not in spite of their own passionate ethical commitments in their personal perspective, but because of these. I hope that claim is both clearer and more plausible now. If people see their own personal ethical commitments in a certain light, as modeled by the challenge conception of ethics, then they can also come to see how these convictions are parasitic on justice; why they must therefore accept a resource-based conception of justice; why the only appropriate resource-based conception, for ethical liberals, is an egalitarian one; how that conception of justice condemns ethical intolerance; and why the paternalistic objection to that last conclusion, which is based on the idea that people's lives can be made better against their own convictions, is mistaken. I also said, long ago, that the argument that disclosed tolerance as a theorem, in this way, would itself shape the version of tolerance it endorsed. I hope that claim is also clearer and more plausible now. Liberal equality is neutral about first-person, not third-person, ethics, and only insofar as first-person ethics does not embody antiliberal political principles.

Epilogue

I am very much aware that the argument of these lectures lacks a dimension I might mention now: a historical dimension. I have made no effort, nor am I in any way competent, to explore the implications of my central argument for or in intellectual history. I believe that the challenge model dominates Greek ethics, particularly Aristotelian ethics, and that in the modern period it has played a crucial part, in indistinct battle with ethical skepticism, in the development of humanist ethics. The model of impact, on the contrary, seems to me prominent in many forms of theological ethics and in various forms of utilitarian ethics, including those usually regarded as the most direct enemies of theology. Whatever sense or cogency these opaque remarks might have, I do not mean them to suggest what I earlier denied: that religious or utilitarian ethics can have no place in the model of challenge. The idea that living skillfully means recognizing and entering into an appropriate relationship with some conception of God, or that it means recognizing and responding to human misery, are not only possible interpretations of the challenge model but, for many people, compelling interpretations of it. I mean only that many of the political implications people have drawn from theological or utilitarian ethics makes sense only if these are understood on the different model of impact.

Equality of What?

Amartya Sen

Discussions in moral philosophy have offered us a wide menu in answer to the question: equality of what? In this lecture I shall concentrate on three particular types of equality, viz., (i) utilitarian equality, (ii) total utility equality, and (iii) Rawlsian equality. I shall argue that all three have serious limitations, and that while they fail in rather different and contrasting ways, an adequate theory cannot be constructed even on the *combined* grounds of the three. Towards the end I shall try to present an alternative formulation of equality which seems to me to deserve a good deal more attention than it has received, and I shall not desist from doing some propaganda on its behalf.

First a methodological question. When it is claimed that a certain moral principle has shortcomings, what can be the basis of such an allegation? There seem to be at least two different ways of grounding such a criticism, aside from just checking its *direct* appeal to moral intuition. One is to check the *implications* of the principle by taking up particular cases in which the results of employing that principle can be seen in a rather stark way, and then to examine these implications against our intuition. I shall call such a critique a *case-implication critique.* The other is to move not from the general to the particular, but from the general to the *more* general. One can examine the consistency of the principle with another principle that is acknowledged to be more fundamental. Such prior principles are usually formulated at a rather abstract level, and frequently take the form of congruence with some very general procedures. For example, what could be reasonably assumed to have been chosen under the *as if* ignorance of the Rawlsian "original position," a hypothetical primordial

NOTE: For helpful comments I am most grateful to Derek Parfit, Jim Griffin, and John Perry.

state in which people decide on what rules to adopt without knowing who they are going to be — as if they could end up being any
one of the persons in the community.[1] Or what rules would satisfy
Richard Hare's requirement of "universalizability" and be consistent with "giving equal weights to the equal interests of the
occupants of all the roles."[2] I shall call a critique based on such
an approach a *prior-principle critique*. Both approaches can be
used in assessing the moral claims of each type of equality, and
will indeed be used here.

1. UTILITARIAN EQUALITY

Utilitarian equality is the equality that can be derived from
the utilitarian concept of goodness applied to problems of distribution. Perhaps the simplest case is the "pure distribution problem": the problem of dividing a given homogeneous cake among
a group of persons.[3] Each person gets more utility the larger his
share of the cake, and gets utility *only* from his share of the cake;
his utility increases at a diminishing rate as the amount of his
share goes up. The utilitarian objective is to maximize the sum-
total of utility irrespective of distribution, but that requires the
equality of the *marginal* utility of everyone — marginal utility
being the incremental utility each person would get from an addi-

---

[1] J. Rawls, *A Theory of Justice* (Cambridge: Harvard University Press, 1971),
pp. 17–22. See also W. Vickrey, 'Measuring Marginal Utility by Reactions to Risk',
Econometrica 13 (1945), and J. C. Harsanyi, 'Cardinal Welfare, Individualistic
Ethics, and Interpersonal Comparisons of Utility', *Journal of Political Economy* 63
(1955).

[2] R. M. Hare, *The Language of Morals* (Oxford: Clarendon Press, 1952); 'Ethical
Theory and Utilitarianism', in H. D. Lewis, ed., *Contemporary British Philosophy*
(London: Allen and Unwin, 1976), pp. 116–17.

[3] I have tried to use this format for an axiomatic contrast of the Rawlsian and
utilitarian criteria in 'Rawls versus Bentham: An Axiomatic Examination of the Pure
Distribution Problem', in *Theory and Decision* 4 (1974); reprinted in N. Daniels,
ed., *Reading Rawls* (Oxford: Blackwell, 1975). See also L. Kern, 'Comparative Distributive Ethics: An Extension of Sen's Examination of the Pure Distribution Problem', in H. W. Gottinger and W. Leinfellner, eds., *Decision Theory and Social Ethics*
(Dordrecht: Reidel, 1978), and J. P. Griffin, 'Equality: On Sen's Equity Axiom',
Keble College, Oxford, 1978, mimeographed.

tional unit of cake.[4] According to one interpretation, this equality
of marginal utility embodies equal treatment of everyone's
interests.[5]

The position is a bit more complicated when the total size of
the cake is not independent of its distribution. But even then
maximization of the total utility sum requires that transfers be
carried to the point at which the marginal utility gain of the
gainers equals the marginal utility loss of the losers, after taking
into account the effect of the transfer on the size and distribution
of the cake.[6] It is in this wider context that the special type of
equality insisted upon by utilitarianism becomes assertively distinguished. Richard Hare has claimed that "giving equal weight
to the equal interests of all the parties" would "lead to utilitarianism" — thus satisfying the prior-principle requirement of universalizability.[7] Similarly, John Harsanyi shoots down the non-
utilitarians (including this lecturer, I hasten to add), by claiming
for utilitarianism an exclusive ability to avoid "unfair discrimination" between "one person's and another person's equally urgent
human needs."[8]

The moral importance of needs, on this interpretation, is based
exclusively on the notion of utility. This is disputable, and having
had several occasions to dispute it in the past,[9] I shall not shy away

[4] The equality condition would have to be replaced by a corresponding combination of inequality requirements when the appropriate "continuity" properties do not
hold. Deeper difficulties are raised by "non-convexities" (e.g., increasing marginal
utility).

[5] J. Harsanyi, 'Can the Maximin Principle Serve as a Basis for Morality? A
Critique of John Rawls' Theory', *American Political Science Review* 64 (1975).

[6] As mentioned in footnote 4, the equality conditions would require modification
in the absence of continuity of the appropriate type. Transfers must be carried to the
point at which the marginal utility gain of the gainers from any further transfer is
no more than the marginal utility loss of the losers.

[7] Hare (1976), pp. 116–17.

[8] John Harsanyi, 'Non-linear Social Welfare Functions: A Rejoinder to Professor
Sen', in R. E. Butts and J. Hintikka, eds., *Foundational Problems in the Special Sciences*
(Dordrecht: Reidel, 1977), pp. 294–95.

[9] *Collective Choice and Social Welfare* (San Francisco: Holden-Day, 1970), chapter 6 and section 11.4; 'On Weights and Measures: Informational Constraints in

from disputing it in this particular context. But while I will get on to this issue later, I want first to examine the nature of utilitarian equality without — for the time being — questioning the grounding of moral importance entirely on utility. Even when utility is the sole basis of importance there is still the question as to whether the size of *marginal* utility, irrespective of *total* utility enjoyed by the person, is an adequate index of moral importance. It is, of course, possible to define a metric on utility characteristics such that each person's utility scale is coordinated with everyone else's in a way that equal social importance is simply "scaled" as equal marginal utility. If interpersonal comparisons of utility are taken to have no descriptive content, then this can indeed be thought to be a natural approach. No matter how the relative social importances are arrived at, the marginal utilities attributed to each person would then simply reflect these values. This can be done explicitly by appropriate interpersonal scaling,[10] or implicitly through making the utility numbering reflect choices in situations of *as if* uncertainty associated with the "original position" under the additional assumption that ignorance be interpreted as equal probability of being anyone.[11] This is not the occasion to go into the technical details of this type of exercise, but the essence of it consists in using a scaling procedure such that marginal utility measures are automatically identified as indicators of social importance.

This route to utilitarianism may meet with little resistance, but it is non-controversial mainly because it says so little. A prob-

---

Social Welfare Analysis', *Econometrica* 45 (1977). See also T. M. Scanlon's arguments against identifying utility with "urgency" in his 'Preference and Urgency', *Journal of Philosophy* 72 (1975).

[10] For two highly ingenious examples of such an exercise, see Peter Hammond, 'Dual Interpersonal Comparisons of Utility and the Welfare Economics of Income Distribution', *Journal of Public Economics* 6 (1977): 51–57; and Menahem Yaari, 'Rawls, Edgeworth, Shapley and Nash: Theories of Distributive Justice Re-examined', Research Memorandum No. 33, Center for Research in Mathematical Economics and Game Theory, Hebrew University, Jerusalem, 1978.

[11] See Harsanyi (1955, 1975, 1977).

lem arises the moment utilities and interpersonal comparisons thereof are taken to have some independent descriptive content, as utilitarians have traditionally insisted that they do. There could then be conflicts between these descriptive utilities and the appropriately scaled, essentially normative, utilities in terms of which one is "forced" to be a utilitarian. In what follows I shall have nothing more to say on utilitarianism through appropriate interpersonal scaling, and return to examining the traditional utilitarian position, which takes utilities to have interpersonally comparable descriptive content. How moral importance should relate to these descriptive features must, then, be explicitly faced.

The position can be examined from the prior-principle perspective as well as from the case-implication angle. John Rawls's criticism as a preliminary to presenting his own alternative conception of justice took mostly the prior-principle form. This was chiefly in terms of acceptability in the "original position," arguing that in the postulated situation of *as if* ignorance people would not choose to maximize the utility sum. But Rawls also discussed the violence that utilitarianism does to our notions of liberty and equality. Some replies to Rawls's arguments have reasserted the necessity to be a utilitarian by taking the "scaling" route, which was discussed earlier, and which — I think — is inappropriate in meeting Rawls's critique. But I must confess that I find the lure of the "original position" distinctly resistible since it seems very unclear what precisely would be chosen in such a situation. It is also far from obvious that prudential choice under *as if* uncertainty provides an adequate basis for moral judgment in *un*original, i.e., real-life, positions.[12] But I believe Rawls's more direct critiques in terms of liberty and equality do remain powerful.

Insofar as one is concerned with the *distribution* of utilities, it

[12] On this, see Thomas Nagel, 'Rawls on Justice', *Philosophical Review* 83 (1973), and 'Equality' in his *Mortal Questions* (Cambridge: Cambridge University Press, 1979).

follows immediately that utilitarianism would in general give one little comfort. Even the minutest gain in total utility *sum* would be taken to outweigh distributional inequalities of the most blatant kind. This problem would be avoidable under certain assumptions, notably the case in which everyone has the *same* utility function. In the pure distribution problem, with this assumption the utilitarian best would require absolute equality of everyone's total utilities.[13] This is because when the marginal utilities are equated, so would be the total utilities if everyone has the same utility function. This is, however, egalitarianism by serendipity: just the accidental result of the marginal tail wagging the total dog. More importantly, the assumption would be very frequently violated, since there are obvious and well-discussed variations between human beings. John may be easy to please, but Jeremy not. If it is taken to be an acceptable prior-principle that the equality of the distribution of total utilities has some value, then the utilitarian conception of equality — marginal as it is — must stand condemned.

The recognition of the fundamental diversity of human beings does, in fact, have very deep consequences, affecting not merely the utilitarian conception of social good, but others as well, including (as I shall argue presently) even the Rawlsian conception of equality. If human beings are identical, then the application of the prior-principle of universalizability in the form of "giving equal weight to the equal interest of all parties" simplifies enormously. Equal marginal utilities of all — reflecting one interpretation of the equal treatment of needs — coincides with equal total utilities — reflecting one interpretation of serving their overall interests equally well. With diversity, the two can pull in opposite directions, and it is far from clear that "giving equal weight to

---

[13] The problem is much more complex when the total cake is not fixed, and where the maximization of utility sum need not lead to the equality of total utilities unless some additional assumptions are made, e.g., the absence of incentive arguments for inequality.

the equal interest of all parties" would require us to concentrate only on one of the two parameters — taking no note of the other.

The case-implication perspective can also be used to develop a related critique, and I have tried to present such a critique elsewhere.[14] For example, if person A as a cripple gets half the utility that the pleasure-wizard person B does from any given level of income, then in the pure distribution problem between A and B the utilitarian would end up giving the pleasure-wizard B more income than the cripple A. The cripple would then be doubly worse off: both since he gets less utility from the same level of income, *and* since he will also get less income. Utilitarianism must lead to this thanks to its single-minded concern with maximizing the utility sum. The pleasure-wizard's superior efficiency in producing utility would pull income away from the less efficient cripple.

Since this example has been discussed a certain amount,[15] I should perhaps explain what is being asserted and what is not. First, it is *not* being claimed that anyone who has lower total utility (e.g., the cripple) at any given level of income must of necessity have lower marginal utility also. This must be true for some levels of income, but need not be true everywhere. Indeed, the opposite could be the case when incomes are equally distributed. If that were so, then of course even utilitarianism would give the cripple more income than the non-cripple, since at that point the cripple would be the more efficient producer of utility. My point is that there is no guarantee that this will be the case, and more particularly, if it were the case that the cripple were not only worse off in terms of total utility but could convert income into utility less efficiently everywhere (or even just at the point of

[14] *On Economic Inequality* (Oxford: Clarendon Press, 1973), pp. 16–20.

[15] See John Harsanyi, 'Non-linear Social Welfare Functions', *Theory and Decision* 6 (1976): 311–12; Harsanyi (1977); Kern (1978); Griffin (1978); Richard B. Brandt, *A Theory of the Good and the Right* (Oxford: Clarendon Press, 1979), chapter 16.

equal income division), then utilitarianism would compound his disadvantage by settling him with less income on top of lower efficiency in making utility out of income. The point, of course, is not about cripples in general, nor about all people with total utility disadvantage, but concerns people — including cripples — with disadvantage in terms of both total *and* marginal utility at the relevant points.

Second, the descriptive content of utility is rather important in this context. Obviously, if utilities were scaled to reflect moral importance, then wishing to give priority to income for the cripple would simply amount to attributing a higher "marginal utility" to the cripple's income; but this — as we have already discussed — is a very special sense of utility — quite devoid of descriptive content. In terms of descriptive features, what is being assumed in our example is that the cripple can be helped by giving him income, but the increase in his utility as a consequence of a marginal increase in income is less — in terms of the accepted descriptive criteria — than giving that unit of income to the pleasure-wizard, when both have initially the same income.

Finally, the problem for utilitarianism in this case-implication argument is not dependent on an implicit assumption that the claim to more income arising from disadvantage must dominate over the claim arising from high marginal utility.[16] A system that gives some weight to both claims would still fail to meet the utilitarian formula of social good, which demands an exclusive concern with the latter claim. It is this narrowness that makes the utilitarian conception of equality such a limited one. Even when utility is accepted as the only basis of moral importance, utilitarianism fails to capture the relevance of overall advantage for the requirements of equality. The prior-principle critiques can be supplemented by case-implication critiques using this utilitarian lack

---

[16] Such an assumption is made in my Weak Equity Axiom, proposed in Sen (1973), but it is unnecessarily demanding for rejecting utilitarianism. See Griffin (1978) for a telling critique of the Weak Equity Axiom, in this exacting form.

of concern with distributional questions except at the entirely marginal level.

2. TOTAL UTILITY EQUALITY

Welfarism is the view that the goodness of a state of affairs can be judged entirely by the goodness of the utilities in that state.[17] This is a less demanding view than utilitarianism in that it does not demand — in addition — that the goodness of the utilities must be judged by their sum-total. Utilitarianism is, in this sense, a special case of welfarism, and provides one illustration of it. Another distinguished case is the criterion of judging the goodness of a state by the utility level of the worst-off person in that state — a criterion often attributed to John Rawls. (*Except* by John Rawls! He uses social primary goods rather than utility as the index of advantage, as we shall presently discuss.) One can also take some other function of the utilities — other than the sum-total or the minimal element.

Utilitarian equality is one type of welfarist equality. There are others, notably the equality of total utility. It is tempting to think of this as some kind of an analogue of utilitarianism shifting the focus from marginal utility to total utility. This correspondence is, however, rather less close than it might first appear. First of all, while we economists often tend to treat the marginal and the total as belonging to the same plane of discourse, there is an important difference between them. Marginal is an essentially *counter-factual* notion: marginal utility is the additional utility that *would be* generated if the person had one more unit of income. It contrasts what is observed with what allegedly would be observed if something else were different: in this case if the income had been one unit greater. Total is not, however, an inherently counter-factual concept; whether it is or is not would

---

[17] See Sen (1977), and also my 'Welfarism and Utilitarianism', *Journal of Philosophy* 76 (1979).

depend on the variable that is being totalled. In case of utilities, if they are taken to be observed facts, total utility will not be counter-factual. Thus total utility equality is a matter for direct observation, whereas utilitarian equality is not so, since the latter requires hypotheses as to what things would have been under different postulated circumstances. The contrast can be easily traced to the fact that utilitarian equality is essentially a consequence of sum *maximization*, which is itself a counter-factual notion, whereas total utility equality is an equality of some directly observed magnitudes.

Second, utilitarianism provides a complete ordering of all utility distributions — the ranking reflecting the order of the sums of individual utilities—but as specified so far, total utility equality does not do more than just point to the case of absolute equality. In dealing with two cases of non-equal distributions, something more has to be said so that they could be ranked. The ranking can be completed in many different ways.

One way to such a complete ranking is provided by the lexicographic version of the maximin rule, which is associated with the Rawlsian Difference Principle, but interpreted in terms of utilities as opposed to primary goods. Here the goodness of the state of affairs is judged by the level of utility of the worst-off person in that state; but if the worst-off persons in two states respectively have the same level of utility, then the states are ranked according to the utility levels of the second worst-off. If they too tie, then by the utility levels of the third worst-off, and so on. And if two utility distributions are matched at each rank all the way from the worst off to the best off, then the two distributions are equally good. Following a convention established in social choice theory, I shall call this *leximin*.

In what way does total utility equality lead to the leximin? It does this when combined with some other axioms, and in fact the analysis closely parallels the recent axiomatic derivations of the Difference Principle by several authors.[18] Consider four utility levels a, b, c, d, in decreasing order of magnitude. One can argue that in an obvious sense the pair of extreme points (a, d) displays greater inequality than the pair of intermediate points (b, c). Note that this is a purely *ordinal* comparison based on ranking only, and the exact magnitudes of a, b, c, and d make no difference to the comparison in question. If one were *solely* concerned with equality, then it could be argued that (b, c) is superior — or at least non-inferior — to (a, d). This requirement may be seen as a strong version of preferring equality of utility distributions, and may be called "utility equality preference." It is possible to combine this with an axiom due to Patrick Suppes which captures the notion of *dominance* of one utility distribution over another, in the sense of each element of one distribution being at least as large as the corresponding element in the other distribution.[19] In the two-person case this requires that state x must be regarded as at least as good as y, *either* if each person in state x has at least as much utility as himself in state y, *or* if each person in state x has at least as much utility as the *other* person in state y. *If*, in addition, at least one of them has strictly more, then of course x could be declared to be strictly better (and not merely at least as good). If this Suppes principle and the "utility equality preference" are combined, then we are pushed in the direction of leximin. Indeed, leximin can be fully derived from these two principles by requiring that the approach must provide a com-

---

18 See P. J. Hammond, 'Equity, Arrow's Conditions and Rawls' Difference Principle', *Econometrica* 44 (1976); S. Strasnick, 'Social Choice Theory and the Derivation of Rawls' Difference Principle', *Journal of Philosophy* 73 (1976); C. d'Aspremont and L. Gevers, 'Equity and Informational Basis of Collective Choice', *Review of Economic Studies* 44 (1977); K. J. Arrow, 'Extended Sympathy and the Possibility of Social Choice', *American Economic Review* 67 (1977); A. K. Sen, 'On Weights and Measures: Informational Constraints in Social Welfare Analysis', *Econometrica* 45 (1977); R. Deschamps and L. Gevers, 'Leximin and Utilitarian Rules: A Joint Characterization', *Journal of Economic Theory* 17 (1978); K. W. S. Roberts, 'Possibility Theorems with Interpersonally Comparable Welfare Levels', *Review of Economic Studies* 47 (1980); P. J. Hammond, 'Two Person Equity', *Econometrica* 47 (1979).

19 P. Suppes, 'Some Formal Models of Grading Principles', *Synthese* 6 (1966).

plete ordering of all possible states no matter what the interpersonally comparable individual utilities happen to be (called
"unrestricted domain"), and that the ranking of any two states
must depend on utility information concerning *those* states only
(called "independence").

Insofar as the requirements other than utility equality preference (i.e., the Suppes principle, unrestricted domain, and independence) are regarded as acceptable — and they have indeed
been widely used in the social choice literature — leximin can
be seen as the natural concomitant of giving priority to the conception of equality focussing on total utility.

It should be obvious, however, that leximin can be fairly easily
criticised from the prior-principle perspective as well as the case-
implication perspective. Just as utilitarianism pays no attention
to the force of one's claim arising from one's disadvantage, leximin ignores claims arising from the *intensity* of one's needs. The
ordinal characteristic that was pointed out while presenting the
axiom of utility equality preference makes the approach insensitive to the magnitudes of potential utility gains and losses.
While in the critique of utilitarianism that was presented earlier
I argued against treating these potential gains and losses as the
only basis of moral judgment, it was *not* of course alleged that
these have no moral relevance at all. Take the comparison of
(a, d) vis-a-vis (b, c), discussed earlier, and let (b, c) stand for
$(3, 2)$. Utility equality preference would assert the superiority of
$(3, 2)$ over $(10, 1)$ as well as $(4, 1)$. Indeed, it would not distinguish between the two cases at all. It is this lack of concern
with "how much" questions that makes leximin rather easy to criti-
cise *either* by showing its failure to comply with such prior-
principles as "giving equal weight to the equal interest of all
parties," *or* by spelling out its rather austere implications in
specific cases.

Aside from its indifference to "how much" questions, leximin
also has little interest in "how many" questions — paying no

attention at all to the number of people whose interests are over-ridden in the pursuit of the interests of the worst off. The worst-off position rules the roost, and it does not matter whether this goes against the interests of one other person, or against those of a million or a billion other persons. It is sometimes claimed that leximin would not be such an extreme criterion if it could be modified so that this innumeracy were avoided, and if the interests of *one* worse-off position were given priority over the interests of exactly *one* better-off position, but not necessarily against the interests of *more than one* better-off position. In fact, one can define a less demanding version of leximin, which can be called leximin-2, which takes the form of applying the leximin principle *if* all persons other than two are indifferent between the alterna-tives, but not necessarily otherwise. Leximin-2, as a compromise, will be still unconcerned with "how much" questions on the magnitudes of utilities of the two non-indifferent persons, but need not be blinkered about "how many" questions dealing with numbers of people: the priority applies to one person over exactly one other.[20]

Interestingly enough, a consistency problem intervenes here. It can be proved that given the regularity conditions, viz., un-restricted domain and independence, leximin-2 logically entails leximin in general.[21] That is, given these regularity conditions, there is no way of retaining moral sensitivity to the number of people on each side by choosing the limited requirement of leximin-2 without going all the way to leximin itself. It appears that indifference to *how much* questions concerning utilities im-plies indifference to *how many* questions concerning the number of

---

[20] Leximin — and maximin — are concerned with conflicts between positional priorities, i.e., between ranks (such as the "worst-off position," "second worst-off posi-tion," etc.), and not with interpersonal priorities. When positions coincide with per-sons (e.g., the *same* person being the worst off in each state), then positional conflicts translate directly into personal conflicts.

[21] Theorem 8, Sen (1977). See also Hammond (1979) for extensions of this result.

people on different sides. One innumeracy begets another.

Given the nature of these critiques of utilitarian equality and total utility equality respectively, it is natural to ask whether some *combination* of the two should not meet both sets of objections. If utilitarianism is attacked for its unconcern with inequalities of the utility distribution, and leximin is criticised for its lack of interest in the magnitudes of utility gains and losses, and even in the numbers involved, then isn't the right solution to choose some mixture of the two? It is at this point that the long-postponed question of the relation between utility and moral worth becomes crucial. While utilitarianism and leximin differ sharply from each other in the use that they respectively make of the utility information, both share an exclusive concern with utility data. If non-utility considerations have any role in either approach, this arises from the part they play in the determination of utilities, or possibly as surrogates for utility information in the absence of adequate utility data. A combination of utilitarianism and leximin would still be confined to the box of welfarism, and it remains to be examined whether welfarism as a general approach is *itself* adequate.

One aspect of the obtuseness of welfarism was discussed clearly by John Rawls.

In calculating the greatest balance of satisfaction it does not matter, except indirectly, what the desires are for. We are to arrange institutions so as to obtain the greatest sum of satisfactions; we ask no questions about their source or quality but only how their satisfaction would affect the total of well-being. . . . Thus if men take a certain pleasure in discriminating against one another, in subjecting others to a lesser liberty as a means of enhancing their self-respect, then the satisfaction of these desires must be weighed in our deliberations according to their intensity, or whatever, along with other desires. . . . In justice as fairness, on the other hand, persons accept in advance a principle of equal liberty and they do this without a knowledge of their more particular ends. . . . An individual who finds that he enjoys seeing others in positions of lesser liberty understands that he has no claim whatever to this enjoyment. The pleasure he takes in other's deprivation is wrong in itself: it is a satisfaction which requires the violation of a principle to which he would agree in the original position.[22]

It is easily seen that this is an argument not merely against utilitarianism, but against the adequacy of utility information for moral judgments of states of affairs, and is, thus, an attack on welfarism in general. Second, it is clear that as a criticism of welfarism — and *a fortiori* as a critique of utilitarianism — the argument uses a principle that is unnecessarily strong. If it were the case that pleasures taken "in other's deprivation" were not taken to be wrong in itself, but simply *disregarded*, even then the rejection of welfarism would stand. Furthermore, even if such pleasures were regarded as valuable, but *less* valuable than pleasures arising from other sources (e.g., enjoying food, work, or leisure), welfarism would still stand rejected. The issue — as John Stuart Mill had noted — is the lack of "parity" between one source of utility and another.[23] Welfarism requires the endorsement not merely of the widely shared intuition that any pleasure has some value — and one would have to be a bit of a kill-joy to dissent from this — but also the much more dubious proposition that pleasures must be relatively weighed *only* according to their respective intensities, irrespective of the source of the pleasure and the nature of the activity that goes with it. Finally, Rawls's argument takes the form of an appeal to the prior-principle of equating moral rightness with prudential acceptability in the original position. Even those who do not accept that prior principle could reject the welfarist no-nonsense counting of utility irrespective of all other information by reference to other prior principles, e.g., the irreducible value of liberty.

[22] Rawls (1971), pp. 30–31.
[23] John Stuart Mill, *On Liberty* (1859), p. 140.

The relevance of non-utility information to moral judgments is the central issue involved in disputing welfarism. Libertarian considerations point towards a particular class of non-utility information, and I have argued elsewhere that this may require even the rejection of the so-called Pareto principle based on utility dominance.[24] But there are also other types of non-utility information which have been thought to be intrinsically important. Tim Scanlon has recently discussed the contrast between "urgency" and utility (or intensity of preference). He has also argued that "the criteria of well-being that we actually employ in making moral judgments are objective," and a person's level of well-being is taken to be "independent of that person's tastes and interests."[25] These moral judgments could thus conflict with utilitarian — and more generally (Scanlon could have argued) with welfarist — moralities, no matter whether utility is interpreted as pleasure, or — as is increasingly common recently — as desire-fulfilment.

However, acknowledging the relevance of objective factors does not require that well-being be taken to be independent of tastes, and Scanlon's categories are *too* pure. For example, a lack of "parity" between utility from self-regarding actions and that from other-regarding actions will go beyond utility as an index of well-being and will be fatal to welfarism, but the contrast is not, of course, independent of tastes and subjective features. "Objective" considerations can count along with a person's tastes. What is required is the denial that a person's well-being be judged *exclusively* in terms of his or her utilities. If such judgments take into account a person's pleasures and desire-fulfilments, but also certain objective factors, e.g., whether he or she is hungry, cold, or oppressed, the resulting calculus would still be non-welfarist. Welfarism is an extremist position, and its denial can take many different forms — pure and mixed — so long as totally ignoring non-utility information is avoided.

[24] Sen (1970), especially chapter 6. Also Sen (1979).
[25] T. M. Scanlon (1975), pp. 658–59.

Second, it is also clear that the notion of urgency need not work only *through* the determinants of personal well-being — however broadly conceived. For example, the claim that one should not be *exploited* at work is not based on making exploitation an additional parameter in the specification of well-being on top of such factors as income and effort, but on the moral view that a person deserves to get what he — according to one way of characterizing production — has produced. Similarly, the urgency deriving from principles such as "equal pay for equal work" hits directly at discrimination without having to redefine the notion of personal well-being to take note of such discriminations. One could, for example, say: "She must be paid just as much as the men working in that job, not primarily because she would otherwise have a lower level of well-being than the others, but simply because she is doing the *same* work as the men there, and why should she be paid less?" These moral claims, based on non-welfarist conceptions of equality, have played important parts in social movements, and it seems difficult to sustain the hypothesis that they are purely "instrumental" claims — ultimately justified by their indirect impact on the fulfilment of welfarist, or other well-being-based, objectives.

Thus the dissociation of urgency from utility can arise from two different sources. One disentangles the notion of personal well-being from utility, and the other makes urgency not a function only of well-being. But, at the same time, the former does not require that well-being be independent of utility, and the latter does not necessitate a notion of urgency that is independent of personal well-being. Welfarism is a purist position and must avoid any contamination from either of these sources.

3. RAWLSIAN EQUALITY

Rawls's "two principles of justice" characterize the need for equality in terms of — what he has called — "primary social goods." [26] These are "things that every rational man is presumed to want," including "rights, liberties and opportunities, income and wealth, and the social bases of self-respect." Basic liberties are separated out as having priority over other primary goods, and thus priority is given to the principle of liberty which demands that "each person is to have an equal right to the most extensive basic liberty compatible with a similar liberty for others." The second principle supplements this, demanding efficiency and equality, judging advantage in terms of an index of primary goods. Inequalities are condemned unless they work out to everyone's advantage. This incorporates the "Difference Principle" in which priority is given to furthering the interests of the worst-off. And that leads to maximin, or to leximin, defined not on individual utilities but on the index of primary goods. But given the priority of the liberty principle, no trade-offs are permitted between basic liberties and economic and social gain.

Herbert Hart has persuasively disputed Rawls's arguments for the priority of liberty,[27] but with that question I shall not be concerned in this lecture. What is crucial for the problem under discussion is the concentration on bundles of primary social goods. Some of the difficulties with welfarism that I tried to discuss will not apply to the pursuit of Rawlsian equality. Objective criteria of well-being can be directly accommodated within the index of primary goods. So can be Mill's denial of the parity between pleasures from different sources, since the sources can be discriminated on the basis of the nature of the goods. Furthermore, while the Difference Principle is egalitarian in a way similar to leximin, it avoids the much-criticised feature of leximin of giving more income to people who are hard to please and who have to be deluged in champagne and buried in caviar to bring them to a

[26] Rawls (1971), pp. 60–65.

[27] H. L. A. Hart, 'Rawls on Liberty and Its Priority', *University of Chicago Law Review* 40 (1973); reprinted in N. Daniels, ed., *Reading Rawls* (Oxford: Blackwell, 1975).

normal level of utility, which you and I get from a sandwich and beer. Since advantage is judged not in terms of utilities at all, but through the index of primary goods, expensive tastes cease to provide a ground for getting more income. Rawls justifies this in terms of a person's responsibility for his own ends.

But what about the cripple with utility disadvantage, whom we discussed earlier? Leximin will give him more income in a pure distribution problem. Utilitarianism, I had complained, will give him *less*. The Difference Principle will give him neither more nor less on grounds of his being a cripple. His utility disadvantage will be irrelevant to the Difference Principle. This may seem hard, and I think it is. Rawls justifies this by pointing out that "hard cases" can "distract our moral perception by leading us to think of people distant from us whose fate arouses pity and anxiety." [28] This can be so, but hard cases do exist, and to take disabilities, or special health needs, or physical or mental defects, as morally irrelevant, or to leave them out for fear of making a mistake, may guarantee that the *opposite* mistake will be made.

And the problem does not end with hard cases. The primary goods approach seems to take little note of the diversity of human beings. In the context of assessing utilitarian equality, it was argued that if people were fundamentally similar in terms of utility functions, then the utilitarian concern with maximizing the sum-total of utilities would push us simultaneously also in the direction of equality of utility levels. Thus utilitarianism could be rendered vastly more attractive if people really were similar. A corresponding remark can be made about the Rawlsian Difference Principle. If people were basically very similar, then an index of primary goods might be quite a good way of judging advantage. But, in fact, people seem to have very different needs varying with health, longevity, climatic conditions, location, work

[28] John Rawls, 'A Kantian Concept of Equality', *Cambridge Review* (February 1975), p. 96.

conditions, temperament, and even body size (affecting food and clothing requirements). So what is involved is not merely ignoring a few hard cases, but overlooking very widespread and real differences. Judging advantage purely in terms of primary goods leads to a partially blind morality.

Indeed, it can be argued that there is, in fact, an element of "fetishism" in the Rawlsian framework. Rawls takes primary goods as the embodiment of advantage, rather than taking advantage to be a *relationship* between persons and goods. Utilitarianism, or leximin, or — more generally — welfarism does not have this fetishism, since utilities are reflections of one type of relation between persons and goods. For example, income and wealth are not valued under utilitarianism as physical units, but in terms of their capacity to create human happiness or to satisfy human desires. Even if utility is not thought to be the right focus for the person–good relationship, to have an entirely good-oriented framework provides a peculiar way of judging advantage.

It can also be argued that while utility in the form of happiness or desire-fulfilment may be an *inadequate* guide to urgency, the Rawlsian framework asserts it to be *irrelevant* to urgency, which is, of course, a much stronger claim. The distinction was discussed earlier in the context of assessing welfarism, and it was pointed out that a rejection of welfarism need not take us to the point in which utility is given no role whatsoever. That a person's interest should have nothing directly to do with his happiness or desire-fulfilment seems difficult to justify. Even in terms of the prior-principle of prudential acceptability in the "original position," it is not at all clear why people in that primordial state should be taken to be so indifferent to the joys and sufferings in occupying particular positions, or if they are not, why their concern about these joys and sufferings should be taken to be morally irrelevant.

4. BASIC CAPABILITY EQUALITY

This leads to the further question: Can we not construct an adequate theory of equality on the *combined* grounds of Rawlsian equality and equality under the two welfarist conceptions, with some trade-offs among them. I would now like to argue briefly why I believe this too may prove to be informationally short. This can, of course, easily be asserted *if* claims arising from considerations other than well-being were acknowledged to be legitimate. Non-exploitation, or non-discrimination, requires the use of information not fully captured either by utility or by primary goods. Other conceptions of entitlements can also be brought in going beyond concern with personal well-being only. But in what follows I shall not introduce these concepts. My contention is that *even* the concept of *needs* does not get adequate coverage through the information on primary goods and utility.

I shall use a case-implication argument. Take the cripple again with marginal utility disadvantage. We saw that utilitarianism would do nothing for him; in fact it will give him *less* income than to the physically fit. Nor would the Difference Principle help him; it will leave his physical disadvantage severely alone. He did, however, get preferential treatment under leximin, and more generally, under criteria fostering total equality. His low level of total utility was the basis of his claim. But now suppose that he is no worse off than others in utility terms despite his physical handicap because of certain other utility features. This could be because he has a jolly disposition. Or because he has a low aspiration level and his heart leaps up whenever he sees a rainbow in the sky. Or because he is religious and feels that he will be rewarded in after-life, or cheerfully accepts what he takes to be just penalty for misdeeds in a past incarnation. The important point is that despite his marginal utility disadvantage, he has no longer a total utility deprivation. Now not even leximin — or any other notion of equality focussing on total utility — will do much for him. If we still think that he has needs as a cripple that should be catered to, then the basis of that claim clearly rests neither in high marginal utility, nor in low total utility, nor — of course — in deprivation in terms of primary goods.

It is arguable that what is missing in all this framework is some notion of "basic capabilities": a person being able to do certain basic things. The ability to move about is the relevant one here, but one can consider others, e.g., the ability to meet one's nutritional requirements, the wherewithal to be clothed and sheltered, the power to participate in the social life of the community. The notion of urgency related to this is not fully captured by either utility or primary goods, or any combination of the two. Primary goods suffers from fetishist handicap in being concerned with goods, and even though the list of goods is specified in a broad and inclusive way, encompassing rights, liberties, opportunities, income, wealth, and the social basis of self-respect, it still is concerned with good things rather than with what these good things *do* to human beings. Utility, on the other hand, *is* concerned with what these things do to human beings, but uses a metric that focusses not on the person's capabilities but on his mental reaction. There is something still missing in the combined list of primary goods and utilities. If it is argued that resources should be devoted to remove or substantially reduce the handicap of the cripple despite there being no marginal utility argument (because it is expensive), despite there being no total utility argument (because he is so contented), and despite there being no primary goods deprivation (because he has the goods that others have), the case must rest on something else. I believe what is at issue is the interpretation of needs in the form of basic capabilities. This interpretation of needs and interests is often implicit in the demand for equality. This type of equality I shall call "basic capability equality."

The focus on basic capabilities can be seen as a natural extension of Rawls's concern with primary goods, shifting attention from goods to what goods do to human beings. Rawls himself motivates judging advantage in terms of primary goods by referring to capabilities, even though his criteria end up focussing on goods as such: on income rather than on what income does, on the "social bases of self-respect" rather than on self-respect itself, and so on. If human beings were very like each other, this would not have mattered a great deal, but there is evidence that the conversion of goods to capabilities varies from person to person substantially, and the equality of the former may still be far from the equality of the latter.

There are, of course, many difficulties with the notion of "basic capability equality." In particular, the problem of indexing the basic capability bundles is a serious one. It is, in many ways, a problem comparable with the indexing of primary good bundles in the context of Rawlsian equality. This is not the occasion to go into the technical issues involved in such an indexing, but it is clear that whatever partial ordering can be done on the basis of broad uniformity of personal preferences must be supplemented by certain established conventions of relative importance.

The ideas of relative importance are, of course, conditional on the nature of the society. The notion of the equality of basic capabilities is a very general one, but any application of it must be rather culture-dependent, especially in the weighting of different capabilities. While Rawlsian equality has the characteristic of being both culture-dependent and fetishist, basic capability equality avoids fetishism, but remains culture-dependent. Indeed, basic capability equality can be seen as essentially an extension of the Rawlsian approach in a non-fetishist direction.

5. CONCLUDING REMARKS

I end with three final remarks. First, it is not my contention that basic capability equality can be the sole guide to the moral good. For one thing morality is not concerned only with equality.

For another, while it is my contention that basic capability equality has certain clear advantages over other types of equality, I did not argue that the others were morally irrelevant. Basic capability equality is a partial guide to the part of moral goodness that is associated with the idea of equality. I have tried to argue that as a partial guide it has virtues that the other characterisations of equality do not possess.

Second, the index of basic capabilities, like utility, can be used in many different ways. Basic capability equality corresponds to total utility equality, and it can be extended in different directions, e.g., to leximin of basic capabilities. On the other hand, the index can be used also in a way similar to utilitarianism, judging the strength of a claim in terms of incremental contribution to *enhancing* the index value. The main departure is in focussing on a *magnitude* different from utility as well as the primary goods index. The new dimension can be utilised in different ways, of which basic capability equality is only one.

Last, the bulk of this lecture has been concerned with rejecting the claims of utilitarian equality, total utility equality, and Rawlsian equality to provide a sufficient basis for the equality-aspect of morality — indeed, even for that part of it which is concerned with needs rather than deserts. I have argued that none of these three is sufficient, nor is any combination of the three.

This is my main thesis. I have also made the constructive claim that this gap can be narrowed by the idea of basic capability equality, and more generally by the use of basic capability as a morally relevant dimension taking us beyond utility and primary goods. I should end by pointing out that the validity of the main thesis is not conditional on the acceptance of this constructive claim.

Incentives, Inequality, and Community

G. A. Cohen

... the rulers of mankind ... maintain side by side two standards of social ethics, without the risk of their colliding. Keeping one set of values for use, and another for display, they combine, without conscious insincerity, the moral satisfaction of idealistic principles with the material advantages of realistic practice.

— R. H. Tawney, *Equality*

I. The Incentive Argument, The Interpersonal Test, and Community

1.

In March of 1988, Nigel Lawson, who was then Margaret Thatcher's chancellor of the exchequer, brought the top rate of income tax in Britain down, from 60 to 40 percent. That cut enlarged the net incomes of those whose incomes were already large, in comparison with the British average, and, of course, in com-

Many friends and colleagues commented helpfully, and in some cases at magnanimous length, on earlier versions of the material forming these lectures. For perceptive admonitions at various Oxford meetings I thank Ronald Dworkin, Susan Hurley, Thomas Nagel, Derek Parfit, Thomas Scanlon, Samuel Scheffler, and Joseph Raz. For (often voluminous) letters of criticism, I thank Richard Arneson, John Baker, Annette Barnes, Gerald Barnes, Christopher Bertram, Akeel Bilgrami, Giacomo Bonanno, Joshua Cohen, Gerald Dworkin, Jon Elster, Keith Graham, Daniel Hausman, Ted Honderich, Will Kymlicka, Andrew Levine, Kasper Lippert-Rasmussen, Murray MacBeath, John McMurtry, David Miller, Michael Otsuka, Derek Parfit, Philip Pettit, Thomas Pogge, Janet Radcliffe-Richards, John Roemer, Amelie Rorty, Miles Sabin, Robert Shaver, William Shaw, Seana Shiffrin, Hillel Steiner, Joseph Stiglitz, Robert Ware, Martin Wilkinson, Alan Wertheimer, Andrew Williams, Joseph Wolff, and Erik Wright. My greatest debt is to Arnold Zuboff, who devoted countless hours to arguing with, and correcting, me, and I am particularly grateful to Samuel Scheffler for his incisive criticism at the seminar following the lectures. I should add that some of the argumentation of the lectures is anticipated in these articles about Rawls: Thomas Grey, "The First Virtue," *Stanford Law Review* 25 (January 1973); Jan Narveson, "A Puzzle about Economic Justice in Rawls' Theory," *Social Theory and Practice* 4, no. 1 (1976); and Joseph Carens, "Rights and Duties in an Egalitarian Society," *Political Theory* 14, no. 1 (February 1986).

parison with the income of Britain's poor people. Socialists hated the tax cut, and a recent policy document says that the Labour party would, effectively, restore the pre-1988 rate.[1]

How might the Lawson tax cut be defended? Well, economic inequality is no new thing in capitalist society, so there has been plenty of time for a lot of arguments to accumulate in favor of it. We hear, from the political right, that rich people are entitled to their wealth: to part of it because they produced it themselves — but for them, it would not have existed — and to the rest of it because it was transferred to them voluntarily by others who were themselves entitled to it because they produced it, or because they received it as a gift or in voluntary trade from others who were themselves entitled to it because . . . (and so on). (Some who hold that view also think that it is because it establishes moral desert that production justifies title, while others find the entitlement story compelling even when the idea of desert plays no role in it.) And then there is the utilitarian proposition, affirmed not only on the right but in the center, that inequality is justified because, through dynamizing the economy, it expands the gross national product and thereby causes an increase in the sum of human happiness.

Left-wing liberals, whose chief representative in philosophy is John Rawls, reject these arguments for inequality: they do not accept the principles (entitlement, desert, and general utility) which figure in their major premises.[2] But the right and center

---

[1] Strictly speaking, the top tax would be raised to 50 percent, but the ceiling on National Insurance contributions would be removed, and the effect of the two measures would be the same as that of raising the income tax to 59 percent and leaving National Insurance alone.

[2] To be more precise, they reject those principles *at the relevant fundamental level*. The qualification is necessary because left-wing liberals recognize desert and entitlement as (derivative) rules of legitimate reward in schemes of contribution and compensation which are not *grounded* in notions of desert and entitlement. (See John Rawls, *A Theory of Justice* [Cambridge: Harvard University Press, 1971], pp. 103, 310–15; and Thomas Scanlon, "The Significance of Choice," in *The Tanner Lectures on Human Values*, Vol. 8 [Salt Lake City: University of Utah Press, 1988], pp. 188, 203. For a recent statement of nuanced views on desert and entitlement,

sometimes offer an additional argument for inequality, to the major premise of which the liberals are friendly. That major premise is the principle that inequalities are justified when they render badly off people as well off as it is possible for such people to be.[3] In one version of this argument for inequality — and this version of it is the topic of these lectures — their high levels of income cause unusually productive people to produce more than they otherwise would; and, as a result of the incentives enjoyed by those at the top, the people who end up near the bottom are better off than they would be in a more equal society. This was one of the most politically effective justifications of the unequalizing policy of Thatcher Conservatism. We were ceaselessly told that movement contrary to that policy, in a socialist egalitarian direction, would be bad for badly off people, by advocates of a regime which seems itself to have brought about the very effect against which its apologists insistently warned.[4]

Left-wing liberals deny the factual claim that the vast inequalities in Britain or America actually do benefit the badly off, but they tend to agree that if they did, they would be justified, and they defend inequalities that really are justified, in their view, by the incentive consideration. That is a major theme in John Rawls's work. For Rawls, some people are, mainly as a matter of genetic and other luck, capable of producing more than others are, and it is right for them to be richer than others if the less fortunate are caused to be better off as a result.[5] The policy is warranted by what Rawls calls the difference principle, which endorses all and

---

see John Rawls, *Justice as Fairness: A Briefer Restatement* [Cambridge: Harvard University, 1989, manuscript], pp. 54, sec. 2, and 57 n. 34; I do not understand the doctrine presented in the latter place).

[3] For extensive use of this principle, see F. A. Hayek, *The Constitution of Liberty* (Chicago: University of Chicago Press, 1960), chap. 3, and esp. pp. 44–49.

[4] Strong support for that charge comes from *Punishing the Poor: Poverty under Thatcher*, by Kay Andrews and John Jacobs (London: Macmillan, 1990).

[5] See Rawls, *A Theory of Justice*, pp. 15, 102, 151, 179, 546; Rawls, *Justice as Fairness*, pp. 57, 89.

only those social and economic inequalities that are good for the worst off, or, more generously, those inequalities that either make the worst off better off or do not make them worse off: in this matter there is a certain ambiguity of formulation in Rawls, and in what follows I shall take the difference principle in its more generous form, in which it allows inequalities that do not help but also do not hurt the worst off.[6]

Back now to the socialist egalitarians, who did not like the Lawson tax cut. Being to the left of left-wing liberals, socialist egalitarians are also unimpressed by the desert, entitlement, and utility justifications of inequality. But it is not so easy for them to set aside the Rawlsian justification of inequality. They cannot just dismiss it, without lending to their own advocacy of equality a fanatical hue which they could not themselves on reflection find attractive.

Socialist egalitarians say that they believe in equality. We might well think that they count as egalitarians because equality

---

[6] Statements of the difference principle display ambiguity along two dimensions. There is the ambiguity remarked in the text above, between inequalities that *do not harm* and inequalities that *help* the badly off, and there is the further ambiguity between *mandated* and *permitted* inequalities. These distinctions generate the following matrix:

	Mandated		Permitted
Helping ones are	1	→	2
Non-harming ones are	3	→	4

Since what is mandated is permitted, and what helps does not harm, there exist the implications among possible interpretations of the principle indicated by the arrows above, and there are five logically possible positions about which inequalities are mandated and which allowed: all are mandated (1,2,3,4); helping ones are mandated, and others forbidden (1,2); none are mandated and only helping ones are permitted (2); none are mandated and all non-harming ones are permitted (2,4); helping ones are mandated and all non-harming ones are permitted (1,2,4). Rationales can be provided for each of these five points of view, and I believe that there are traces of all of them in the letter and/or spirit of various Rawlsian texts. (Although, as I have said, I take the difference principle in a form in which it allows *all* non-harming inequalities, my critique of Rawls is consistent with his holding any of the positions distinguished above: it depends only on his allowing helping inequalities and forbidding harming ones, and that stance is a constituent in each of the five positions).

is their premise. But the structure of that premise is too simple to accommodate the thought that gets them going politically, which is: why should some people be badly off, when other people are so *well* off? That is not the same as the colorless question, Why should some people be better off than others? for in that question there is no reference to absolute levels of condition, hence no reference to anyone being badly off, as opposed to just *less* well off than other people are. Maybe some egalitarians would maintain their zeal in a world of millionaires and billionaires in which no one's life is hard, but the politically engaged socialist egalitarians that I have in mind have no strong opinion about inequality at millionaire/billionaire levels. What they find wrong is that there is, so they think, unnecessary hardship at the lower end of the scale. There are people who are badly off and who, they believe, would be better off under an equalizing redistribution. The practically crucial feature of the situation is that the badly off are worse off than anyone needs to be, since an equalizing redistribution would enhance their lives.

For these egalitarians, equality would be a good thing because it would make the badly off better off. They do not think it a good thing about equality that it would make the well off worse off. And when their critics charge them with being willing, for the sake of equality, to grind everyone down to the level of the worst off, or even lower, they do not say, in response: well, yes, let us grind down if necessary, but let us achieve equality on a higher plane if that is possible. Instead, what they say is somewhat evasive, at the level of principle; they just deny that it is necessary, for the sake of achieving equality, to move to a condition in which some are worse off and none are better off than now. Were they more reflective, they might add that, if leveling down were necessary, then equality would lose its appeal. Either it would make the badly off worse off still, in frustration of the original egalitarian purpose, or it would make the badly off no better off, while others are made worse off to no evident purpose. Relative to their initial inspiration, which is a concern about badly off people, an inequality is mandatory if it really is needed to improve the condition of the badly off, and it is permissible if it does not improve but also does not worsen their condition.

Accordingly, these egalitarians lose sight of their goal, their position becomes incoherent or untrue to itself, if, in a world with badly off people, they reject the difference principle and cleave to an egalitarianism of strict equality. (Given the priorities and emphases that I have attributed to them, they should, strictly speaking, affirm as fundamental neither equality nor the difference principle but this complex maxim: make the badly off well off, or, if that is not possible, make them as well off as possible. But, on a modestly demanding interpretation of what it means to be well off, and on a realistic view of the world's foreseeable resource prospects, the practical consequences of the complex maxim are those of the difference principle.) We might conclude that the socialist egalitarians that I have in mind should not be called "egalitarians," since (if I am right) equality is not their real premise. But that conclusion would be hasty, and I shall say more about the property of the name "egalitarian" in a moment.

For my part, I accept the difference principle, in its generous interpretation (see above), but I question its application in defense of special money incentives to talented people. Rawlsians think that inequalities associated with such incentives satisfy the principle. But I believe that the idea that an inequality is justified if, through the familiar incentive mechanism, it benefits the badly off is more problematic than Rawlsians suppose; that, at least when the incentive consideration is isolated from all reference to desert or entitlement, it generates an argument for inequality that requires a model of society in breach of an elementary condition of community. The difference principle can be used to justify paying incentives that induce inequalities only when the attitude of talented people runs counter to the spirit of the difference principle itself: they would not need special incentives if they were themselves unambivalently committed to the principle. Accordingly, they must be thought of as outside the community upholding the principle when it is used to justify incentive payments to them.[7]

Speaking more generally, and somewhat beyond the limited brief of these lectures, I want to record here my doubt that the difference principle justifies *any* significant inequality, in an unqualified way. The principle allows an inequality only if the worst off could not benefit from its removal. And I believe that it is in general more difficult than liberals suppose to show that the worst off could not benefit from removal of an inequality, and hence in general more difficult than liberals think it is to justify an inequality at the bar of the difference principle. The worst off benefit from incentive inequality in particular only because the better off would, in effect, go on strike if unequalizing incentives were withdrawn. This inequality benefits the badly off only within the constraint set by the inegalitarian attitude, and the consequent behavior, of the well off, a constraint that they could remove. And an inequality can also benefit the badly off within a constraint set, not by inegalitarian attitudes per se, but by preexisting unequal structure. Thus, in a country with state medical provision, the inequality of treatment that comes from allocating a portion of hospital resources to high-fee-paying patients who get superior care benefits the badly off when some of the revenue is used to raise standards throughout the service. The unequal medical provision helps poor people, but only against the background of a prior income inequality (which no doubt itself reflects further structural inequality

---

[7] Although I shall press against left-wing liberals the thought that community cannot tolerate the inequalities that they endorse, I need not deny that enormous inequalities coexisted with community in premarket societies. For, if that was indeed true, then the coexistence was possible because of general acceptance, and, more particularly, because of acceptance by the less well off of ideologies of destiny and place which left-wing liberals do not countenance. That community can go with inequality when people believe things that liberals regard as false does not show that they can go together in a society possessed of a modern consciousness.

and inegalitarian attitude) that has not, within this argument, it-self been shown to benefit them.

The farther back one goes, temporally and causally, in the con-struction of the feasible set, the more one encounters open possi-bilities that were closed by human choice, and the harder it is to identify inequalities that do not harm the badly off. Bringing the two cases distinguished above together, I conjecture that social in-equalities will appear beneficial to or neutral toward the interest of those at the bottom only when we take as given unequal struc-tures and/or inequality-endorsing attitudes that no one who affirms the difference principle should unprotestingly accept.[8]

Now if all that is right, then we might, in the end, in a round-about way, vindicate the application of the term "egalitarian" to the socialists that I have had in mind, provided that they are will-ing to tolerate a formulation of their position along lines just fore-shadowed. For we might say that a person is an egalitarian if he applies the difference principle in circumstances in which there exist badly off (as opposed to just less well off) people *and* he believes that what the principle demands, in those circumstances, is equality itself, if, that is, he believes that in the long run, and prescinding from rooted inegalitarian attitudes and practices, there *are*, in such circumstances, no social inequalities that do not harm the worst off. Equality appears, at first, to be a premise. It is then rejected, *as* a premise, when the reason for wanting equality is clarified: it is rejected in favor of the difference principle (or, strictly, the more complex maxim stated at p. 268 above). But, now grounded in (something like) the difference principle, it re-asserts itself as a conclusion, for our world, in these times, and for the foreseeable future.

---

[8] We can also say that inequalities are necessary to improve the condition of the badly off when we take for granted, not, as above, causal, but moral imperatives. Thus incentives can indeed be judged necessary to raise the condition of the badly off when elements of the desert and entitlement rationales that left-wing liberals re-ject are affirmed.

2.

I return to Rawls and the difference principle in Part III of these lectures. Right now I want to focus on Nigel Lawson's tax cut, and on the incentive case against canceling it, the case, that is, for maintaining rewards to productive people at the existing high level. And I shall consider that case only with respect to those who, so it is thought, produce a lot by exercising skill and talent, rather than by investing capital. Accordingly, the argument I shall examine applies not only to capitalist economies but also to economies without private ownership of capital, such as certain forms of market socialism. Of course, there also exists an incentive argument for high returns to capital investment, but I am not going to address that argument in these lectures.

Proponents of the incentive argument say that when productive people take home modest pay, they produce less than they otherwise do, and, as a result, relatively poor and badly off people are worse off than they are when the exercise of talent is well rewarded. Applied against a restoration of the top tax to 60 percent, the argument runs as follows:

> Economic inequalities are justified when they make the worst off people materially better off. [Major, normative premise]
>
> When the top rate of tax is 40 percent, (*a*) the talented rich produce more than they do when it is 60 percent, and (*b*) the worst off are, as a result, materially better off. [Minor, factual premise]
>
> Therefore, the top tax should not be raised from 40 percent to 60 percent.

It is immaterial to present concerns how the circumstance alleged to obtain in part *a* of the minor premise of the argument is supposed to occasion the result described in part *b*. One possibility is that the rich work so much harder when the tax rate goes down that the tax take goes up, and more is available for redis-

tribution. Another is that, when the rich work harder, they produce, among other things, (better) employment opportunities for
badly off people.

I am going to comment negatively on the incentive argument,
but my criticism of it will take a particular form. For I shall focus
not, directly, on the argument as such, but on the character of certain utterances of it. Accordingly, I shall not raise questions about
the validity of the argument, or about the truth of its premises,
save insofar as they arise (and they do) within the special focus
just described. And I shall not, in particular, pursue possible
doubts about the minor, factual, premise of the argument. I shall
question neither claim *a*, that the supposedly talented rich are
more productive when they are more generously rewarded, nor
claim *b*, that the badly off benefit from the greater productivity
of the well off affirmed in *a*. I do not aim to show that the minor
premise of the incentive argument is false.

The critique that follows is not of everything that could be
called an incentive, but only of incentives that produce inequality
and which are said to be justified because they make badly off
people better off. I raise no objection against incentives designed
to eliminate a poverty trap, or to induce people to undertake particularly unpleasant jobs. It is not constitutive of those incentives
that they produce inequality. My target is incentives conferring
high rewards on people of talent who would otherwise not perform as those rewards induce them to do. I believe that the familiar liberal case for incentives of that kind has not been thoroughly
thought through.

3.

I said that I would criticize the incentive argument by focusing
on certain utterances of it. For I believe that, although the argument may sound reasonable when it is presented, as it usually is,
and as it was above, in blandly impersonal form, it does not sound
so good when we fix on a presentation of it in which a talented

rich person pronounces it to a badly off person. And the fact that the argument undergoes this devaluation when it occurs in that interpersonal setting should affect our assessment of the nature of the society that the incentive justification by implication recommends.

A normative argument will often wear a particular aspect because of who is offering it and/or to whom it is being addressed. When reasons are given for performing an action or endorsing a policy or adopting an attitude, the appropriate response by the person(s) asked so to act or approve or feel, and the reaction of variously placed observers of the interchange, may depend on who is speaking and who is listening. The form, and the explanation, of that dependence vary considerably across different kinds of case. But the general point is that there are many ways, some more interesting than others, in which an argument's persuasive value can be speaker-audience-relative, and there are many reasons of, once again, different degrees of interest, why that should be so.

Before describing a form of dependence (of response on who is addressing whom) that operates in the case of the incentive argument, and in order to induce a mood in which we think of arguments in their contexts of delivery, I list a few examples of the general phenomenon:

(*a*) I can argue that the driver over there should not be blamed for just now making a right turn on a red light, since he does not know that the rules are different outside California. But he cannot, at the moment, make that very argument, entirely sound though it may be.

(*b*) You want the fishing rod for recreation, and I need it to get my next meal. I know that you are so unstoical that you will be more upset if you do not get to fish than I will be if I do not get to eat. So I let you have the rod, and I cite your hypersensitivity to disappointment as my reason. It would be a lot less good for you to give that as a reason why you should have the rod.

(*c*) I might persuade my fellow middle class friend that, because my car is being repaired, and I consequently have to spend hours on the buses these days, I have a right to be grumpy. The same conclusion, on the same basis, sounds feeble when the audience is not my friend but a carless fellow bus passenger who is forced to endure these slow journeys every day.

(*d*) As designers of advertisements for charitable causes know, our ordinary self-serving reasons for not giving much (we need a new roof, I'm saving for my holiday, I'm not actually *very* rich) sound remarkably lame when we imagine them being presented to those for whom our lack of charity means misery and death.[9]

(*e*) And such quotidian reasons also sound feeble when they are presented to people whose sacrifice for the cause is much larger than the one the speaker is excusing himself from offering.[10]

---

[9] "How do you tell a person dying of hunger that there's nothing you can do?" (*Action Aid* leaflet, 1990).

[10] An exploitation of (inter alia) this particular relativity occurred in an advertisement of 1943 whose purpose was to promote the purchase of war bonds. In March 1944 the advertisement won a prize for its contribution to the war effort.

The top third of the ad's space pictures an American prisoner of war in a bleak cell. Below the picture, we find the following text:

WILL YOU WRITE A LETTER to a Prisoner of War . . . tonight?

Maybe he's one of Jimmie Doolittle's boys. Perhaps he was left behind when Bataan fell. Anyway, he's an American, and he hasn't had a letter in a long, long time.

And when you sit down to write, tell *him* why you didn't buy your share of War Bonds last pay day.

"Dear Joe," you might say, "the old topcoat was getting kind of threadbare, so I . . ."

No, cross it out. Joe might not understand about the topcoat, especially if he's shivering in a damp Japanese cell.

Let's try again. "Dear Joe, I've been working pretty hard and haven't had a vacation in over a year, so . . ."

Hell, better cross that out, too. They don't even get vacations where Joe's staying.

Well, what are you waiting for? Go ahead, write the letter to Joe. *Try* to write it, anyhow.

But mister, if somehow you find you can't finish that letter, will you, at least, do this for Joe? Will you up the amount of money you're putting into War Bonds and keep buying your share from here on in? (1945 *Britannica Book of the Year* [*A Record of the March of Events* of 1944] [Chicago: Encyclopaedia Britannica, 1945], p. 22).

A word about the form of this ad, and about the sources of its motivating power (if it did the motivating it should have done to deserve the prize it won).

(*f*) Since the pot should not call the kettle black, an employee may be unimpressed when a routinely tax-evading well-heeled superior dresses him down because of his modest appropriations from petty cash.

The examples show that arguments vary in their capacity to satisfy because of variations in people's epistemic (*a*) or moral

---

The ad is directed not, of course, at one person but at a large set of people, all the people in the condition of material life and personal intention of the civilian that the ad sketches. Yet the ad speaks as though to one person and it has that single person address a single member of the set of POWs. The content of the ad implies that civilians as such have some kind of obligation to POWs as such. But the ad aims to convey the obligation falling on many by selecting one individual from each of the two groups and figuring forth an encounter between them. Notice, moreover, that the ad would have sacrificed little or nothing of its purpose and power if its personal references had been pluralized, if, that is, the civilian had spoken of *our* threadbare coats, run-down sheds, and lacks of vacation, to an imagined *assembly* of POWs. (Compare first-person plural presentation of the incentive justification, by a rich person, or by all of them in unison, to all the poor people).

The ad makers thought that they could expose the insufficiency of the reasons civilians give themselves for not buying bonds by portraying a civilian offering them to Joe. And they were right that it is easier to face yourself when you decide for the stated reasons not to buy bonds if you do not have to face Joe at the same time.

The power of the ad to move the reader is multiply determined, mingling elements that go into types *c*, *d*, and *e* above. The ad simulates an immediacy between the civilian and Joe, such immediacy being one rhetorical effect of casting an argument in interpersonal form. And then, immediacy having been secured, there are two or three separable things, mixed here in a powerful cocktail, on which the ad relies: that Joe and I are members of the same community, and he is suffering; that Joe and I are coparticipants in an immensely important enterprise in which at least the *quality* of my life and that of the members of my family is at stake; and that Joe is a moral hero — look what he has given, for the sake of the mentioned enterprise, compared with the modest thing that I resist giving. These considerations combine to make me feel answerable to Joe. The ad says that although it sounds quite reasonable for a person to choose a new coat before buying more bonds, the burden of wearing a threadbare coat carries no justificatory weight when it is compared with the burden Joe carries: that, so the ad implies, explains the shame a civilian would feel in telling Joe that his threadbare coat was a good reason for not buying more bonds.

Finally, a comment on the role of immediacy, which, so I noted, is one source of the advertisement's power. Immediacy can contribute to persuasion in cases where what is rendered immediate is not a person (or a group) that is addressed. We do not speak to animals, but arguments justifying their use in certain experiments might be hard to deliver in the lab while those experiments are in train. We also do not speak to trees, but it might be harder to justify the size of the Sunday edition of the *New York Times* when one is standing in a majestic forest. So: having to face a person when uttering an argument is a special case of immediacy, not part of its general form, and it is perhaps not crucial to the ad's power that the POW is *addressed*, as opposed to just on scene when the argument is presented.

(*e, f*) or social (*c*) position, or because of issues of tact and embarrassment (*c, d, e*) and immediacy (*d*), or because being generous is more attractive than being grabby (*b*). I shall not here attempt a systematic taxonomy of ways that arguments subside in different sorts of interpersonal delivery. Instead, I pass to a type of case which is of special interest here, since the incentive argument belongs to it.

4.

In this type of case, an argument changes its aspect when its presenter is the person, or one of the people, whose choice, or choices, make one or more of the argument's premises true. By contrast with other presenters of the same argument, a person who makes, or helps to make, one of its premises true can be asked to justify the fact that it is true.[11] And sometimes he will be unable to provide a satisfying justification.

For a dramatic example of this structure, consider the argument for paying a kidnapper where the child will be freed only if the kidnapper is paid. There are various reasons for not paying. Some concern further consequences: maybe, for example, more kidnapping would be encouraged. And paying could be thought wrong not only in some of its consequences but in its nature: paying is acceding to a vile threat. You will nevertheless agree that, because so much is at stake, paying kidnappers is often justified. And the argument for paying a particular kidnapper, shorn of qualifications needed to neutralize the countervailing reasons mentioned a moment ago, might run as follows:

Children should be with their parents.

Unless they pay him, this kidnapper will not return this child to its parents.

So, this child's parents should pay this kidnapper.

---

[11] As opposed to the claim that it is true, which every presenter of the argument can be asked to justify.

Now, that form of the argument is entirely third-personal: in that form of it, anyone (save, perhaps, someone mentioned in the argument) might be presenting it to anyone. But let us now imagine the kidnapper himself presenting the argument, to, for example, the child's parents. (What will matter here is that he is doing the talking, rather than that they are doing the listening: the latter circumstance achieves prominence in section 11 below.) The argument that follows is the same as that given above, by an unimpeachable criterion of identity for arguments: its major premise states the same principle and its minor premise carries the same factual claim:

Children should be with their parents.

I shall not return your child unless you pay me.

So, you should pay me.

Notice, now, that despite what we can assume to be the truth of its premises and the validity of its inference, discredit attaches to anyone who utters this argument in the foregoing interpersonal setting, even though uttering the same argument in impersonal form is, in most cases,[12] an innocent procedure. And there is, of course, no mystery about why the argument's presenter attracts discredit in the exhibited interpersonal case. He does so because the fact to which he appeals, which is that you will get your child back only if you pay, is one that he deliberately causes to obtain: he makes that true, and to make that true is morally vile.

When he presents the argument, the kidnapper shows himself to be awful, but it is hardly necessary for us to reflect on his utterance of the argument to convince ourselves that he merits disap-

---

[12] I express myself in that cautious way because, apart from the case, if you want to allow it, in which the kidnapper himself uses the impersonal form of the argument, referring to himself as "he," there is the case of a person who puts it forth and conveys (for example, by his tone) that he is quite insensitive to the countervailing (if properly overridden) considerations, and/or that he sees nothing untoward in the kidnapper's threat, and/or that he sees human dealings on the model of interaction of impersonal forces.

proval. Independently of any such reflection, we amply realize that the kidnapper's conduct is wrong, and we need not be particularly scandalized by his frank avowal of it. Indeed, in certain instances a kidnapper's presentation of the argument will be a service to the parents, because sometimes his utterance of the argument's minor premise will, for the first time, put them in the picture about how to get their child back. One can even imagine a maybe slightly schizoid kidnapper suddenly thinking, "Omigod, I've forgotten to tell the kid's parents!" and experiencing some concern for them, and for the child, in the course of that thought.

Yet although what is (mainly) bad about the kidnapper is not his voicing the argument, but his making its minor premise true, he should still be ashamed to voice the argument, just because he makes that premise true. The fact that in some cases he would do further ill not to voice the argument does not falsify the claim that in all cases he reveals himself to be ghastly when he does voice it.

In the kidnapper argument, there are two groups of agents, the kidnapper and the parents, both referred to in the third person in the initial presentation of the argument, and referred to in the first and second persons in its revised presentation. Consider any argument that refers to distinct groups of people, A and B. There are many different ways in which such an argument might be presented. It might be uttered by members of A or of B or of neither group, and it might be addressed to members of either group or of neither. And all of that applies to the incentive argument, with the groups being talented rich people on the one hand and the worst off on the other. In my treatment of the incentive argument I shall mainly be interested in the case where a talented rich person puts it forward, sometimes no matter to whom and sometimes where it matters that poor people are his audience; and at one point I shall consider the opposite case, where a poor person addresses the argument to a talented rich one.

The incentive argument has something in common with the kidnapper argument, even though there are major differences between withholding a hostage and withholding labor until one gets the money one desires. But before looking more carefully at similarities and contrasts between the kidnapper and incentive arguments, I want to explain why the word "community" appears in the title of these lectures.

5.

In its familiar use, "community" covers a multitude of conditions, and I shall introduce the particular condition that I have in mind by relating it to the concept of a *comprehensive justification*.

Most policy arguments contain premises about how people will act when the policy is, and is not, in force. Schemes for housing, health, education, and the economy typically operate by altering agents' feasible sets, and their justifications usually say what agents facing those sets can be expected to choose to do.

Consider, then, a policy, P, and an argument purportedly justifying it, one of whose premises says that a subset, S, of the population will act in a certain fashion when P is in force. We engage in what might be called *comprehensive assessment* of the profferred justification of P when we ask whether the projected behavior of the members of S is itself justified. And *comprehensive justification* of P obtains only if that behavior is indeed justified.[13]

"We should do A because they will do B" may justify our doing A, but it does not justify it comprehensively if they are not justified in doing B, and we do not provide a comprehensive justification of our doing A if we set aside as irrelevant the question whether they are justified in doing B. Thus, insofar as we are expected to treat the incentive argument as though no question arises about the justification of the behavior of the talented rich that its minor premise describes, what we are offered may be a justification, but it is not a comprehensive justification, of the incentives policy.

---

[13] It follows, harmlessly, that penal policies adopted to reduce the incidence of crime lack comprehensive justification. The very fact that such a policy is justified shows that all is not well with society.

Now, a policy argument provides a comprehensive justification only if it passes what I shall call the *interpersonal test*. This tests how robust a policy argument is, by subjecting it to variation with respect to who is speaking and/or who is listening when the argument is presented. The test asks whether the argument could serve as a justification of a mooted policy when uttered by any member of society to any other member. So, to carry out the test, we hypothesize an utterance of the argument by a specified individual, or, more commonly, by a member of a specified group, to another individual, or to a member of another, or, indeed, the same, group. If, *because* of who is presenting it, and/or to whom it is presented, the argument cannot serve as a justification of the policy, then whether or not it passes as such under other dialogical conditions, it fails (*tout court*) to provide a comprehensive justification of the policy.

A salient way that arguments fail, when put to this test, and the only mode of test failure that will henceforth figure in these lectures, is that the speaker cannot fulfill a demand for justification that does not arise when the argument is presented by and/or to others. So, to anticipate what I shall try to show, the incentive argument does not serve as a justification of inequality on the lips of the talented rich, because they cannot answer a demand for justification that naturally arises when they present the argument, namely, *why* would you work less hard if income tax were put back up to 60 percent? The rich will find that question difficult no matter who puts it to them, but I shall often focus on the case where their interlocutors are badly off people, because in that setting the question, and the difficulty the rich have with it, may lead to further dialogical development that carries further illumination.

When the justification of policies that mention groups of people is presented in the usual way, with exclusively third-person reference to groups and their members, the propriety of the question why various people are disposed to act as they do is not always apparent. It becomes evident when we picture the relevant people themselves rehearsing the argument, and sometimes more so when the audience is a strategically selected one. The test of interpersonal presentation makes vivid that the justification of policy characteristically depends on circumstances that are not exogenous with respect to human agency.

And so to community. I began by observing that there is more than one kind of community, and I must now specify the kind that is relevant to present concerns. First, though, a few points about the semantics of the word "community."

Like "friendship," "community" functions both as a count noun and as a mass noun. It is a count noun when it denotes sets of people variously bound or connected (the European community, London's Italian community, our community) and it is a mass noun when we speak of how much community there is in a certain society, when we say that some action enhances or reduces, or some attitude honors or violates, community, and so on.

A community, one could say, is a set of people among whom there is community: that is how the count-notion and the mass-notion are linked. "Community" is in this respect like "friendship": a friendship is a relationship in which friendship obtains. Notice that friends can do and feel things that are inconsistent with friendship without thereby dissolving their friendship. There can be a lapse of friendship in a friendship without that friendship ceasing to be. But there cannot (enduringly) be *no* friendship in a friendship. And all that is also true of community: there can be violations and lapses of community in a community, but there cannot be no community in a community.

In addition to community in the adjectivally unqualified sense where it is analogous not only in form but also in content to friendship, there are specific types of community, some of which do, while others do not, contribute to community in the just denoted sense. And types of community (mass-wise) distinguish types of community (count-wise). Linguistic community, or community of language, constitutes a linguistic community as such;

community of nationality establishes a national community; and community of interest in stamps binds the philatelic community.

The form of community that concerns me here, which I shall call *justificatory community*, prevails in justificatory communities. And justificatory community, though something of a concocted notion, contributes to community *tout court*, that is, to community in the full (adjectivally unqualified) sense sketched a moment ago. A justificatory community is a set of people among whom there prevails a norm (which need not always be satisfied) of comprehensive justification. If what certain people are disposed to do when a policy is in force is part of the justification of that policy, it is considered appropriate to ask them to justify the relevant behavior, and it detracts from justificatory community when they cannot do so. It follows that an argument for a policy satisfies the requirement of justificatory community, with respect to the people it mentions, only if it passes the interpersonal test. And if all arguments for the policy fail that test, then the policy itself evinces lack of justificatory community, whatever else might nevertheless be said in its favor.

Now, an argument fails the interpersonal test, and is therefore inconsistent with community, if relevant agents *could* not justify the behavior the argument ascribes to them. What if the agents are actually asked to justify their stance and, for one reason or another, they refuse to do so? Then the argument in question does not necessarily fail the test, for it might be that they could justify their stance. But if their reason for refusing to justify it is that they do not think themselves accountable to their interrogators, that they do not think that they *need* provide a justification, then they are forswearing community with the rest of us in respect of the policy issue in question. They are asking us to treat them like a set of Martians in the light of whose predictable aggressive, or even benign, behavior it is wise for us to take certain steps, but whom we should not expect to engage in justificatory dialogue.

To employ the interpersonal test and to regard its failure as indicative of a lack of community is to presuppose nothing about which particular collections of people constitute communities in the relevant sense. Some may think that there is no reason why there should be community between rich and poor in a society, and they may therefore regard failure of the test as uninteresting, or, if interesting, then not because it shows lapse of community. Others, by contrast, might think that community ought to obtain among all human beings, so that it would stain a policy argument advanced by rich countries in North-South dialogue if it could not pass muster in explicit I-thou form.[14] The thesis associated with the interpersonal test is that, if a policy justification fails it, then anyone proposing that justification in effect represents the people it mentions as *pro tanto* out of community with one another. Whether they should be in community with one another is a separate question. That depends on a doctrine, not to be articulated here, about what the proper boundaries of a community are. In my own (here undefended) view, it diminishes the democratic character of a society if it is not a community in the present sense, since we do not make policy *together* if we make it in the light of what some of us do that cannot be justified to others.

It is often said that it is unrealistic to expect a modern society to be a community, and it is no doubt inconceivable that there should be a standing disposition of warm mutual identification between any pair of citizens in a large and heterogeneous polity. But community here is not some soggy mega-*Gemeinschaftlichkeit*. Instead, my claim about the incentive justification is that, to appropriate a phase of Rawls's, it does not supply "a public basis

[14] In *Justice as Fairness* (p. 152 n. 28) Rawls expresses a view which has a bearing on how wide community can be: "the allegiance to, or the motivational support needed, for the difference principle to be effective presupposes a degree of homogeneity among peoples and a sense of social cohesion and closeness that cannot be expected in a society of states." This implies that there is sufficient such closeness domestically. (Three further contrasts between the single- and multi-society cases that Rawls sketches in the footnote seem to me to fail, but none of them matter here.)

in the light of which citizens can justify to one another their common institutions" and that the justification is therefore incompatible with what Rawls calls "ties of civic friendship." [15]

Now some examples of the battery of concepts introduced above.

Under the premiership of Harold Wilson, some economic policies were justified by reference to the intentions of the so-called "gnomes of Zurich," the international bankers who, it was said, would react punitively to various government decisions. It was a mark of their *foreign* status that economic policy had to *placate* those bankers, and although it might have been thought that they should behave differently, it would not have been considered appropriate for the British government to call upon them to do so. But such a call would surely be appropriate in the case of people conceived as belonging to our own community. Nor should members of our own community need to be *placated* by our community's policies: when justified, their demands should be satisfied, but that is a different matter.

An example that for some readers may be close to home: the policy argument that rates of pay to British academics should be raised, since otherwise they will succumb to the lure of high foreign salaries. We can suppose that academics are indeed disposed to leave the country because of current salary levels. The issue of whether, nevertheless, they should emigrate is pertinent to the policy argument when they are regarded as fellow members of community who owe the rest a justification for decisions that affect the welfare of the country. And many British academics with an inclination to leave who put the stated policy argument contrive to avoid that issue by casting the minor premise of the argument in the third person. They say: "Academics will go abroad," not: "We'll go abroad."

The connection between sharing community membership and being open to requests for justification comes out nicely in an ex-

---

[15] John Rawls, "Kantian Constructivism in Moral Theory," *Journal of Philosophy* 77, no. 9 (September 1980): 561; Rawls, *A Theory of Justice*, p. 536.

ample of current interest. The Moscow generals might address the Lithuanian independence movement leaders as follows: "Widespread bloodshed is to be avoided. If you persist in your drive for independence, we shall intervene forcefully, and there will be widespread bloodshed as a result. You should therefore abandon your drive for independence." The Lithuanian leaders might now ask the generals to justify their conditional intention to intervene forcefully. If the generals brush that question aside, they forswear justificatory community with the Lithuanians.

The Lithuanian leaders might produce a parallel argument: "Widespread bloodshed is to be avoided. If you intervene forcefully, we shall nevertheless persist in our drive for independence, and there will be widespread bloodshed as a result. You should therefore abandon your plan to intervene forcefully." And the Lithuanians, too, might feel no obligation to justify their intentions to the generals. If, on the other hand, both sides labor under such a sense of obligation, they will enter a justificatory exchange in which each tries to show that the other's minor premise, whether true or not, should be false.

6.

The interpersonal test focuses on an utterance of an argument, but what it tests, through examination of that utterance, is the argument itself. If lack of community is displayed when the rich present the incentive argument, then the argument itself (irrespective of who affirms it) represents relations between rich and poor as at variance with community. It follows, if I am right, that the incentive argument can justify inequality only in a society where interpersonal relations lack a communal character, in the specified sense.

Sometimes, as, for example, in the kidnapper case, the interpersonal test will be a roundabout way of proving an already evident point (in the kidnapper case, that there is significant lack of community between the kidnapper and the parents). But in other cases the test will illuminate, and I believe that the incentive argu-ment is one of them. The argument is generally presented in thoroughly third-personal terms and, relatedly, as though no ques-tion arises about the attitudes and choices of the rich people it mentions. When, by contrast, we imagine a talented rich person himself affirming the argument, then background issues of equality and obligation come clearly into view, and, if I am right, the rich are revealed to be out of community with the poor in respect of the economic dimension of their lives. So we see more deeply into the character of the incentive argument when we cast it in the selected I-thou terms.

Now, an important qualification. I say that the incentive argu-ment shows itself to be repugnant to community when it is offered *on its own* by well-off people. I insert that phrase because the present case against the argument lapses when the argument appears in combination with claims about desert, and/or with Nozick-like claims about a person's entitlements to the reward his or her labor would command on an unfettered market. I do not myself accept that sort of compound justification of incentive inequality, but I do not here contend that it fails the interpersonal test. My target here is the unadorned or naked use of the incentive justification. It is often used nakedly, and with plenty of emphasis that it is being used nakedly. That emphasis occurs when advo-cates say it is an advantageous feature of the incentive justification that it employs no controversial moral premises about desert or entitlement. (Notice that, since John Rawls rejects use of desert and entitlement to justify inequalities, the Rawlsian endorsement of incentives takes what I call a naked form.)

The sequence of claims that I make goes as follows: The tal-ented rich cannot justify the fact that the minor premise of the (naked) incentive argument is true. If they cannot justify the truth of its minor premise, then they cannot use the argument as a justification of inequality. If they cannot use it as a justification of inequality, then it cannot be used as a justification within community. If it cannot be used as a justification within community, then anyone who uses it (in effect) represents society as at variance with community when he does so.

II. Testing the Incentive Argument

7.

The kidnapper argument discredits its advocate when the kidnapper puts it forward himself because, as I said (see sec. 4), he *makes* it true that the parent gets their child back only if they pay, and to make that true is morally vile.

Accordingly, to discredit first-person affirmation of the incentive argument in a parallel way, I must defend two claims. First, that in a sufficiently similar sense, the rich *make* it true that they will not work as hard at 60 percent tax as they do at 40 percent: I have to show that the minor premise[16] of the incentive argument owes its truth to their decisions and intentions. (I say *sufficiently* similar, because there undoubtedly are some significant differences here, consequent on the fact that the rich are not an individual but a group, and a group with shifting membership: at the end of this section I address some of the complication which that fact generates.) And it also needs to be shown that, deprived as they here are of recourse to the considerations of desert and entitlement that are set aside in a naked (see sec. 6) use of the incentive argument, the rich cannot justify making the stated proposition true. I am not, of course, obliged to maintain, even then, that their making it true puts them on a moral par with kidnappers, but just that, if their posture is defensible, then its defense rests on grounds of the sort that a naked user of the incentive argument forgoes.

I turn to my first task, which is to show that the talented rich do make the factual premise of the argument true. Let us ask: if

---

[16] Or, strictly, part *a* of that premise: part *b* is true only if others — for example, the government — act in certain required ways. But for simplicity I shall continue to speak of the rich making the factual minor premise (*tout court*) true.

that premise is true, then why is it true? Is it true because the rich are *unable* to work at 60 percent as hard as they do at 40? Or is it true because they are *unwilling* to work that hard at 60 percent? If the truth of the premise reflects inability, then we cannot say that, in the relevant sense, the rich *make* the premise true. An inability explanation of the truth of the premise means that the rich could not, by choosing differently, make the premise false.

There are two forms that an inability claim might take. In the first form of the claim, the rich cannot work hard unless they consume things that cost a great deal of money.

Now, it might well be true that without enough money to buy superior relaxation some high-talent performances would be impossible: perhaps the massively self-driving executive does need, to be effective, more expensive leisure between one day's work and the next than he can get living in ordinary accommodation on an average wage. (When I say that he might *need* high-quality leisure, I refer not to his preference ordering or utility function but to what it is physically and/or psychologically possible for him to do. That kind of capacity limitation interacts causally with a person's utility function, but it is not identical with it or an aspect of it. But the income gap which that consideration would justify is surely only a fraction of the one that obtains even at 60 percent top tax. The extra money which executives (and so forth) get at 40 percent can hardly be required to finance whatever luxuries we might imagine that they strictly *need* to perform at a high level: they could afford those necessary luxuries with what they have left even when they pay at 60 percent tax.

In a different version of the claim that the rich could not work as hard at 60 percent tax as they do at 40 percent, what they are said to need is not the goods that only a lot of money will buy but the *prospect* of getting those goods or that money: the high reward is now said to be indispensable to *motivation*, or morale. (You eventually give the biscuit to the performing dog so that the same procedure will work again next time, and not because the dog needs the calories it gets from the biscuit to enable it to go on performing.) This motivation story does not say that, unless they are handsomely paid, the rich will *choose* not to work very hard: the proposition that they have a real choice in the matter is just what the inability claim is designed to contradict. What is rather meant is that the allure of big bucks sustains, and is needed to sustain, the motivational drive required for heavy effort: the rich just cannot *get* themselves to work as hard when they expect to be taxed at 60 percent as they can get themselves to work when they expect to be taxed at 40 percent.

Now, in my opinion, there is not much truth in this contention: it represents people of talent as more feeble than, on the whole, they are. It is not likely to be lack of power to do otherwise that causes the rich to take longer holidays, to knock off at five instead of at six, or not to bother trying to get one more order, those being the things that they do when the income tax rises, if the minor premise of the incentive argument is true. The tax rise means that the rich face a new and less appealing schedule of the costs and benefits of alternative courses of action, and they will, of course, find it harder to raise up enthusiasm for choices that now promise smaller rewards. It does not follow that they cannot make, and effectively pursue, those choices.

Still, I say that there is not much, not no, truth in the contention mooted here. For I recognize that a perception that reward is "too low" can cause, at least somewhat independently of the will, a morose reluctance which operates as a drag on performance. But we should ask what brings about that disabling perception. And if two of its prominent causes were its only causes, then, as I shall now try to explain, the "motivation" version of the inability contention would be disqualified.

One thing that causes a dispiriting feeling that reward is too low is disappointed expectation. Socialized as they have been in a severely unequal society, the talented rich of course anticipate a handsome return for their exertions. They will therefore be downcast when such return is not forthcoming, even when they do not judge that they deserve or are otherwise entitled to it. But it is not unlikely that they also do make judgments like that. They think that they have a right to golden rewards if they work hard, and so powerful is that belief that it can act as a further cause of low morale: it can make the thought of working hard at 60 percent tax fill them with a truly disabling dismay.

Now, an inability to work hard at 60 percent tax (in people who, *ex hypothesi*, routinely work that hard at 40 percent) that reflects habituated expectation, or judgment of entitlement, or both, cannot count here, in rebuttal of the claim that optional decisions of the talented rich make the minor premise of the incentive argument true. Consider, first, the habituation factor. We are here engaged in a ground-level investigation of a certain justification of inequality. It is therefore inappropriate, by way of contribution to that justification, to cite mere habituation to unequal rewards. Habits can change,[17] and they are therefore beside the point in a fundamental inquiry. And the causal force of belief in the rightness of high reward (which helps to sustain the habitual expectation) must also be ignored here. For we are here envisaging the talented rich uttering the incentive argument in its naked form, in which invocation of entitlement is pointedly eschewed. There would, accordingly, be a kind of pragmatic inconsistency if the rich had to cite their own belief in entitlement when rejecting the claim that the truth of the minor premise of the argument

---

[17] If not always at the level of the individual, then certainly at the social level, through reformed structures of education. And even if the relevant habits could not change, that would have more implications for the practice than for the theory of justice. As Rawls says, "We do not consider the strains of commitment that might result from some people having to move from a favored position in an unjust society to a less favored position (either absolutely or relatively or both) in this just society. . . . The strains of commitment test applied to cases of hypothetical transition from unjust societies is irrelevant" ("Reply to Alexander and Musgrave," *Quarterly Journal of Economics*, 1974, p. 653, and see Rawls, *Justice as Fairness*, p. 44, on the role of education in sustaining a just society: the relevant strains of commitment are those that survive a socialization process that instills egalitarian principles in the young).

reflects what they are themselves willing and unwilling to do.[18]

If the "motivation" variant of the inability claim depended entirely on habit and normative belief, we could safely set it aside. We could say that if it is true, it is compromised in the present context by what its truth rests on, that it does not furnish an appropriate reason for saying that talented rich people could not work as hard at 60 percent tax as they do at 40. The claim might help to silence moralistic charges against the present generation of talented rich people, but it could not contribute to a robust vindication of inequality in human society.

Now I firmly believe that such truth as the inability claim possesses does depend, entirely, on factors of habit and ideology that, for the stated reasons, must here be ruled out. I think it hard to believe otherwise, when one focuses on the inability claim proper, as opposed to the claim, with which it is readily confused, that the talented rich have a *right* not to work as hard at 60 percent tax as they do at 40 percent. Nevertheless, I have not shown that there exist no relevant deeper restrictions on motivation, and, in the seminar following these lectures, I was rightly taken to task on this score by Samuel Scheffler, who did not reject my conclusion, but who emphasized that it had not been demonstrated, not, at any rate, in the general case, where the issue is not whether these particular people could keep their shoulders to the wheel under the contemplated tax rise, but whether *some* significant inequalities are required, in general, for optimal economic motivation.

For all that I had shown, so Scheffler said, incentives might elicit motives that could not "be summoned at will," that nothing

---

[18] That particular inconsistency would not attach to naked use of the argument by a third party who cites (without endorsing) the belief of the rich in their entitlements as what happens to explain the truth of the argument's minor premise. But reference to that belief would nevertheless be unacceptable when the argument for inequality is pitched at a fundamental level. If the rich are unable to work as hard at 60 percent tax as they do at 40 because they believe that they should be paid more if they work harder, then the stated incapacity cannot, without bizarre circularity, figure in an argument which would justify the proposition that it is *fundamentally right* that they be paid more for working harder.

else would induce, and that would enable agents to perform better than they otherwise could. To illustrate the form of his objection, he cited the "runner who needs competition to achieve his fastest times," and people who work best under the pressure, adversity, or challenge. The compelling examples warn against being simple-minded about psychological feasibility. They show that what people are able to do depends on the reasons they have for doing it: with different reasons, the adrenalin flows to different extents. And Scheffler concluded that a fully adequate reply to the inability claim would have to include "at least the rudiments of a serious psychology of egalitarianism . . . a realistic account of the human motivational resources and mechanisms that egalitarian . . . institutions would expect to engage."

I accept this criticism, which calls for a program of work that manifestly cannot be accomplished here. It needs to be shown that a society of people who believe in equality and act accordingly is reproducible, that it is not fated to collapse under disintegrative strains. Such societies seem to be possible on a small scale, and we need to explore what constraints of human nature and organization make them difficult — as they undoubtedly are — on a larger scale, and whether those difficulties approach impossibility. As a practical proposal, normative egalitarianism indeed requires a corresponding psychology. If the research program to which the Scheffler objection points were to deliver negative results, equality might still be a tenable value, but it could not, unmodified, represent a policy goal.

In pursuing such a program, in the search for possible equality-supporting "human motivational resources and mechanisms," it is not inappropriate to reflect on the other (nonincentive) examples that illustrate the form of Scheffler's objection. For they all involve a drive to perform well, whether as an end in itself or as a way of impressing others, and/or oneself. The motivation in question contrasts with the search for gains which, like money, are quite external to the performance itself. The examples remind us that the desire to achieve, to shine, and, yes, to outshine, can elicit enormous effort even in the absence of pecuniary motivation. Of course, many would say that such nonpecuniary mechanisms just replace money inequality by status inequality, and that is yet another large challenge to which I cannot respond fully here.[19] Notice, though, that the notion of "replacement" is somewhat unapt, since money inequality itself generates status inequality. Status is not, moreover, redistributable in the same way that material resources are, and it therefore does not raise the same issues as money inequality does for an egalitarianism whose inspiration (see sec. 1 above) is that some people lead unnecessarily hard lives.

And there is another consideration to be borne in mind: in estimating what it would be like for a person to accept a salary that is much lower than what full exercise of market power would provide, the strain to think about is the one he would feel when, *ex hypothesi*, people like him are accepting similarly modest salaries. We are talking about an egalitarian society, not about a population of talented people each of whom is a unique moral hero.

That is the best I can do, right now, by way of facing up to the prodigious task Scheffler set me. So, realizing that some of the required case has not been proven, I nevertheless now set the motivation claim aside, and, with all the relevant implied *caveats*, I conclude that the reason why the minor premise of the incentive argument is true (if it is true) is that the executive and his like are *willing* to work hard only at a 40 percent top tax rate.

But, before we ask whether that choice is justified, let me address the complication that, even if each talented individual chooses not to work hard at a 60 percent tax, no such individual makes the minor premise of the incentive argument true, since its truth requires that many such individuals make similar choices.

---

[19] For an ingenious attempt to meet it, see Joseph Carens, *Equality, Moral Incentives, and the Market* (Chicago: University of Chicago Press, 1981). There are substantial flaws in Carens's book, but it is, in my view, a profound and pioneering work.

Here, then, is a disanalogy with the case of the kidnapper, since he makes the minor premise of his argument true all by himself.

In response to this important point, I shall say only two things here. First, notice that an individual talented rich person is relevantly analogous to a member of a large band of kidnappers, who could also truthfully say: it will make no, or not much, difference if I change my choice. Yet, if a member of such a band puts the kidnapper argument in the first-person pural, if he says, "Giving *us* the money is the only way you will get your child back," then the fact that he is only (a dispensable) one of the "us" who together ensure that the child is held captive does not make his posture justifiable. And it is similarly true that if what the rich together cause could not be justified if one rich person caused it, then being only one rich person and not all of them would not suffice to make one's behavior justifiable. One might not be *as* responsible as when one achieves something without assistance, but one also could not say that the result had nothing to do with one's actions.[20]

And whatever the complex truth may be about individual responsibility for a collectively produced result, I am not here primarily interested in commenting on the moral character of rich people. My primary interest is in an argument which, I claim, fails the interpersonal test. Rich people may benefit from a practice on which they have little occasion to reflect. If we here (counterfactually) imagine them trying to justify that practice by recourse to the incentive argument, it is in order to investigate not, in the first instance, how blameworthy they are, but how that argument fares in the light of a norm of justificatory community.

---

[20] For a case which bears on the issue dealt with in the foregoing paragraph, see Derek Parfit's "harmless torturers" at p. 80 of his *Reasons and Persons* (Oxford: Clarendon Press, 1984). If someone objects that the talented rich are unlike the just-imagined kidnappers in not being an organized group, then, so I believe, reflection on Parfit's case shows that they need not be one for my purposes. And one could also put forward a persuasive case of relatively unorganized kidnappers, where all that is essential to the analogy is restored, but I shall spare you the rococo detail.

8.

In its standard presentation, the incentive argument is put forward as though it is irrelevant to its assessment whether the rich are justified in making its minor premise true, and as though it would be inappropriate to put that question to them. I have protested that the question can be considered inappropriate only if the rich are conceived as inaccessible third persons who do not belong to the society for which the incentive policy is proposed. It does not follow that what the rich do could not be justified, that the neglected question, having been raised, could not be answered satisfactorily. In this section I explore possible answers to it.

The relevant part of the premise (that is, part *a*) says that, if the top tax rises to 60 percent, the talented rich will work less hard than they do now, when the top tax is 40 percent. And, so we have concluded, that is because they will then *choose* to work less hard. As a result of that choice, the badly off will be worse off than they were before (by the truth of part *b* of the minor premise of the incentive argument), and, a fortiori, worse off than they would be if the talented rich maintained at 60 percent tax the effort they put in at 40 percent. On the factual assumptions behind the minor premise of the argument, the ordering of benefit to the badly off from the three work/tax packages just mentioned is as follows:

1 The talented rich work *w* at 60 percent tax
2 The talented rich work *w* at 40 percent tax
3 The talented rich work *w-x* at 60 percent tax,

where *w* is the amount the rich choose to work at 40 percent and *x* the amount by which they reduce their input if the tax rises to 60 percent.

We must now ask whether the choices of rich people, which make 3 rather than 1 true if the tax rises, and thereby make the badly off worse off than when the tax is low, can be justified, when notions of desert and entitlement are not allowed to figure in justifications.

In certain cases, where working just as hard at 60 percent tax as one did at 40 percent would mean an oppressive existence, the choice that the rich make is undoubtedly justified. Think of those harried and haggard Yuppies, or overworked surgeons, who really would lead miserable lives if the massive amount of work that they do were not compensated by the massive amount of income that leads them to choose to work that hard. We can set such "special burden" cases aside, not because they do not exist, but because of the nature of the justification of the talented rich person's choice in this sort of case.

Let me explain. In the present exercise, the incentive argument is supposed to justify inequality. But when special burden is invoked, what we get is not a justification of an inequality, all things considered, that incentives produce, but a denial that they do produce an inequality, all things considered. That is so because, when we compare people's material situations, we must take into account not only the income they get but also what they have to do to get it. Accordingly, if the talented rich could plausibly claim special burden, the move to the 40 percent tax which induced them to work harder might also be required for the sake of equality: where work is specially arduous, or stressful, higher remuneration is a counterbalancing equalizer, on a sensible view of how to judge whether or not things are equal. Since I oppose only those incentives that induce unambiguous inequalities, my opposition retires in face of the special burden case, and I acknowledge that, where special burden holds, the rich have a persuasive answer to the question why they make the minor premise of the incentive argument true.

My primary target, as a philosopher, is a pattern of justification, from which the incentive argument deviates when special burden holds. But, as a politically engaged person, I also have another target: the real-world inequality that is actually defended on incentive grounds. And because I also have that second target, I have to claim that the special burden case is statistically uncommon. But I do not find that difficult to do, since I am confident that, if talented rich people were to provide, at 60 percent tax, the greater effort we are supposing them to supply at 40 percent, then a large majority of them would still have not only higher incomes but also more fulfilling jobs than ordinary people enjoy.[21]

Since I propose to cast no doubt on the truth of the minor premise of the incentive argument, I must now set aside another case, that in which well-paid talented people so enjoy their work or are so dedicated to making money that they would actually work no less hard after a tax rise. Such people are bluffing if, in the hope of inducing a political effect, they announce that a tax rise would lead them to work less. But in their case, and, a fortiori, in the case of talented people whose labor supply curve is in the relevant range not merely vertical but backward-bending, the minor premise of the incentive argument is false, since these people will *not* work less hard if the tax goes up, and this case is therefore out of bounds here.

Summarizing and extending the foregoing discussion, I now ask you to look at a table that depicts three positions that the talented rich person might be thought to be in. Of the three cases that appear in the table, two are, for different reasons, irrelevant to our purposes, the special burden case because it poses no problem for the egalitarian point of view (and is in any event not

---

[21] Anyone who dissents from that statistical assessment is invited to settle for the following more modest claim, which will suffice here: although it is difficult to tell how much any given individual enjoys or disenjoys his work, it is false that jobs demanding talent are, on the whole, less satisfying. Accordingly, the consideration of burden cannot justify the fact that on the whole they command much more pay.

It is an important point, for Rawls, that the talented are fortunate to be talented, and that is partly because the exercise of talent in work is satisfying. Accordingly, Rawlsians are not well placed to adduce the special burden consideration in support of the justice of incentives. As Robert Nozick remarks, "Rawls is *not* imagining that inequalities are needed to fill positions that everyone can do equally well, or that the most drudgery-filled positions that require the least skill will command the highest income" (*Anarchy, State, and Utopia* [New York: Basic Books, 1974], p. 188).

widely instantiated), and the case of bluff, because in that case the minor premise of the incentive argument is false. So, from now on, let us focus on what is called the standard case in the table.

In the table, w denotes the amount which the rich actually work at 40 percent, and w-x denotes some significantly smaller amount. In all three case, the rich prefer working w at 40 percent to working w-x at 60 percent. This preference may not be readily apparent, but we can demonstrate[22] that they have it. For they choose to work w, rather than w-x, when the tax is 40 percent,

Benefit to the (currently) badly off	Preference orderings of the rich across three work/tax packages
	The standard case
2	Work w at 40%
3	Work w-x at 60%
1	Work w at 60% (and be much better off than others are)
	The bluff case
2	Work w at 40%
1	Work w at 60%
3	Work w-x at 60% (and be much better off than others are)
	The special burden case
2	Work w at 40%
3	Work w-x at 60%
1	Work w at 60% (and be worse off than others are as a result)

[22] On the usual economists' assumptions, which are innocent here, that choice tracks preference, and that wide choice is preferred to narrow.

and they must prefer *w-x* at 40 percent to *w-x* at 60, since work is the same and income is higher in the first package. It follows that the rich prefer working harder at 40 percent to working less hard at 60.

The preference orderings of the rich are identical in the standard and special burden cases. The difference between those cases (which is formulated in parentheses) lies in the comparison between the lot of the rich and that of other people when the rich are at the bottom of that preference ordering. This comparison reflects both income level and quality of work experience: were they to work as hard at 60 percent as they do at 40, the rich would in the special burden case be worse off than others are, but in the standard case they would still be much better off than others are. The ordering of benefit to the badly off from the various work-tax packages (which is given by the numbers in the column on the left, and which is the same in all three cases) is based on the assumption that part *b* of the minor premise of the incentive argument is true (so "*w* at 40 percent" ranks above "*w-x* at 60 percent") and on the further assumption that, if the rich worked as hard at 60 as they do at 40, then that would bring still further benefit to the poor (so "*w* at 60 percent" ranks above "*w* at 40 percent").

The interpersonal test has talented rich people *themselves* uttering the incentive argument. Now, for present purposes, the talented rich do not fall under the bluff case, in which the minor premise is false: they really will work less if the tax goes up. And, if we follow a distinction that has found favor with philosophers, the rich do not *threaten* anything if they utter the incentive argument, since, in the recommended distinction, you merely *warn* that you will do *A* when you are bent on doing *A* independently of the leverage you get from saying that you will do it. Notice that, in the recommended distinction, a kidnapper who likes children merely *warns* if he would actually prefer (for nonstrategic reasons) to keep the child if he is not paid: this shows that, under the recommended distinction, nonthreatening warnings can be very unpleasant.

So imagine, now, a set of highly paid managers and professionals addressing poorly paid workers, unemployed people, and people indigent for various personal and situational reasons, who depend on state welfare. The managers are lobbying against a rise in tax from 40 to 60 percent, and this is what they say:

> Public policy should make the worst off people (in this case, as it happens, you) better off.
>
> If the top tax goes up to 60 percent, we shall work less hard, and, as a result, the position of the poor (your position) will be worse.
>
> So, the top tax on our income should not be raised to 60 percent.

Although these argument-uttering rich may not, for one or other reason, count as *threatening* the poor, they remain people of superior income and form of life who could continue to work as now if the tax rose to 60 percent, and thereby bring more benefit to the poor, while still being much better off than they are, but who would refuse to do that. They say, in effect: we are unwilling to do what we could do to make you better off and yet still be much better off, ourselves, than you are. We realize that, at the present level of fuel allowance, many of you will be very cold this winter.[23] If the tax went up to 60 percent and we worked no less hard in response, revenue for fuel expenditure could rise, and some of you would be more comfortable. But in fact we would work less, and you would be worse off, following such a tax rise.

Having presented their argument, the rich are not well placed to answer a poor person who asks: "Given that you would still be much better off than we are if you worked as you do now at the 60 percent tax, what justifies your intention to work less if the tax

---

[23] According to Robin Cook, MP, Labour spokesman on health, in the severe winter of 1991 there were 4,000 more deaths of old people than are usual in such a period.

rises to that level?" For these rich people do not say that they deserve a lot because of their prodigious effort, or merit more because of their higher contribution to production. There is in their approach no appeal to such controversial moral premises, and many of them would think that, being free of such premises, their argument is consequently less vulnerable. And they cannot respond by saying that the money inequality which they defend is necessary to make the poor better off, since it is they who make it necessary, and the question put by the poor asks, in effect, what their justification is for making it necessary.

The incentive argument does furnish the poor with a reason to accept the inequality that it recommends. For the poor can take it as given that the rich are determined to sustain the intentions that make the argument work. But the argument cannot operate like that for the rich themselves: since they cannot treat their own choices as objective data, they cannot take it as given that the minor premise of the argument is true. Correspondingly, and unlike the poor, they need a justification not for accepting but for imposing the inequality that the argument defends.

But it might be said that the rich can indeed respond convincingly to the poor, and without advancing the controversial claims about desert and entitlement that are here ruled out. They can say: "Look, it simply would not be worth our while to work that hard if the tax rate were any higher, and if you were in our shoes you would feel the same way." [24] Would that not be a good answer to the question the poor pose?

As I shall presently allow, there is some power in this answer. But its rhetorical cast makes it seem more powerful than it is.

Notice, to begin with, that the first part ("Look . . . higher") of the quoted plea has no independent interest, no interest, that is, which is independent of the associated claim that the poor, if

---

[24] This piece of dialogue comes from Samuel Scheffler's seminar commentary on these lectures. Scheffler pressed the challenge to which the rest of this section is a response.

better placed, would feel (and act) as the rich now do. For it is a presupposition of the challenge the poor put to the rich that the latter do prefer, and intend, to work less hard if the tax goes up, and in speaking of what is "worth their while" the rich can only be reminding the poor of those preferences and intentions: they cannot mean, for example, that they are paid nothing, or paid badly, if they work hard at a 60 percent rate of tax.

So the burden of the rhetorically presented justificatory move is that a typical poor person would behave just as the rich, on the whole, do. But there is something that the poor person can say in reply. He can say: "Neither of us really knows how I would behave. Not all rich people market maximize as a matter of course, and I hope that, if I were rich, I would not belong to the vast majority that do, especially if I retained a lively sense of what it is like to be in the condition I am now actually in." (A slave need not be impressed when a master says: "Had you been born into the slaveholder class, you too would have lived well and treated your slaves like slaves." Such counterfactual predictions do not show that what people at a certain social level typically choose to do is justifiable.[25]

Suppose, now, that the rich abandon the vivid but problematic "you'd do the same in my shoes" style of justification. Suppose they just say (this being the content of the text to note 24, without its rhetorical cast) that, even when desert and entitlement are set aside, only an extreme moral rigorist could deny that *every person has a right to pursue self-interest to some reasonable extent* (even when that makes things worse than they need be for badly off people).

I do not wish to reject the italicized principle, which affirms what Samuel Scheffler has called an "agent-centered prerogative."[26] But a modest right of self-interest seems insufficient to

[25] I have always thought that the right reply to a white South African who says, to an anti-Apartheid advocate, "You would see things differently if you were in my position," is: "Quite: I'm sure it does blind one's vision."

[26] See his *Rejection of Consequentialism* (Oxford: Clarendon Press, 1982).

justify the range of inequality, the extremes of wealth and poverty, that actually obtain in the society under discussion. Entitlement or desert might justify vast differences between rich and poor: no limit to the inequality they might endorse is inscribed in them. This is particularly clear in the case of the entitlement principle that I am absolute owner of my own labor power. When my power to produce is conceived as fully private property, I may do with it as I will and demand what I may for its use. A proportionately greater attention to one's own interest, as opposed to that of others, is more limited in its justificatory reach, and it seems unlikely to justify the existing contrast of luxury and want.

Now, it might be objected that, in characterizing the position of the less well off as one of deprivation or want, I am unfairly tilting the balance against the incentive argument. To such an objection I have three replies.

First, I am in this part concerned with a real political use of the incentive argument. Reference to real circumstances is therefore entirely appropriate.

Second, the incentive argument is quite general. It should therefore apply no matter how badly off the badly off are, both absolutely and relatively to the well off. Accordingly, it is methodologically proper to focus on particularly dramatic cases of its application.

And it is precisely when the condition of the badly off is especially wretched that the *major* premise of the incentive argument can pass as compelling. Where the worst off are not too badly off, it looks more fanatical to assign absolute priority to their claims. But the stronger the case for ameliorating the situation of the badly off is, the more discreditable (if I am right) the incentive argument is on the lips of the rich. So the argument is most shameful where, at first sight, it is most apt.

Now, a world that implements John Rawls's *two* principles of justice will not display the degree of inequality that characterizes contemporary Britain. Accordingly, the foregoing attempt to neutralize the agent-prerogative defense of the incentive argument in its common use will not serve to defeat it as a defense of the Rawlsian use of the argument, and more will be said about that later.

9.

The resolve of talented rich people to produce less if the tax rises makes the factual premise of the incentive argument true and ensures that the poor are poorer than they otherwise would be. I have argued that, within the restriction of naked use of the incentive argument, the rich cannot justify making its factual premise true. There is consequently an impression of incoherence when *they* employ the argument in defense of low taxes on top salaries: for the more disposed they are to affirm its normative premise, the less disposed they should be to make its factual premise true.[27] The argument stands up only because the agents mentioned in its minor premise do not act as one would expect people who put forward its major premise to act. If they did so act, they would not make the minor premise of the argument true, it would then not be true, and the argument would collapse.

For an analogy to the bad faith that comes when the rich themselves propound the argument, think of kidnappers who say that, since the safety of the hostage should be of paramount concern, its loved ones should pay for its release. That structurally similar — and risible — posture is portrayed in the film *Ruthless People*, in which frustrated kidnappers express outrage against the husband

---

[27] This claim, that affirmation of the major premise of the argument by the talented rich *does not cohere* with their disposition to make its minor premise true, is not identical with (though it is related to) the claim labored above, to wit, that the talented rich *cannot justify* making the minor premise true, when the incentive argument is used nakedly. The incoherence claim depends on what the major premise says, and goes with certain formulations of it only. If the kidnapper changes the major premise of his argument from "children should be with their parents" to "parents should pay to retrieve kidnapped children," the claim about his minor premise survives, but the incoherence claim goes. Analogous results emerge if the rich employ as major premise: "the poor should vote for whatever enhances their interests."

of the unwanted wife whom they hold hostage, when they become apprised of that husband's blithe lack of desire to pay for his wife's release. Or think of a crowd of recently munching strollers who complain about the failure of the city's street-cleaning service as they toss their Big Mac containers into the gutter. There is similar incongruity when talented rich people indignantly condemn parties of the Left for a supposed lack of concern for the poor supposedly shown by the Left's policy of taxing the rich heavily. They can say that such parties are stupid, in light of the terms of cooperation to which they are themselves resolved to stick, but, although that may be true, it is not a reason for *them* to display indignation.

10.

The incentive rationale might convince the poor that they should vote to maintain low taxes. But it does not show them why the rich have made it true that they might be well advised to vote like that. And the poor might refuse to vote that way. They might support Labour and press for higher taxation on high incomes, and not because they do not accept the minor, factual, premise of the incentive argument. On the contrary: they might believe that the minor premise is true, they might notice that its truth reflects the insistence of the rich on an unusually high standard of life and work, and they might want not to condone that insistence but to resist it, even at the cost of their own material self-interest. They would then reject the major premise of the incentive argument. They would say that inequalities that enhance their own position are not justified when the reason why they enhance it is the one that features in the minor premise of the argument.

The poor have *a* reason to respond as the rich suggest, since if they do they prosper better materially, and they might care enough about that to play ball with the rich. But it would not necessarily be irrational for the poor to reject what the rich suggest and forgo the promised material gain. It is not necessarily irrational (and it is sometimes felt to be morally imperative) to refuse to deal with a person who wields power in an untoward way even if, should you accede to the proposal he makes, you would be materially better off. That is not necessarily irrational both because how well off you are is not a matter of your material situation alone, and because how well off you are is not the only matter it is rational for you to care about. (That low-income people sometimes care about other things, such as retaining their self-respect and not collaborating with what they think unfair, is shown in their frequent willingness to hold out on strike for higher wages beyond the point where that could be thought rational in income-maximizing terms.)

Still, the indignant poor might, as I said, care enough about prospective extra income to fall in with what the rich propose. They could think: we want to improve our modest lot, so it is entirely reasonable for us to accept the enhanced-incentives proposal. But they could not say to the rich: yes, your proposal is entirely reasonable. If the rich could claim that they *need* extra money to perform better or that without superior pay a superior performance would mean that they live bleak lives, then the poor could accede to the proposal of the rich in the dimension of I-thou interaction. In the case that I am envisaging (that is, in the standard case of the table), resisting their proposal is one way of treating the rich as a set of thous, rather than as a powerful opaque force. If the rich could be regarded as external things, like machines, or bits of nature, it would then be irrational for the poor not to accept their proposal. It is irrational to be angry with a lofty mountain, to think "I'm damned if I'm going to climb you or walk around you to get where I want to go," since, unless you are an animist, your relationship to a mountain properly takes an I-it form. But the poor know that the rich are persons, and they may regard them as fellow members of community who can be asked, face to face, for justification. And then rejection by the poor of the proposal made by the rich is not necessarily irrational: uncooperative anger is one rational response to what the rich say.

11.

The incentive argument is not problematic (in the particular way that I say it is) when it is thought acceptable to view the rich as outside the community to which the poor belong. But sometimes, in Britain, anyway, many of the rich themselves are eager to invoke community, when, for example, they react with (real or fake) horror to militant agitation among the poor. (Maybe some of the rich think that "belong to the same community as" denotes a nonsymmetrical relation.)

Of course, particular talented people can affirm the incentive argument without difficulty, by declaring that they personally lack the disposition attributed to members of their class in the argument. But if the argument is going to pass muster as a justification of unequal reward within community, then putting it forward in the first person, and without such disavowal, should not be problematic.

In the third person, the minor premise of the argument just predicts how the rich will behave, and it can show misunderstanding of the speaker's message to demand a justification of that behavior: the speaker is not responsible for it, and he might himself be disposed to condemn it. But to affirm the minor premise of the argument with full first-person force is to declare, or, what suffices for present purposes, to manifest, an intention, and a demand for justification is therefore in order. Observe the difference between these two interchanges, each of which follows assertion of the minor premise of the argument to a poor person, in the first case *by* a poor person, or by some third party.

Poor person: But they, the rich, should not demand so much.

Reply: That has nothing to do with me. The fact is that they do.

That is a valid reply to the poor person's lament. But now consider an analogous interchange following a first-person presentation of the premise:

> Poor person: But you, the rich, should not demand so much.
>
> Reply: That has nothing to do with me. The fact is that we (I, and the others) do.

Here the very incoherence of the reply confirms the aptness of the challenge against which it strains.

Finding it difficult to provide a convincing reply, the rich may represent their own optional attitudes and decisions *as* given facts. They might say to the poor, "Look, we all have to accept the reality of the situation." Yet it is not an exogenous reality which they are asking the poor to recognize. In this rhetoric of the rich, a declaration of intention masquerades as a description of something beyond choice: the rich present *themselves* in third-personal terms, in alienation from their own agency.[28]

For an analogous self-misrepresentation, consider how absurd it would be for the kidnapper to say: "Gee, I'm sorry, but the fact is that unless you pay I will not release your child." If he says that in factual style, and not as a piece of macabre humor, his remark expresses an estrangement from his own intention which means that he is crazy.

And I believe that there is also something weird going on when the will of a class is depicted by its members as *just* a sociological fact. The rich man sits in his living room, and he explains, in a detached style that says that *his* choices have nothing to do with the matter, why the poor should vote against higher taxes on the rich. Here, too, there is alienation, but, because it is less ob-

---

[28] This is not a rerun of the inability claim, which we left behind at the end of section 7. That claim acknowledges that the rich form and execute a set of intentions, but denies that they could form and/or execute certain alternative ones. In the motif of alienation, the very fact of intentional agency is concealed, or at least obscured.

vious than the alienation of the single kidnapper that I just portrayed, you do not have to be completely crazy to slip into it. It is easy to slip into *this* alienation because each rich person's individual choice lacks salience, lost as it is among the millions of similar choices typical of members of his class: he participates in a practice so familiar that it gets treated as part of, or on a par with, the course of nature. In a reflective moment he might be appalled by the situation of the badly off, but he reifies the intentions of rich people (his own included), which frustrate their claim to priority, into hard data which social policy must take as parametric. He is unalive to the fact that his own decisions contribute to the condition he describes, a condition which is the upshot of a vast number of personal choices, but which he describes in the impersonal discourse of sociology or economics.

Recall the crazy kidnapper, who says, "Gee, I'm sorry." The child's parents might display a corresponding craziness. They do so if they treat the kidnapper's intention as an objective fact not only for them but even for him. And then they think of his demand as just what they happen to have to pay to get their child back, and maybe one of them says to the kidnapper, as to a possibly sympathetic bystander: "Well, £5000 *is* a lot of money, as I'm sure you'll agree, but it's less, after all, than what it cost to have Sally's adenoids removed, and, as you've pointed out, it is her *life* that's at stake."

And these reflections also have a bearing on the incentive argument. I have said that the incapacity of that argument to serve as a justification of inequality when the rich present it to the poor shows that the argument presupposes a lack of community between them. And I have just now also said that when the rich deliver it in a certain cast or tone, they imply that they do not qualify as choosing human agents. In considering that second point, it may be instructive to contemplate a presentation of the incentive argument that we have not yet considered, one in which a poor person addresses a set of rich ones. Now the minor premise will say: if the top tax rises to 60 percent, *you* will work less hard, and we shall consequently be worse off. If the poor speaker says that in an objective tone of voice, his rich listeners might, as a result, feel the weirdness that comes when someone predicts your behavior as though you have no control over it. Some of the listeners might even protest: "Hey, wait a minute. We would like at least to *try* not to work less if the tax rises." And the poor speaker might counter: "You're not likely to stick to that resolution. *Please* vote against the tax rise." In his insistence on the truth of the incentive argument's minor premise, this poor person would be setting his face against community, or against the capacity for agency of his listeners, or against both.

III. INCENTIVES AND THE DIFFERENCE PRINCIPLE

12.

I have thus far scrutinized a defense of the inequalities of an actually existing capitalist society (Great Britain) that occurs in ordinary political discourse. I now leave the vernacular context and turn to a text-based examination of John Rawls's difference principle. It is certain that Rawls would not endorse the particular inequalities that prevail in Britain. But his own defense of inequality has significant elements in common with the case for Lawson's tax cut, and much of my criticism of the latter also bears against Rawls's views.

It is usually supposed, and it is evidently supposed by Rawls himself, that his affirmation of the difference principle is consistent with his endorsement of the inequalities that come with special incentives to people of talent. But I shall argue that, when true to itself, Rawlsian justice condemns such incentives, and that no society whose members are *themselves* unambivalently committed to the difference principle need use special incentives to motivate talented producers.

In these lectures I have been concerned to distinguish between inequalities that are necessary, apart from human choice, to make the worst off better off, and inequalities that are necessary to that end only given what some people's intentions are. And this distinction, between, as one might say, intention-relative and intention-independent necessities, generates a question about how we are to take the word "necessary" in John Rawls's difference principle. When he says that inequalities are just if they are necessary to improve the position of the worst off,[29] does he countenance only inequalities that are necessary (to achieve the stated end) apart from people's intentions, or also, and more liberally (in more than one sense of that term), inequalities such as those that are necessary when talented people lack a certain sort of commitment to equality and are set to act accordingly? We confront here two readings of the difference principle: in its *strict* reading, it counts inequalities as necessary only when they are, strictly, necessary, necessary, that is, apart from people's chosen intentions. In its *lax* reading, it countenances intention-relative necessities as well. So, for example, if an inequality is needed to make the badly off better off but only *given* that talented producers operate as self-interested market maximizers, then that inequality is endorsed by the lax, but not by the strict, reading of the difference principle.

I shall argue that each of these incompatible readings of the principle is nourished by material in Rawls's writings, so that he has, in effect, two positions on the matter. His comments on the spirit in which people in a just society affirm the difference principle point to the strict, "intention-independent" reading of it: that reading goes with his remarks about "full compliance," the dignity of the badly off, and fraternity. Yet, by endorsing incentives, Rawls treats inequalities whose necessity is relative to the intentions of talented people as acceptable to the difference prin-

---

[29] That is one part of the difference principle. Another part says that inequalities are unjust if they worsen the position of the worst off, and, on the generous interpretation of the principle (see sec. 1 above), a third part says that they are (not un)just if they have no effect on the worst off.

ciple: he proceeds as though he affirms the principle in its lax interpretation.

13.

Before turning to Rawls's texts, I want to argue that the strict interpretation of the difference principle is mandatory *if* we suppose that the people in the society in which it is applied are themselves attached to the idea of justice that the principle articulates and are motivated by it in their daily lives. In other words: if we begin with an uninterpreted statement of the principle, where it is ambiguous across strict and lax interpretations, *and* we suppose that all of the people in the society it governs comply wholeheartedly with it, by which I mean that they are concerned to ensure that their own conduct is just in the sense defined by the principles, then what they comply with is the principle in its strict interpretation.

In such a society, the difference principle affects the motivation of citizens in economic life. It controls their expectations about remuneration, that is, what they will regard as acceptable pay for the posts they are invited to fill. It is generally thought that the difference principle would be used by government to modify the effect of choices which are not themselves influenced by the principle, but, so I claim, in a society of wholehearted commitment to the principle, there cannot be so stark a contrast between public and private choice. Instead, citizens want their own economic behavior to satisfy the principle, and they help to sustain a moral climate in which others want the same. I show in the next section that much of what Rawls says commits him to such an understanding of the difference principle, even though his approval of incentives embodies a rejection of that understanding, since approving of incentives means accepting the difference principle in its lax form, and in that form it can be satisfied in a society where it has no direct influence on economic motivation.

Suppose I am a doctor, contemplating a hospital post which I know I could obtain at, say, £40,000 a year. I also believe that, if — and only if — I took something in the region of £15,000 for filling it, then any difference between my reward and what the less well paid get would be justified by what I strictly need to do the job, or by its special burdens. Then how can I say, with a straight face, that justice forbids inequalities that are detrimental to the badly off *and* be resolved to act justly in my own life, unless, should I indeed go for this particular job, I offer myself at £15,000 and thereby release £25,000 for socially beneficial use?[30]

I might say: "Look, I *am* concerned about the less well off, but I do not have to devote my whole life to them. It is right for government to serve their interests by taxing me, but I should also be allowed to pursue my own *self*-interest, and that is why I feel justified in taking the salary that hospitals have to offer to attract physicians like me."

But this reply is not sustainable here.

First, notice that I cannot mean the reply in a spirit of apologetic self-criticism, for I am here, *ex hypothesi*, resolved to act justly. Under that hypothesis, I must show that my behavior is not unjust, not that it is an understandable compromise between justice and self-interest. I have to show that the inequalities caused by what I and other professionals choose to do are not unjust, even though they make the lot of the badly off worse than it needs to

---

[30] People who favor a lax interpretation of the difference principle have suggested that I could say that my giving up the £25,000 would deliver little benefit to any particular person. Yet that need not be so: if it be required that my sacrifice make a palpable difference to some particular person or particular people, then channels which do not fragment its impact could be devised. But the requirement is anyhow misconceived. For one could argue, by the same token, against those who support the difference principle in its lax interpretation, that it is pointless to collect income tax from one person in particular, since that too makes no significant difference to any individual.

And this is anyway not the central issue here. For the appropriate question here is not: what, irrespective of the character of the society in which he finds himself, is the moral obligation of a talented individual who believes in Rawlsian justice? The right question is: what would a *society* that is just by the lights of the difference principle be like? How, among other things, would talented people in *general* behave in such a society? If, as I am claiming, they would in general take jobs for modest salaries, then each could reflect that, together with others, he or she is making a massive difference to (what would otherwise be) badly off people.

be. Consequently, I am claiming that some inequality is just because it reflects legitimate pursuit of self-interest on the part of people with a fortunate endowment of talent. I am saying that justice is itself a compromise or balance between self-interest and the claims of equality.

As I indicated earlier (see sec. 8), I do not aim to impugn the integrity of a conception of justice which allows the agent a certain self-regarding prerogative. But the doctor's reply is meant not merely to articulate a defensible conception of justice, but to reconcile his claim to be wholeheartedly committed to the difference principle's idea of economic justice with his lax reading of that principle. We must ask whether his reply accomplishes that result.

Now, Rawls does not speak of distributive justice as a compromise of the contemplated sort,[31] but our question is whether he might, whether, that is, he could vindicate the lax difference principle along the lines of the doctor's reply. And I do not think that he could, since the reply turns on what is here the wrong distinction. The reply defends assistance to the badly off moderated by the pursuit of self-interest, as opposed to a more total devotion to them. But that is not the same as the distinction between benefiting the badly off by virtue of what I pay in taxes and through other by-products of self-seeking activity, and benefiting them in less contingent fashion. The government, pursuing the lax difference principle, might tax me more, or less, than whatever should count as a reasonable compromise between self-interest and service. If it taxed me more than that, I would, according to the reply, have reason of legitimate self-interest to object, and the reply therefore represents the difference principle as (at times) too demanding, even in its lax form. And if government taxed me less than what a reasonable compromise would dictate, then I could not say that the laxness in the principle I affirm was justified

[31] It would be a mistake to think that the priority of liberty over the difference principle makes for such a compromise. Among the reasons why it does not do so is that we are not here concerned with coercive restrictions, in the name of justice, on the doctor's liberty, but with what would count as a just use of his liberty.

on compromise grounds: for on those grounds it would then be too lax.[32]

In short, the compromise idea will not in general draw the same line as the lax difference principle does. Defended along compromise lines, the lax difference principle is at best an imperfect proxy for a just balance, and not, what it is supposed to be, a fundamental principle of justice. The compromise idea is, simply, different from the idea that inequalities are justified if they are necessary to benefit the badly off, given that agents are (or might be) self-regarding maximizers on the market. Accordingly, the lax difference principle cannot be what agents committed to difference-principle justice affirm: from their point of view, it draws an arbitrary line between serving oneself and serving others.

We are left with the strict difference principle,[33] which government cannot by itself implement. For the strict difference principle to prevail, there needs to be an ethos informed by the principle in society at large. Therefore, a society (as opposed to its government) does not qualify as committed to the difference principle unless it is indeed informed by a certain ethos, or culture of justice. Ethoses are, of course, beyond the immediate control of legislation, but I believe that a just society is normally impossible without one,[34] and Rawls himself requires that there be a nur-

[32] With a certain distribution of talent, the inequalities allowed by the lax difference principle could be quite large, of a size that is intuitively incongruent with the central Rawlsian idea that the gifted owe their special powers to mere good fortune. How can *they* be thoroughly just people, think themselves merely lucky to have the assets they do, and nevertheless take as much advantage of them as they can on the market? Of course, there are also distributions of talent under which the inequalities might be quite small. But they are not small as a matter of principle, and it is no defense of a supposed fundamental principle, when its consistency with certain consequences generates criticism, to show that it lacks those consequences in practice. So defended, the principle is not, as intended, fundamental, but warranted because, given the facts, it serves more fundamental aims.

[33] I do not mean that there is no other game in town, but just that there is no third way of playing the difference principle game. (A further alternative would be the strict difference principle constrained by an agent-centered prerogative. But the added constraint *modifies* — it does not interpret — the difference principle.)

[34] For example, because of problems of asymmetrical information and incentive compatibility that are familiar to economists, and that are crudely illustrated by the

turance and cultivation of appropriate attitude in the just society that he describes.

In a culture of justice shaped by the difference principle, talented people would not expect (what they usually have the power to obtain) the high salaries whose level reflects high demand for their talent (as opposed to the special needs or special burdens of their jobs). It follows that the difference principle in a society of just people would not induce the inequality it is usually thought (e.g., by Rawls) to produce, and it would not, in particular, justify incentive payments in the "standard" sense of that phrase (see the table above), that is, payments not to compensate for unusually arduous work, but to draw talent to jobs that are not in general especially grueling. In a just society, where justice is defined by the difference principle in its preinterpreted form, the difference principle will prevail in its strict interpretation.

(It is not true that, in the society I have in mind, a person would have to worry about unfortunate people every time he made an economic decision. Liberals would regard that as oppressive,[35] and, whether or not they are right, one function of the egalitarian ethos is to make conscious focus on the worst off unnecessary. What rather happens is that people internalize, and — in the normal case — they unreflectively live by, principles which restrain the pursuit of self-interest and whose point is that the less fortunate gain when conduct is directed by them.)

14.

On the lax interpretation of what the difference principle demands, it is satisfied when everyone gets what he can through self-

---

propensity of the productive to withdraw labor when taxes rise too high. Under abnormal conditions, justice might be consistent with universal self-interested maximizing: if, for example, talents and utility functions are identical, then initial equality of tangible assets might be considered sufficient for justice. On a Dworkinian view, that would be so even with different utility functions.

[35] See, e.g., Thomas Nagel, "Libertarianism without Foundations," in J. Paul, ed., *Reading Nozick* (Totowa, N.J.: Rowman and Littlefield, 1981), pp. 199–200.

seeking behavior in a market whose rewards are so structured by taxation and other regulation that the worst off are as well off as any scheme of taxed and regulated market rewards can make them. On my view of what it means for a society to institute the principle, people would mention norms of equality when asked to explain why they and those like them are willing to work for the pay they get. This strict interpretation conflicts with Rawls's endorsement of unequalizing incentives. Yet, as I now propose to show, the strict interpretation of the principle coheres with a number of significant general characterizations of justice to be found in Rawls's work.

It is very important in the present connection that Rawls's theory describes what he calls a well-ordered society, one, that is, whose citizens display full and willing compliance with the demands of justice. In a well-ordered society each person acts out of a sense of justice informed by the principles of justice not merely at the ballot box but as he goes about his daily business.

So much is clear from many passages in Rawls's writings. We are told not only that "everyone accepts, and knows that others likewise accept, the same first principles of right and justice," which might, by itself, be consistent with a ballot box view of their commitment, but also that the parties "in everyday life . . . affirm and act from [those] first principles of justice." [36] Full compliance with the principles means that they act *from* them, in everyday life, "in the course," as Rawls also puts it, "of their daily lives." [37] And their "full autonomy is achieved" partly through "acting *from* these principles as their sense of justice dictates." [38] Citizens are strongly committed to acting that way. They "have a highest-order desire, their sense of justice, to *act* from the principles of jus-

[36] Rawls, "Kantian Constructivism," p. 521.

[37] Ibid., p. 528. Cf. Rawls, *A Theory of Justice*, p. 253: they "knowingly act on the principles of justice in the ordinary course of events."

[38] Rawls, "Kantian Constructivism," p. 528, emphasis added.

tice." [39] They "have a desire to express their nature as free and equal moral persons, and this they do most adequately by acting *from* the principles that they would acknowledge in the original position. When all strive to comply with these principles and each succeeds, then individually and collectively their nature as moral persons is *most* fully realized, and with it their individual and collective good." [40]

Now, such statements seem to me to imply that the economic motivation of Rawlsian citizens is influenced by the difference principle. How could they act like maximizing incentive seekers if in "*their daily lives*" they act "*from*" a principle which directs primary concern for the badly off? Can we say that they act *from* such a principle in their daily lives just because they support taxation which is shaped by the principle and which aims to modify the results of their acting *from* maximizing motives? Such support might show that you respect the claim of the principle against you, but it surely does not suffice as proof of your being inspired by it as part of a sense of justice on which you operate in your daily life.[41] How could your "nature as [a] moral person" count as "*most* fully realized" when you go for as much as you can get in your own market choices,[42] and merely endorse application of the principle by the government in imperfect moderation of the

[39] Ibid., p. 532, emphasis added.

[40] Rawls, *A Theory of Justice*, p. 528, emphases added.

[41] Rawls says that "citizens have a normally effective sense of justice, that is, one that enables them to understand and to apply the principles of justice, and for the most part to act from them as their circumstances require (*Justice as Fairness*, p. 154). Why would they have to apply the principles themselves to their own circumstances if just behavior consisted in obeying laws designed to effect an implementation of those principles?

[42] How does the economic behavior of a maximizer who is committed to the lax difference principle differ from that of a maximizer who is not? It might be said that, unlike the latter, the former is willing to maximize only when and because the principle is in force. But that is not necessarily true: people who believe that the lax difference principle should be instituted may have various views about what they should do in a society in which it is not. And even if our believer would indeed behave nonmaximizingly if the principle were not in force, that hardly shows that he "strive[s] to comply with" the difference principle in his "daily life."

inequality which the choices of people like you tend to cause?

Consider this passage from *A Theory of Justice*: "by abstaining from the exploitation of the contingencies of nature and social circumstances within a framework of equal liberty, persons express their respect for one another in the very constitution of their society." [43] If that is so, then it seems to me that in the Rawlsian society there will not be incentive seekers, since they do exploit their contingent talent and social advantages, and the passage says that people who do that show a lack of the respect for other people that the constitution of their society requires. If you deny that the passage has this implication, then you must make one or other of two implausible claims. You must claim either that (1) despite what the passage says, Rawlsianly just talented people might exploit the contingency of their superior talent, or that (2) contrary to what seems evident, talented market-maximizers do not engage in such exploitation.[44]

Think about it this way. On a Rawlsian view, there is no reason of basic principle why the talented should earn more than the untalented. It is merely that things (supposedly) fall out that way, when the difference principle is applied. So imagine that we address the talented rich people, and we ask them why they do not give the above-average parts of their incomes to people of below-average income, when, *ex hypothesi*, they would have compliantly accepted the resulting post-giveaway incomes had the difference principle happened to mandate them. What could they say? They

---

[43] Rawls, *A Theory of Justice*, p. 179, and see, generally, pp. 72–75.

[44] It has been claimed, against my interpretation of the quoted passage, that it speaks of an expression of mutual respect when persons choose their constitution and not, as I have supposed, when they act in the society it constitutes. But there is no scope of "abstaining from the exploitation of the contingencies of nature and social circumstance" at the stage of constitutional choice, since, at that point, no one knows what those contingencies are. This and other phrases (not quoted above) in the paragraph from which the passage is drawn establish that the objection is misguided, that Rawls is here commenting on people's choices in real life rather than in the original position. He is speaking about how things are "when society follows these principles" (ibid., p. 179).

certainly could not say that they were abstaining from exploitation of their talent advantages, and we could not say that they live under "a conception of justice that nullifies the accidents of natural endowment and the contingencies of social circumstance as counters in the quest for . . . economic advantage." [45]

15.

Rawls believes that a just society, on the lax understanding of how it operates, honors the dignity of the worst off, since, so he says, they know that they are caused to be as well off as they could be. But that is an illusion. For they are as well off as they could be only *given* the self-seekingness of those who are better off, and maybe far better off, than they.

Joshua Cohen is a strong advocate of the difference principle. He draws a contrast between a society ruled by that principle and one whose rule is a basic minimum for all and then laissez-faire. Cohen disparages the basic minimum/laissez-faire arrangement because of how weak its "affirmation of [the] worth" of the worst-off individuals is. For if I am one of them in such a society, "then I know that I could do better if those who are better off were prepared to forgo some of their advantages. And I know that this loss of advantage to me is not just for a stretch of time but covers the course of my entire life. Others know this, and know that I know it, and so on. Still they accept the advantages." [46] Yet Cohen fails to see that all those things can be said about the less gifted in a society ruled by the lax difference principle, where talented people demand, and get, incentive payments. In such a society, clear-thinking unfortunate people know that they "could do better if those who are better off were prepared to forgo some of their advantages." Cohen describes a badly placed person in a Rawlsian society reflecting with satisfaction that "other citizens act from maximin" (that is, in this context, from the principle of putting

[45] Rawls, *A Theory of Justice*, p. 15.
[46] Joshua Cohen, "Democratic Equality," *Ethics*, July 1989, p. 743.

the interests of the badly off first) and thereby "display a concern for my good and the good of those to whom I am attached." [47] But the badly placed person can enjoy such a reflection only on my revisionary conception of the character of a Rawlsian society. When the difference principle in its standard, lax, interpretation prevails, it is not in general true that citizens "act from maximin," and the inequalities that come as a result might challenge the sense of self-worth of those who are at the bottom. If they succeed in sustaining that sense, that will not be because of their perception of how the better off regard them.

Joshua Cohen's remarks are in the spirit of the Rawls passage which says that "the least favored man," here called B, "can accept A's being better off since A's advantages have been gained in ways that improve B's prospects. If A were not allowed his better position, B would be even worse off than he is." [48] The second sentence of this passage does not compel agreement with the first, since, with everything else equal, A could have refrained from seizing the full complement of the advantages he was able to seize, and then B would have been better off than he is. It indicates how little A cares about B's lot that he refuses to improve B's bad prospects without the advantages he gets in the course of doing so.

The mistake in Cohen's comment on the difference principle shows that, given his own lax application of it, Rawls is wrong to represent it as a realization of the value of fraternity, which he glosses as "the idea of not wanting to have greater advantages unless this is to the benefit of others who are less well off. . . . Members of a family commonly do not wish to gain unless they can do so in ways that further the interests of the rest. Now wanting to act on the difference principle has precisely this consequence." [49] But "wanting to act on the difference principle" has the stated consequence only if we interpret the principle strictly. For wanting

[47] Ibid., p. 746.
[48] Rawls, *A Theory of Justice*, p. 103.
[49] Ibid., p. 105.

not "to gain unless they can do so in ways that further the interests of the rest" is incompatible with the drive for enrichment motivating market maximizers.

We should note an ambiguity in the phrase "not wanting to have greater advantages unless this is to the benefit of others who are less well off." A person of that description does not want to gain unless others thereby do. Does that mean: unless they gain something (no matter how little)? But that is not the maximin concept. Or does it mean: unless none of his gain means that theirs is less than it need be? But, provided that the feasible set is sufficiently ample, that means going for equality.[50]

A society of maximizers with taxation and regulation dictated by the lax difference principle is necessarily preferable from the point of view of the worst off to a laissez-faire society; but in neither society is the conduct of high fliers consistent with the essentially socialist value of fraternity or with motivation informed by the difference principle. Rawls must give up either his approval of incentives to the exercise of talent or his ideals of dignity, fraternity, and the full realization of persons' moral natures. I think the ideals are worth keeping.[51]

[50] Let me illustrate this point. Two brothers, A and B, are at benefit levels 6 and 5, respectively, in New York, where they live. If they moved to Chicago, their levels would rise to 10 and 6. If they moved to Boston, they would rise to 8 and 7. Is fraternity, as Rawls means to characterize it, consistent with A proposing that they move to Chicago? If so, it is a thin thing. Or is Rawlsian fraternity strictly maximizing? In that case, Boston is the choice, and, in a feasible set with no bar to redistribution, equality is the result.

[51] It might be thought that, beyond his commitment to those ideals, Rawls has further reason to reject incentives and the lax difference principle, to wit, that the risk aversiveness which induces the parties in the original position to select the difference principle would also incline them to prefer its strict form. For two reasons, I have not used this argument. The first reason is that I seek to pursue my case against the part of Rawls to which I object by invoking Rawlsian ideas with which I agree, and I agree neither that principles chosen in the original position are ipso facto just nor that its parties would choose a maximin strategy and, therefore, if the foregoing suggestion is sound, the strict difference principle. The second reason is that the strict difference principle *might* be thought to imply a principle, or set of principles, "for individuals," as Rawls uses that phrase, and it is difficult to say both whether it does and whether, if it does, the principle or principles are of the right type to be chosen in the original position: see Rawls, *A Theory of Justice*, pp. 108–10, 115, 135.

16.

At one point, Rawls comments on the view that "the greater expectations allowed to entrepreneurs encourages [*sic*] them to do things which raise the long-term prospects of the laboring class." [52] He does not (quite) endorse that factual claim, but he says that, if, as he shows he believes, it is true, then the difference principle recommends the rewards generating those greater expectations and the "initial inequality in life prospects" associated with them.

There are other passages to relevantly similar effect,[53] and there is no point quoting them all here. But I do want to quote and comment on a remark by Rawls which might be read as an attempt to anticipate and deflect the line of criticism that I have developed.

Following one of his incentives-endorsing passages, Rawls says: "One might think that ideally individuals should want to serve one another. But since the parties are assumed not to take an interest in one another's interests, their acceptance of those inequalities is only the acceptance of the relations in which men stand in the circumstances of justice. They have no grounds for complaining of one another's motives." [54] It might be said, on the basis of this passage, that my critique of Rawls displays misunderstanding of the role of principles of justice, as he conceives them. Those principles, it might be said, are rules observed by fair-minded people in their mutually advantageous interaction, fair-minded people who may or may not *care* about one another, but who qualify as just as long as they observe the rules. They go beyond justice if they do care about one another, and in demanding that the difference principle be strict I am demanding more than justice.

[52] Ibid., p. 78.

[53] See ibid., pp. 151, 157, 279; Rawls, *Justice as Fairness*, pp. 44, 46; Rawls, "Distributive Justice," in P. Laslett and W. G. Runciman, eds., *Philosophy, Politics and Society*, 3d series (Oxford: Basil Blackwell, 1967), p. 67.

[54] Rawls, *A Theory of Justice*, p. 151. For more on "mutual disinterest," see Rawls, *Justice as Fairness*, p. 62.

But that line of thought seems to me untenable. For it wrongly attributes to people in the achieved, just society the mutual indifference that characterizes the specially tailored persons of Rawls's original position, in which the principles that are to govern the just society are chosen. In the original position mutual indifference is assumed for methodological reasons, to derive justice from rational self-interest under a veil of ignorance constraint. But it does not follow that the principles chosen by the mutually indifferent parties of the original position are consistent with mutual indifference when they operate as rules of interaction in a functioning society. And to attribute mutual indifference to people in the realized society is, surely, to contradict the idea that their relations partake of fraternity, as Rawls describes that condition (see sec. 15 above).[55] People who, like "members of a family," "do not wish to gain unless they can do so in ways that further the interests of the rest" are not people who take no interest in one another's interests. How could a person who takes no interest in the interests of others want advantages for himself only if his enjoyment of them benefits the less well off (see sec. 15)?

17.

Rawls says that "a person in the original position would concede the justice of [the] inequalities [required for incentives]. Indeed, it would be short-sighted of him not to do so."[56] Now, the phrasing of this contention is curious, since we normally think of short-sightedness as poor perception not of justice but of one's own interests.[57] And I point out this infelicity in the formulation

---

[55] Rawls himself distinguishes similarly between people's attitudes to one another in the original position and in society when he writes that "although the parties in the original position take no interest in each other's interests, they know that in society they need to be assured by the esteem of their associates. Their self-respect and their confidence in the value of their own system of ends cannot withstand the indifference . . . of others" (*A Theory of Justice*, p. 338).

[56] Ibid., p. 151.

[57] A person in the original position does not, in any case, ask himself what is *just*. He asks himself what, given his ignorance, is the best choice from the point of view of his interests.

because I believe that it reflects an unresolved tension in the Rawlsian architectonic, one that underlies the difficulties exposed in these lectures. That underlying tension is between a *bargaining* conception and a *community* conception of social relationships. (There are conceptions which fall between those two, with elements of each, but, as I read Rawls, both of them appear in his work, in relatively pure forms.)

But let us ignore the infelicitous phrasing in the passage, and concentrate on the implied claim that it would be a mistake not to concede the justice of incentive inequalities. My reply to that claim, a reply that by now is entirely predictable, is that, *if* we are talking within the assumption of full compliance, then we need not and should not concede either that incentive inequalities are required to motivate performance or that they are just. Let us now, however, retire the heady assumptions of full compliance and a widespread sense of justice. Consider, instead, a society like the United States, where fortunate people learn to expect more than they would get when the difference principle prevails in a comprehensive way. In that case, we might agree that it would be a mistake not to concede incentive inequalities. If we need inequalities to "encourage effective performance" [58] then it might be folly not to have them, but it does not follow that having them is a requirement of basic justice, where a *basic* principle of justice is one that has application in a society where, as in Rawls's, everyone always acts justly.

Although his primary topic is justice under full compliance, Rawls also treats his principles as standards for assessing actually existing society.[59] In my view, the difference principle, conceived as one that would govern a just society, condemns as unjust those existing inequalities which are necessary to benefit the worst off where that necessity reflects the intentions of the talented rich; but, given that the inequalities are necessary, albeit for the stated

[58] Rawls, *A Theory of Justice*, p. 151.
[59] See ibid., pp. 245–46.

reason, to remove them would be reckless. Along with Nikolai Bukharin, I would have said to the kulaks: "Enrich yourselves!" without supposing (any more than Bukharin did) that I was thereby voicing a demand of justice. If we are concerned about the badly off, then we should sometimes concede incentives, just as we should sometimes satisfy even a kidnapper's demands. We are not then acting on the difference principle in its strict interpretation, in which it is a principle of justice governing a society of just people who are inspired by it. We are acting on the lax version of the difference principle, which endorses incentives and which has application in societies of the familiar unjust kind. On the assumption that they are indeed unavoidable, incentive payments may be justified, but it does not follow that no injustice occurs when they are provided. (One might say, to a child's guardian: the kidnapper is unjustly threatening the safety of the child, and justice to the child therefore demands that you pay him. And one might say, to legislators in a structurally unequal society: the talented are unjustly indifferent to the plight of the poor, and justice to the poor therefore demands that you do not impose very high taxation.)

The policy of paying productive people plenty to get them to produce so that badly off people will be better off is rational when productive people are resolved to serve only if they are richly rewarded. But their stance is then unjust by the very standard which the difference principle itself sets. Accordingly, on a strict view of Rawlsian justice, the difference principle in its lax interpretation, which does mandate the incentives policy, is not a basic principle of justice but a principle for handling people's injustice. It is not a basic principle of justice, since it confers benefit on market maximizers who offend against justice. We might call it a principle of damage limitation in the field of justice.[60]

When doing so limits the damage, it is wise to run society on lax difference principle lines, but it is also wise to recognize that

---

[60] Or, a "principle for meeting injustice" (ibid., p. 246).

society is not then based on justice. A related and more general point is that one should not suppose that, as Rawls says in *A Theory of Justice*, "justice is *the* first virtue of social institutions," where that means that "laws and institutions . . . must be reformed or abolished if they are unjust." [61] For sometimes justice is unattainable, and we do well to settle for something else. When there is no way to get the child back without paying, when a just outcome is not to be had, then paying, which makes all (kidnapper, parents, child) better off than refusing to pay, is almost certainly preferable, although in some cases, with less at stake, we might prefer to forgo the Pareto improvement, in order not to accede to an unjust demand.

Similarly, and according to an ancient Marxist wisdom, justice is not the first virtue of institutions in conditions of scarcity. Under those conditions a just distribution may be impossible to achieve, since powerful people will block it. In that case striving for justice may make everyone worse off, and unjust laws and institutions should not be "reformed or abolished." And scarcity in the Marxist sense is not poverty of supply, but the wider circumstance that, to secure what might be a quite reasonable supply, most people must spend most of their time engaged in labor that interferes with self-realization.

Under such a condition, and it is a huge and difficult question whether we are still in it, it might be right to tolerate, and even, sometimes, to nourish, incentive motivation, despite the fact that it contradicts justice. Sometimes, the difference principle, in its lax interpretation, can be recommended as a first virtue of social institutions, because we cannot get justice, and the injustice that goes with incentives is the best injustice we can get.

18.

My principal contention about Rawls is that (potential) high fliers would forgo incentives properly so-called in a full compli-

---

[61] Ibid., p. 3, my emphasis.

ance society governed by the difference principle and characterized by fraternity and universal dignity. I have not rejected the difference principle in its lax reading *as* a principle of public policy: I do not doubt that there are contexts where it is right to apply it. What I have questioned is its description as a principle of (basic) justice, and I have deplored Rawls's willingness to describe those at the top end of a society governed by it as undergoing the fullest possible realization of their moral natures. My own socialist-egalitarian position was nicely articulated by John Stuart Mill in his *Principles of Political Economy*. Contrasting equal payment with incentive-style payment according to product ("work done"), Mill said that the first

> appeals to a higher standard of justice, and is adapted to a much higher moral condition of human nature. The proportioning of remuneration to work done is really just, only in so far as the more or less of the work is a matter of choice; when it depends on natural difference of strength or capacity, this principle of remuneration is in itself an injustice: it is giving to those who have; assigning most to those who are already most favoured by nature. Considered, however, as a compromise with the selfish type of character formed by the present standard of morality, and fostered by the existing social institutions, it is highly expedient; and until education shall have been entirely regenerated, is far more likely to prove immediately successful, than an attempt at a higher ideal.[62]

Rawls's lax application of his different principle means "giving to those who have." He presents the incentive policy as a feature of the just society, whereas it is in fact, and as Mill says, just "highly expedient" in society as we know it, a sober "compromise

[62] John Stuart Mill, *Principles of Political Economy*, book 2, chap. 1, sec. 4, in J. M. Robson, ed., *Collected Works of John Stuart Mill*, vol. 2 (Toronto: University of Toronto Press, 1965), p. 210. In chapter 5 of his *Utilitarianism* Mill argues, at great length, that justice is a species of expediency. But here the self-same principle of remuneration is, under the stated conditions, both "highly expedient" and "an injustice." It is a nice question whether that conjunction of designations is compatible with everything that Mill says in *Utilitarianism*.

with the selfish type of character" formed by capitalism.[63] Philoso-phers in search of justice should not be content with an expedient compromise. To call expediency *justice* goes against the regenera-tion to which Mill looked forward at the end of this fine passage.

[63] For sapient criticism of Rawls along these lines, see Allen Buchanan, *Marx and Justice* (Totowa, N.J.: Rowman and Littlefield, 1982), pp. 127–28. According to Mill, "the deep-rooted selfishness which forms the general character of the exist-ing state of society is so deeply rooted only because the whole course of the existing institutions tends to foster it" (*Autobiography* [New York: New American Library, 1965], pp. 168–69). See, for further pertinent references, Richard Ashcraft, "Class Conflict and Constitutionalism in J. S. Mill's Thought," in Nancy Rosenblum, ed., *Liberalism and the Moral Life* (Cambridge: Harvard University Press, 1989), pp. 117–18.

Contributors

Quentin Skinner is Professor of Political Science at the University of Cambridge and a Fellow of Christ's College. He is a Fellow of the British Academy and of the Royal Historical Society. His important book, *The Foundations of Modern Political Thought*, won the Wolfson Literary Prize in 1979. Professor Skinner delivered "The Paradoxes of Political Liberty," as the 1984 Tanner Lecture at Harvard University.

T. M. Scanlon is Professor of Philosophy at Harvard University and taught for many years at Princeton University. He is the author of many influential articles in moral and political philosophy, including "Contractarianism and Utilitarianism," and was one of the founding editors of *Philosophy and Public Affairs*. Professor Scanlon delivered "The Significance of Choice," as the 1986 Tanner Lecture at Oxford University.

John Rawls is Professor of Philosophy at Harvard University. His *A Theory of Justice* (1971) was widely acclaimed as a landmark work in moral and political philosophy. More recently, he has published a sequel, *Political Liberalism* (1993). Professor Rawls delivered "The Basic Liberties and Their Priority," which also appears as a chapter in *Political Liberalism,* as the 1981 Tanner Lecture at the University of Michigan.

Ronald Dworkin is Professor of Jurisprudence at Oxford University and a Fellow of University College, as well a Professor of Law at New York University. Previously, he was Hohfeld Professor of Jurisprudence at Yale University. His books include *Taking Rights Seriously* (1977), *A Matter of Principle* (1986), *Law's Empire* (1988), and *Life's Dominion: An Argument about Abortion, Euthanasia and Individual Freedom* (1993). Professor Dworkin delivered "Foundations of Liberal Equality," as the 1988 Tanner Lecture at Stanford University.

Amartya Sen is Lamont University Professor of Economics at Harvard University. Before that, he was the Drummond Professor of Political Economy at Oxford University, and Fellow of All Souls College. His books include *Choice of Techniques* (1960), *Collective Choice and Social Welfare* (1970), *On Economic Inequality* (1973), *On Ethics and Economics* (1987), and *Inequality Reexamined* (1992). Professor Sen delivered "Equality of What?" as the 1979 Tanner Lecture at Stanford University.

G. A. Cohen is the Chichele Professor of Social and Political Theory at Oxford University and Fellow of All Souls College. Previously, he was a Lecturer and then a Reader in Philosophy at University College, London. He is the author of *Karl Marx's Theory of History: A Defense* (1978), and *History, Labor and Freedom* (1978). Professor Cohen delivered "Incentives, Inequality, and Community," as the 1991 Tanner Lecture at Stanford University.